STORMWATER MANAGEM
FOR LAND DEVELOPMEN

STORMWATER MANAGEMENT FOR LAND DEVELOPMENT
Methods and Calculations for Quantity Control

THOMAS A. SEYBERT

WILEY

JOHN WILEY & SONS, INC.

For general information on our other products and services or for technical support, please contact our Customer Care Department within the United States at (800) 762-2974, outside the United States at (317) 572-3993 or fax (317) 572-4002.

Wiley also publishes its books in a variety of electronic formats. Some content that appears in print may not be available in electronic books. For more information about Wiley products, visit our web site at www.wiley.com.

Library of Congress Cataloging-in-Publication Data:

Seybert, Thomas A.
    Stormwater management for land development: methods and calculations for quantity control / Thomas A. Seybert.
        p. cm.
    ISBN-13: 978-0-471-72177-2 (cloth)
    ISBN-10: 0-471-72177-8 (cloth)
    1. Urban runoff—Management. 2. Land use—Environmental aspects. 3. Water quality management. I. Title.
TD657.S49 2006
628.2—dc22

                                                                                2006000885

Printed in the United States of America

10 9 8 7 6 5 4 3 2

To my loving wife and best friend, Chris

CONTENTS

PREFACE

Stormwater Management for Land Development: Methods and Calculations for Quantity Control, was written in response to the need for a book that covers the basic methods of hydraulics and hydrology used in land development design. The structure of the book is placed in three segments: fluid mechanics and hydraulics, watershed analysis and basic hydrologic methods, and stormwater design for conveyance and detention. The book is intended as a text for engineering and engineering technology students at the baccalaureate level. It is specifically written for academic programs where a single fluid mechanics and hydrology course is used to present stormwater management methods. In addition to academic use, the text is intended as a desktop reference for professionals engaged in stormwater runoff calculations, conveyance design, and detention design. It is recognized that in professional practice, the majority of stormwater calculations are done with specialized commercial software. However, the practitioner must understand the methods behind the software, and this book explains the origin and application of many of these computerized methods.

The need for a texbook like this became apparent to me while teaching portions of the Penn State University continuing education short course titled *Computational Methods in Stormwater Management.* The short course, which was first started in 1978 by hydrology faculty in the Department of Civil Engineering at Penn State, is intended for consulting engineers, municipal engineers, landscape architects, surveyors, and other professionals engaged in the design or review of stormwater management plans. I joined the short course teaching staff in 1984, and many attendees would ask me to recommend a single reference that includes basic coverage of hydraulic and hydrologic methods in stormwater design. I was not aware of any single book that would fill the need. For the short course, notes in a three-ring binder were prepared and distributed to the attendees as their stormwater reference. These notes were developed by various graduate students and faculty at Penn State, and I developed four or five of the sections over the years. In time, accumulation of the sections that I wrote created the foundation for part of this book, mainly the hydrology chapters.

In Pennsylvania, Maryland, and a few other states, surveyors and surveying engineers are allowed, by law, to practice stormwater management design, mainly in connection with subdivision of land for housing or commercial development. In these states, there is a need for continuing education of surveyors to gain the skills necessary to complete reasonable stormwater design with accepted hydraulic and hydrologic methods. To fill this need, I, and my mentor and colleague Gert Aron, developed a set of workshops to cover basic hydraulics and hydrology for surveyors engaged in land development design. The workshops also serve as an exam review for surveyors-in-training who are getting ready to sit for their registration exam. The workshops have been offered over the past 15 years at the Pennsylvania Society of Land Surveyors State Conference, held annually in Hershey, PA. Notes developed for use in this workshop have served as the framework for several parts of this book, mainly the fluid mechanics and hydraulics chapters.

In 1996, I became a faculty member in the Surveying Program, College of Engineering, at Penn State University, Wilkes-Barre campus. One of my immediate duties was to create a course in stormwater management that would be appropriate for baccalaureate surveying graduates who intended to practice surveying in Pennsylvania. A three credit elective course was developed in 1997, and after two modifications, it evolved into a three credit course that contains fifteen weeks of instruction, with the first five weeks focusing on fluid mechanics and hydraulics, the next seven weeks focusing on hydrologic methods, and the last three weeks focusing on stormwater design. I knew that a good textbook for this course was not available, so I began to write a textbook in the Fall of 1998. During each course offering I would try to write a new chapter, and use the draft chapters as a class reference. After a few years of this approach, I had five chapters written, with about seven to go. The following year I was awarded a sabbatical, and during the sabbatical year, I finished the manuscript.

This book covers common methods used in stormwater design for quantity control. The book does not cover design for other stormwater topics such as water quality, groundwater recharge, and stream bank erosion. The original outline of topics for this book did include chapters on innovative methods in stormwater management and stormwater design with best management practices. Unfortunately, these chapters were dropped as the deadline for the manuscript approached. This kept the entire focus of the book on stormwater quantity claculations, which is probably for the better. If inspiration and time come my way, a companion text may be written dealing with these other issues. For now, I plan to concentrate on maintaining and improving this text.

As with any first publication of a technical book, it has been my experience that, even with the closest checking and double checking, some errors will most likely exist in the printed manuscript. As the author, I am responsible for these errors. Questions about the text and possible errata should be directed to me. Example problems have been checked for numerical accuracy, yet it is difficult to discover all errors. Hopefully, the context of a concept will be clear enough such that errors will not impede the understanding of a concept, but simply cause the reader to examine the topic a bit closer.

THOMAS A. SEYBERT

Wilkes-Barre, Pennsylvania

ACKNOWLEDGMENTS

During the time it took me to complete this book, several people were very helpful and encouraging through the process. First and foremost, I am blessed with a very supportive and loving wife, and two wonderful children Beth and Ben. There were many long hours during evenings, weekends, and early mornings during the writing, when I was not able to be with my three favorite people. For their patience, understanding and encouragement, I am very grateful. I also wish to acknowledge my father and mother. They taught me how to embrace work and persevere through a task.

Encouragement for pursuing the book came from several engineering faculty at Penn State Wilkes-Barre. However, the most helpful faculty encouragement came from Chuck Ghilani, Professor of Engineering in the Surveying Program, who, at the time, was in the process of writing his second book for surveying students and professionals. We had many discussions about the book writing process, and these discussions made me realize that I could write a textbook if I put my mind to it. Early draft versions of the manuscript were used and reviewed by baccalaureate students in surveying. Many of the practice problems and example problems were solved by these students. Irene Stubb, staff assistant, read several chapters for grammatical errors and also prepared, in part, some of the tables in the text. Several other chapters were reviewed for format and grammar by my wife, Chris. All through the writing process, she was always willing to help, even at times when she had a dozen other things to do to keep our household running smoothly.

Much of the research for writing this book was performed through the Penn State Library System. Marcia Nelson and Matthew O'Conner, library staff at Penn State Wilkes-Barre, were very helpful in finding reference ma-

pasture, and meadow into impervious surfaces of stone, pavement, and roofing. The addition of impervious area to a site changes the hydrology of that site and the surrounding watershed. The topography of a site is almost always disturbed to accommodate the construction of an impervious structure. Changing topography usually removes natural surface depressions in the landscape that capture, hold, and slowly infiltrate water into the subsurface. Grading of a site usually transforms an undulating vegetated surface into a plane impervious surface or grass lawn. In either case, surface depressions are removed and water that was once captured and infiltrated now accumulates and travels across the landscape to a downstream point.

Natural flow paths that twist and wind across the landscape are usually altered into linear, constant-slope paths that are changed in length and roughness. The change in these flow-path characteristics affect the time required for surface runoff to move across and through the landscape. This change in timing directly affects runoff rates, usually increasing their magnitude and causing an increase in the frequency of flooding.

The addition of impervious area requires a reduction in pervious area that reduces the capacity of a site to infiltrate rainfall. When infiltration capacity is reduced, runoff potential increases and groundwater recharge potential decreases.

1.3 STORMWATER DESIGN CRITERIA

Since the late nineteenth century until the mid-twentieth century, stormwater management was usually considered the successful collection and disposal of increased surface runoff. The solution was usually a comprehensive design of roof gutters, downspouts, swales, curbed gutters, sewer inlets, and sewer pipes to collect, convey, and discharge surface runoff to streams, rivers, lakes, and other water bodies in the most efficient manner possible. The central theme of stormwater management design was to collect and transport the runoff to a nearby body of water as quickly as possible, ridding the developed site of the excess runoff. Little thought was given to the effects of excess runoff and decreased infiltration on the surrounding watershed.

In the 1970s, many states recognized the need to consider the effects of land development on downstream flooding, including local nuisance flooding and larger-scale flood plain overflow. Regulations were put in place to control peak runoff rates. The common regulation required the developer to release no more runoff flow after development than was coming from the site prior to development. The design was focused on peak flow control, which was typically achieved through collection, detention, and slow release of surface runoff through a regulating outlet structure.

In the 1980s, partially as a result of the National Urban Runoff Program (U.S. EPA, 1983), more attention was placed on pollution from developed land, with particular emphasis on nonpoint source pollution. As a result, sev-

Figure 1.1 Channel and roadway flooding caused by upstream land development (courtesy of F. Thornton, Darby Creek Valley Association, Delaware County, PA).

eral states and municipalities required developers to address the polluted runoff issue. Suspended solids in runoff were identified as a primary transport mechanism for nonpoint source pollutants such as copper, zinc, lead, nitrogen, phosphorous, and others. Therefore, many stormwater management designs included measures to remove sediment in runoff. The capture, detention, and very slow release of the first flush of runoff was considered one of the most effective measures to allow sediment in the runoff to settle out, thus reducing the pollutant load to downstream waters.

Temperature increase in nearby streams was also brought to the attention of land development designers. As cool fresh rainfall travels across a black, hot, summer sunned parking lot, the water temperature can increase dramatically. Even small changes in stream temperature can cause a bad environment for fresh-water aquatic life, particularly fish. The concept of cooling runoff through stormwater management design was thrown into the mix.

In the early 1990s to the turn of the twenty-first century, additional issues were recognized. They included increased streambank erosion and reduced groundwater recharge. Streambank erosion was attributed to the extended release of target design flows from flow-control facilities. Although these facilities provided some measure of flood control, they inadvertently delivered to the downstream channel a design release rate over a longer period of time. The design release rate was almost always at a velocity that was bank-erosive for a longer duration than had naturally occurred before development. In almost all regions where peak flow mitigation was required, excessive streambank erosion became more prevalent. Shrinking groundwater storage levels

Figure 1.2 A sediment forebay used to capture the first flush of runoff (courtesy of R. Traver, Villanova Urban Stormwater Partnership, Villanova University).

in urbanized areas prompted many state and local officials to examine the effect of land development on groundwater recharge. Obviously, if rainfall is being converted into large amounts of surface runoff, then the amount of infiltration must be reducing. Several states and local municipalities are now requiring a developed site to include a design for providing groundwater recharge areas.

In summary, the issues that must be addressed in a stormwater management plan have changed over the past half century, as illustrated in Table 1.1. Mere collection and disposal of runoff has transformed into runoff collection with peak flow control, volume control, groundwater recharge, water quality treatment, downstream channel protection, or a combination of these. A good stormwater management plan will address all of these issues through a comprehensive design.

1.4 COMPREHENSIVE AND INNOVATIVE DESIGN

To develop a better stormwater management plan, the prospective site must be evaluated prior to the design of roadways, lots, building locations, and

Figure 1.3 Stream bank erosion caused by upstream stormwater detention facilities (courtesy of Cahill Associates, West Chester, PA).

other development features. Preservation of natural vegetation, reduction of impervious areas, and protection of high-infiltration soils are just some of the elements of stormwater design that should be considered prior to the selection and design of management structures.

Very early in the planning and design process, the site should be examined to identify the constraints and opportunities for smart design. Constraints may

Figure 1.4 Groundwater recharge through an infiltration trench (courtesy of P. DeBarry, Borton-Lawson Engineering, Wilkes-Barre, PA).

TABLE 1.1 Progressive Change in Stormwater Design Issues during the Past Half Century

Stormwater Design Issue	Approximate Timeline				
	Pre-1970	1975	1985	1995	2000
Flooding within project site	X	X	X	X	X
Flooding outside project site		X	X	X	X
Surface water quality			X	X	X
Temperature			X	X	X
Groundwater recharge				X	X
Stream bank erosion					X

include poorly drained soils, steep slopes, unstable soils, shallow soils, high water table, wetlands, riparian buffer zones, utility easements, and certain property covenants. Opportunities may be well-drained soils, wooded areas, panoramic views, surface water ponds, and old hedge rows. Old structures of historical significance, such as a one-room schoolhouse, stone barn, field-stone walls, covered bridge, stone arch bridge, and well-maintained farm buildings, can also be used as land development opportunities.

During the evaluation process some constraints might be turned into op-portunities. Riparian buffers can be used to the advantage of the development if the buffer zone is maintained and utilized for walking paths, observation points, park benches, and other parklike facilities. Wetlands can be protected and still used to enhance property value if development is worked around the wetland area and the wetland is highlighted as a natural area within the de-velopment. The perimeter of a small cluster of woods might be used as the back lot lines of a circle of several homes, and preserved as a community asset and natural area.

Beyond opportunities and constraints, conservation design should be used. These methods are anything that reduces disturbed areas, protects streams and natural drainage paths, and minimizes impervious cover. Example methods are open space design and cluster housing. Figure 1.5 shows a developed site maintaining open (green) space and protecting the natural drainage paths. This type of design reduces the impact of development on the site hydrology. There are other methods that can be used, many of which are mentioned in several state stormwater management manuals, including those of New York, Mary-land, Virginia, and Georgia.

For the developer, this design approach may be more costly in terms of engineering fees, yet in the end, a cleverly designed plan that takes advantage of site opportunities and utilizes open space design can reduce surface area needed for an expansive detention facility. This will, in turn, open up space for other use, such as additional building lots or conservation space that will enhance the market value of the developed property.

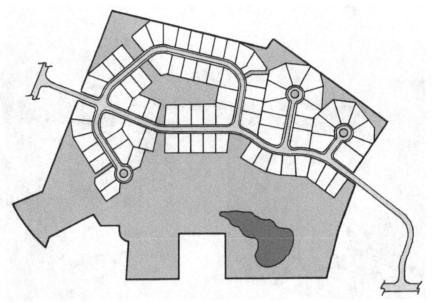

Figure 1.5 Open space design is used to reduce the effect of development (courtesy of Atlanta Regional Commission).

The worst approach to stormwater design is to think solely in terms of maximum number of postage-stamp lots that can fit into a property, with the stormwater management design treated as a last-minute addition to the design. In this approach, integration of the opportunities available to assist in minimizing the negative impact of the development is usually lost. The stormwater plan is typically reduced to an uninspired design of concrete curb gutters, inlets, pipes, and a pond stuck in the lowest corner of the site. Admittedly, detention facilities are difficult to avoid in stormwater design, and almost always necessary. Curb gutters are often required, with no option for the designer. Yet, if stormwater management is a first priority in the design process, the size of a detention pond can be reduced, and the negative effect of necessary conventional development structures like curb gutters and detention ponds can be minimized.

Sometimes innovative stormwater design is not readily accepted by counties or municipalities because the review agency is simply not familiar with the design benefits and new design methods. In the creation of any stormwater management plan, it is almost always beneficial to the designer and the review agency to have a preliminary meeting, very early in the design process, with the reviewer to discuss a general stormwater management scheme for the site. At this time, innovative methods can be presented, with expected benefits and design methods explained. Many times, a conversation like this will make the entire design and approval process much simpler.

Figure 1.6 A retention basin in a professional office park (courtesy of S. Brown, Penn State University).

1.5 BOOK ORGANIZATION

The impacts of development are mitigated in some way through structural devices or nonstructural land use practices. In all cases, the selection and design of these structures or practices are based on the estimation of surface runoff rates and volumes for the pre-development and post-development site conditions. Methods for analyzing flow rates and depths across the landscape are necessary. Sizing of conveyance structures and storage facilities is almost always necessary. Therefore, a fundamental understanding of surface hydrology, fluid flow, and methods to model both are necessary.

To support quantity calculations used in stormwater design, this book is organized into three groups of chapters, providing coverage of: (1) basic fluid mechanics, (2) fundamental surface hydrology, and (3) stormwater design methods, with all three sections geared toward stormwater management design for land development.

The first group includes chapters 2 through 4, which deal with fundamental methods in fluid mechanics. Chapter 2 deals with basic fluid properties and the analysis of fluids at rest, including static pressure and forces on submerged surfaces. Chapter 3 includes methods used to analyze fluid that is moving in a closed flow system. Chapter 4 covers fundamental methods of hydraulic analysis used in open channel flow. The material provides general fluid mechanics knowledge and a foundation for the design of conveyance structures in a typical stormwater management plan.

The second group includes chapters 5 through 10, which present hydrologic topics that are directly related to stormwater quantity control. Chapter 5 covers the hydrologic cycle and the hydrologic characteristics of watersheds that are important to standard stormwater calculations. Chapter 6 gives an overview of rainfall, providing data sources for design rainfall and methods to create design storms. Chapter 7 covers watershed time of concentration, presenting several methods and illustrating the most popular methods used. Chapter 8 presents the common runoff depth and peak flow estimation methods used in stormwater design, namely the NRCS and Rational methods. Chapter 9 explains fundamental concepts in hydrographs, including the unit hydrograph. This is followed with an explanation of the NRCS unit hydrograph and Rational hydrograph methods. Finally, Chapter 10 covers fundamental routing methods used for channel and detention basin routing.

The third group includes chapters 11 and 12, which covers procedures used to design stormwater management structures for collection, conveyance, storage, and release of surface runoff. Chapter 11 deals mainly with the analysis and design of swales, channels, pipes, and culverts. Chapter 12 deals specifically with the sizing of detention facilities and the design of multiple-stage outlet structures.

There are many other topics that must be addressed in stormwater management. This book, however, is intended to cover the most common computational methods for stormwater runoff estimation and analysis that supports stormwater management. Other chapters may be added in future editions of this text to address other elements of stormwater design.

REFERENCES

Atlanta Regional Commission. 2001. *Georgia Stormwater Management Manual: Volume 2.* Atlanta, GA, http://www.georgiastormwater.com.

DeBarry, P. A. 2004. *Watersheds: Processes, Assessment and Management.* Hoboken, NJ: John Wiley and Sons.

Maryland Department of the Environment. 2000. *Maryland Stormwater Design Manual, Volumes I & II.* Baltimore, MD: Water Management Division, http://www.mde.state.md.us.

New York State Department of Environmental Conservation. 2003. *Stormwater Management Design Manual.* Albany, NY, http://www.dec.state.ny.us.

Pennsylvania Department of Environmental Protection. 2006. *Pennsylvania Stormwater and BMP Manual (draft).* Harrisburg, PA, http://www.dep.state.pa.us.

Schueler, T. 1987. *Controlling Urban Runoff: A Practical Manual for Planning and Designing Urban BMPs.* Washington, DC: MWCOG.

U.S. Environmental Protection Agency. 1983. *Results of the Nationwide Urban Runoff Program, Volume 1—Final Report.* Washington, DC: Office of Water, 159 pp.

Virginia Department of Conservation and Recreation. 1999. *Virginia Stormwater Management Handbook, Volumes I & II.* Richmond, VA: Division of Soil and Water Conservation, http://www.dcr.virginia.gov/sw/stormwat.htm.

CHAPTER 2

FLUID PROPERTIES AND BASIC STATICS

2.1 INTRODUCTION

Fluids can be managed and engineered to perform many tasks. The hydraulic brake system in an automobile uses an oil-based fluid to transform a force applied on the brake pedal into a force applied through the brake pads and rotors, which slows the automobile. A forced-air heating and cooling system is used to distribute, through a blower and ductwork, warm or cool air generated by a heat pump to various locations in the building. Both of these examples illustrate the manipulation of a fluid to perform a certain task. Managing the volume, rate, and flow-path of surface water runoff on a land development site is no different. Sometimes we wish to divert runoff away from a building. Sometimes we must contain runoff in a structure, hold it for a while, and release it later at a slower rate. We may wish to protect a road from flooding at a stream crossing, so we must determine a correct pipe size to handle the expected stream flow. All of these tasks require some type of fluid-flow calculation and engineering design. Therefore, a fundamental understanding of water as a stationary or flowing fluid is important to support good stormwater management calculations and design.

A fluid is a substance that easily changes form when external forces are applied or removed. It is also a *continuum*—that is, a whole and continuous substance that cannot be easily separated into parts. This property of a fluid gives the substance some unique characteristics, which will be discussed later. In very general terms, fluids can be categorized as either *compressible* or *incompressible*. Gasses are compressible. They expand or contract to fill the space available for occupancy. When you pump air into a bicycle tire, a certain amount of air is being moved from a larger space to a smaller space. To do this the air must compress, thus increasing the pressure inside the tire. Examples of compressible fluids include air, steam, helium, oxygen, and methane. Liquids are considered incompressible. When moved from one space to another, a liquid maintains the same volume necessary for storage in either space. If the space is too large, the container is not filled. If the space is too small, there is an overflow. In reality, all fluids are compressible, but in the practical range of most engineering use, liquids are incompressible. Examples of incompressible fluids include water, gasoline, oil, antifreeze, and milk.

The study of water flow is given the special title of *hydraulics,* which is the specialized area of fluid mechanics that is used in stormwater runoff modeling. Hydraulic flow is incompressible and much easier to model than compressible. An *ideal* fluid is one that is assumed to be incompressible and frictionless, and it is used for developing theory or demonstration. Many times in engineering, we can treat water (stormwater) as an ideal fluid because it is a reasonable approximation in the given application.

2.2   UNITS

Currently, metric units are seldom used in stormwater design in the United States. Therefore, in this text U.S. customary units will be the preferred unit. Both unit systems require unit definition for the physical quantities encountered in common fluid mechanics study. They are length, mass, force, and time. The U.S. Customary System is a force-based system of pounds (lbs), feet (ft), and seconds (s). The International System (SI) is a mass-based system of kilograms (kg), meters (m), and seconds (s). Table 2.1 is a comparison of the two systems for four fundamental physical quantities used in fluid mechanics.

Units can be used many times to assist in the solution of a problem. Simply knowing the units of the desired outcome may indicate the necessary inputs. Dimensional analysis is a method in fluid mechanics devoted to simplification of complex fluid phenomenon. It is often used in fluid mechanics experimentation. Although we will not use such methods in this text, it is important to

TABLE 2.1   Primary Units for Physical Properties in Two Systems of Units

Quantity	International System (metric)	U.S. Customary System (foot)
Length	meter (m)	foot (ft)
Mass	kilogram (kg)	slug (lb-s^2/ft^4)
Force	Newton (N) (kg-m/s^2)	pound (lb)
Time	second (s)	second (s)

always keep track of units to make sure that they are compatible and consistent with the given application. Length can be expressed in feet, but it can also be expressed in miles (mi) or inches (in). Area, which is length squared, can be expressed in square feet (ft^2), but it can also be expressed in acres (ac) or square miles (mi^2). Table 2.2 shows some of the common units encountered in fluid mechanics and hydrology, with some appropriate conversions. Metric units are provided as a matter of interest only. The remainder of this book will deal almost exclusively with U.S. customary units.

Example 2.1   A pipeline that extends over a distance of 12.5 miles carries a fluid that is known to flow at a rate of 4.5 ft/s. How many hours will it take fluid to flow from one end of the pipe to the other?

Solution:

$$\text{Time} = \frac{\text{Distance}}{\text{Velocity}}$$

$$T = \frac{12.5 \text{ mi} \times 5280 \text{ ft/mi}}{4.5 \text{ ft/s} \times 3600 \text{ s/hr}} = 4.07 \text{ hrs}$$

In this simple example, the known units of the expected answer aid in the solution of the problem. The distance was converted from miles to feet and the velocity was converted from ft/s to ft/hr. The units of miles, feet, and seconds canceled in the calculation, leaving the sole unit of hours in the final result. Simply knowing the units of an answer aids in the solution of the problem.

The equation used in the solution of Example 2.1 is a simple physics relation that is dimensionally homogenous. This means that the parameters in the equation (distance and velocity) have units that will yield a reasonable unit for the variable (time). It is worth noting that most equations in fluid mechanics are based on physics and thus dimensionally homogeneous. However, in stormwater management, many equations are based on statistical analysis (empirical) and are often not dimensionally homogeneous. It is very

TABLE 2.2   Common Units and Conversions Used in Fluid Mechanics and Hydrology

Variable	U.S. Customary Units	Metric Units	Conversions
Distance	foot (ft) mile (mi)	meter (m) kilometer (km)	0.3048 m/ft 1.609 km/mi 5280 ft/mi 1000 m/km
Rainfall and runoff depth	inches (in)	millimeters (mm)	1 in = 25.4 mm
Surface area	feet^2 (ft^2) acres (ac) square miles (mi^2)	meters^2 (m^2) hectares (ha) kilometers^2 (km^2)	1 ac = 43,560 ft^2 1 mi^2 = 640 ac 1 ha = 1000 m^2 1 km^2 = 100 ha 1 ha = 2.471 ac
Storage volume (ponds and reservoirs)	feet^3 (ft^3) acre-inch (ac-in) acre-feet (ac-ft) ft^3/s/hr (cfs-hr) ft^3/sec/day (cfs-day)	meters^3 (m^3)	1 acre-ft = 43,560 ft^3 1 cfs-hr = 3600 ft^3 1 cfs-hr = 1 ac-in 1 cfs-days = 2 ac-ft
Water volume	gallons (gal) feet^3 (ft^3)	meters^3 (m^3) liters (l)	1 ft^3 = 7.48 gal 1 gal = 3.785 l
Water weight	pounds (lbs)	kilogram-meter/ second^2 (kg-m/s^2), Newton (N)	1 gal = 8.34 lb
Flow rate, runoff rate, and stream flow	feet^3/second (ft^3/s, cfs) gallons/minute (gpm)	meters^3/second (cms) liters/second (l/s)	1 cfs = 28.32 l/s 1 cfs = 448.8 gpm
Rainfall rate	inches/hour (in/hr) ft^3/sec/ac (cfs/ac)	millimeters/hour (mm/hr)	1 in/hr = 1 cfs/ac
Pressure	pound/inch^2 (psi), feet (of water)*	kilogram/meter^2 (kg/m^2), Pascal (Pa)	1 psi = 2.31 ft of water*

*The concept of pressure expressed in the units of feet is explained in Chapter 3.

important that students of stormwater methods be mindful of parameter units as defined by the method, and take great care to use the appropriate units.

2.3 FLUID PROPERTIES

A few fundamental properties of fluids must be understood before beginning any type of study on fluid flow. These properties are mass, density, specific weight, and viscosity. There are other useful properties of fluids, but these are the ones used most often in hydraulics.

Mass measures the ability of a body to resist motion. A body with a large mass can resist motion better than a body with a smaller mass. Mass is related to the *weight* through Newton's second law of motion, which states that force is equal to mass times acceleration ($F = ma$). In this case, the force is weight and the acceleration is gravity, thus giving us the fundamental relation of

$$W = mg \tag{2.1}$$

where W = gravity force (weight) that acts through a body (lb) [N]
$\quad m$ = mass of a body (slugs or lb-s^2/ft) [kg]
$\quad g$ = acceleration due to gravity (32.2 ft/s^2) [9.81 m/s^2]

The acceleration due to gravity, or simply gravity, is often called the *gravitational constant*. In reality, gravity varies with geographic location and is not a constant. Yet, the variation is small enough that we do not worry about this variation in hydraulic calculations.

Density is simply mass per unit volume and is a handy property in comparing motion resistance of several different substances. The relation defining density is

$$\rho = \frac{m}{V} \tag{2.2}$$

where ρ = density (slugs/ft^3 or lb-s^2/ft^4) [kg/m^3]
$\quad m$ = mass of a body (slugs or lb-s^2/ft) [kg]
$\quad V$ = volume of a body (ft^3) [m^3]

The Greek letter ρ (rho and pronounced "row") is used to represent this property. The density of water at 34°F (4°C) is 1.94 lb-s^2/ft^4 or 1000 kg/m^3, and these are the commonly used values. The temperature of 4°C is a temperature used when defining the physical properties of water because it is the temperature where water density is greatest. Water density decreases as temperature increases, yet through the practical range of temperatures for stormwater runoff, density varies from 1.94 at 32°F to 1.92 at 120°F. This variation is so small that we simply neglect it.

One might question 120°F as an upper limit on the expected range of temperature for stormwater runoff. It has been observed that runoff from large areas paved with asphalt during a hot summer day can reach water temperatures as high as 120°F. This is one of the reasons why fish usually do not survive in a stream next to a shopping mall. Most fresh-water fish cannot survive significant water temperature variations even for short durations.

Specific weight is similar to density. It is weight per unit volume. The relation is

$$\gamma = \frac{W}{V} \tag{2.3}$$

where γ = specific weight (lb/ft³) [kg-s²/m]
  W = weight of a body (lb) [N]
  V = volume of a body (ft³) [m³]

The Greek letter γ (gamma) is used to represent this property. The specific weight of water is commonly given as 62.4 lb/ft³. Just like density, however, specific weight varies with temperature (62.4 at 32°F to 61.7 at 120°F). Again, we neglect the variation because it is only about a 1% change, well within the expected accuracy of stormwater design methods. This specific weight tells us that if a large bucket of water weighs about 50 lb, the bucket has a volume capacity of less than one cubic foot. The common three-gallon bucket holds about 0.4 ft³.

Because density and specific weight are similar, another useful relation is available. If we take Equations 2.2 and 2.3, solve each for V, and then equate, we will get this relation:

$$\gamma = \rho g \tag{2.4}$$

This equation relates specific weight to density (specific mass) through the acceleration due to gravity. It is a convenient relation that is used often in fluid mechanics.

Specific gravity is a dimensionless parameter that allows a quick comparison of the density (or specific weight) of a substance to water. This can be handy if we are concerned about flotation or certain buoyancy effects in hydraulic structures. Specific gravity is defined as follows:

$$s.g. = \frac{\rho_{substance}}{\rho_{water} \ @ \ 4°C} = \frac{\gamma_{substance}}{\gamma_{water} \ @ \ 4°C} \tag{2.5}$$

where $s.g.$ = specific gravity (no units)

and ρ and γ are as defined earlier. The specific gravity of water is obviously 1.00 at 4°C. If a substance has a specific gravity less than one, then it is lighter than water and will float. If a substance has a specific gravity greater than one, then it is heavier than water and will sink. Specific gravity of water does change with temperature, but like density and specific weight, it is not a significant change.

Table 2.3 provides the average values of specific gravity, density, and specific weight for several common fluids at 68°F.

Viscosity is a fluid property that requires a bit more explanation. It is very important in the determination of friction losses in fluid flow. Viscosity represents the ability of a fluid to resist internal motion and motion along a solid boundary. The internal motion can also be described as relative motion between adjacent layers of fluid elements. The Greek letter μ (mu, pronounced "mew") is the common symbol used to represent viscosity, which is more properly referred to as *dynamic viscosity.*

The concepts of shear stress are used to explain and define viscosity. The Greek letter τ (tau, pronounced like "cow" with a t instead of c) is used to represent shear stress. Consider a fluid trapped between two surfaces, such as within the space between a smaller drum inserted inside a slightly larger drum, as shown in Figure 2.1. If we hold the outer drum stationary and rotate the inner drum with a constant velocity in a counter-clockwise direction, we can observe a velocity profile in the trapped fluid along line A–B, with the stationary surface at B and the constant velocity surface at A.

The velocity of the water in the trapped space will vary between zero at the stationary boundary B to a velocity at A equal to the velocity of the moving boundary. If the velocity is changing along line A–B through the different water layers in the fluid, then certain water layers must move faster than others, and thus there is relative motion between layers in the water. If we think of these layers as small, independent units of water rubbing against each other as they move, then the idea of shear stress (friction) between the

TABLE 2.3 Average Values of Density, Specific Weight, and Specific Gravity for Common Fluids at 68°F

Substance	Specific Gravity	Density (slugs/ft³)	Specific Weight (lb/ft³)
Gasoline	0.680	1.32	42.4
Motor oil	0.887	1.72	55.3
Linseed oil	0.930	1.80	58.0
Water	1.000	1.94	62.4
Seawater	1.030	1.99	64.3
Ethylene glycol	1.100	2.13	68.6
Carbon tetrachloride	1.590	3.08	99.2
Mercury	13.54	26.2	849

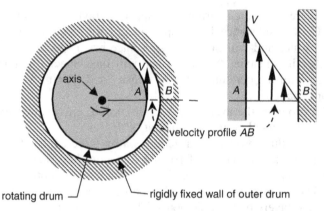

Figure 2.1 Schematic of velocity profile created by a rotating drum viscometer.

layers is easy to envision. This is a simplified explanation of what happens in fluid flow. When velocity varies between adjacent fluid elements, frictional resistance occurs internally. Viscosity is a measure of this frictional resistance. It is the proportionality constant between shear stress in adjacent layers of a fluid and the associated velocity change between those layers. This simple relation is often used to define viscosity:

$$\tau = \mu \frac{\Delta v}{\Delta y} \tag{2.6}$$

where τ = shear stress in the fluid (lb/ft³) [kg-s²/m]
  μ = dynamic viscosity, or simply viscosity (lb-s/ft²) [N-s/m²]
  Δv = change in velocity between two adjacent layers (ft/s) [m/s]
  Δy = change in distance between two adjacent layers (ft) [m]

From Equation 2.6 we can see that if μ is large, then shear stress between fluid elements is large. When shear stress is large, which makes viscosity large, the fluid has a greater ability to resist movement. Thus, a fluid with a high viscosity will flow slower than a fluid with a low viscosity in the same flow system. This equation holds for Newtonian fluids only, meaning that the velocity profile is linear through the flow region. For someone who works with several types of fluids, this may be important. Some fluids are non-Newtonian—that is, the velocity profile is not linear through the vertical profile region, and in these cases, Equation 2.6 is not valid. Thankfully, water can be considered a Newtonian fluid and the simple viscosity relation of Equation 2.6 applies.

The dynamic viscosity of water changes significantly within the practical range of temperature for stormwater flow, varying from 3.66×10^{-5} lb-s/ft² at 32°F to 1.14×10^{-5} lb-s/ft² at 120°F. This represents a viscosity variation over 200 percent. Figure 2.2 shows the variation in dynamic viscosity for the temperature range of water as a liquid.

One might think that water temperature is a critical property of the fluid when designing stormwater drainage structures. As it turns out, in drainage design we generally use a common fluid temperature of 50°F, which gives a viscosity of about 2.7×10^{-5} lb-s/ft^2. If a pipe is designed to carry a certain flow using this value of viscosity, it will easily convey that same flow at higher temperatures. Engineers often prefer numbers that are easy to remember, which makes the value of viscosity at 68°F (about 2×10^{-5}) a handy choice. Viscosity is used in estimating friction losses in stormwater conveyance systems. Yet friction losses are usually minor losses in a conveyance system, and therefore the relatively gross approximation of the value of viscosity for all water temperatures is acceptable.

One stormwater management structure where viscosity can affect design is an infiltration facility that must operate in warm and cold temperatures. These structures experience high friction losses in the infiltration process. The viscosity of water can reduce infiltration capacity by as much as 50 percent for cold weather as compared to warm weather. In this case, viscosity variation is important and must be considered in the design.

It is very common in fluid mechanics equations to encounter the ratio of viscosity over density. So, as a matter of convenience, the property of *kinematic viscosity* was created, and is simply defined as

$$\nu = \frac{\mu}{\rho} \tag{2.7}$$

where ν = kinematic viscosity (ft^2/s) [m^2/s]

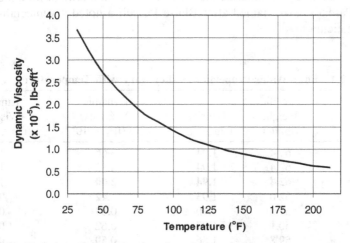

Figure 2.2   Variation of dynamic viscosity of water for the temperature range of 32°F to 212°F.

and the other two terms are as previously defined. The Greek letter ν (nu, pronounced new) is used for kinematic viscosity. The logic behind the use of ν is that it is easier to look up one property in a table (ν) than it is to look up two (μ and ρ).

Table 2.4 provides tabulated values of specific weight, density, dynamic viscosity, and kinematic viscosity for the liquid range of water. Note that all properties decrease in magnitude with increasing temperature. In stormwater management design, we usually neglect the effect of temperature on these properties and adopt a single value for each property as design constants. The values offered at 50°F are commonly used as these design constants. The values presented in the 68°F row are not in strict mathematical agreement, but they are simple to remember and sufficiently accurate for many calculations.

2.4 PRESSURE

The study of water at rest is *fluid statics*. Forces and pressures exerted by standing (static) water are important in many aspects of civil engineering design. In stormwater design, there may be times when we are interested in computing the force of standing water on a headwall, retaining wall, or flap gate in an outlet structure.

Because a fluid is a continuum, it has the ability to exert pressure in all directions. Two fundamental laws are useful in understanding fluids at rest. First, the pressure on a very small fluid element exerted by surrounding fluid elements is constant, that is, the pressure is uniform in all directions as illustrated in Figure 2.3. Second, when fluid is contained by a solid boundary, the pressure acts perpendicular to the solid boundary, as shown in Figure 2.4. Figures 2.3 and 2.4 summarize these two fundamental laws of fluid mechanics called Pascal's laws, named after Blaise Pascal, a noted seventeenth-century mathematician.

TABLE 2.4   Four Water Properties as they Vary with Temperature

Temperature °F	Specific Weight (lb/ft³)	Density (slugs/ft³)	Dynamic Viscosity (lb-s/ft², × 10⁻⁵)	Kinematic Viscosity (ft²/s, × 10⁻⁵)
32	62.4	1.94	3.66	1.89
50	62.4	1.94	2.72	1.40
68*	**62.4**	**1.94**	**2.00**	**1.00**
100	62.0	1.93	1.42	0.74
150	61.2	1.90	0.89	0.47
200	60.1	1.87	0.62	0.34
212	59.8	1.86	0.59	0.32

*The values for viscosity are approximate but easily remembered.

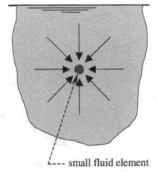

L--- small fluid element

Figure 2.3 Fluid is a continuum and exerts constant pressure in all directions.

Pressure can be defined as the amount of force exerted by a fluid on a unit area. A unit area is a convenience term, such as one square inch or one square foot. The general relation used to express fluid pressure is

$$p = \frac{F}{A} \tag{2.8}$$

where p = pressure (lb/ft^2)
    F = force (lb)
    A = area (ft^2)

Equation 2.8 is a basic relation in fluid mechanics and can be used to solve several practical problems. We can use this equation to compute specific forces exerted by a fluid.

Example 2.2 Consider a large rectangular tank of dimensions 12 by 24 feet at the base and 8 feet high holding 7 feet of water, as shown in Figure 2.5. Compute the pressure exerted on the tank bottom.

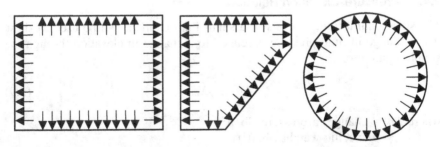

Figure 2.4 Pressure acts perpendicular to solid boundaries.

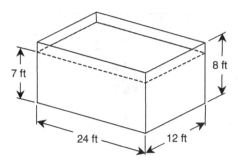

Figure 2.5   Sketch of tank for Examples 2.2 and 2.3.

Solution: Equation 2.8 says that pressure is force divided by area. The force exerted on the tank bottom area is the total weight of the water in the tank. In this case, the force is volume multiplied by specific weight. Assuming the specific weight of water is 62.4 lb/ft³, the force would be

$$F = (12 \text{ ft})(24 \text{ ft})(7 \text{ ft})(62.4 \text{ lb/ft}^3) = 125{,}800 \text{ lb}$$

The bottom area of the tank is

$$A = 12 \text{ ft} \times 24 \text{ ft} = 288 \text{ ft}^2$$

The pressure can be computed as

$$p = \frac{F}{A} = \frac{125{,}800 \text{ lb}}{(288 \text{ ft}^2)(144 \text{ in}^2/\text{ft}^2)} = 3.03 \text{ lb/in}^2$$

The pressure on the bottom of the tank is uniform across the entire area. Each square inch of tank bottom is carrying 3.03 pounds of force. We can confirm this later after examining the laws of static forces on submerged bodies, which depend on understanding the pressure-elevation relationship of fluids at rest. These laws also allow us to solve Example 2.2 in a simpler fashion.

2.4.1 Pressure-Elevation Relation

The static equilibrium analysis of a small fluid element can be used to show that a change in fluid pressure is related to a change in elevation through the simple relation of

$$\Delta p = \gamma \Delta z \tag{2.9}$$

where Δp = change in pressure (lb/ft²)
     γ = specific weight (lb/ft³)
     Δz = change in elevation or height (ft)

This formula is often written in a simpler form that drops the delta symbol and relates pressure to fluid depth instead of elevation change:

$$p = \gamma h \tag{2.10}$$

where p = pressure (lb/ft^2)
     h = depth of fluid (ft)

Equations 2.9 and 2.10 are applicable for fluids that are homogeneous and at rest. Clean water is homogeneous. Sediment-laden water is not really homogeneous, yet we often analyze it as such. A thick water/sludge is nonhomogeneous, and in this case Equation 2.9 does not apply. Pressure is force per unit area, as defined in Equation 2.8. The units of fluid pressure that are commonly used include lb/in^2 (psi), lb/ft^2, and inches of mercury, which can be converted directly to a force per unit area by using Equation 2.8. If we examine Equations 2.9 and 2.10, we can make the following observations:

- Pressure varies linearly with depth.
- Elements of a liquid at the same elevation must have the same pressure.
- An increase in elevation of a body within a liquid will cause a decrease in surrounding pressure, and vice versa.

Example 2.3   Solve Example 2.2 using Equation 2.10.

Solution: The fluid depth in the tank is 7 feet. The fluid has a specific weight of 62.4 lb/ft^3. Therefore, using Equation 2.10 we can solve for pressure:

$$p = \frac{(62.4 \text{ lb/ft}^3)(7 \text{ ft})}{144 \text{ in}^2/\text{ft}^2} = 3.03 \text{ lb/in}^2$$

The solution to Example 2.2 is quicker using Equation 2.10 as compared to Equation 2.7. This leads us directly to one of Pascal's notable discoveries. Pascal proposed that pressure does *not* depend on fluid volume. Pressure is driven by fluid depth, or column height. The pressure at the bottom of a one-inch diameter vertical tube that holds 5 feet of water is the same pressure that we should expect at the bottom of a 45-ft diameter swimming pool that holds 5 feet of water. The volume stored above a surface does not affect the pressure on that surface. Figure 2.6 shows the configuration of several different fluid containers that all experience the same pressure at the container bottom. This observation was contrary to popular belief at the time of its discovery, and therefore it was labeled Pascal's paradox.

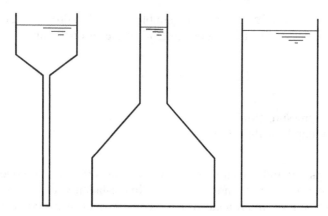

Figure 2.6 Several containers illustrate Pascal's paradox, with the same pressure at the bottom.

2.4.2 Reference Pressure

Equation 2.9 gives *change* in pressure, so it requires a reference pressure to get a total pressure at some point in space. Pressure can be measured with respect to an absolute vacuum, which has pressure equal to zero. It is a consistent reference, but it is not readily accessible. Pressure can also be measured relative to the atmosphere, which is very accessible. However, this reference varies with elevation and temperature. Most pressures encountered in engineering are measured by common pressure gages that are referenced to the atmosphere. The relationship between absolute pressure and gage pressure is

$$p_{absolute} = p_{gage} + p_{atmosphere} \qquad (2.11)$$

Absolute pressure is always positive. Gage pressure can be positive or negative. The pressure in the atmosphere is typically assumed to be 14.7 lb/in² [101.3 kPa], with a practical variation between 13.8 and 15.3 lb/in² (absolute). This variation in air pressure does not significantly affect pressure calculations for water in most civil engineering design, and certainly has little affect on stormwater management design.

Atmospheric pressure is often reported in inches (or millimeters) of mercury, typically in the range of 28 to 31 inches. Mercury barometers are typically used to measure atmospheric pressure, and mercury weighs about 849 lb/ft³. Using Equation 2.10, we can compute the pressure (lb/in² or psi) generated by a 30-inch column of mercury as

$$p = \gamma h = \frac{(849 \text{ lb/ft}^3)(30 \text{ in})}{1728 \text{ in}^3/\text{ft}^3} = 14.7 \text{ lb/in}^2$$

As always in fluid mechanics, attention must be given to consistent units. In this case, the volume in cubic feet must be converted to volume in cubic inches through the conversion factor of 1728 in³/ft³ to get the answer in the units of lb/in² (psi).

Meteorologists, physicists, and engineers have long adopted the short-cut method of expressing pressure in terms of a height of fluid. The meteorologist usually uses mercury. The civil engineer usually uses water. The mechanical engineer often uses oil. The key thing to remember is that pressure can be expressed in inches or feet, but it is understood that the pressure really has units of force per unit area as illustrated in the previous calculation.

Example 2.4 Consider an open cylindrical tank that is 5 feet in diameter, 15 feet high, and holding 13 feet of water shown in Figure 2.7. The barometric pressure surrounding the tank is reported as 28.2 inches of mercury. Determine: (a) the gage pressure (psi) at the bottom of the tank and (b) the absolute pressure (psi) at the bottom of the tank.

Solution:

(a) $p_{gage} = \gamma_{water} h = \dfrac{(62.4 \text{ lb/ft}^2)(13 \text{ ft})}{(144 \text{ in}^3/\text{ft}^3)} = 5.63 \text{ lb/in}^2$

(b) $p_{atmosphere} = \gamma_{mercury} h = \dfrac{(849 \text{ lb/ft}^2)(28.2 \text{ in})}{1728 \text{ in}^3/\text{ft}^3} = 13.86 \text{ lb/in}^2$

$p_{absolute} = p_{gage} + p_{atmosphere} = (5.63 + 13.86) \text{ lb/in}^2 = 19.49 \text{ lb/in}^2$

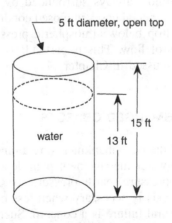

Figure 2.7 Water tank of Examples 2.4 and 2.5.

Example 2.5 For the tank in Example 2.4, the water depth remains 13 feet but the atmospheric pressure changes to 31.1 inches of mercury. Determine the absolute pressure (psi) at the bottom of the tank.

Solution:

$$P_{\text{atmosphere}} = \gamma_{\text{mercury}} h = \frac{(849 \text{ lb/ft}^2)(31.1 \text{ in})}{1728 \text{ in}^3/\text{ft}^3} = 15.28 \text{ lb/in}^2$$

$$P_{\text{absolute}} = P_{\text{gage}} + P_{\text{atmosphere}} = (5.63 + 15.28) \text{ lb/in}^2 = 20.91 \text{ lb/in}^2$$

Examples 2.4 and 2.5 illustrate a few things. First, keeping track of units is important. The input parameters were given in pounds and feet. The desired output was in pounds and inches. We had to apply the simple conversions of ft^3 to in^3 and ft^2 to in^2. Also, the examples illustrate the effect of atmospheric pressure variation on an absolute pressure. In this case, the absolute pressure at the bottom of the tank changed $(20.91 - 19.49)/19.49 \times 100 = 7.3\%$ due to a change in atmospheric pressure. Seven percent variation is significant, yet the two problems use values of atmospheric pressure that represent the extreme variation that one would expect in the atmosphere. Most times this change in absolute pressure due to atmospheric pressure variation is not significant. If we are concerned about the structural integrity of the tank, we must realize that the *pressure difference* experienced by the tank bottom and walls is what drives the structural design. So, as long as the atmospheric pressure surrounding the tank, at any given time, is the same on all sides, the loading on the tank will be the same. With this in mind, gage pressure is adequate for most engineering design purposes and, as you may suspect, we almost always use gage pressure in civil engineering design, simply because our design project is almost always surrounded by a uniform atmospheric pressure. There are some special cases in closed conduit design where trapped air in the conduit can drop below atmospheric pressure and the trapped air may affect that analysis of flow. This is particularly true in culvert analysis and design, which is discussed in Chapter 11.

2.5 FORCES ON SUBMERGED OBJECTS

The complete design of dams, embankments, retaining walls and other structural devices in a stormwater management plan depend on the computation of forces due to fluid pressure, earth pressure, or a combination of both. Rigorous structural analysis is necessary when loss of personal property and human life due to structural failure is a concern. Such analysis is beyond the scope of this text. However, for many stormwater structures a simple understanding of the magnitude of forces experienced by the structure is often sufficient to determine the engineering feasibility of that structure. Forces caused by static fluid on a structure are determined by computing the pressure on the submerged object and converting that pressure to a force. The fundamental pressure-elevation relation of Equations 2.9 and 2.10 is commonly used to assist in fluid force calculations. Sophisticated fluid pressure problems often require the use of integral calculus or finite element methods. However, many situations can be analyzed through the use of a simple analysis of forces and basic engineering mechanics.

2.5.1 Flat Horizontal Surfaces

The computation of hydrostatic force on flat horizontal surfaces relies directly on the pressure relation of Equation 2.8 and pressure-elevation relation of Equation 2.10. When water pressure acts on one side of a flat surface while the other side of that surface is open to the atmosphere, a hydrostatic force occurs. Often in hydraulic structures we are concerned about uplift forces. Such is the case when water pressure is acting on the underside of a horizontal surface while air (zero pressure) is in contact with the upper side of the same horizontal surface. A simple computation of hydrostatic uplift force is best illustrated by example.

Example 2.6 A watertight concrete manhole as shown in Figure 2.8 is used to change the direction of flow in a storm sewer piping network. The manhole is 10 feet deep and is installed in a region near a wetland, where the depth

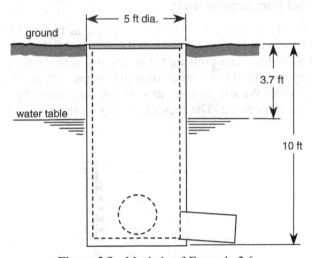

Figure 2.8 Manhole of Example 2.6.

to water table is 3.7 feet. The manhole is cylindrical and has an outside diameter of 5 feet, which is constant for its entire depth. Compute the hydrostatic uplift force acting on the manhole due to the high water table.

Solution: Equation 2.8 states that force is the product of pressure and area. The pressure acting upward on the bottom of the manhole is defined by Equation 2.10.

$$p = \gamma h = (62.4 \text{ lb/ft}^3)(10 - 3.7 \text{ ft}) = 393 \text{ lb/ft}^2$$

The area of the bottom of the manhole is

$$A = \frac{\pi d^2}{4} = \frac{\pi (5 \text{ ft})^2}{4} = 19.63 \text{ ft}^2$$

Thus, the force is

$$F = (393 \text{ lb/ft}^2)(19.63 \text{ ft}^2) = 7720 \text{ lb}$$

In order for the manhole to remain stationary, the weight of the manhole and any overburden soil above the manhole must weigh more than 7720 lb. In this case, a quick calculation on the volume of the reinforced concrete manhole, with a 0.5 ft wall thickness and a standard cast-iron cover, reveals that the manhole weighs approximately 12,000 lb. Thus we can conclude that the manhole will most likely not move due to the hydrostatic uplift force.

2.5.2 Vertical Rectangular Walls

Consider a simple rectangular vertical wall shown in Figure 2.9. The width dimension of the wall is perpendicular to the sketch.

Equation 2.10 states that pressure varies linearly with depth, and therefore we must compute a fluid pressure distribution on the submerged area before resolving the force. We will assume atmospheric pressure to be zero and use it as the reference pressure. The pressure acting on the wall at the air-water

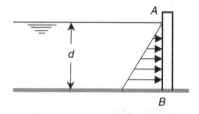

Figure 2.9 Pressure variation on a rectangular vertical wall.

interface (point A) is zero. Thus, the pressure varies linearly (straight-line), beginning at zero and increasing to the pressure at the bottom of the wall (point B), which can be computed using $P_B = \gamma h_B$. The resulting pressure distribution on the wall is a simple triangle and the average pressure on the wall is

$$P_{average} = \frac{p_A + p_B}{2} = \frac{0 + \gamma h_B}{2} = \frac{\gamma h_B}{2}$$

Here, h_B is defined as d in the sketch, and therefore the relation simply becomes

$$P_{average} = \frac{\gamma d}{2} \tag{2.12}$$

We know from Equation 2.8 that $F = pA$, so the force on the wall becomes

$$F = \left(\frac{\gamma d}{2}\right) A \tag{2.13}$$

where F = force exerted on the wall by the fluid (lb)
    γ = specific weight of the fluid (lb/ft³)
    d = depth of fluid acting against the wall (ft)
    A = the surface area of the wall in contact with the fluid (ft²)

The area of the wall in contact with the water is simply the product of depth and width. This is the simple relation used to compute the force of a fluid on a vertical rectangular wall. The average pressure calculation uses a triangular-shaped prism, as shown in Figure 2.10, which assumes a rectangular wall. If the wall is not rectangular in shape, then this equation is not valid.

Equation 2.13 gives us the magnitude of the force exerted on the wall, but it is also important to know the point of application of this force and its line

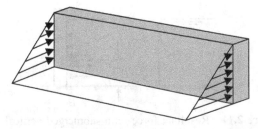

Figure 2.10 Pressure prism for a rectangular vertical wall.

of action. Pascal's laws tell us that the force must act perpendicular to solid boundaries, so the line of action must be perpendicular to the wall. The point of application turns out to be through the centroid of the pressure prism (also known as the center of pressure) acting on the wall. For vertical rectangular walls, the centroid of the pressure prism occurs at $d/3$ from the bottom of the wall, measured along the vertical as shown in Figure 2.11 (point C). In summary, the force due to fluid pressure, acting on a vertical rectangular wall has three characteristics:

- The magnitude of the force is equal to $\gamma dA/2$.
- The line of action is perpendicular to the wall.
- The point of application is at $d/3$ above the bottom of the wall, measured along the vertical.

Example 2.7   A vertical rectangular wall that is 24 feet wide acts as a flood prevention barrier along a street near a river. The maximum expected water depth against the wall during flooding is 4.5 feet. Compute the force exerted on the wall by the maximum expected water depth and also report its point of application with respect to the bottom of the wall.

Solution: Using Equation 2.13, we have

$$F = \left(\frac{\gamma d}{2}\right) A$$

$$F = \frac{(62.4 \text{ lb/ft}^3)(4.5 \text{ ft})(4.5 \text{ ft})(24 \text{ ft})}{2} = 15{,}200 \text{ lb}$$

The force acts perpendicular to the wall at a location y, measured from the bottom of the wall:

$$y = \frac{d}{3} = \frac{4.5 \text{ ft}}{3} = 1.5 \text{ ft}$$

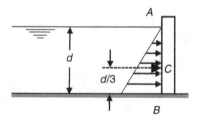

Figure 2.11   Resultant force on a submerged vertical wall.

The computed force would act 1.5 feet from the bottom of the wall, and since the wall is rectangular and horizontally symmetrical, the force would act at the mid-width location, or 12 feet from either end of the wall. More often, structural engineers express uniform loading in terms of a unit foot when the structure is prismatic—that is, it is uniform in cross-section for the full length of the wall. In this example, the load on the wall per foot is

$$F_{\text{per foot}} = \left(\frac{15,200 \text{ lb}}{24 \text{ ft}}\right) = 633 \text{ lb/ft}$$

2.5.3 Other Submerged Areas

The vertical rectangular wall is a special case of a more general solution for forces on submerged areas. As submerged areas become more irregular and complex in orientation and design, so do the methods of analysis. Ultimately, the methods of integral calculus will solve most problems of force on a submerged area. Such topics are beyond the objective of this text. However, to understand the limitations of the methods presented here, a broader understanding of the topic is valuable. The coverage of these topics can be found in any good engineering fluid mechanics textbook, such as Street et al. (1996). Mott (2006) has a practically oriented treatment of the topic for submerged plane areas and curved surfaces.

2.6 BUOYANT FORCE

The methods of computing forces on submerged areas can be used to determine the hydrostatic uplift force on a submerged object. This hydrostatic uplift force is commonly called the *buoyant force*. Buoyant force can be computed by the following relation:

$$F_{\text{b}} = \gamma_{\text{f}} V_{\text{d}} \qquad (2.14)$$

where F_{b} = buoyant force (lb)
γ_{f} = specific weight of the fluid (lb/ft^3)
V_{d} = volume displaced by the immersed body (ft^3)

This simple relation can be used to compute approximate uplift forces on buried stormwater structures, such as pipes, tanks, and catch basins that are installed in areas with a high water table.

Example 2.8 For the manhole of Example 2.6, compute the uplift force by using Equation 2.14.

Solution: The water displacement volume of the manhole is

$$V_d = (10 - 3.7 \text{ ft}) \frac{\pi(5 \text{ ft})^2}{4} = 123.7 \text{ ft}^3$$

And the buoyant force is

$$F_b = \gamma_f V_d = (62.4 \text{ lb/ft}^3)(123.7 \text{ ft}^3) = 7720 \text{ lb}$$

The buoyant force equation gives the same result as the solution in Example 2.6, and it is a bit simpler to solve. Either method is acceptable here, but in problems where geometry is more complex, the buoyant force equation may be easier to use.

PROBLEMS

2.1   A newly constructed wet detention pond has a storage capacity of 3.5 ac-ft. The contractor decides to fill the pond by drawing water from a nearby stream using a pump. The pump delivers water at a constant rate of 400 gpm. How many hours will it take to fill the pond using this pump?

2.2   In kinematics, the distance traveled by a body starting from rest can be expressed by the relation $d = \frac{1}{2}at^2$, where a is acceleration and t is time. A tractor-trailer is observed moving up a long, gradually inclined mountain road starting from rest. It travels 2.7 miles in 7.8 minutes. Assume the vehicle acceleration is constant during the entire time of observation. Determine the acceleration in ft/s^2 and in mi/hr/s.

2.3   Gasoline has a specific gravity of 0.680. If the gasoline tank of a pickup truck holds 30 gallons, how much weight is added to the truck with a full tank versus an empty tank?

2.4   A three-gallon bucket weighing 0.5 of a pound is filled with a liquid. The bucket with liquid weighs 22.7 pounds. Determine the specific weight and specific gravity of the liquid. Is the liquid lighter or heavier than water? Based on this information, what is your best guess as to the identity of the liquid?

2.5   Consider the viscosity of water. Which will pour down a sink drain quicker: 2 gallons of boiling hot water (210°F) or 2 gallons of ice cold water (35°F)? Explain your answer.

2.6   A cylindrical tank on a firetruck is 14 feet long and has a 6-foot diameter. Determine the storage capacity of the tank in gallons and the weight of the water in a full tank, in tons.

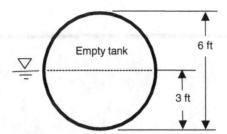

Figure 2.12 Cylindrical tank of Problem 2.10.

2.7 If the atmospheric pressure is reported to be 27.8 inches of mercury (s.g. = 13.6), what is the atmospheric pressure in psi? Is this high, average, or low in terms of atmospheric pressure?

2.8 A rectangular concrete box inlet has the outside dimensions of 3.0 feet wide, 5.0 feet long, and 7.5 feet deep. It is placed flush with grade in a soil that has a high water table. At its extreme condition the water table is only 2.0 feet from the soil surface. Compute the uplift force (buoyant force) on this concrete box due to this high water table.

2.9 If the walls and bottom of the concrete box inlet in Problem 2.8 are 6 inches thick, determine if the uplift force will cause the box to move upward. Assume reinforced concrete weighs 150 lb/ft^3. Assume the box is covered with a metal grate that weights 150 lbs.

2.10 An empty cylindrical steel tank (Figure 2.12) has a diameter of 6 feet and length of 30 feet. It is placed in a river on its side and is observed to float in the water with a draft of about 3.0 feet. Determine:

a. The weight of the tank, assuming that the buoyant force equals the tank weight.

b. The wall thickness of the tank if steel has a specific weight of 490 lb/ft^3.

REFERENCES

1. Daugherty, R. L., J. B. Franzini, and E. J. Finnemore. 1985. *Fluid Mechanics with Engineering Applications,* 8th ed. New York: McGraw-Hill, ISBN 0-07-15441-4.

2. Brater, E. F., H. W. King, J. E. Lindell, and C. Y. Wei. 1996. *Handbook of Hydraulics,* 7th ed. New York: McGraw-Hill, ISBN 0-070-07247-7.

3. Mott, R. L. 2006. *Applied Fluid Mechanics,* 6th Ed. Upper Saddle River, NJ: Prentice-Hall, ISBN 0-13-114680-7.

4. Street, R. L., G. Z. Watters, and J. K. Vennard. 1996. *Elementary Fluid Mechanics,* 7th ed., New York: John Wiley & Sons, ISBN 0-471-01310-2.

CHAPTER 3

━━━━━━━━━━━━━━━━━━━━━━━━━━━━━━━━━

FLUID FLOW

3.1 INTRODUCTION

Fluid flow is the study of fluid in motion, which is also called *fluid dynamics.* Dynamics is commonly broken into two parts: kinematics and kinetics. Kinematics is the part of dynamics that deals with distance, velocity, acceleration, and time. Kinematics does not answer the question of why the motion occurs, but instead describes the motion of the body in terms of translation and rotation. Kinetics, by contrast, is that part of science that deals with the effect of forces on a body. Kinetics deals with force, mass, and acceleration. The methods presented here are related to both kinematics and kinetics.

There are three fundamental conservation methods used in fluid mechanics: mass, energy, and momentum. In this text, we will investigate only mass and energy methods, although momentum methods are useful in some specialized applications in stormwater design. Conservation of mass is a kinematic relationship and conservation of energy is a kinetic relationship. Understanding these two basic conservation methods is necessary for understanding and analyzing fluid flow in stormwater management structures.

There are two basic types of fluid flow, namely pressure flow and open channel (gravity) flow. *Pressure flow* typically occurs in closed conduits, such as a pipe or culvert that is flowing at full capacity. Pressure flow requires the flowing fluid to exert some fluid pressure on all boundaries of the closed conduit and has the defining parameters of pressure, area, velocity, elevation, and energy loss. *Open channel flow*, also known as free surface flow, occurs in open conduits or channels such as a river, stream, swale, curb gutter, or ditch. Closed conduits such as pipes and culverts that flow partially full are also classified as open channel flow. The presence of a free surface (air to water interface) within the conduit establishes the condition of open channel flow in any conveyance structure.

In stormwater management design, open channel flow is the most common type of flow encountered. Overland flow, gutter flow, swale flow, some pipe flow and all stream flow (natural channel or man-made) is a form of open channel flow. Pressure flow can exist in storm sewers and culverts. Outlet structures for detention ponds are mostly pressure flow devices.

3.2 FLOW RATE

Before discussing conservation of mass or energy, the concept of flow rate must be understood. Flow rate is a means of quantifying the movement of fluids with respect to time. In fluid mechanics, there are three fundamental flow rates that can be used, based on the way the fluid is measured—volume, mass, or weight. These three flow rates, with equations and units, are summarized in Table 3.1.

In Equations 3.1 to 3.3, v is the average velocity of the fluid, A is the flow area of the flow conduit, ρ is fluid density, and γ is fluid specific weight. Volume flow rate is most often used when dealing with water. With gasses, mass flow rate is convenient because density is more likely to change in a compressible gas. When weight is more important than volume, as in structural design, weight flow rate is used. Note that all three flow rate equations contain a velocity term, which is a kinematic parameter. In stormwater management and surface water flow analysis, we are always interested in the

TABLE 3.1 Three Forms of Flow Rate in Fluid Mechanics

Flow Rate	U.S. Customary Units	Equation	
Volume	ft³/s	$q = vA$	(3.1)
Mass	slug/s	$M = \rho vA$	(3.2)
Weight	lb/s	$W = \gamma vA$	(3.3)

volume or volume flow rate of runoff. Therefore, we use exclusively the volume flow rate relation of Equation 3.1.

Example 3.1   Consider a 24-inch circular pipe flowing full of water. If the velocity of flow in the pipe is 2.0 ft/s, determine (a) the volume flow rate, (b) the mass flow rate, and (c) the weight flow rate. Assume that the pipe inside diameter is the nominal diameter of the pipe.

Solution: The flow area of the conduit is the cross-sectional area of the 24-inch (2-ft) diameter pipe. Thus area is computed as follows:

$$A = \frac{\pi D^2}{4} = \frac{\pi (2)^2}{4} = 3.14 \text{ ft}^2$$

The volume flow rate is simply v times A or

$$q = vA = (2 \text{ ft/s})(3.14 \text{ ft}^2) = 6.28 \text{ ft}^3/\text{s}$$

The mass flow rate is the volume flow rate times the density of water.

$$M = \rho vA = \rho q = (1.94 \text{ slugs/ft}^3)(6.28 \text{ ft}^3/\text{s}) = 12.2 \text{ slugs/s}$$

The weight flow rate is the volume flow rate times the specific weight of water.

$$W = \gamma vA = \gamma q = (62.4 \text{ lb/ft}^3)(6.28 \text{ ft}^3/\text{s}) = 392 \text{ lb/s}$$

3.2.1 Steady Flow

Flow can be classified as either *steady* or *unsteady*. For volume flow analysis, steady flow means that the flow rate does not change with time. Flow in a garden hose connected to a common residential spigot can be considered steady flow. As long as the spigot valve is open and we don't touch it, the flow is steady. Even if the garden hose is in two segments, say a ¾-inch segment attached to a ½-inch segment, the flow is still steady. The flow going into the hose through the spigot at the ¾-inch end is the same as the flow coming out of the hose at the open ½-inch end.

Unsteady flow is flow that varies with time. During the time we open and close the spigot to the hose, the flow is unsteady; that is, the flow is increasing (while we open the valve) or decreasing (while we close the valve). Steady flow is more elementary than unsteady flow. Many engineering applications in stormwater design can be considered steady flow. The flow in a stormwater pipe or diversion swale (ditch) is usually treated as steady flow, and the methods presented in this chapter apply. However, the design of the outlet structure of a detention pond is unsteady flow. As a detention pond fills during a rainfall event, flow through the outlet structure increases with time. As a detention pond drains after a rainfall event ends, the flow through the structure decreases with time, usually from a maximum flow to zero. Differencing methods must be used to model the flow through a detention facility. This method is covered in chapters 10 and 12.

3.2.2 Uniform Flow

We can also classify flow as either uniform or nonuniform. *Uniform flow* means that the flow velocity does not change with location along the flow path. Conversely, *nonuniform flow* has velocity that changes as the water travels along its flow path. Steady flow in a closed conduit that changes in cross-sectional area from smaller size to larger size can be considered non-uniform flow. As the flow moves from the smaller section to the larger section, the flow velocity must decrease. This particular case is called steady-nonuniform flow. The flow is constant, but the velocity changes. The product of velocity and area in each section remains the same. This condition is a good illustration of the continuity relation, which is discussed later. Steady uniform flow is the easiest flow type to model and, thankfully, it is the flow type most commonly assumed in many analysis and design situations in stormwater management.

3.3 CONSERVATION OF MASS

The law of conservation of mass says that mass can neither be created nor destroyed. In many hydraulic calculations it can be applied as a simple accounting mechanism. For a control volume in a fluid-flow system, the law of conservation of mass can be written in equation form:

$$q_{in} - q_{out} = \frac{\Delta S}{\Delta t} \tag{3.4}$$

where q_{in} = flow rate into the system (ft^3/s)

q_{out} = flow rate out of the system (ft^3/s)

$\Delta S/\Delta t$ = change in storage in the system with respect to time (ft^3/s)

The common control volume example that helps explain this relation is a water storage tank with an inflow pipe and an outflow pipe. The inflow pipe is providing a flow rate that is different (larger or smaller) than the outflow pipe. Since the inflow is different than the outflow, the water volume (storage) in the tank will change (increase or decrease) with time. Equation 3.4 can be used to calculate the change in storage in the tank for a finite period of time.

Example 3.2   A water storage tank shown in Figure 3.1 has water flowing in at a constant rate of 490 gpm. At the same time, a pump is used to remove water from the tank at an approximately constant rate of 630 gpm. What is the change in storage in the tank over a period of 45 minutes?

Solution: Using the units of gallons and minutes:

$$q_{in} - q_{out} = \frac{\Delta S}{\Delta t}$$

$$\Delta S = (q_{in} - q_{out})\Delta t$$

$$\Delta S = (490 \text{ gpm} - 630 \text{ gpm}) \, 45 \text{ min} = (-140)(45) = -6300 \text{ gal}$$

The negative sign indicates that the storage volume has decreased by 6300 gallons during the 45-minute period.

A common control volume in stormwater management is the detention pond, as shown in Figure 3.2. The flow rate into the pond can be from more than one source. Inflow can be a point source such as a pipe or culvert, or it can be a distributed source, such as rainfall. The outflow from a control volume is sometimes referred to as a *sink*. For a pond, the sink can be a point sink, such as an outlet pipe, or it can be distributed such as infiltration through the pond bottom. Of course, we would not want significant infiltration through the pond embankment. That could lead to structural failure. In any case, one must evaluate all significant sources and sinks that contribute flow into or out of the control volume and account for them in the mass conservation relation. The difference will result in either an increase in storage (inflow greater than outflow) or a decrease in storage (outflow greater than inflow) in the detention pond.

The example of a detention pond as a control volume is an interesting one, yet it is a significant task to analyze mass conservation in a detention pond. The relation requires q_{in} and q_{out} to be relatively constant for the duration of

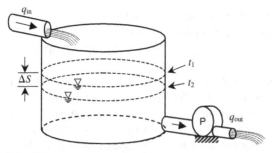

Figure 3.1   Water storage tank with constant inflow and outflow.

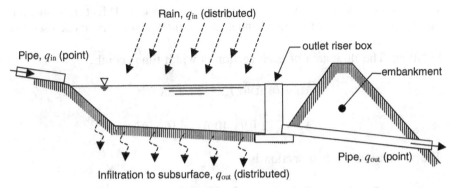

Figure 3.2   Sketch of a detention pond with inflows and outflows.

the time period, Δt. For a typical detention pond, this is true only for very short time periods. Therefore, to use Equation 3.4, it must be solved repetitively over small time intervals, using the results of a previous calculation as input to the next calculation. In this scenario, the equation solution is referred to as a *discretized solution*. The discretization process takes a nonlinear (nonuniform) function and solves it in short time intervals, such that the nonlinear function is approximately equal to a linear function. This method is utilized in the channel and basin routing methods of Chapter 10.

The *continuity equation* is a special case of conservation of mass that assumes the flow into the system is the same as the flow out of the system. In this case, the change in storage in the control volume is zero and a simpler relation applies.

$$q_{in} = q_{out} \tag{3.5}$$

In this simplified equation, if flow is constant in the system, we can apply the flow rate Equation 3.1 and rewrite continuity as

$$v_1 A_1 = v_2 A_2 \tag{3.6}$$

where v = average cross-sectional velocity of the fluid (ft/s)
A = cross-sectional flow area in the conveyance device (ft^2)

This is a handy equation when a steady flow moves from one conduit to another, as in the case of stormwater moving from a 24-inch pipe to a 30-inch pipe, or from a storm sewer to an open channel.

Example 3.3   Water flows in a rectangular open channel that is 4 feet wide and lined with concrete. The flow depth is measured as 0.72 feet. The channel changes to a second rectangular section that is 12 feet wide and is lined with stone rip-rap. The flow depth in the 12-foot section is 1.40 feet. If a flow rate of 24.5 ft³/s is constant in the channel, determine the velocity in each section.

Solution: The flow area of each section is width times depth.

$$A_1 = (4 \text{ ft})(0.72 \text{ ft}) = 2.88 \text{ ft}^2$$

$$A_2 = (12 \text{ ft})(1.40 \text{ ft}) = 16.8 \text{ ft}^2$$

The velocity in the first section is

$$v_1 = \frac{q}{A_1} = \frac{24.5}{2.88} = 8.51 \text{ ft/s}$$

The velocity in the second section is

$$v_2 = \frac{q}{A_2} = \frac{24.5}{16.8} = 1.46 \text{ ft/s}$$

3.4 ENERGY METHODS

Fluid energy is a very important concept in fluid mechanics. Many useful fluid motion equations are derived from energy concepts. When a fluid flows from one location to another, it requires energy to move the fluid. The conservation of energy law states that energy cannot be created or destroyed, but can change forms.

Energy methods are derived from the basic physical concept of work of a force, which simply defined is

$$w = Fd \qquad (3.7)$$

where w = work of a force (lb-ft)
$\quad F$ = applied force (lb)
$\quad d$ = distance through which the force is applied (ft)

The units of work and energy are lb-ft. Some people like to flip the units to ft-lb. Work is typically visualized as the movement of an object of some weight (mass) through a distance. The classic example is a box of weight w moved through a distance d. The key phrase in the definition of d in the work equation is "through which." This requires the distance of movement of the force to be measured along the same path as the direction of the force. Thus, for a box of weight w, the gravity force of the box is being moved. If the box is moved along a horizontal plane, the weight of the box performs no work since the movement is perpendicular to the gravity force. However, if the box is moved along a vertical plane, then the box does work and can be computed by Equation 3.7.

In fluid mechanics, the object being moved is a fluid. Since fluid is a continuum, it is best viewed as a small fluid element of unit weight, such as an imaginary 1-lb fluid element. For this reason, energy is defined in the units of pound-foot per pound (lb-ft/lb) of fluid moved. For convenience the unit of fluid energy is shortened to simply feet of fluid. It is often easier to think of fluid energy in terms of feet (depth or height) than in terms of lb-ft/lb (energy units).

In fluid flow, the three major energy forms are potential energy, kinetic energy, and static energy. They are described in terms of fluid height, also known as energy head. The term *head* in this application means the height of a water column necessary to replace an equivalent fluid pressure, as defined by $p = \gamma h$.

3.4.1 Potential Energy (Elevation Head)

Potential energy, or energy of elevation, is that energy attributed to the position of the fluid with respect to an elevation datum. It is simply defined as

$$h_z = z \qquad (3.8)$$

where h_z = potential energy or elevation head (ft)
     z = elevation of the fluid with respect to a datum (ft)

Again, think of elevation energy as ft-lbs of energy per pound of water. If water is moved to a higher elevation, then work is done on the water or in simpler terms, energy has been added to the water. Therefore, as the water element rises in elevation, it gains energy. As it drops in elevation, it loses energy.

3.4.2 Kinetic Energy (Velocity Head)

Kinetic energy is that energy attributed to the velocity (motion) of the fluid and is often referred to as the dynamic head or velocity head. A unit weight (one pound) of fluid moving at velocity v has kinetic energy or velocity head, expressed mathematically as

$$h_v = \frac{v^2}{2g} \qquad (3.9)$$

where h_v = velocity head (ft)
  v = velocity of the fluid (ft/s)
  g = gravitation constant (32.2 ft/s²)

Notice in this equation that the units for h_v work out to be units of length, or feet of water.

3.4.3 Static Energy (Pressure Head)

Static energy or pressure head is a special form of potential energy and represents the amount of energy trapped in the fluid due to fluid pressure. It is defined by rearranging the static pressure relation of Equation 2.10 to

$$h_s = \frac{p}{\gamma} \qquad (3.10)$$

where h_s = pressure head (ft)
  p = pressure of the fluid (lb/ft²)
  γ = specific weight of the fluid, water (62.4 lb/ft³)

Pressure head is often simply referred to as the static head because it represents that segment of energy that results from static pressure in the fluid. Fluid pressure represents an ability of the fluid to do work. It exists in closed conduit flow where pressure is exerted on all surfaces of the conduit. Like elevation head and velocity head, static pressure head is expressed in length units, typically feet.

3.4.4 Total Fluid Energy

To determine the total energy of a fluid element at any point in a fluid flow system, we sum the three basic fluid energies. For a fluid element of unit weight with pressure p, velocity v, and elevation z, the total energy E, of the fluid element is

$$E = h_z + h_v + h_s \qquad (3.11)$$

Substituting Equations 3.8, 3.9, and 3.10 gives

$$E = z + \frac{v^2}{2g} + \frac{p}{\gamma} \qquad (3.12)$$

Equation 3.12 is the basic energy relation in fluid mechanics. Its discovery is attributed to the eighteenth-century Swiss physicist Daniel Bernoulli. It is commonly seen in engineering practice in the rearranged form of

$$E = \frac{p}{\gamma} + \frac{v^2}{2g} + z \tag{3.13}$$

Example 3.3 A 4-inch water pipe carries 800 gpm with a line pressure of 22 psi. The pipe is 17 feet above a local elevation datum. Determine the total energy of the fluid in the pipe with respect to the local datum.

Solution: Using Equation 3.10,

$$h_s = \frac{p}{\gamma} = \frac{22 \text{ lb/in}^2}{62.4 \text{ lb/ft}^3} \times \frac{144 \text{ in}^2}{\text{ft}^2} = 50.8 \text{ ft}$$

Area is computed using simple geometry.

$$A_4 = \frac{\pi D^2}{4} = \frac{\pi 0.333^2}{4} = 0.0872 \text{ ft}^2$$

Using the volume flow equation, velocity can be computed.

$$v = \frac{q}{A} = \frac{400 \text{ gal/min}}{0.0872 \text{ ft}^2} \times \frac{\text{ft}^3}{7.48 \text{ gal}} \times \frac{\text{min}}{60 \text{ s}} = 10.2 \text{ ft/s}$$

Finally, total energy is computed using Equation 3.13.

$$h_v = \frac{v^2}{2g} = \frac{(10.2 \text{ ft/s})^2}{2 \times 32.2 \text{ ft/s}^2} = 1.6 \text{ ft}$$

$$h_z = z = 17 \text{ ft}$$

$$E = \frac{p}{\gamma} + \frac{v^2}{2g} + z = 50.8 + 1.6 + 17 = 69.4 \text{ ft}$$

Keep in mind that this energy of 69.4 feet is energy per unit weight of the fluid. It represents 69.4 lb-ft of energy per pound of fluid moved.

3.5 BERNOULLI EQUATION

The law of the conservation of energy for fluids states that the total energy of a given fluid element must remain constant as it moves through a flow system. Fluids typically move from a higher energy condition to a lower energy condition, unless the system contains a pump. To evaluate the tendency of a fluid to move requires an investigation of total energy, which includes pressure, velocity, and elevation. If we decide to track an element of fluid through a system, the law of energy conservation allows us to claim that the total energy of the fluid element will remain constant throughout the system. So as the fluid moves from point 1 to point 2, we can state

$$E_1 = E_2 \qquad (3.14)$$

$$\frac{p_1}{\gamma} + \frac{v_1^2}{2g} + z_1 = \frac{p_2}{\gamma} + \frac{v_2^2}{2g} + z_2 \qquad (3.15)$$

This equation is commonly called the *Bernoulli equation*. It was derived for an ideal fluid where the fluid experiences no losses or gains in energy while flowing from point 1 to point 2. Such losses or gains could be due to friction, fluid motor, turbine, heat exchanger, or pump. In practice, this equation is applicable when the losses or gains are small and therefore negligible.

Consider the fluid system shown in Figure 3.3. Water is flowing from an elevated tank through a pipe system to another tank at a lower elevation. If the flow is considered ideal, the conservation of energy law states that fluid energy is the same at points 1, 2, 3, and 4. Static pressure may change, velocity may change, and elevation may change, but the sum of these three energy forms will not change.

Knowing that energy is conserved helps us in the solution of fluid flow problems. We can write the Bernoulli equation between any two points in the system as long as the flow is ideal or can be approximated by ideal flow.

Example 3.4 A 16-foot diameter water tank is 12 feet high and holds 9 feet of water. The tank is drained by a 4-inch diameter pipe, as shown in

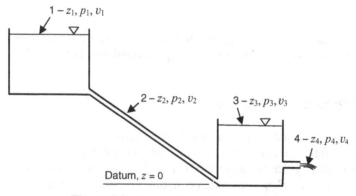

Figure 3.3 Two tanks and pipe system.

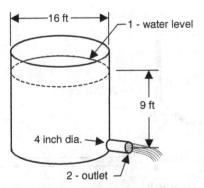

Figure 3.4 Tank of Example 3.4.

Figure 3.4. Assume that the flow is ideal, with no energy loss. Determine the velocity of the water discharging from the pipe.

Solution: The free water surface is an excellent point to compute total energy since water pressure is zero, the downward velocity is practically zero (16-foot tank diameter is very large compared to the 4-inch diameter discharge pipe) and the height of water above the discharge pipe is known. In this case we can set the elevation datum through the discharge pipe centerline. If we evaluate energy in the discharge jet, just immediately outside the pipe, we know that pressure is zero (no solid boundaries surrounding the flow) and elevation is zero, based on our arbitrary assignment of the elevation datum. Thus, we can write

$$\frac{p_1}{\gamma} + \frac{v_1^2}{2g} + z_1 = \frac{p_2}{\gamma} + \frac{v_2^2}{2g} + z_2$$

Since p_1, v_1, p_2 and z_2 equal zero, the equation reduces to

$$z_1 = \frac{v_2^2}{2g}$$

Solving for v_2 we get

$$v_2 = \sqrt{2g\,z_1} = \sqrt{2 \times 32.2 \text{ ft/s}^2 \times 9 \text{ ft}} = 24.1 \text{ ft/s}$$

Example 3.5   Consider the water reservoir and piping system shown in Figure 3.5. The reservoir is open to the atmosphere and is drained by a 24-inch diameter pipe, which eventually reduces to a 12-inch diameter jet before discharging to the atmosphere. A pressure gage is attached to the 24-inch line at point 2 as shown. If the flow is considered ideal, determine (a) the system flow rate and (b) the pressure reading on the gage at point 2 in psi.

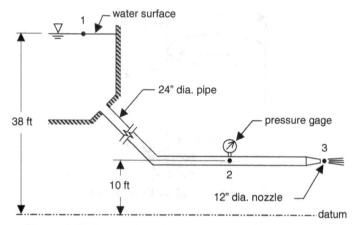

Figure 3.5   Reservoir and piping system of Example 3.5.

Solution: To determine system flow, let's determine the velocity of flow through the 12-inch jet using points 1 and 3 in the system.

$$\frac{p_1}{\gamma} + \frac{v_1^2}{2g} + z_1 = \frac{p_3}{\gamma} + \frac{v_3^2}{2g} + z_3$$

At point 1, p_1 and v_1 are zero, while z_1 is 38 feet. At point 3, p_3 is zero and z_3 is 10 feet, leaving v_3 as the only unknown in the equation.

$$38 \text{ ft} = \frac{v_3^2}{2 \times 32.2 \text{ ft/s}^2} + 10 \text{ ft}$$

$$v_3 = \sqrt{2 \times 32.2 \ (38 - 10) \text{ ft}} = 42.5 \text{ ft/s}$$

The area of the jet is

$$A_3 = \frac{\pi D_3^2}{4} = \frac{\pi (1)^2}{4} = 0.785 \text{ ft}^2$$

Knowing the velocity and flow area at the 12-inch jet, we can compute the flow using

$$q = v_3 A_3 = 42.5 \text{ ft/s} \times 0.785 \text{ ft}^2 = 33.3 \text{ ft}^3/\text{s}$$

The pressure at point 2 is the pressure in the horizontal segment of the 24-inch pipe. We know the total energy at point 1, and we can use continuity to compute the velocity at point 2.

$$v_2 A_2 = v_3 A_3$$

$$v_2 = v_3 \frac{A_3}{A_2} = v_3 \left(\frac{\frac{\pi D_3^2}{4}}{\frac{\pi D_2^2}{4}} \right) = v_3 \frac{D_3^2}{D_2^2}$$

$$v_2 = (42.5 \text{ ft/s}) \frac{(12 \text{ in})^2}{(24 \text{ in})^2} = 10.62 \text{ ft/s}$$

As a matter of convenience, we can compute the velocity head at 2.

$$\frac{v_2^2}{2g} = \frac{(10.62 \text{ ft/s})^2}{2 \times 32.2 \text{ ft/s}^2} = 1.75 \text{ ft}$$

Now we can write the Bernoulli equation from point 1 to point 2, and solve for p_2.

$$\frac{p_1}{\gamma} + \frac{v_1^2}{2g} + z_1 = \frac{p_2}{\gamma} + \frac{v_2^2}{2g} + z_2$$

$$38 \text{ ft} = \frac{p_2}{62.4 \text{ lb/ft}^3} + 1.75 \text{ ft} + 10 \text{ ft}$$

$$p_2 = 62.4 \text{ lb/ft}^3 (38 \text{ ft} - 1.75 \text{ ft} - 10 \text{ ft}) \left(\frac{\text{ft}^2}{144 \text{ in}^2} \right) = 11.4 \text{ psi}$$

3.6 ENERGY LOSSES

Anytime fluid flow changes direction the fluid increases in turbulence. The turbulence increase causes flow element interaction and energy loss in the form of heat. In traditional flow systems these losses are called minor losses and are due to valves, fittings, bends, and any other in-line apparatus that causes flow lines in the fluid to become more irregular. Also, as the fluid passes along the solid boundary of the flow conduit the fluid encounters conduit surface resistance, causing friction losses. Other losses can occur in a fluid flow system, but in stormwater flow analysis these are the two most important energy losses.

3.6.1 Reynolds Number

To properly analyze friction losses, the flow must be characterized as either laminar or turbulent. In a closed conduit, fluid velocity is zero immediately next to the pipe wall, and maximum at the pipe center line. In laminar flow all fluid particles follow a straight path with respect to the boundary (pipe wall), as shown in Figure 3.6. Friction resistance is provided by viscous shear between slower and faster fluid layers. The flow is characterized as smooth, quiet, and usually low velocity. In turbulent flow, eddies are caused by pipe-wall roughness. Shear between slower and faster layers and fluid particles moving laterally in a random fashion causes additional internal flow resistance. Flow lines are irregular with noisy flow.

The occurrence of laminar or turbulent flow is numerically characterized by flow velocity, pipe diameter, and fluid viscosity through the Reynolds number, N_R. It is computed as

$$N_R = \frac{vD\rho}{\mu} \tag{3.16}$$

where N_R = Reynolds number, dimensionless
$\quad\quad D$ = characteristic flow dimension or pipe diameter (ft)
$\quad\quad v$ = the fluid velocity (ft/s)
$\quad\quad \rho$ = fluid density (lb-s/ft^4, slugs/ft^3)
$\quad\quad \mu$ = dynamic viscosity of the fluid (lb-s/ft^2)

Deeper study of the Reynolds number reveals that it is the dimensionless ratio of inertia forces to viscous forces of a fluid element. The inertia force from Newtonian mechanics is mass times acceleration. The viscous force is fluid shear stress as defined in Equation 2.6 multiplied by shear area. When viscous forces are greater than inertia forces the internal friction dominates and the flow is smooth, quiet, and laminar. In simpler terms, the internal friction forces are strong enough to maintain fluid element shape and keep the flowing elements in order and under control. Flow lines are generally very regular and smooth. Flow elements move in a regulated orderly fashion. When

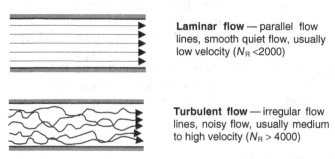

Laminar flow — parallel flow lines, smooth quiet flow, usually low velocity ($N_R < 2000$)

Turbulent flow — irregular flow lines, noisy flow, usually medium to high velocity ($N_R > 4000$)

Figure 3.6   Characteristics of laminar and turbulent pipe flow.

the inertia forces are greater than viscous forces, the inertia dominates internal friction and the flow is disorderly, irregular, and turbulent. In simpler terms, the mass of flowing water overpowers the internal friction forces' capability to hold the water element together. It disperses, mixing with adjacent water elements in a semi-chaotic fashion. Flow lines criss-cross, with some local reverse flow occurring.

The ratio of dynamic viscosity over density in Equation 3.16 can be replaced with kinematic viscosity to provide a more convenient form of Equation 3.16,

$$N_R = \frac{vD}{\nu} \tag{3.17}$$

where ν = the kinematic viscosity of the fluid, ft^2/s

Flow regime tends to be laminar when $N_R < 2000$ and turbulent when $N_R > 4000$. Between these two limits the flow characterization is difficult to determine, and this region is often called the *transitional zone*. For most practical situations in surface water flow, the flow characterization is turbulent. Therefore, the discussion of friction losses will be restricted to turbulent flow.

Example 3.6 Water is flowing at a rate of 50 gpm. The water temperature is 50° F. Determine the Reynolds number if the water is flowing in a pipe of (a) 48-inch diameter and (b) 8-inch diameter. Characterize each flow as laminar or turbulent.

Solution: Flow is converted to units of ft^3/s, areas are computed in units of ft^2, and velocities are determined using the volume flow equation.

$$q = 50 \text{ gpm} \times \frac{1 \text{ ft}^3/s}{448.8 \text{ gpm}} = 0.111 \text{ ft}^3/s$$

$$A_{48} = \pi \frac{(4 \text{ ft})^2}{4} = 12.57 \text{ ft}^2, \quad A_8 = \pi \frac{(0.667 \text{ ft})^2}{4} = 0.349 \text{ ft}^2$$

$$v_{48} = \frac{q}{A_{48}} = \frac{0.111 \text{ ft}^3/s}{12.57 \text{ ft}^2} = 0.00883 \text{ ft/s},$$

$$v_8 = \frac{q}{A_8} = \frac{0.111 \text{ ft}^3/s}{0.349 \text{ ft}^2} = 3.18 \text{ ft/s}$$

Reynolds number for the 48-inch pipe is

$$N_{R,48} = \frac{v_{48}D_{48}}{\nu} = \frac{(0.00883 \text{ ft/s})\,(4 \text{ ft})}{1.4 \times 10^{-5} \text{ ft}^2/\text{s}} = 2523$$

The flow in the 48-inch pipe is in the transitional zone and cannot be categorized as laminar or turbulent.

Reynolds number for the 8-inch pipe is

$$N_{R,8} = \frac{v_8 D_8}{\nu} = \frac{3.18 \text{ ft/s} \times 0.667 \text{ ft}}{1.4 \times 10^{-5} \text{ ft}^2/\text{s}} = 151{,}500$$

The flow in the 8-inch pipe is turbulent.

This example illustrates the rarity of laminar flow occurring in typical water flow. A flow velocity of 0.00883 ft/s, which is practically crawling, was not laminar flow.

3.6.2 Friction Losses

The head loss due to friction in a given length L of pipe can be computed by the Darcy–Weisbach equation:

$$h_f = f \frac{L}{D} \frac{v^2}{2g} \tag{3.18}$$

where h_f = head loss due to friction (ft)
$\ f$ = friction factor
$\ L$ = length of pipe (ft)
$\ D$ = pipe diameter (ft)
$\ v$ = fluid velocity (ft/s)
$\ g$ = gravitational constant (ft/s^2)

In this equation, the friction factor f is determined through a chart called the Moody Diagram, using the Reynolds number N_R and the relative roughness of the pipe. Relative roughness of the pipe is defined as the ratio of the pipe roughness ε to the pipe diameter D. Pipe roughness is a property of the pipe material and commonly provided by the pipe manufacturer. Typical values of pipe roughness are shown in Table 3.2 and the Moody diagram is shown in Figure 3.7 and Appendix D.

Equation 3.18 is sufficient to determine (1) friction loss over a given pipe length for a given flow rate, (2) the flow rate through a pipe, or (3) the pipe diameter necessary to carry a given flow rate. Each problem type has a different solution approach. Three examples are provided to illustrate these computations.

TABLE 3.2 Typical Values of Pipe Roughness, ε

Material	ε, ft
Plastic	0.010×10^{-4}
Commercial steel	1.5×10^{-4}
Galvanized iron	5.0×10^{-4}
Cast iron	8.5×10^{-4}
Finished concrete	40×10^{-4}
Rough concrete	100×10^{-4}

Example 3.7 A 6-inch pipe of commercial steel is carrying 2 ft³/s of water at 50°F. Estimate the head loss due to friction over a 1000-foot length.

Solution: The average velocity of the pipe is the ratio between the flow rate and the pipe cross-sectional area:

$$v = \frac{2 \text{ ft}^3/\text{s}}{\frac{\pi}{4} 0.5^2 \text{ ft}^2} = 10.2 \text{ ft/s}$$

The kinematic viscosity at 50°F is 1.4×10^{-5} ft²/s, and the Reynolds number is

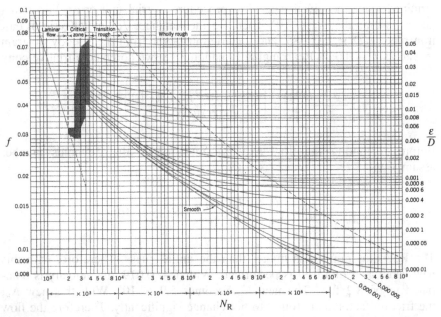

Figure 3.7 The Moody diagram is used to determine the friction factor, f (see Appendix D).

$$N_R = \frac{Dv}{\nu} = \frac{(0.5 \text{ ft})(10.2 \text{ ft/s})}{1.4 \times 10^{-5} \text{ ft}^2/\text{s}} = 3.6 \times 10^5$$

The relative roughness is

$$\frac{\varepsilon}{D} = \frac{0.00015 \text{ ft}}{0.5 \text{ ft}} = 0.0003$$

For these values of N_R and ε/D, the Moody diagram gives a roughness co-efficient $f = 0.017$, and the head loss is

$$h_f = f \frac{L}{D} \frac{v^2}{2g} = 0.017 \times \left(\frac{1000 \text{ ft}}{0.5 \text{ ft}} \right) \times \frac{(10.2 \text{ ft/s})^2}{2(32.2 \text{ ft/s}^2)} = 55 \text{ ft}$$

Therefore, 55 feet of head is lost in 1000 feet of pipe.

Example 3.8   In a 12-inch cast iron pipe, a head loss of 2 feet per 100 feet of pipe length is available. How much water, at 50°F, can the pipe supply?

Solution: This is somewhat more complicated than the previous example, because the velocity is not known and thus Reynolds number cannot be de-termined from the given data. The procedure is trial and error. For a first guess, assume that $N_R \approx 10^5$. Then, for the roughness/diameter ratio of cast iron pipe, $\varepsilon/D = 0.00085$, and the friction factor from the Moody diagram is read as $f = 0.022$. Rearranging Equation 3.18, we compute a trial velocity

$$v = \left[\frac{2g \, h_f \, D}{f \, L} \right]^{\frac{1}{2}} = \left[\frac{2(32.2 \text{ ft/s}^2)(2 \text{ ft})(1 \text{ ft})}{(0.022)(100 \text{ ft})} \right]^{\frac{1}{2}} = 7.7 \text{ ft/s}$$

Before computing the flow rate, we must check the Reynolds number assumption.

$$N_R = \frac{(1 \text{ ft})(7.7 \text{ ft/s})}{(1.4 \times 10^{-5} \text{ ft}^2/\text{s})} = 5.5 \times 10^5$$

The Reynolds number is higher than the initial guess. Therefore, with this new value a second trial is performed. With $f = 0.019$, the velocity is computed to be 8.2 ft/s. The new N_R becomes 5.9×10^5. With this new N_R, the friction factor, f, is found to not change significantly. Therefore the flow rate is

$$q = vA = v\frac{\pi}{4}D^2 = (8.2 \text{ ft/s})\left(\frac{\pi}{4}\right)(1)^2 = 6.4 \text{ ft}^3/\text{s}$$

The pipe can supply 6.4 ft³/s of water at 50°F.

Example 3.9 A commercial steel pipe must carry a flow rate of 50 ft³/s of water at 50°F under a total head loss gradient of 0.5 percent, or 1 foot in 200 feet of length. What is the required pipe size? Assume standard pipe diameters are in increments of 2 inches.

Solution: In this case, neither the relative roughness ε/D, nor Reynold's number are known. Therefore, we will use common sense and engineering judgment and assume a 30-inch (2.5 feet) diameter, and compute the resulting head loss. The velocity and Reynolds number based on our first assumption are

$$v = \frac{50 \text{ ft}^3/\text{s}}{\left(\dfrac{\pi}{4}\right)(2.5 \text{ ft})^2} = 10.2 \text{ ft/s}$$

$$N_R = \frac{(2.5 \text{ ft})(10.2 \text{ ft/s})}{(1.4 \times 10^{-5} \text{ ft}^2/\text{s})} = 1.8 \times 10^6$$

The friction factor from the Moody diagram is

$$\frac{\varepsilon}{D} = \frac{0.00015 \text{ ft}}{2.5 \text{ ft}} = 0.00006$$

$$f = 0.0125$$

Using the Darcy equation, head loss is computed as

$$h_f = 0.0125\left(\frac{200 \text{ ft}}{2.5 \text{ ft}}\right)\frac{(10.2 \text{ ft/s})^2}{2(32.2 \text{ ft/s}^2)} = 1.62 \text{ ft}$$

The head loss is too high, so the pipe size is increased to 34 inches (2.83 feet), and we try again.

$$v = \frac{50}{\frac{\pi}{4} 2.83^2} = 7.95 \text{ ft/s}$$

$$N_R = \frac{2.83 \times 7.95}{1.4 \times 10^{-5}} = 1.6 \times 10^6, \frac{\varepsilon}{D} = \frac{0.00015 \text{ ft}}{2.83 \text{ ft}} = 0.000053, f = 0.0125$$

$$h_f = 0.0125 \left(\frac{200 \text{ ft}}{2.83 \text{ ft}}\right) \frac{(7.95 \text{ ft/s})^2}{2(32.2 \text{ ft/s}^2)} = 0.87 \text{ ft}$$

This is about 13% lower than the specified 1-foot head loss. Therefore, a 34-inch pipe should be adequate.

3.6.3 Minor Losses

In addition to head losses due to pipe friction, there are head losses due to fittings, bends, and valves. These items cause the flow lines to change direction. Direction change causes fluid elements to increase internal friction stress, and therefore, energy loss occurs. The losses are expressed by the equation

$$h_m = K \frac{v^2}{2g} \tag{3.19}$$

where h_m = minor head loss (ft)
    K = loss coefficient

Notice that energy lost due to minor piping elements is directly related to velocity head. This is similar to the case of friction losses, where the $f \times L/D$ term can be thought of as a loss coefficient, K. For minor piping elements, the loss coefficient is determined through experimental studies of each bend or fitting. Table 3.3 lists coefficients for some common fittings. It should be noted that the globe valve, with its very high coefficient, is often installed as a pressure-reducing device.

TABLE 3.3 Loss Coefficients for Common Pipe Fittings

Fitting Type	K
Standard 90° bend	0.9
Standard tee	1.8
Gate valve (fully open)	0.2
Globe valve (fully open)	10.0

Combining Equations 3.18 and 3.19, the combined head loss due to friction and minor losses between points 1 and 2 in a pipe system is expressed as:

$$h_{L_{1-2}} = h_f + \Sigma h_m = \left(f\frac{L}{D} + \Sigma K\right)\left(\frac{v^2}{2g}\right) \tag{3.20}$$

If the pipe in Example 3.7 had contained four 90-degree bends and one gate valve, the total head loss would have been

$$h_L = \left\{(0.017)\frac{(1000 \text{ ft})}{(0.5 \text{ ft})} + [(4 \times 0.9) + 0.2]\right\}\left(\frac{(10.2 \text{ ft/s})^2}{2(32.2 \text{ ft/s}^2)}\right)$$

$$= (34 + 3.8) \times 1.62 \text{ ft} = 61 \text{ ft}$$

From this calculation, you can see why the minor losses are called minor. Usually, the number of fittings, transitions, bends, and values in a system are small. In this example calculation, the minor losses had a total K factor of 3.8, while friction had an equivalent K factor of 34, about nine times larger. Other losses that are common are entrance, exit, contraction, and expansion losses. These are more common in stormwater management applications.

When water moves from a larger body of water into a pipe or conveyance structure, the flowing water encounters an *entrance loss* due to flow lines changing directions to enter the reduced flow area. The typical situation is a submerged pipe draining an impounded water body, such as a lake, tank, or flooded area above a roadway embankment. The geometry of the inlet to the pipe can cause significantly different energy losses. Figure 3.8 shows three

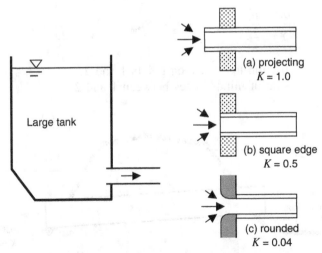

Figure 3.8 Varying geometric conditions for entrance losses.

different entrance conditions causing three different energy losses. Depending on entrance shape, the loss coefficient K changes dramatically. A projecting inlet forces water to sharply bend anywhere from 0 to 180 degrees in flow direction to get into the pipe. A square-edge entrance requires water flow to sharply bend between 0 and 90 degrees. A smooth entrance allows water to gradually bend around a corner. A smooth entrance can reduce a culvert design diameter based solely on the increased efficiency of getting water into the pipe. There are many other entrance geometries available in culvert design. Selection of the entrance geometry is important because it can significantly increase culvert flow capacity and therefore must be considered. The negative aspect of a smooth entrance geometry is construction cost. Therefore, entrance efficiency should always be balanced against cost. Culvert design is discussed in more detail in Chapter 11.

When water flows from a pipe and discharges into a larger body of water where velocity is zero, the energy in the water drops by one velocity head. This is called an *exit loss*. This condition can occur in tanks, reservoirs, ponds, and also in culvert design. Figure 3.9 illustrates a culvert under a roadway experiencing an exit loss on the downstream side. In this figure it is assumed that the standing water is essentially at rest, compared to the pipe velocity.

3.7   GENERAL ENERGY EQUATION

When it is not possible to consider flow as ideal, the minor losses and friction losses must be included in any energy calculation. A more general energy equation can be created by incorporating Equation 3.20 into the Bernoulli equation to account for these losses:

$$\frac{p_1}{\gamma} + \frac{v_1^2}{2g} + z_1 - h_{f_{1-2}} - \Sigma h_{m_{1-2}} = \frac{p_2}{\gamma} + \frac{v_2^2}{2g} + z_2 \qquad (3.21)$$

where $h_{f,1-2}$ = friction loss between points 1 and 2
$\Sigma h_{m,1-2}$ = sum of minor losses between 1 and 2

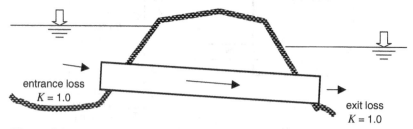

Figure 3.9   Culvert experiencing a projected entrance loss and an exit loss.

If a pump or fluid motor was part of the system, then additional terms would be added to the equation. However, for the analysis of many flow systems, including the vast majority of stormwater flow systems, this equation is adequate.

Example 3.10 Determine the velocity in the 4-inch discharge pipe of Example 3.4 if flow is not considered ideal and a square-edged entrance loss is included in the energy equation.

Solution: We can assume no friction losses because the discharge pipe is very short, and thus Equation 3.21 becomes

$$\frac{p_1}{\gamma} + \frac{v_1^2}{2g} + z_1 - K\frac{v_2^2}{2g} = \frac{p_2}{\gamma} + \frac{v_2^2}{2g} + z_2$$

where $K = 0.5$ and p_1, v_1, p_2, and z_2 again equal zero. The equation further reduces to

$$z_1 = \frac{v_2^2}{2g} + K\frac{v_2^2}{2g} = 1.5\frac{v_2^2}{2g}$$

Solving for v_2,

$$v_2 = \sqrt{\frac{2g\,z_1}{1.5}} = \sqrt{\frac{2 \times 32.2 \text{ ft/s}^2 \times 9 \text{ ft}}{1.5}} = 19.6 \text{ ft/s}$$

This calculation shows that the assumption of ideal flow caused an error in analysis of about 4.5 ft/sec, or 23 percent in the velocity and therefore, the ideal flow assumption for Example 3.4 was not appropriate.

Example 3.11 The smooth concrete culvert of Figure 3.10 has a diameter of 24 inches and a flow velocity of 4.5 ft/s. If the pipe is known to flow full, determine the total energy lost due to the combined effect of the square-edged entrance, friction, and exit.

Solution: The Reynolds number is

$$N_R = \frac{Dv}{\nu} = \frac{(2 \text{ ft})(4.5 \text{ ft/s})}{(1.4 \times 10^{-5} \text{ ft}^2/\text{s})} = 6.4 \times 10^5$$

For smooth concrete pipe, $\varepsilon = 0.001$ and thus

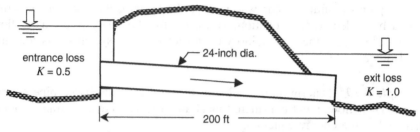

Figure 3.10   Culvert for Example 3.11.

$$\frac{\varepsilon}{D} = \frac{0.001 \text{ ft}}{2 \text{ ft}} = 0.0005$$

From the Moody diagram with $N_R = 6.4 \times 10^5$ and $\varepsilon/D = 0.0005$, read $f = 0.0175$. With $K_{\text{entrance}} = 0.5$ and $K_{\text{exit}} = 1.0$, total energy lost is

$$h_L = \left(f \frac{L}{D} + \Sigma K \right) \left(\frac{v^2}{2g} \right)$$

$$h_L = \left\{ (0.0175) \frac{(200 \text{ ft})}{(2 \text{ ft})} + [0.5 + 1.0] \right\} \left(\frac{(4.5 \text{ ft/s})^2}{2(32.2 \text{ ft/s}^2)} \right)$$

$$h_L = (1.75 + 1.5) \times 0.314 \text{ ft} = 1.02 \text{ ft}$$

This calculation suggests that the difference in water-surface-elevation between the upstream side and downstream side of this culvert is about 1 foot.

3.8 THE ORIFICE

Surface flow can be controlled or measured through several devices. The most common devices used in stormwater management design are the weir and the orifice. The *weir* is a gravity flow device and will be covered in Chapter 4. The *orifice* is a control device used in pressure flow. It is commonly used in the design of outlet structures for stormwater detention facilities.

The driving mechanism behind flow through an orifice is static water pressure, or *head*. The static head on the upstream side of the orifice is usually converted completely into dynamic head (velocity head) on the downstream side. Figure 3.11 shows a sketch of an orifice discharging freely to the atmosphere. If we assume ideal flow, and write the Bernoulli equation between points 1 and 2, we start with

$$\frac{p_1}{\gamma} + \frac{v_1^2}{2g} + z_1 = \frac{p_2}{\gamma} + \frac{v_2^2}{2g} + z_2. \qquad (3.22)$$

We can set p_1 and v_1 equal to zero, and z_1 equal to H. At point 2, p_2 and z_2 equal zero. Thus, the equation reduces to

$$0 + 0 + H = 0 + \frac{v_2^2}{2g} + 0 \qquad (3.23)$$

Solving for v_2 and dropping the subscript 2, we get

$$v = \sqrt{2gH} \qquad (3.24)$$

Flow is velocity times area, so flow through an orifice, assuming ideal flow, reduces to

$$q_o = A\sqrt{2gH} \qquad (3.25)$$

As it turns out, orifice flow is not ideal. The flow lines through the orifice must bend up to 90 degrees around the edge of the orifice. This bending action causes the flow lines to contract, creating a discharge stream with an effective diameter smaller than the diameter of the orifice. This smaller diameter causes an associated reduction in effective flow area. Thus, the ideal equation is modified by adding a discharge coefficient to account for this reduction in flow area. This modification to Equation 3.25 gives the classical orifice flow equation

$$q_o = C_o A\sqrt{2gH} \qquad (3.26)$$

where q_o = flow rate through the orifice (ft^3/s)
   C_o = orifice discharge coefficient
   A = area of the orifice (ft^2)
   g = gravitational constant (32.2 ft/s^2)
   H = depth of water above the center of the orifice (ft)

Figure 3.11 shows the orifice geometric area, A and the orifice effective flow area, A_e. The discharge coefficient for an orifice is commonly reported as 0.60. In reality, this coefficient varies between 0.58 and 0.62 but the nominal value of 0.60 is more than adequate for stormwater management design. As a reminder, this equation works only for the orifice that discharges freely to the atmosphere. A submerged orifice or partially submerged orifice on the downstream side does not follow Equation 3.26. Such conditions must be

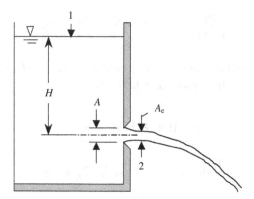

Figure 3.11   An orifice discharging freely to the atmosphere.

modeled using energy methods for the specific condition, taking into account pressure head on the downstream side of the orifice.

Example 3.12   A 2-inch-diameter orifice is used to release water from a steel tank. The centerline elevation of the orifice opening is 98.45 feet. The water surface in the tank has an elevation of 106.05 feet. Determine the flow through the orifice.

Solution: The static pressure head acting on the orifice opening is the elevation difference:

$$H = 106.05 - 98.45 = 7.60 \text{ ft}$$

The flow area of the orifice is

$$A = \frac{\pi D^2}{4} = \frac{\pi \left(\dfrac{2 \text{ in}}{12 \text{ in/ft}} \right)^2}{4} = 0.0218 \text{ ft}^2$$

Flow is computed as

$$q_o = C_o A \sqrt{2gH}$$

$$q_o = (0.6)(0.0218 \text{ ft}^2)\sqrt{2(32.2 \text{ ft/s}^2)(7.60 \text{ ft})} = 0.289 \text{ ft}^3/\text{s}$$

Example 3.13   A two-stage, concrete riser box is used to regulate flow through a stormwater detention facility. The box has two circular orifice openings as shown in Figure 3.12. Both orifices discharge freely without the effects

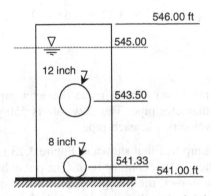

Figure 3.12   Concrete riser box with two circular orifices.

of submergence. Determine the flow through the riser box if the water surface elevation in the pond is 545.00 feet.

Solution: When the water surface is at 545.00 feet, both orifice openings are discharging flow. For the lower orifice, stage 1, the driving head and flow area are

$$H_1 = 545.00 - 541.33 = 3.67 \text{ ft}$$

$$A_1 = \frac{\pi D_1^2}{4} = \frac{\pi (0.667 \text{ ft})^2}{4} = 0.349 \text{ ft}^2$$

Assuming an orifice coefficient of 0.6, the flow through stage 1 is

$$q_{o,1} = C_o A_1 \sqrt{2g\,H_1} = (0.6)(0.349 \text{ ft}^2)\sqrt{2(32.2 \text{ ft/s}^2)(3.67 \text{ ft})} = 3.22 \text{ ft}^3/\text{s}$$

For the second orifice, stage 2, the driving head and area are

$$H_2 = 545.00 - 543.50 = 1.50 \text{ ft}$$

$$A_2 = \frac{\pi D_2^2}{4} = \frac{\pi (1.0 \text{ ft})^2}{4} = 0.785 \text{ ft}^2$$

Assuming an orifice coefficient of 0.6, the flow through stage 2 is

$$q_{o,2} = C_o A_2 \sqrt{2g\,H_2} = (0.6)(0.785 \text{ ft}^2)\sqrt{2(32.2 \text{ ft/s}^2)(1.5 \text{ ft})} = 4.63 \text{ ft}^3/\text{s}$$

The total flow through the riser box is the sum of the flow in the two stages:

$$q = q_{o,1} + q_{o,2} = 3.22 + 4.63 = 7.85 \ \text{ft}^3/\text{s}$$

PROBLEMS

3.1   Water is flowing in an 8-inch inside diameter pipe that reduces to a 3-inch inside diameter pipe. The flow rate is 550 gpm. Determine the average flow velocities in each pipe.

3.2   A hand well pump like that shown in Figure 3.13 is used to draw water from a springhouse on a country farm. The pump has a 3-inch diameter plunger. When drawn, the plunger pushes water out of a 1½-inch diameter spigot. Assume that there is no leakage past the plunger or check valve. Determine (a) the flow rate of water in gpm from the hand pump for a 9-in/s draw on the plunger, and (b) the flow velocity in the 1½-inch diameter spigot.

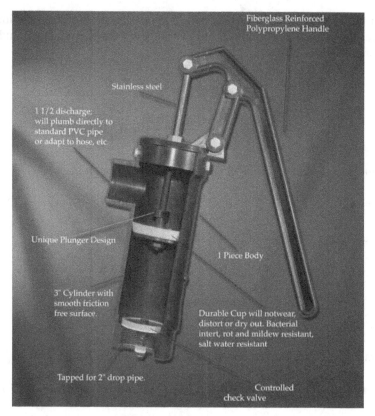

Figure 3.13   Hand pump (courtesy of Survival Unlimited www.survivalunlimited. com).

3.3 An infiltration basin is similar to a stormwater detention basin, except the bottom is designed to allow significant exfiltration from the pond to the subsurface. The basin is monitored for surface inflow and surface outflow. For a particular steady-flow condition, the pond inflow from a storm sewer pipe is measured as 1.10 ft³/s. The pond outflow through a riser box outlet discharge pipe is measured as 0.77 ft³/s. The basin bottom is flat and has a surface area of 0.285 acres. Assume that stormwater leaves the pond through infiltration to the soil and this exfiltration is uniform across the basin bottom. Compute the infiltration velocity in inches per hour.

3.4 A 3-foot-diameter culvert is used for a highway stream crossing, as shown in Figure 3.14. The water surface elevation on the upstream side of the culvert is 970.1 feet. The downstream side of the culvert discharges to the atmosphere. The culvert invert elevations are 965.6 feet on the upstream side and 964.0 feet on the downstream side. Assume pressure flow throughout the culvert. Neglect friction and minor losses (ideal flow). Compute the flow through the pipe in ft³/s.

3.5 Water flows in a circular pipe at a rate of 10 gpm. Determine the Reynolds number and classify the flow as laminar, transitional, or turbulent if the diameter is (a) 15 inches, (b) 8 inches, and (c) 6 inches. Use a kinematic viscosity of 1.40×10^{-5} ft²/s.

3.6 Compute the head loss in a smooth plastic pipe under pressure flow, having an inside diameter of 24 inches and carrying a flow of 19.5 ft³/s, for a length of 1200 ft. Use a kinematic viscosity of (a) 1.67×10^{-5} ft²/s (40°F) and (b) 5.03×10^{-6} ft²/s (140°F).

3.7 A smooth concrete pipe is needed to carry a water flow of 60 ft³/s for a distance of 900 feet. Determine the minimum diameter if the pipe can cause only 2.5 feet of head loss due to friction. Use a kinematic viscosity of 1.40×10^{-5} ft²/s. Select your diameter from the nominal pipes of 18, 24, 30, 36, 42, 48, 54, and 60 inches.

3.8 Solve Example 3.4, taking into account the entrance loss at the inlet of the 4-inch diameter pipe. Assume the entrance is (a) projecting, (b) square edge, and (c) rounded.

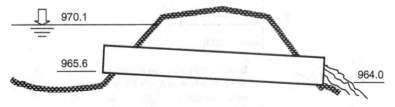

Figure 3.14 Problem 3.4.

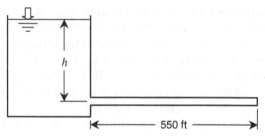

Figure 3.15 Problem 3.9.

3.9 Water flows at 50°F from a storage tank through 550 feet of 6-inch schedule 40 steel pipe (inside diameter = 0.5054 ft) as shown in Figure 3.15. Calculate the head required above the pipe inlet to produce a volume flow-rate of 2.5 ft³/s. Consider the entrance and pipe friction losses in your calculation.

3.10 A commercial steel pipe having an 8-inch inside diameter is used to release water from a reservoir, as shown in Figure 3.16. The water discharges as a free jet to the atmosphere. If the flow is to be maintained at 5 ft³/s, determine the required reservoir depth, h. Consider friction and minor losses in your solution and use a kinematic viscosity of 1.40×10^{-5} ft²/s.

3.11 A 6-inch diameter circular orifice experiences 14.5 feet of static pressure head on the center of its opening. Calculate the flow through the orifice.

3.12 Two rectangular orifices mounted in a concrete riser box are used to control flow from a stormwater detention facility, as shown in Figure

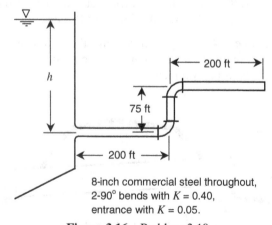

Figure 3.16 Problem 3.10.

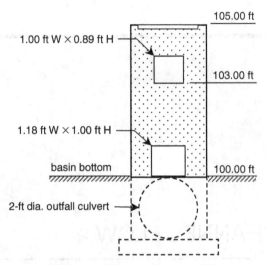

105.00 ft

1.00 ft W × 0.89 ft H

103.00 ft

1.18 ft W × 1.00 ft H

basin bottom

100.00 ft

2-ft dia. outfall culvert

Figure 3.17 Riser box of Problem 3.12 (courtesy of T. F. Smith, PE, PLS, Conver and Smith Engineering, Royersford, PA).

3.17. Determine the flow through the riser box if the water surface elevation in the pond is (a) 102.5 feet and (b) 104.5 feet. Assume both orifices have discharge coefficients of 0.6 and flow discharges freely without experiencing any submergence.

REFERENCES

American Society of Civil Engineers, 1992. *Design and Construction of Urban Stormwater Management Systems.* ASCE Manual and Reports of Engineering Practice No. 77, ISBN 0-87262-855-8.

Brater, E. F., H. W. King, J. E. Lindell, and C. Y. Wei. 1996. *Handbook of Hydraulics,* 7th ed. New York: McGraw-Hill, ISBN 0-070-07247-7.

Daugherty, Robert L., J. B. Franzini, and E. J. Finnemore. 1985. *Fluid Mechanics with Engineering Applications,* 8th ed. New York: McGraw-Hill, ISBN 0-07-15441-4.

Mott, R. L. 2006. *Applied Fluid Mechanics,* 6th ed. Upper Saddle River, NJ: Prentice-Hall, ISBN 0-13-114680-7.

Street, Robert L., Gary Z. Watters, and John K. Vennard. 1996. *Elementary Fluid Mechanics,* 7th ed. New York: John Wiley & Sons, ISBN 0-471-01310-2.

OPEN CHANNEL FLOW

4.1   INTRODUCTION

Open channel flow occurs when the top boundary of the fluid is exposed to the atmosphere. Pressure on the top boundary is always constant and assumed to be zero (gage pressure). This boundary is often called the *free surface,* because it is free from contact with a solid boundary. Open channel flow occurs naturally in shallow gullies, streams, and rivers. In stormwater management design, open channel flow occurs in rain gutters, storm sewers flowing partially full, roadside ditches, curb gutters, flow diversion swales, and man-made channels. Open channel flow can be very complicated because the upper flow boundary (free surface) can move up or down, depending on the slope, roughness, and geometric shape of the channel. To perform proper open channel flow analysis and design, a broad understanding of possible flow types is necessary.

4.2 FLOW CLASSIFICATIONS

Open channel flow can be classified in several different ways. Just like pressure flow, open channel flow can change with time and space. However, here we are typically looking at flow rate (q) and flow depth (y).

Steady flow occurs in a channel when flow rate is constant. Conversely, *unsteady flow* occurs when flow rate is changing, either increasing or decreasing. A change in flow rate is usually caused by a lateral inflow, either at a single point or uniformly along the flow path. *Uniform flow* in a channel occurs when flow depth is constant for all sections along the flow path. For uniform flow to exist, the channel must be *prismatic*—that is, have a consistent shape all along the channel reach. Conversely, *nonuniform flow* occurs when depth varies along the flow path. As flow travels down the channel, flow depth may increase or decrease, depending on variations in channel slope, roughness, section geometry, or flow. With these two classifications of steady–unsteady and uniform–nonuniform, all types of open channel flow can be placed into one of four categories.

Steady uniform flow is the simplest flow to analyze and requires constant flow and constant depth. A man-made flow diversion, such as a prismatic stormwater swale around a building or parking lot is a good example of a flow channel that is designed to carry steady uniform flow. The channel section is almost always prismatic or assumed prismatic. Figure 4.1 gives a simple illustration of a profile view and cross-section of a prismatic channel carrying steady uniform flow.

Steady nonuniform flow occurs when flow rate is constant and the flow depth changes from section to section. Figure 4.2 gives two schematic profiles of flow with changing depth. This flow type occurs often in nature where stream and river channels carry essentially a constant flow but the section geometry changes. Most natural streams widen and narrow as they meander across the Earth's surface. With the widening and narrowing, flow depths typically decrease and increase, causing the flow to be nonuniform. This flow type is more difficult to analyze than steady uniform flow.

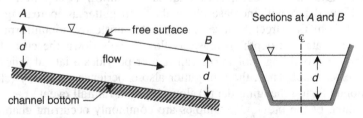

Figure 4.1 Profile and section of steady uniform flow where depth is constant and the channel bottom is parallel to the free surface.

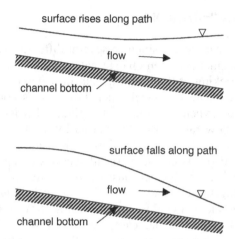

Figure 4.2 Profiles of nonuniform flow where depth is changing. Flow can be steady (constant) or unsteady (changing).

Unsteady uniform flow is a theoretical possibility, but highly unlikely to occur in practical applications. Flow rate would be changing but flow depth would remain constant. This would require a delicate balance, with a changing section geometry to match a changing flow rate, without changing flow depth. This flow type could possibly be created in a controlled laboratory environment, but it would be difficult. Therefore, anytime we refer to uniform flow in practice, it is always understood to be steady uniform flow.

Unsteady nonuniform flow occurs when flow rate and depth are changing. This is the most complex channel flow to analyze. Natural streams of any significant length experience lateral inflow from surface runoff or subsurface groundwater. Increasing stream flow along the path creates unsteady flow. The nonprismatic characteristic of most natural channels guarantees the flow to be nonuniform as well. In the urban environment, a curb gutter is a good example of a channel that carries unsteady nonuniform flow. When rainfall hits a paved street, runoff will travel to and along the gutter. As the gutter flow travels along the curb, additional lateral inflow is captured from the street. Flow depth will increase along the curb gutter as increasing flow is captured from the street surface. This creates unsteady nonuniform flow— that is, the rate and depth increase as flow travels down the curb. Rainfall dripping off a building roof into a rain gutter provides a lateral inflow along the gutter channel. Thus, the rain gutter also experiences unsteady (changing rate) nonuniform (changing depth) flow during a rainfall event.

All three of the previous examples are commonly occurring channel-flow situations in stormwater. However, in these situations and the majority of channel-flow situations encountered in stormwater management design, we often assume the flow to be steady and uniform. In natural channels, it is common to analyze segments of a river or stream such that lateral inflow does not change the channel flow appreciably. Section geometry is commonly averaged in some approximate fashion for the segment. For man-made channels like the curb gutter or rain gutter, we typically choose a single peak design-flow and hold it as constant. The associated design-flow depth becomes the maximum flow depth expected in the channel. All flows prior to the peak and after the peak will result in lower flow depths, making the geometry adequate for all anticipated flow conditions. The geometry is commonly applied to the entire flow path to create a prismatic design.

4.3 HYDRAULIC RADIUS AND DEPTH

Hydraulic radius and hydraulic depth are two characteristic parameters of open channel flow. *Hydraulic radius* is defined as

$$R_h = \frac{A}{P} \tag{4.1}$$

where A = channel section flow area (ft^2)
P = wetted perimeter of the flow section (ft)

The wetted perimeter is the flow boundary distance along the channel cross-section that comes in contact with water. Figure 4.3 illustrates flow area and wetted perimeter for a typical trapezoidal channel. Hydraulic radius is an indicator of channel efficiency. For efficient flow, it is desirable to maximize flow area to increase conveyance and minimize the flow boundary to reduce frictional resistance. Thus, larger values of hydraulic radius indicate a more efficient section.

Hydraulic depth is defined as

$$y_h = \frac{A}{T} \tag{4.2}$$

where A = channel section flow area (ft^2)
T = width of the free surface (top width) of the flow section (ft)

Compared to hydraulic radius, hydraulic depth is the flow area divided by the nonwetted perimeter of the flow section. Top width of a trapezoidal channel is shown in Figure 4.3.

Example 4.1 Figure 4.4 shows a channel section that has the approximate shape of a trapezoid where the bottom width is 7.5 feet and the left and right side slopes are approximately 1 horizontal to 1 vertical (1H:1V). The flow

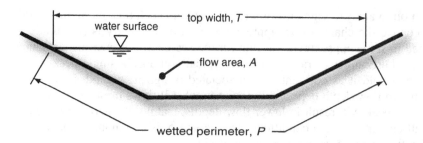

Figure 4.3 Flow area, wetted perimeter, and top width for a trapezoidal channel section.

depth in the channel is 2.8 feet. Determine the hydraulic radius and hydraulic depth for this section.

Solution: For a trapezoid, the area can be computed using three regular geometric shapes of a triangle, rectangle, and triangle. The two triangles are equal in shape with leg dimensions of 2.8 feet and 2.8 feet. The rectangle section has the dimension of 7.5 feet by 2.8 feet. Thus, the area is

$$A = (2.8)(7.5) + 2\left[\frac{1}{2}(2.8)(2.8)\right] = 28.8 \text{ ft}^2$$

The wetted perimeter is the bottom width plus the length of the two side slopes. The Pythagorean theorem is used to compute the side slopes, and thus the wetted perimeter is

$$P = 7.5 + 2\sqrt{2.8^2 + 2.8^2} = 15.4 \text{ ft}$$

Top width of the channel is simply

$$T = 2.8 + 7.5 + 2.8 = 13.1 \text{ ft}$$

Thus, hydraulic radius and hydraulic depth are

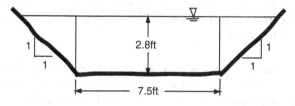

Figure 4.4 Trapezoidal section of Example 4.1.

$$R_h = \frac{A}{P} = \frac{28.8}{15.4} = 1.87 \text{ ft}$$

$$y_h = \frac{A}{T} = \frac{28.8}{13.1} = 2.20 \text{ ft}$$

Example 4.2 Express the hydraulic radius and hydraulic depth of a circular pipe flowing half full in terms of pipe diameter, D.

Solution: For a circular pipe flowing half full, $A = \dfrac{\pi D^2}{8}$, $P = \dfrac{\pi D}{2}$, and $T = D$:

$$R_h = \frac{A}{P} = \frac{\left(\dfrac{\pi D^2}{8}\right)}{\left(\dfrac{\pi D}{2}\right)} = \frac{D}{4}$$

$$y_h = \frac{A}{T} = \frac{\left(\dfrac{\pi D^2}{8}\right)}{d} = \frac{\pi D}{8}$$

Example 4.2 shows that hydraulic radius for a circular section flowing half full is $D/4$. Performing these same calculations for a pipe flowing full will show that hydraulic radius for a circular pipe flowing full also gives hydraulic radius equal to $D/4$. This is a handy relation to remember; however, it is not a general rule for all flow depths in a circular section. Hydraulic radius and depth for other flow depths must be solved directly using Equations 4.1 and 4.2, or through the use of a hydraulic elements graph, which is presented in Section 4.8.

4.4 FLOW BEHAVIOR

Open channel flow is basically controlled by viscosity, gravity, and inertia. As discussed in Chapter 3, viscosity of water is directly related to frictional resistance and causes the flow to be laminar, transitional, or turbulent.

As in pressure flow, the Reynolds number is used to characterize open channel flow as laminar or turbulent. It represents the ratio of inertial forces to viscous forces, as expressed by Equation 3.17, which is repeated here for convenience:

$$N_R = \frac{vD}{\nu} \tag{3.17}$$

where v = mean velocity of the flow (ft/s)

D = characteristic flow dimension (ft)

v = kinematic viscosity (ft²/s)

In the equation, the characteristic flow dimension, D, for open channel flow is the hydraulic radius of the channel, R_h. In pipe flow, the transition range from laminar to turbulent flow is when N_R is between 2000 and 4000. Since the hydraulic radius of a pipe flowing full (or half full) is one-fourth the pipe diameter, the transition range from laminar to turbulent flow in open channels should be about one-fourth that of pipe flow, or between $N_R < 500$ and $N_R > 1000$. Experimental data presented by Chow [1959] shows that this range is actually closer to $N_R < 500$ and $N_R > 2000$.

The Reynolds number is not the only dimensionless number for characterizing open channel flow. The effect of gravity forces relative to inertial forces is also used as a dimensionless ratio called the *Froude number, N_F*, which is defined as

$$N_F = \frac{v}{\sqrt{gy_h}}$$ (4.3)

where v = mean velocity of the flow (ft/s)

g = acceleration due to gravity (ft/s²)

y_h = hydraulic depth (ft)

In the Froude number, the mean velocity represents the inertia force. The square root of g times y_h represents the gravity force. Thus, when N_F is less than one, the gravity force dominates the inertia force and flow is defined as *subcritical*. Flow has a lower velocity and is sometimes observed as smooth or tranquil. When N_F is greater than one, the inertia force dominates the gravity force and flow is defined as *supercritical*. Flow has a higher velocity and is observed to be rapid or bombarding. When N_F is one, neither force dominates the other and flow is *critical*. This is the break point between subcritical and supercritical flow.

Using both the Reynolds and Froude numbers, open channel flow can be classified into four flow regimes as shown in Table 4.1. Transitional flow is not used in the classification because it is very difficult to define. In the

TABLE 4.1 Open Channel Flow Regimes Based on Froude and Reynolds Numbers

Flow Classification	N_F	N_R
subcritical-laminar	<1	<500
subcritical-turbulent	<1	>2000
supercritical-laminar	>1	<500
supercritical-turbulent	>1	>2000

rigorous study of open channel flow these four classifications are very useful. However, in stormwater management design, Froude number is often used by itself for characterizing flow as simply subcritical or supercritical.

Example 4.3   If the channel section of Example 4.1 is known to have a flow velocity of 4.5 ft/s, characterize the flow as laminar or turbulent and subcritical or supercritical. Assume the water temperature is 68°F.

Solution: The section has R_h = 1.87 feet and y_h = 2.20 feet. The Reynolds number and Froude number for the section are:

$$N_R = \frac{vD}{\nu} = \frac{v\,4R_h}{\nu} = \frac{(4.5 \text{ ft/s})4(1.87 \text{ ft})}{1.00 \times 10^{-5} \text{ ft}^2/\text{s}} = 3.4 \times 10^6, \text{ flow is turbulent.}$$

$$N_F = \frac{v}{\sqrt{gy_h}} = \frac{4.5 \text{ ft/s}}{\sqrt{32.2 \text{ ft/s}^2)(2.20 \text{ ft})}} = 0.53, \text{ flow is subcritical.}$$

Units were carried in this example to illustrate the dimensionless properties of the Reynolds and Froude numbers.

Using the laminar flow limit of N_R < 500 and kinematic viscosity of 1×10^{-5}, channel flow will be laminar only when the product of velocity and R_h is less than 0.00125 ft²/s. This is a very small number and shows that laminar flow rarely exists in open channel flow.

4.5 STEADY UNIFORM FLOW

In stormwater management, steady uniform flow is a commonly assumed condition in open channel analysis and design. With steady uniform flow, depth and mean velocity are constant in time and space. Figure 4.5 implies, for the condition of $y_1 = y_2$ and $v_1 = v_2$, that the water surface must be parallel to the channel bottom slope. Flow depth under these conditions is known as *normal depth*. This condition typically occurs in man-made channels or natural channels where the section geometry is prismatic. In nature, true steady uniform flow does not occur that often. Yet for short time frames or short flow-path segments, steady uniform flow is a very good approximation to real-world conditions.

Gravity provides the driving force for this flow through the slope of the channel bottom. The gravity force driving the flow is the component of the weight of the water parallel to the channel bottom. If the channel slope is expressed in terms of θ, then this driving force can be expressed as $w \sin \theta$. In uniform flow, velocity is constant, so acceleration is zero. For nonaccelerated flow, an equal and opposite resisting force to the gravity force must be present. This force is frictional resistance of the channel section against the water. Figure 4.5 shows uniform steady flow in an open channel. Here, the

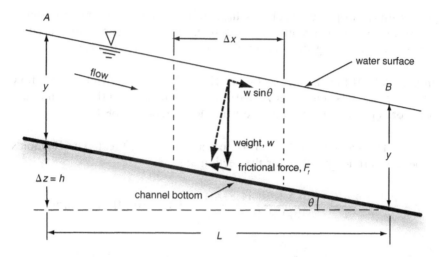

Figure 4.5 Forces acting on a flow element of length Δx.

friction force, F_f, must equal the gravity force $w \sin \theta$. Therefore, the fundamental physics equation that defines uniform flow in a channel is

$$F_f = w \sin \theta \tag{4.4}$$

In practice we never use this relation. Instead, using physical and geometric equalities, mathematical substitutions, algebraic manipulation, and experimental observations, this equation is transformed into what is commonly known as the Manning equation. Robert Manning performed the experimental observations to relate a channel roughness coefficient to channel resistance. In its U.S. standard form, the equation is

$$v = \frac{1.49}{n} R_h^{2/3} S^{1/2} \tag{4.5}$$

where v = mean channel velocity (ft/s)
$\quad\;\; n$ = channel roughness coefficient
$\quad R_h$ = hydraulic radius (ft)
$\quad\;\; S$ = channel bottom slope (ft/ft)

For those who are interested, the complete transformation of Equation 4.4 into Equation 4.5 is provided in Appendix A.

Many times flow is needed instead of mean velocity. Combining $q = vA$ with Equation 4.5 gives the other commonly reported form of Manning's equation as

$$q = \frac{1.49}{n} A \, R_{\text{h}}^{2/3} \, S^{1/2} \tag{4.6}$$

where q is expressed in ft^3/s and A is the flow area in ft^2. Manning's experiments were run under uniform channel geometry (prismatic) and uniform flow conditions. In practice, the equation has been applied successfully to nonprismatic channels. These nonprismatic channels are channel sections typically found in nature, where the channel geometry changes somewhat, but not significantly. A good understanding of each of the variables is necessary for proper use of the equation.

4.5.1 Channel Slope

Channel bottom slope, S, can be estimated using the equation

$$S = \Delta h / L \tag{4.7}$$

where Δh is vertical drop along the channel and L is the channel length, as shown in Figure 4.5. It is worth noting that S represents the constant rate of energy loss (feet of head, h, per foot of channel length, L) in the channel flow. In natural channels, the bottom slope is seldom uniform, and the average water surface slope is often a better estimate.

To estimate slope, elevation change and channel length are commonly determined from topographic maps or field survey. The estimation of slope is often assumed to be without significant error, yet studies by Johnson (1996) have suggested that variation in estimation of this parameter can be as much as 25 percent when estimating elevation change and channel length from topographic maps. Therefore, when practical, good-quality field survey data are preferred over general topographic maps to compute channel slope.

4.5.2 Flow Area and Hydraulic Radius

These two parameters are based on section geometry. For man-made regular channels, section shapes are typically computed by knowing the design-flow depth and the section shape. Common section shapes are circular, rectangular, triangular and trapezoidal. The geometric properties of several channel sections are shown in Table 4.2 and the associated geometries are shown in Figure 4.6. A close review of the table shows that the rectangular and triangular sections are special cases of the trapezoidal section. A rectangular section is a trapezoidal section where $z = 0$. A triangular section is a trapezoidal section where $b = 0$. Consequently, the design professional only needs to remember the trapezoidal and circular section properties. The parabolic section geometry (not shown) has more complex property equations. In practice,

TABLE 4.2   Geometric Properties of Common Channel Sections

Section Type	Area	Perimeter	Top Width	Hydraulic Radius	Hydraulic Depth
Circular (α = radians)	$\dfrac{(\alpha - \sin \alpha)D^2}{8}$	$\dfrac{\alpha D}{2}$	$(\sin \frac{1}{2} \alpha)D$	$\dfrac{1}{4}\left(1 - \dfrac{\sin \alpha}{\alpha}\right)D$	$\dfrac{(\alpha - \sin \alpha)D}{(\sin \frac{1}{2} \alpha)8}$
Rectangular	by	$b + 2y$	b	$\dfrac{by}{b + 2y}$	y
Triangular	zy^2	$2y\sqrt{1 + z^2}$	$2zy$	$\dfrac{zy}{2\sqrt{1 + z^2}}$	$\dfrac{y}{2}$
Trapezoidal	$(b + zy)y$	$b + 2y\sqrt{1 + z^2}$	$b + 2zy$	$\dfrac{(b + zy)y}{b + 2y\sqrt{1 + z^2}}$	$\dfrac{(b + zy)y}{b + 2zy}$

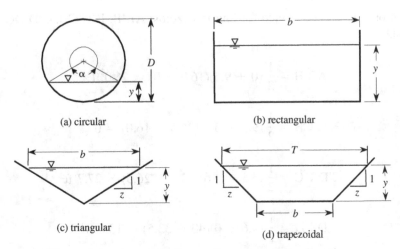

Figure 4.6 Geometric shapes of common channel sections.

it is rarely used because it is more difficult to design and construct in the field.

Natural channel sections are usually irregular in shape, yet are often approximated by the shape of a regular geometric section. For channel sections that are very irregular, geometry is often approximated with a series of points using profile coordinates. Figure 4.7 shows an irregular section that is approximated by five points across the section profile. The area is computed using either the trapezoidal area formula or method of coordinates. The perimeter is computed by using the Pythagorean theorem repetitively to compute individual lengths along the channel bottom or by using coordinates and the distance formula.

Example 4.4 Compute the area and wetted perimeter of the section in Figure 4.7 using the trapezoid formula for area and Pythagorean theorem for wetted perimeter.

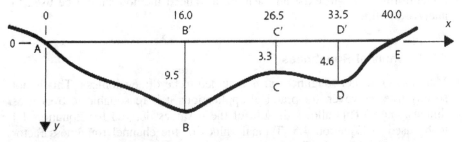

Figure 4.7 Irregular channel cross-section.

Solution: Area is computed for four trapezoids: AB′B, B′C′CB, C′D′DC and D′ED.

$$AB'B = \frac{1}{2}(0 + 9.5)(16.0 - 0) = 76.0 \text{ ft}^2$$

$$B'C'CB = \frac{1}{2}(9.5 + 3.3)(26.5 - 16.0) = 67.2 \text{ ft}^2$$

$$C'D'DC = \frac{1}{2}(3.3 + 4.6)(33.5 - 26.5) = 27.7 \text{ ft}^2$$

$$D'ED = \frac{1}{2}(4.6 + 0)(40 - 33.5) = 15.0 \text{ ft}^2$$

The total area is the sum of the four trapezoids.

$$A = 76.0 + 67.2 + 27.7 + 15.0 = 185.9 \text{ ft}^2$$

The perimeter is computed using the Pythagorean theorem on each line segment that approximates the channel bottom along line ABCDE.

$$P = AB + BC + CD + DE$$

$$P = [16^2 + 9.5^2]^{1/2} + [(26.5 - 16)^2 + (9.5 - 3.3)^2]^{1/2} + [(33.5 - 26.5)^2 + (4.6 - 3.3)^2]^{1/2} + [(40 - 33.5)^2 + 4.6^2]^{1/2}$$

$$P = 18.61 + 12.19 + 7.12 + 7.96 = 45.9 \text{ ft}$$

To use Manning's equation with an irregular-shaped channel, the channel must still be approximately prismatic—that is, the irregular section shape must be relatively constant for the entire length of the channel. If it is not, nonuniform flow will exist and a more advanced method should be used to analyze the flow.

4.5.3 Channel Roughness

Manning's channel roughness n, is assumed to be dimensionless. This is not strictly true; however, for practical applications it is reasonable to treat it as dimensionless. This allows the use of the n values derived for Equation 4.4 to be used in Equation 4.5. Typical values of the channel roughness factor are given in Table 4.3. The values range from very smooth surfaces (0.010) to very rough flow paths (0.4). As a matter of warning, these roughness values

TABLE 4.3   Roughness Coefficient Values for the Manning Equation (ASCE, 1992)

Surface Type	n
CLOSED CONDUITS	
Asbestos-cement pipe	0.011–0.015
Brick	0.013–0.017
Cast iron pipe	
Cement lined and seal coated	0.011–0.015
Concrete (monolithic)	
Smooth forms	0.012–0.014
Rough forms	0.015–0.017
Concrete pipe	0.011–0.015
Corrugated metal pipe	
½ inch × 2 ½ inch corrugations	
Plain	0.022–0.026
Paved invert	0.018–0.022
Spun asphalt lined	0.011–0.015
Plastic pipe (smooth)	0.011–0.015
Vitrified clay	
Pipes	0.011–0.015
Liner plates	0.013–0.017
OPEN CHANNELS	
Lined channels	
Asphalt	0.013–0.017
Brick	0.012–0.018
Concrete	0.011–0.020
Rubble or riprap	0.020–0.035
Vegetation	0.030–0.40*
Excavated or dredged	
Earth, straight and uniform	0.020–0.030
Earth, winding, fairly uniform	0.025–0.040
Rock	0.030–0.045
Unmaintained	0.050–0.140
Natural (minor streams, top width at flood stage < 100 ft)	
Fairly regular section	0.030–0.070
Irregular section with pools	0.04–0.10

*See Chapter 11 for further definition of vegetated channels.

are for open channel flow only and should not be used in sheet flow equations. Sheet flow has a very shallow depth (< 0.05 ft) across a relatively plane surface. Channel flow assumes a flow of significant depth where the depth is much larger than the surface roughness dimension. Sheet flow is discussed in Chapter 7.

Selection of a roughness value can be difficult. Several factors should be considered in the selection process. These factors include: (1) channel surface regularity in terms of condition and type; (2) section size and shape variations;

(3) channel obstructions such as weeds, rock, and debris; (4) vegetation effect on flow, and (5) channel meandering. In the same study mentioned earlier, Johnson (1996) reported that channel roughness estimates can vary anywhere from 5 to 35 percent, depending on personal interpretation of the channel characteristics and condition.

Cowan (1956) offered a structured method for estimating channel roughness in medium to small natural channels based on the five listed factors. In this method, a value for n can be computed by

$$n = (n_0 + n_1 + n_2 + n_3 + n_4)m_5 \qquad (4.8)$$

where n_0 is a basic value of n, and n_1 through n_4 are corrections for surface irregularities, section shape and size variations, obstructions, and vegetation and flow conditions, respectively. The modifier m_5 accounts for channel meandering. A summary computation list for this method is provided in Table 4.4. The table gives some indication of the effect of each variable on the final channel roughness. Further description of this method is presented

TABLE 4.4   Values for Computing Roughness n by Equation 4.11 (Cowan, 1956)

Variable	Description	Values
Basic material, n_0	Earth	0.020
	Rock cut	0.025
	Fine gravel	0.024
	Course gravel	0.028
Surface irregularity, n_1	Smooth	0.000
	Minor	0.005
	Moderate	0.010
	Severe	0.020
Section variation, n_2	Gradual	0.000
	Alternating occasionally	0.005
	Alternating frequently	0.010–0.015
Effect of obstructions, n_3	Negligible	0.000
	Minor	0.010–0.015
	Appreciable	0.020–0.030
	Severe	0.040–0.060
Vegetation, n_4	Low	0.005–0.010
	Medium	0.010–0.025
	High	0.025–0.050
	Very high	0.050–0.100
Degree of meandering, m_5	Minor	1.00
	Appreciable	1.15
	Severe	1.30

by Chow (1959) and McCuen (2005). Even if this method is not used, it helps to reinforce the need to consider channel characteristics other than channel surface description before choosing a roughness value from a table.

Example 4.5 Using Cowan's method, estimate the channel roughness for a mountain stream that flows through a natural rock-cut, containing a moderate amount of surface irregularity, with gradual section variation, appreciable obstructions to flow, low vegetation resistance, and limited meandering.

Solution: From Table 4.4 the following values are selected.

Basic (rock-cut), $n_0 = 0.025$
Irregularity (moderate), $n_1 = 0.010$
Section variation (gradual), $n_2 = 0.000$
Obstructions (minor), $n_3 = 0.012$
Vegetation (low), $n_4 = 0.007$
Meandering (minor), $m_5 = 1.00$

Using Equation 4.8, the channel roughness is estimated as

$$n = (0.025 + 0.010 + 0.000 + 0.012 + 0.007)1.00 = 0.054$$

It is worth noting that this value falls in the middle of the range provided in Table 4.3 (0.030–0.070) for a natural minor stream with a fairly regular section.

Example 4.6 The channel described in Example 4.5 has a section that is approximated reasonably well by a rectangular channel. The base dimension averages 12 feet throughout its length of 2,200 feet. The channel drops 95 feet in this length. If flow depth is observed to be 1.8 feet, estimate the flow rate.

Solution: The slope of the channel is computed using Equation 4.7.

$$S = \frac{\Delta h}{L} = \frac{95 \text{ ft}}{2200 \text{ ft}} = 0.0432 \text{ ft/ft}$$

Table 4.2 is used to compute A, P, and R_h for a rectangular channel.

$$A = by = (12 \text{ ft})(1.8 \text{ ft}) = 21.6 \text{ ft}$$

$$P = b + 2y = 12 \text{ ft} + 2(1.8 \text{ ft}) = 15.6 \text{ ft}$$

$$R_h = \frac{A}{P} = \frac{21.6 \text{ ft}^2}{15.6 \text{ ft}} = 1.38 \text{ ft}$$

Flow is computed using Equation 4.6.

$$q = \frac{1.49}{n} A \, R_h^{2/3} \, S^{1/2} = \frac{1.49}{0.054} (21.6 \text{ ft}^2)(1.38)^{2/3} \, (0.0432 \text{ ft/ft})^{1/2}$$

$$q = 154 \text{ ft}^3/\text{s}$$

4.6 SPECIFIC ENERGY AND CRITICAL DEPTH

Energy necessary to drive open channel flow is provided by gravity through the change in elevation along the channel path. Figure 4.8 shows the energy components of elevation z, flow depth y, velocity head ($v^2/2g$), and head loss between the two sections ($h_{L(1-2)}$) along a path. The general energy equation discussed in Chapter 3 can be applied to an open channel in a manner similar to that of a closed conduit by observing that the total energy at A must equal the total energy at B. The energy equation becomes

$$y_1 + \frac{v_1^2}{2g} + z_1 = y_2 + \frac{v_2^2}{2g} + z_2 + h_{L(1-2)} \tag{4.9}$$

where y = flow depth (ft)
  v = mean channel velocity (ft/s)
  z = channel bottom elevation (ft)
  R_h = hydraulic radius (ft)
  $h_{L(1-2)}$ = channel bottom slope (ft/ft)

Note that flow depth (y) is used in place of pressure head (p/γ) when compared to energy in a closed conduit flow. In open channel flow, water depth causes a static pressure at the bottom of the channel, and it varies linearly from a maximum value at the channel bottom to zero at the free surface. In pressure flow, static pressure is computed for the centerline of the conduit, noting that fluid pressure typically varies very little across the pipe flow section.

In Figure 4.8, the *energy grade line* (EGL) is a plot of total energy in the fluid as a function of path length. This line shows the rate at which energy

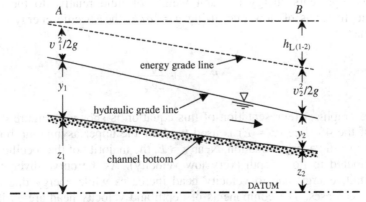

Figure 4.8   Energy components in open channel flow.

is lost along the path. For uniform flow, energy is lost at a constant rate, so the slope of the EGL is parallel to the channel bottom slope. In Manning's equation, the slope term is really the slope of the energy grade line. It just turns out that energy slope for uniform flow is equal to bottom slope, which is relatively easy to compute.

In Figure 4.8, the free surface is a plot of the *hydraulic grade line* (HGL), which is the sum of flow depth and bottom elevation. The HGL is important for some hydraulics calculations, particularly free surface flow in storm sewers, where the flow passes from an upstream pipe through a manhole or inlet box and back into a downstream pipe. A plot of the HGL through a manhole or inlet box will show if the water surface is dropping, which is necessary to maintain uniform flow and avoid backwater effects in the system.

Through a manhole, the water surface can rise as high as the EGL if a significant obstruction is encountered, causing the velocity head to transform into flow depth (pressure head). Such an obstruction might be a sharp change in the flow direction. In cases where the EGL shows water surcharging a manhole or inlet, the pipe design should be changed. The EGL is also important in bridge pier design. The upstream side of a bridge pier is what is commonly called a *stagnation point*. Such points block the flow, converting the flow velocity into a stagnation pressure, or increased water surface. The water height at the upstream side of the pier is approximately equal to normal flow depth plus velocity head, which represents the EGL.

In open channel flow, it is often important to consider energy specific to the flow without consideration of path position. *Specific energy, E,* is defined as the combined energy of flow depth and velocity and expressed as

$$E = y + \frac{v^2}{2g} \tag{4.10}$$

This represents energy per unit weight of fluid relative to the channel bottom. In terms of flow rate, using $v = q/A$, the specific energy equation becomes

$$E = y + \frac{q^2}{2gA^2} \tag{4.11}$$

The graphical representation of this equation is shown in Figure 4.9. The plot of the 45° line ($y = E$) is used to show the upper asymptotic boundary of the specific energy equation. Near $y = E$, the majority of the specific energy is attributed to flow depth (very low velocity). As the curve diverges from this limit, energy due to velocity head increases while energy due to flow depth decreases. The components of depth and velocity head are easily seen on a horizontal line extending from the y-axis to the specific energy curve. The segment from the y-axis to the 45° line is flow depth, and the segment from the 45° line to the specific energy curve is velocity head. Close inspection of the graph shows that the velocity component is always increasing as depth is decreasing.

The diagram shows that for any specific energy, there are two possible flow depths. These depths are called *alternate depths* since either can occur in the channel section, depending on slope and roughness. The graph also shows that a minimum specific energy exists. This is where the critical flow depth,

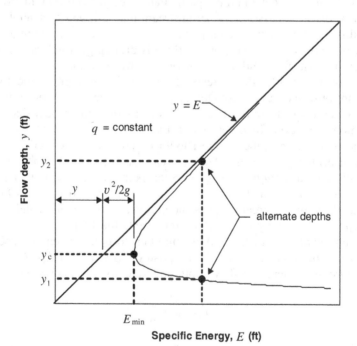

Figure 4.9 Typical specific energy diagram for open channel flow.

y_c occurs. Critical depth defines the break-point between supercritical and subcritical flow.

As you might guess, for any specific energy greater than the minimum, the larger alternate depth (y_2) represents subcritical flow and the smaller alternate depth (y_1) represents supercritical flow. For uniform flow in a prismatic channel, roughness and slope variation can cause the depth to change from subcritical to supercritical, and vice versa. Steeper slope and lower channel roughness increase the possibility of supercritical flow. Flatter slope and higher channel roughness typically cause subcritical flow.

For the condition of minimum specific energy, an expression for critical flow, can be derived from Equation 4.11 using differential calculus. The expression is

$$\frac{q^2}{g} = \frac{A_c^3}{T_c} \tag{4.12}$$

This equation can be used to compute critical depth for a channel.

Example 4.7 Water is flowing in a trapezoidal channel at a rate of 7.5 ft³/s. The channel has a 12-foot bottom width, and the side slopes are 1.5 horizontal to 1 vertical. Calculate critical depth for the channel.

Solution: Using Table 4.2, flow area and top width are expressed in terms of critical depth.

$$A_c = by + zy^2 = 12y_c + 1.5 \ y_c^2$$

$$T_c = b + 2zy = 12 + 2(1.5 \ y_c)$$

Substituting these expressions into Equation 4.12 gives

$$\frac{q^2}{g} = \frac{A_c^3}{T_c}$$

$$\frac{7.5^2}{32.2} = \frac{(12y_c + 1.5y_c^2)^3}{12 + 2(1.5y_c)}$$

$$1.75 = \frac{(12y_c + 1.5y_c^2)^3}{12 + 3y_c}$$

The equation is solved by trial and error for y_c. The value of the right side of the equation is computed based upon a guess at y_c. When the computation yields a value equal to 1.75, the solution is complete.

Trial	y_c	Right Side	Comment
1	0.3	4.039	low
2	0.2	1.182	low
3	0.23	1.804	high
4	0.227	1.733	close
5	0.228	1.757	close enough

$$y_c = 0.23 \text{ ft}$$

Although the equation was solved for depth to the nearest 0.001 feet, it is more logical to report the critical depth to ± 0.01 feet since it is highly unlikely that flow in this channel can be accurately measured any closer than 0.01 feet.

4.7   CHANNEL SIZING

The Manning equation as presented in Equation 4.6 is useful for analyzing flow capacity of a channel. In analysis, the geometry of the channel is known and flow is determined. The equation is also used in design. Channel design factors that must be considered include stability, efficiency, maintenance, and aesthetic appearance. However, the first step in design is sizing. Sizing usually allows selection of geometric properties within certain limitations such as minimum and maximum slope, surface roughness, maximum top width, maximum side slopes, or possibly width of drainage easement.

When sizing a channel, flow is known and channel geometry must be determined. Usually, channel slope is known or cannot be altered very much in the design. Surface roughness is controlled by the proposed channel lining, and is usually assumed or known. To simplify the design process, Equation 4.6 is rearranged to place all geometric parameters of the channel section on the left side of the equation.

$$AR_h^{2/3} = \frac{qn}{1.49\ S^{1/2}} \tag{4.13}$$

Using this equation, the process of sizing is trial and error, where a guess at the section geometry is made and a flow depth is estimated. From this, area and hydraulic radius are computed and the magnitude of the left side of Equation 4.13 is determined. This number is compared to the magnitude of the right side. If these numbers are in agreement, the sizing is complete. If they are not, an adjustment to section geometry is made (usually depth) and area and hydraulic radius are recomputed. The left side is again compared to the right side. The process is repeated until a close match is obtained between the two sides of the equality.

Example 4.8 Determine the basic dimensions of a trapezoidal channel section to carry a flow of 19 ft³/s. The flow depth cannot exceed 1.5 feet and the top width at the maximum water surface cannot exceed 20 feet. Side slope must be at least 3 horizontal to 1 vertical or flatter, and the preferred side slope is 5H to 1V. Channel slope must be held to 0.0185 ft/ft, and the lining has a roughness coefficient of 0.040.

Solution: With flow, roughness, and slope established, Equation 4.13 is simplified to

$$AR_h^{2/3} = \frac{qn}{1.49 \, S^{1/2}} = \frac{(19)(0.040)}{1.49(0.0185)^{1/2}}$$

$$AR_h^{2/3} = 3.75$$

Channel dimensions must be assumed. For beginners, we can arbitrarily say that flow velocity should be around 2 ft/s to protect the channel from erosion. Using continuity, the flow area can be estimated as

$$A = \frac{q}{v} = \frac{19 \text{ ft}^3/s}{2 \text{ ft/s}} = 9.5 \text{ ft}^2$$

A flow area somewhere around 10 ft² is a good starting point. We boldly assume the bottom width to be 10 feet, with side slopes of 5 to 1. For this case, if flow depth is 1 foot, the flow area is 15 ft². It appears this channel has plenty of flow area. Therefore with $b = 10$ feet, $z = 5$, and a variable flow depth, we can create equations for A and P that are a function of y only.
From Table 4.2,

$$A = by + zy^2 = 10y + 5y^2$$

$$P = b + 2y\sqrt{1 + z^2} = 10 + 2y\sqrt{1 + 5^2} = 10 + 10.2y$$

With these equations, a guess at y allows us to compute A, P, R_h and $AR_h^{2/3}$. The solution becomes trial and error.

Trial	y	A	P	R_h	$AR_h^{2/3}$	Comment
1	1	15	20.20	0.743	12.3	high
2	0.5	6.25	15.10	0.555	3.47	low
3	0.55	7.01	15.61	0.587	4.11	high
4	0.52	6.55	15.30	0.568	3.72	almost
5	0.522	6.58	15.32	0.569	3.75	OK

The flow depth of 0.52 feet is well below the maximum allowable depth of 1.5 feet. Using Table 4.2, top width is computed as

$$T = b + 2zy = 10 + 2(5)(0.52) = 15.2 \text{ ft}$$

This is one acceptable channel section size based on the given criteria. Many other configurations are possible, and a smaller section with a larger depth may be desirable. A second solution to this problem is a trapezoidal channel with bottom width of 4 feet, side slopes of 3:1, flow depth of 1.31 feet, and top width of 7.86 feet. Certainly, this solution requires less space for construction, but its deeper flow depth implies a higher velocity and also an increased probability that the channel would scour under full flow conditions. Chapter 11 addresses more fully other design elements of an open channel.

4.8 CIRCULAR CONDUITS FLOWING FULL OR PARTIALLY FULL

When the Manning equation is applied to "barrel full" flow through circular pipes with a diameter of D, the hydraulic radius, R_h, becomes

$$R_h = \frac{A}{P} = \frac{\frac{\pi}{4} D^2}{\pi D} = \frac{D}{4} \tag{4.14}$$

For this special case, substituting the area equation and Equation 4.14 into Equation 4.6, the Manning equation takes the form of

$$q = \frac{0.46}{n} D^{8/3} S^{1/2} \tag{4.15}$$

If q and S are known, the equation can be solved for the diameter of the pipe in inches, giving

$$D_{min} = 16\left(\frac{qn}{S^{1/2}}\right)^{3/8} \text{ (inches)} \tag{4.16}$$

Equation 4.16 is a design equation for circular pipes flowing full under uniform flow with normal depth assumed in the pipe. It is often used for storm sewer design for circular pipes with medium to small diameters. The minimum pipe diameter is computed using flow, slope, and pipe roughness. The designer chooses the next larger standard pipe size to carry the flow. The larger diameter will almost always cause the pipe to flow partially full.

Partially full pipe flow can be analyzed using a hydraulic elements graph, like the one shown in Figure 4.10. The chart shows how area, hydraulic radius, and flow vary with increasing depth in a circular conduit. The hydraulic radius curve shows that hydraulic radius is maximum around a flow depth ratio y/D equal to about 0.80. This is caused by the relatively larger increase in wetted perimeter, as compared to the relatively low increase in flow area between y/D equal to 0.8 and 1.0.

The flow ratio curve shows that the circular conduit carries a maximum flow at a flow depth ratio around 0.94. This is a recognized characteristic of normal flow in circular pipes. The maximum flow capacity is greater at the flow depth $y/D = 0.938$ than it is at full flow. The full flow capacity is usually assumed to be the maximum, however. This provides a small safety factor in design.

Example 4.9   A circular pipe is used to convey flow between two stormwater catch basins. The pipe must carry 27.5 ft³/s, and gravity flow is assumed. The pipe has a slope of 0.037 ft/ft and is made of smooth bore plastic (N12). Recommend a pipe size to carry this flow. Determine the flow capacity of the chosen pipe and the flow depth for the design flow.

Solution: Manning's roughness for N12 plastic pipe is 0.012. Equation 4.15 is used directly to solve for the minimum pipe diameter.

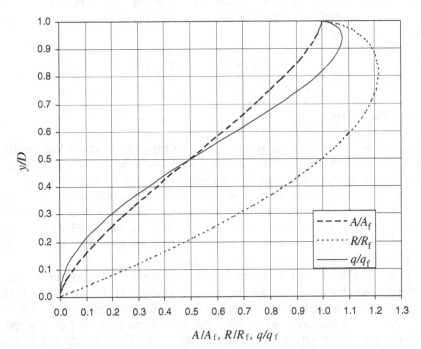

$$A/A_f, \; R/R_f, \; q/q_f$$

Figure 4.10 Hydraulic elements of a circular pipe flowing partially full.

$$D_{min} = 16\left(\frac{qn}{S^{1/2}}\right)^{3/8} = 16\left(\frac{(27.5)(0.012)}{(0.037)}\right)^{3/8}$$

$$D_{min} = 19.6 \text{ inches}$$

Standard diameters for N12 pipe include 15, 18, 24 and 30 inches. A 24-inch-diameter pipe is the minimum standard size that will work.

The full flow capacity of a 24-inch pipe with $n = 0.012$ and $S = 0.037$ ft/ft is

$$q_f = \frac{0.46}{n} D^{8/3} S^{1/2} = \frac{0.46}{0.012}\left(\frac{24}{12}\right)^{8/3} (0.037)^{1/2}$$

$$q_f = 46.8 \text{ ft}^3/\text{s}$$

The design flow depth is found by using the ratio of design flow divided by full capacity flow (q/q_f) and the hydraulics element graph.

$$\frac{q}{q_f} = \frac{27.5}{46.8} = 0.59$$

From Figure 4.10 (hydraulic elements graph) using q/q_f of 0.59 the ratio of y/D is approximately 0.55. Thus the design flow depth in the 24-inch pipe will be approximately

$$y = 0.55(24) = 13.2 \text{ inches}$$

4.9 THE WEIR

The *weir* is a flow measurement device that typically forces a fluid to back up behind a barrier to create a free fall over a wall or a flow regime change through the barrier. When used to measure stream or channel flow, the weir is typically constructed as a long horizontal obstruction across the entire stream, acting like a small dam and creating a wide rectangular flow section. The upstream flow lines must bend upward from the channel bottom to flow over the obstruction, causing an increase in flow velocity. This is the config-uration of a simple *unconstricted rectangular weir*.

When used as a control for the flow of impounded water, as in the case of a stormwater detention facility, the weir is typically constructed as a slotted rectangular opening in a barrier wall. This second weir type is called a *con-stricted rectangular weir* where the flow must bend upward from the pond bottom and also inward at the surface toward the left and right sides of the weir. In either case, the change in velocity through the weir causes the static and dynamic energy to change, allowing the energy equation to be used to compute the velocity of flow at the crest of the weir.

Figure 4.11 shows a sketch of a constricted rectangular weir and the typical flow profile. The crest of the weir is assumed to be sharp and well defined. The water surface is curved downward as it falls over the obstruction causing a free-fall as it discharges to the downstream side of the weir. The free-fall guarantees that the static pressure just below the weir crest is only atmospheric, which is zero gage pressure. This simplifies the solution of the energy equation and gives the theoretical equation for discharge over a weir as

$$q_w = \frac{2}{3} L\sqrt{2gH^3} \tag{4.17}$$

where q_w = flow rate through the weir (ft^3/s)
 L = flow length of the weir (ft)
 H = depth of water over the weir (ft)

The actual flow is different from the theoretical for several reasons. One reason is that flow constrictions at the lip of the weir reduce the actual flow area to an effective flow area. To take real flow effects into account, a coefficient is added to the equation, changing it to

$$q_w = \frac{2}{3} C_w \sqrt{2g} \, LH^{3/2} \tag{4.18}$$

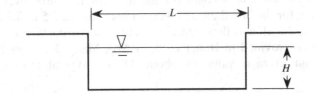

(a) Section of a constricted rectangular weir

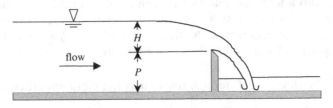

(b) Profile of a rectangular sharp crested weir

Figure 4.11 The rectangular weir.

where C_w = weir discharge coefficient (dimensionless)
   H = flow height of water surface above weir (ft)

The flow height is the elevation difference between the water surface above the weir and the weir crest. The water surface elevation is measured about three or four times H upstream of the weir crest. The weir discharge coefficient varies somewhat with weir geometry and the ratio of H to P (as defined in the sketch), but it is commonly approximated as 0.6 for most practical cases. To simplify the equation, the three leading terms on the right side are merged into one coefficient, and the equation is simplified to the commonly applied form of

$$q_w = C L H^{3/2} \qquad (4.19)$$

With this simplification, the coefficient C includes the square root of the gravitational constant, making Equation 4.19 unit specific. For the U.S. Standard system of units, sharp crested weir flow can be calculated using specific flow equations, as reported by Mott (2006). These equations include the variables P and H as defined in Figure 4.11. However, in stormwater management design practice, most professionals simply use Equation 4.19, setting C to about 3.3 for unconstricted rectangular weirs and 3.1 for constricted rectangular weirs. The reduction of C from 3.3 to 3.1 for the constricted weir is assumed to account for the constriction effect.

The *broad-crested weir* is a special case of the rectangular weir. The flow travels over a measurable width instead of a sharp crest as shown in Figure 4.12. Equation 4.19 is often applied to the broad-crested weir, except the weir coefficient is modified to account for the less efficient flow over the crest. The coefficient for the broad-crested weir varies between 2.5 to 3.3 depending on the crest width W and flow depth H. Values of the coefficient are shown in Table 4.5 as provided in Brater et al. (1996). Many designers in practice simply use an average value of about 3.0 for typical stormwater flow situations.

Example 4.10   A contracted weir is used to measure flow in a stream. The weir is cut into a long concrete barrier with a length of 3.5 feet. The crest of the weir is at elevation 100.00 feet and the water surface elevation of the backwater in the stream behind the weir is 101.85 feet. Assume that the weir has a sharp crest. Estimate the flow in the stream.

Solution: The flow height through the weir is the elevation difference.

$$H = 101.85 - 100.00 = 1.85 \text{ ft}$$

With L = 3.5 ft and C set to 3.1, the flow is computed using Equation 4.19.

TABLE 4.5 Values of C in Equation 4.24 for Broad-crested Weirs (Brater et al. 1996)

Head, H (feet)	Weir Crest Width (feet)										
	0.50	0.75	1.00	1.50	2.00	2.50	3.00	4.00	5.00	10.00	15.00
0.20	2.80	2.75	2.69	2.62	2.54	2.48	2.44	2.38	2.34	2.49	2.68
0.40	2.92	2.80	2.72	2.64	2.61	2.60	2.58	2.54	2.50	2.56	2.70
0.60	3.08	2.89	2.75	2.64	2.61	2.60	2.68	2.69	2.70	2.70	2.70
0.80	3.30	3.04	2.85	2.68	2.60	2.60	2.67	2.68	2.68	2.69	2.64
1.00	3.32	3.14	2.98	2.75	2.66	2.64	2.65	2.67	2.68	2.68	2.63
1.50*	3.32	3.27	3.24	2.99	2.83	2.72	2.66	2.65	2.65	2.65	2.64
2.00	3.32	3.31	3.30	3.03	2.85	2.76	2.72	2.68	2.65	2.64	2.63
3.00	3.32	3.32	3.32	3.32	3.20	3.05	2.92	2.73	2.66	2.64	2.63
4.00	3.32	3.32	3.32	3.32	3.32	3.32	3.07	2.79	2.70	2.64	2.63
5.00	3.32	3.32	3.32	3.32	3.32	3.32	3.32	3.07	2.79	2.64	2.63

*Values interpolated from data reported for H = 1.4 and H = 1.6 feet.

$$q_w = C L H^{3/2}$$

$$q_w = 3.1(3.5)(1.85)^{3/2} = 27.3 \text{ ft}^3/\text{s}$$

Example 4.11 A dam in a small stream near an old grist mill is measured to be 24 feet across, with a width of 1.5 feet at the crest. The weir crest has an elevation of 1197.52 feet and runs the entire length of the dam. The water surface in the dam has an elevation of 1197.95 feet. Estimate the flow in the stream.

Solution: The flow height over the crest is the elevation difference.

$$H = 1197.95 - 1197.52 = 0.43 \text{ ft}$$

With width of 1.5 feet and flow depth of 0.43 feet, C is taken from Table 4.5 as 2.64. With $L = 24$ feet, the flow is computed using Equation 4.19.

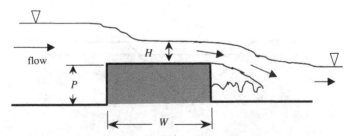

Figure 4.12 The broad-crested weir.

$$q_w = C \, L \, H^{3/2}$$

$$q_w = 2.64(24)(0.43)^{3/2} = 17.86 \text{ ft}^3/\text{s}$$

The *v-notch weir* is similar to the rectangular weir except in geometry. The weir shape is shown in Figure 4.13. It is very useful for measuring or controlling small flows. The general equation for the v-notch weir is derived from the application of the energy equation:

$$q_w = \frac{8}{15} C_w \sqrt{2g} \left(\tan \left(\frac{\theta}{2} \right) \right) H^{5/2} \tag{4.20}$$

where q_w = flow rate through the weir (ft^3/s)
   θ = v-notch angle (degrees)
   H = depth of water over the weir (ft)

The weir discharge coefficient varies with head but not dramatically. A good overall value for C_w for water is about 0.59. Simplifying the equation by combining the first three terms into one gives

$$q_w = 2.52 \tan \left(\frac{\theta}{2} \right) H^{5/2} \tag{4.21}$$

$$q_w = CH^{5/2} \tag{4.22}$$

where all terms are as previously defined. The flow coefficient C in Equation 4.22, is approximately 2.5 for $\theta = 90°$ and 1.0 for $\theta = 45°$. The discharge coefficient for other values of θ can be found in Brater et al. (1996).

Example 4.12   The flow in a small stream is measured through the use of a v-notch weir. The v-notch angle is 90°. The invert elevation of the v-notch is set at 1250.50 feet above datum. A reading from a gage staff sets the elevation of the impounded water behind the weir at 1252.88 feet. Determine the stream flow.

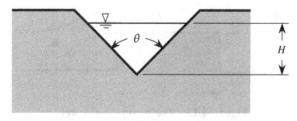

Figure 4.13   Section geometry of the v-notch weir.

Solution: The flow height over the crest is the elevation difference.

$$H = 1252.88 - 1250.50 = 2.38 \text{ ft}$$

The flow is computed using Equation 4.22.

$$q_w = CH^{5/2} = 2.5(2.38)^{2.5} = 21.8 \text{ ft}^3/\text{s}$$

PROBLEMS

4.1 A plastic rain gutter has the dimensions shown in Figure 4.14. The gutter is attached to a building and has a slope of 1/8 inch per foot. Determine the flow capacity of this gutter in gallons per minute if it flows at a depth of 2.5 inches. Assume uniform flow and a roughness coefficient of 0.010.

4.2 For the gutter described in Problem 4.1, determine the flow capacity if the roughness coefficient is increased to 0.017 due to dirt and grime buildup on the inside of the gutter.

4.3 A rectangular channel is flowing at a depth of 0.25 feet. It is 8 feet wide on a slope of 0.050 ft/ft, and is made of brush-finished concrete, having a roughness coefficient of 0.015. Determine the flow rate in the channel.

4.4 The channel of Problem 4.3 changes to a flatter slope of 0.010 ft/ft. At the transition, the concrete lining ends and a rock rip-rap lining having, a roughness of 0.050, is used. Determine the flow depth in the flatter channel section.

4.5 For the channel section described in Problem 4.3, compute the specific energy and classify the flow as either subcritical or supercritical.

4.6 For the channel section described in Problem 4.4, compute the specific energy and classify the flow as either subcritical or supercritical.

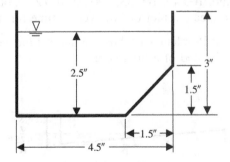

Figure 4.14 Problem 4.1.

4.7   A circular pipe is used as a storm sewer, and uniform flow is assumed. The pipe diameter is 36 inches and made of corrugated metal with roughness of 0.024. The pipe has a slope of 0.012 ft/ft. Determine (a) the pipe flow capacity and (b) the flow in the pipe if the centerline flow depth is 22 inches.

4.8   A circular storm sewer must carry 230 ft³/s, and uniform gravity flow is assumed. The pipe will have a slope of 0.044 ft/ft and is made of reinforced concrete. Recommend a nominal pipe size to carry the flow.

4.9   A circular pipe is used to carry gravity flow between two stormwater catch basins. The pipe must carry 41 ft³/s. The pipe has a slope of 0.032 ft/ft and is made of smooth bore plastic (N12). Determine (a) a nominal pipe size to carry this flow, (b) the flow capacity of the chosen pipe, and (c) the flow depth for the design flow.

4.10   A concrete street and curb gutter has the geometry shown in Figure 4.15. It has a flow-line slope of 0.0225 ft/ft. Determine the capacity of the gutter if the water depth at the curb cannot exceed 0.25 feet.

4.11   A stormwater swale must be constructed to divert surface runoff around a large commercial building. A hydrologic analysis of the site determines that the peak flow expected in the swale is 25 ft³/s. To simplify maintenance, section geometry is triangular with side slopes no steeper than 3:1 or greater than 6:1. The lining is to be mowed grass with a roughness coefficient of 0.035. The top width cannot exceed 20 feet. If the flow-line slope of the swale is set at 0.0135 ft/ft, determine the dimensions of the swale that will meet the design criteria.

4.12   A broad-crested weir is used to measure flow in a stream that discharges to a small lake. The weir crest is topped with a long 12-inch by 12-inch timber that is set perfectly level across the entire width of the stream. The flow path over the timber is 16.5 feet long. The elevation of the weir crest was arbitrarily set to 100.00 feet. A stage/ elevation stick-gage was set about 10 feet upstream of the weir crest in the middle of the stream. Gage readings were taken for ten consecutive days and recorded as follows: 100.45, 100.40, 100.36, 100.33, 100.49, 100.66, 100.40, 100.33, 100.30, 100.28. Compute the flow for each day and create a plot of flow versus time for the stream.

4.13   Use the data of Problem 4.12, but assume that the rectangular weir has a sharp crest instead of a broad crest.

Figure 4.15   Problem 4.10.

4.14 For a v-notch weir and flow condition given in Example 4.12, determine a reasonable weir angle, θ, if it is desired to keep the height of impounded water above the invert of the weir to a maximum depth of 1.5 feet.

REFERENCES

American Society of Civil Engineers. 1992. *Design and Construction of Urban Stormwater Management Systems.* ASCE Manuals and Reports of Engineering Practice No. 77.

Brater, E. F., H. W. King, J. E. Lindell, and C. Y. Wei. 1996. *Handbook of Hydraulics,* 7th ed. New York: McGraw-Hill, ISBN 0-070-07247-7.

Chin, D. A. 2000. *Water-Resources Engineering.* Upper Saddle River, NJ: Prentice-Hall.

Chow, V. T. 1959. *Open Channel Hydraulics.* New York: McGraw-Hill.

Cowan, W. L. 1956. "Estimating Hydraulic Roughness Coefficients." *Agricultural Engineering,* vol. 37: 473–475.

Daugherty, R. L., J. B. Franzini, and E. J. Finnemore. 1985. *Fluid Mechanics with Engineering Applications,* 8th ed. New York: McGraw-Hill.

French, R. H. 1985. *Open Channel Hydraulics.* New York: McGraw-Hill.

Henderson, F. M. 1966. *Open Channel Flow.* New York: Macmillan.

Johnson, P. A. 1996. "Uncertainty of Hydraulic Parameters." *Journal of Hydraulic Engineering,* vol. 112, no. 2, 112–114.

McCuen, R. H. 2005. *Hydrologic Analysis and Design,* 3rd ed. Upper Saddle River, NJ: Pearson Prentice-Hall.

Mott, Robert L. 2006. *Applied Fluid Mechanics,* 6th ed. Upper Saddle River, NJ: Prentice-Hall.

Ramser, C. E. 1929. *Flow of Water in Drainage Channels.* U.S. Department of Agriculture, Technical Bulletin 129.

Scobey, F. C. 1939. *Flow of Water in Irrigation and Similar Canals.* U.S. Department of Agriculture, Technical Bulletin 652.

Street, R. L., G. Z. Watters, and J. K. Vennard, 1996. *Elementary Fluid Mechanics,* 7th ed., New York: John Wiley & Sons.

USDA SCS. 1986. *Engineering Field Handbook—Chapter 7, Grassed Waterways.* NTIS No. PB86-197449/AS.

USDA SCS. 1954. *Handbook of Channel Design for Soil and Water Conservation.* TP-61, Washington, DC, March 1947; Revised June 1954.

CHAPTER 5

HYDROLOGY, WATERSHEDS, AND SOILS

5.1 INTRODUCTION

Hydrology is a study of the gathering, distribution, and movement of water on, above, and below the Earth's surface. It is a very broad area of study, covering many aspects of quantification of water in the environment. There are three general study areas in hydrology—namely, surface water, climatology, and groundwater. Within surface water there are many specialized topics dealing with snow, forests, agricultural lands, urban regions, and other areas of study. Hydrology for land development traditionally has been treated as a segment of the surface water study area, with an emphasis in urban hydrology. Therefore stormwater management hydrology is a very narrow segment of a very broad subject. Stormwater management has typically been thought of as the design of systems to handle the increased gathering and movement of water on the earth's surface caused by land development activities. This general focus still remains today; however, recent developments in stormwater management require land development designers to have some understanding of the effects that land development has on both climate change and groundwater supply.

Hydrology has a complexity that can be attributed mainly to the nature of the earth-environment systems that are studied. The systems are the atmosphere, the Earth's surface, and the Earth's subsurface, each of which contains its own unique array of system-defining parameters. The physical interaction of each system in the process of water movement convolutes the movement to a highly variable process dependent on many parameters that are difficult to quantify and model. So, somewhat like the challenge a meteorologist has to provide an accurate weather forecast, the hydrologist has a difficult task when it comes to analyzing and evaluating water movement.

5.2 THE HYDROLOGIC CYCLE AND WATER BUDGET

The natural beginning point for a study of hydrology is the hydrologic cycle. In simple terms, the *hydrologic cycle* is an accounting process for the movement of water in the atmosphere, on the surface, and beneath the surface of the Earth. Figure 5.1 is a depiction of this accounting.

The elements of the cycle include precipitation or rainfall (P), evaporation (E), transpiration (T), infiltration (I), runoff (R), groundwater flow (G), and storage (S). Each of these elements are described as follows:

- Precipitation—rainfall and possibly snow
- Evaporation—return of water to the atmosphere that is stored on the surface, in the form of wetted vegetation and surfaces, surface depressions, and larger water bodies such as streams, rivers, ponds, and lakes
- Transpiration—uptake of water by vegetation from the soil to the atmosphere
- Infiltration—percolation of surface storage into the soil and near subsurface
- Groundwater flow—accumulation of infiltrated water in the deeper subsurface that flows through the porous media to replenish groundwater storage or return to the surface to feed streams, rivers, ponds, and lakes
- Runoff—excess surface storage that accumulates faster than surface infiltration occurs, exceeds the capacity of surface depressions, and moves along the surface to streams, rivers, ponds, and lakes
- Storage—any of a number of mechanisms that hold water on the surface including wetting of vegetation and other surfaces (often called *interception*), small surface-depression storage, and surface storage in larger bodies of water such as streams, rivers, ponds, and lakes

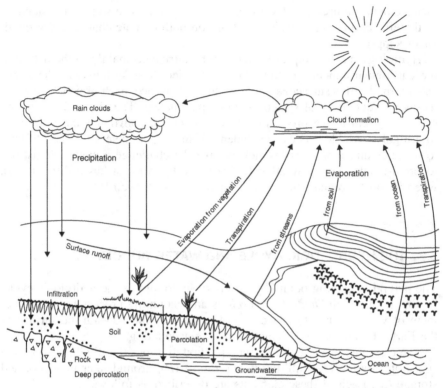

Figure 5.1   The hydrologic cycle (NRCS, NEH 630, Chapter 4).

The process of accounting for all of these elements of the hydrologic cycle requires the definition of a control surface or space, through which elements pass, and identifying each as an inflow or outflow. For surface water hydrology, a certain portion of the Earth's surface is taken as the control space. For this control space, precipitation and groundwater returning to the surface become inflows, and evaporation, transpiration, infiltration, and runoff become outflows. Storage becomes neither an inflow or outflow but simply a holding mechanism until evaporation or infiltration occur. Mathematically we can write a mass balance equation that summarizes this accounting. The conservation of mass principle, mentioned in Chapter 3, can be applied, which states that inflow minus outflow equals change in storage. Therefore, we have

$$(P + G) - (E + T + I + R) = \Delta S \qquad (5.1)$$

If we write each element as a flow (ft^3/s), then storage must also take on the units of ft^3/s, and expressed as storage change per unit of time, $\Delta S/\Delta t$. Rearranged, Equation 5.1 becomes

$$P + G - E - T - I - R = \frac{\Delta S}{\Delta t} \qquad (5.2)$$

This is a common version of the hydrologic budget for general surface water flow. It is used to evaluate any or all of the equation parameters. Depending on the application, the duration of the modeled event can vary widely from a few minutes to several years.

In stormwater management, surface water hydrology focuses on extreme rainfall and runoff events over relatively short time periods. Rainfall amounts commonly range from one to several inches over time periods of 5 minutes to 24 hours. For these very short time periods, several of the parameters in Equation 5.2 become insignificant in the analysis. Groundwater flow, evaporation, and transpiration are very slow moving processes that require larger time periods to become significant in an analysis. Since the typical stormwater modeling duration is very short, we simply neglect the effect of G, E, and T. If we are usually interested in solving for runoff, Equation 5.2 can be rearranged and simplified to

$$R = P - I - \frac{\Delta S}{\Delta t} \qquad (5.3)$$

Therefore, to model stormwater runoff, it is important to have good rainfall information and good methods to model infiltration and surface storage. In essence, this is true of most runoff models, as we will see in Chapter 8.

Example 5.1 A 2,000-square-mile watershed has the following hydrologic record for a given year:

Measured precipitation = 26.2 inches
Average rate of stream flow out of the watershed = 1200 ft³/s
Average rate of stream flow into the watershed = 0
Average drop in groundwater table over watershed = 1.7 inches (porosity of aquifer taken into account)
Surface storage is negligible.

Solution: Using the general hydrologic budget Equation 5.2, estimate the volume of water that evaporated and transpired from the watershed during the year of record. Assume that there is no significant groundwater flow loss to adjacent watersheds.

$$P + G - E - T - I - R = \frac{\Delta S}{\Delta t}$$

Infiltration is reflected in either stream flow or groundwater volume, so it is removed from the equation. Runoff out of the watershed is computed as

$$R = \frac{(1200 \text{ ft}^3/\text{s})(3600 \text{ s}/\text{hr})(24 \text{ hr}/\text{day})(365 \text{ day}/\text{yr})(12 \text{ in}/\text{ft})}{(2000 \text{ mi}^2)(640 \text{ ac}/\text{mi}^2)(43,560 \text{ ft}^2/\text{ac})} = 8.1 \text{ inches}$$

$$E + T = P + G - R - \frac{\Delta S}{\Delta t} = 26.2 - 1.7 - 8.1 - 0 = 16.4 \text{ inches}$$

5.3 WATERSHEDS

Surface runoff modeling depends on the designation of a region or area as the study focus. The concept of a watershed is used to establish an area of water study. A watershed is an area bounded peripherally by a divide, with all the area eventually draining to a point, usually a location in a swale, stream, or river. This point is often called the *point-of-interest,* or, *watershed outlet,* and is the low point in the watershed. As an example, consider a level site with a paved parking lot surrounded by concrete curbs along the perimeter. The lot is graded in a manner to allow all runoff to travel to a low point. A stormwater inlet or curb-cut is placed at this low point to collect runoff and remove it from the parking area. The parking lot in Figure 5.2 is a very

Figure 5.2 This very small watershed comprises a paved parking lot bounded by curb gutters. The curb opening in the foreground acts as the watershed outlet (T. Seybert).

small watershed that has a concrete curb as the boundary and a stormwater inlet as the outlet. On the other hand, consider the city of New Orleans. It is the outlet point of the Mississippi River watershed, with its boundary defined in the east by portions of the Appalachian Mountain range and in the west by portions of the Rocky Mountain range. The watershed is huge and very complex. Both are watersheds, and both can be analyzed for runoff using the appropriate hydrologic models. Most hydrologic analyses for stormwater design deals with watersheds that range from a few thousand square feet to several square miles.

Each watershed has its own specific hydrologic characteristics that affect the movement of water. In stormwater management, these parameters include the watershed boundary, drainage area, drainage path, surface slope, land use, surface roughness, and soil characteristics. Each of these must be defined as well as possible in order to adequately model surface runoff.

5.3.1 Boundary Delineation

The first step in watershed definition is the determination of the watershed boundary. Boundary definition begins with the selection of a point of interest for the analysis of surface runoff. A good topographic map or topographic survey for the area around and upstream of this point is then used for delineation. The boundary is delineated by starting at the point of interest, traversing along the map perpendicular to the map contours that define the direction of maximum surface slope. The line initially follows a path that increases in elevation, but at some point the line will cross contour lines of decreasing elevation. The rule is to always follow a ridge line, such that elevation is always less to the left and right of the path. The old adage of "water runs downhill" is often used to find the ridge line. Surface locations to the left and right of the constructed watershed boundary are constantly checked to determine the direction of surface runoff. If runoff from the surface eventually reaches the point of interest, then that location is part of the watershed and remains inside the watershed boundary. If the runoff does not drain to the point of interest, then that location is not part of the watershed and remains outside the watershed boundary. This constant checking continues, keeping the watershed boundary perpendicular to the contours, until the boundary returns and closes on the point of interest. Figures 5.3 and 5.4 show the delineation of two different watersheds: one for the road crossing of a stream and the other for the outlet of a lake.

As a matter of interest, water does not always run downhill. In reality, it moves from a place of higher total energy to a place of lower total energy (see chapters 3 and 4). For common surface runoff this total energy is almost exclusively defined by surface elevation, since velocity head and pressure head are essentially zero. So, it is probably more accurate to say, "*overland flow* runs downhill." Of course in the context of all that is important in hydrology, this is really a semi-trivial observation.

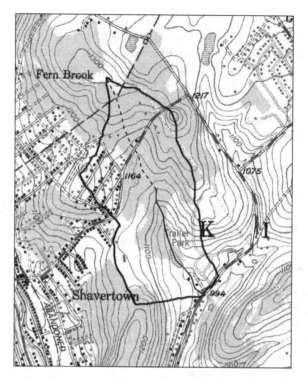

Figure 5.3   Drainage delineation for a road crossing of a stream.

5.3.2   Area

Every drainage area has critically important geometric parameters that define surface runoff. The three most commonly used geometric parameters are area, length, and slope.

Area is the most important watershed characteristic for surface runoff modeling. It defines the "size of the bowl" available for collecting rainfall to generate runoff. Area is determined as a result of the watershed delineation. The area inside the watershed boundary is measured by any means available. If a geographic information system (GIS) in conjunction with a digital elevation model (DEM) is being used to assist in the runoff modeling, the watershed area inside the watershed boundary is automatically computed as an attribute of the boundary line.

If paper maps are used for boundary delineation, then several methods are available to compute area. The most popular method would be the use of a *digitizer* attached to a GIS or computer aided drafting (CAD) system. The digitizer is essentially used to convert the paper boundary into a digital file that can be evaluated in a GIS or CAD system for area of a polygon. Two common manual methods are the polar planimeter and the method of grid cells.

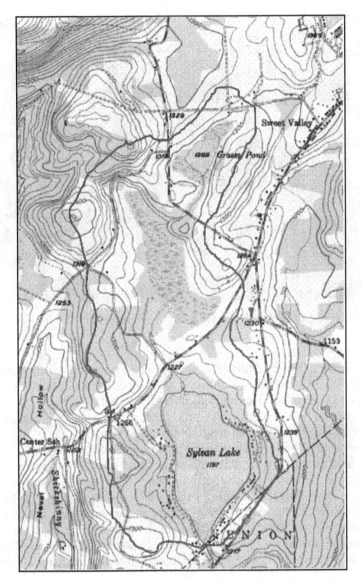

Figure 5.4 Sylvan Lake watershed with boundary delineation.

The *polar planimeter* is a mechanical desktop device that measures small areas with very good precision. A measurement wheel attached to a pivoting arm adds and subtracts polar distances that sum to the magnitude of the planimetered area in square inches or square centimeters (see Figure 5.5). Using the map scale, the area is converted into map units to establish watershed drainage area. There are several different versions of the polar planimeter. Some have analog displays, like that shown in Figure 5.4, and some have

Figure 5.5 Polar planimeter used for measuring area (T. Seybert).

digital displays. Some require the planimeter to be anchored to a stationary point on the planimetering surface. Others operate unteathered and move freely across the planimetering surface. All are older technology, and even though they are easy to use and very precise, the more modern computer digitizer can do the same job, with similar precision.

The *method of cells* requires the use of a light table or window. The paper map is held against the illuminated surface and traced onto a piece of grid paper. Using the traced boundary, the number of grid cells inside the closed polygon is determined, combining partial cells as best as possible. Each grid cell is known to represent so many square inches or square centimeters on the paper. Thus, a simple multiplication of the number of cells times cell area will result in a total area in square inches or square centimeters. Map scale is used to convert the square inch/centimeter area into an area in map units.

Example 5.2 Using the watershed boundary of Figure 5.6, determine the area of the watershed in acres and square miles. The map has been modified in size from the original due to a photocopy process; however, each cell is known to represent 460 by 460 feet of map area.

Solution: A simple counting of full and partial grid cells reveals that there are approximately 202 full cells within the boundary. The area of each cell in map units is

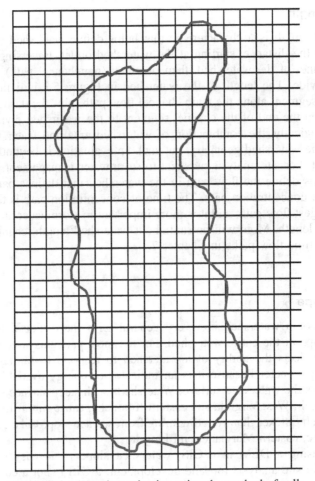

Figure 5.6 Area determination using the method of cells.

$$A_{cell} = 460 \text{ ft} \times 460 \text{ ft} = 211,600 \text{ ft}^2$$

Thus, the watershed area is

$$A = \frac{(202 \text{ cells})(211,600 \text{ ft}^2/\text{cell})}{43,560 \text{ ft}^2/\text{ac}} = 981 \text{ ac}$$

In square miles the area is

$$A = \frac{981 \text{ ac}}{640 \text{ ac}/\text{mi}^2} = 1.53 \text{ mi}^2$$

5.3.3 Length

Watershed length is a characteristic that helps define watershed shape. It is defined as the distance, starting at the watershed outlet, traversing along the main channel of the watershed, then overland (nonchannel path) to the watershed divide. The length of the watershed in Figure 5.3 is defined by the solid line segment along the main channel flow path, plus the dashed line that travels from the end of the channel segment to the watershed divide.

Hydrologically, the combination of watershed area and watershed length helps define watershed geometry, but such an evaluation is beyond the scope of this text. For site analysis pursuant to stormwater management, watershed length helps define the flow path in the watershed that defines part or all of the time of concentration path. The time of concentration path is the hydraulically longest flow path, and it is more important in stormwater analysis than watershed length. More will be said about watershed length, channel length, and travel time flow paths in Chapter 7.

5.3.4 Slope

The slope of a watershed is a very general term that reflects the average surface slope of the entire watershed. For the most part, this watershed characteristic reflects the ability of a watershed to respond to rainfall. It is an important parameter because it is an indicator of energy available to move water across the watershed surface. Watersheds with steep surface slopes, like those found in West Virginia and eastern Kentucky, cause runoff to travel and collect much quicker than runoff coming from surface slopes like those found in Delaware, eastern Maryland, and Florida.

When using a DEM in a GIS, watershed slope is an easy calculation. However, in site analysis for land development, a GIS is not a common tool simply because digital data are not readily available for small sites and are somewhat expensive to generate for the small-scale job. For paper maps, watershed slope is best estimated by computing surface slope for several overland flow paths in the watershed and computing a mathematical average.

Slope is simply computed as presented in Equation 4.7, which is repeated here for convenience.

$$S = \Delta h / L \tag{4.7}$$

where Δh is elevation change along the overland path and L is the path length. Figure 5.7 shows a possible selection of overland flow paths that could be used to estimate watershed slope for the watershed of Figure 5.3. End contours are used to obtain elevation difference, and map scale is used to establish path length. All slopes are averaged to get watershed slope.

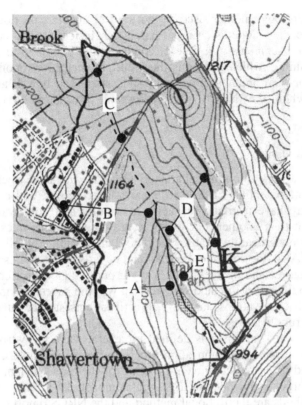

Figure 5.7 Watershed slope is determined by averaging several slope paths.

Example 5.3 For the watershed shown in Figure 5.7, determine the average watershed slope. Use the five paths, A through E, identified in the figure.

Solution: Each path is evaluated for elevation change and scaled for length. Slopes are computed using Equation 4.7. The results are summarized in Table 5.1.

TABLE 5.1 Slope Calculations for Example 5.3

Path	Δh (ft)	L (ft)	Slope (ft/ft)
A	1140 − 1040 = 100	1000	0.100
B	1220 − 1120 = 100	1250	0.080
C	1280 − 1180 = 100	980	0.102
D	1220 − 1080 = 140	920	0.152
E	1160 − 1040 = 120	670	0.179
Average			0.123

Most hydrologic models used in stormwater analysis do not specifically call for watershed slope as an input parameter. Instead, the slope of the various flow path segments in a time of concentration path is used to determine watershed timing, which in turn is the input parameter for runoff estimation. More will be said about average watershed slope and how it affects runoff modeling when the NRCS unit-hydrograph procedure is discussed in Chapter 8.

5.3.5 Land Use

Land use is a very important characteristic of a watershed when evaluating surface runoff potential. Land use dictates surface cover, and a certain type of cover may have a greater capacity to capture and hold water during a rainfall event than another. For example, a dense stand of trees with heavy ground litter underneath will absorb and hold much more rainfall than a paved parking lot. Also, the roughness of the land cover surface affects runoff rates. The same dense stand of trees with heavy ground litter will offer much more resistance to flow over the land surface than will the paved parking lot. Based on these two observations, land use directly affects surface runoff volumes and surface runoff rates.

Land use and land cover is defined in several ways in hydrologic runoff modeling. The most common approach is to assign a runoff coefficient to land use, and have that coefficient account for the effect of land use change on runoff volumes and rates in a particular model. Two common runoff coefficient methods are the Rational method and the NRCS runoff curve number method.

In the Rational method, runoff coefficients, C, range in magnitude between 0 and 1, with 0 representing a no runoff condition and 1 represents the condition where all rainfall is converted to runoff. Land use conditions of commercial/industrial, suburban residential, and unimproved, may have C values of 0.95, 0.55, and 0.15, respectfully. This C value is used directly to estimate runoff peak flow. With some modification and basic assumptions, this peak flow can be used to estimate runoff volume for simple watersheds. These methods are discussed in detail in Chapter 8.

In the NRCS curve number method, a curve number (CN) is assigned to a particular land use, with an associated hydrologic condition of the surface, and an associated hydrologic soil type reflecting subsurface capacity to affect runoff rates and volumes. The method is called the *soil cover complex method*. However, it is commonly referred to simply as the *curve number method*. In this method, a CN value is assigned to a certain soil cover complex. The CN value is used to compute a soil storage capacity, which in turn is used to compute watershed initial abstraction and runoff volume. CN values range from 40 to 98, where 98 is the condition of very high runoff potential and 40 is the condition of very low runoff potential. This method is also discussed in detail in Chapter 8.

Land use data are often determined from typical USGS 7.5 minute quadrangle maps. The map in Figure 5.3, which is a portion of a USGS 7.5 minute quadrangle map, shows white areas with streets and houses (residential), white areas that are blank (open meadow or agricultural), and green (shaded) areas that are blank (wooded). This information, in combination with a site visit, is an easy way to establish land use. Beyond the USGS map, digital orthophoto quad quadrangle (DOQQ) images can be used to estimate land use. Figure 5.8 shows a portion of a DOQQ than contains a small lake with wooded, agricultural, residential, and other land use areas. These images, which are available from the USGS and other data sites on the Internet, are possible sources for determining land use. Care must be taken when using these data sources because they are dated, and significant land use change may have occurred at the site since the production of the image. Without a doubt, the best method for establishing land use is to perform a ground survey, using a recently created topographic survey as a base map. If the site is large enough, it may be cost-effective to obtain the services of a photogrammetric mapping company to perform an aerial survey of the site.

5.4 SOILS AND INFILTRATION

The ability of a watershed to store water through the infiltration process is directly related to soil water characteristics. Soils provide porous space for storage of infiltrated water (rainfall). They can be highly variable from watershed to watershed in terms of porosity and depth. The determination of the characteristics of the soil can be critical in any hydrologic analysis.

5.4.1 Soil Profiles

Soils vary in characteristics with depth, and this variation can affect infiltration capability. A soil profile is used to define soil characteristics as they change with depth. In the field, soil profiles are often observed by making a backhoe cut from three to six feet deep, depending on soil depth. A backhoe cut is nothing more than a hole dug in the ground by a backhoe, creating a shear wall on one side for examination of the soil with depth.

Most soil profiles consist of several layers of distinctly different material. These layers have been standardized by name as the O, A_1, A_2, B, C, and R horizons, as depicted in Figure 5.9.

The O horizon is on the Earth's surface and contains mostly organic ground litter, such as leaves, twigs, and other decaying organic matter. The A_1 horizon contains mostly topsoil, which is high in organic material and supports the growth of vegetation. The A_2 layer is a zone of leaching that is very thin. It is the region where infiltrating water dissolves soluble matter. This leaching zone, if it exists, is often very clearly marked with lines of colored mottling in the soil. The B horizon contains a mixture of humus and minerals. The

Figure 5.8 A portion of a DOQQ for a site in northeastern Pennsylvania.

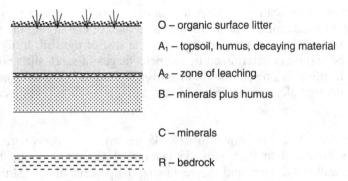

O – organic surface litter

A_1 – topsoil, humus, decaying material

A_2 – zone of leaching

B – minerals plus humus

C – minerals

R – bedrock

Figure 5.9 Soil horizons in a soil profile.

minerals come from the soil parent material. The C horizon contains minerals only, and is bounded on its bottom by the R layer, which is typically unfractured bedrock that is essentially impermeable. Not every profile contains each of these layers. Some profiles may skip the A_2 layer, or the separation between the B and C layers may not be well defined. A good soil survey may include other specialized horizons not mentioned here. However, the idea behind all of this is that soils vary with depth, and this variation affects how a soil responds to water infiltration and water storage.

5.4.2 Soil Texture

Texture is a characteristic of a soil that reflects particle sizes of mineral rock, based on a gradation of the soil. There are several classification systems for texture evaluation, including those of the USDA (U.S. Department of Agriculture), AASHTO (American Association of State Highway and Transportation Officials), and the Unified Classification Systems. Each system provides a process for classifying soils by texture name. The USDA system separates particles sizes into four primary categories of gravel, sand, silt, and clay, based on particle size diameter. The range for each category is

Texture	Gravel	Sand	Silt	Clay
Diameter (mm)	70 - - - - - - 2 - - - - - - 0.05 - - - - - - 0.002 - - - - - - 0			

Sand is further subdivided into five groups of very coarse, coarse, medium, fine, and very fine.

Sand Subtexture	Very Coarse	Coarse	Medium	Fine	Very Fine
Diameter (mm)	2 - - - - - 1 - - - - - 0.5 - - - - - 0.25 - - - - - 0.1 - - - - - 0.05				

The other classification systems use similar particle diameter limits, categories, and subcategories. Each provides a method of classifying the physical property of soil that describes average particle size of the soil. In the USDA system, the texture is determined by the percentages of sand, silt, and clay in the soil. If gravel is present, the term *gravel* is used as a texture modifier. A soil texture triangle, as shown in Figure 5.10, is used to establish classification.

Example 5.4   A soil is known to have 35 percent of its mass with particle diameters greater than 0.05 mm, 55 percent of the particles are between 0.05 mm and 0.002 mm, and the remaining 10 percent of the particles are smaller than 0.002 mm. Using the texture triangle of Figure 5.10, determine the texture of this soil.

Solution: The data show that 35 percent of the soil is sand, 55 percent is silt, and 10 percent is clay. Using the texture triangle Figure 5.10, sand is plotted at 35 percent and a line is drawn up and to the left along the grid lines. Silt

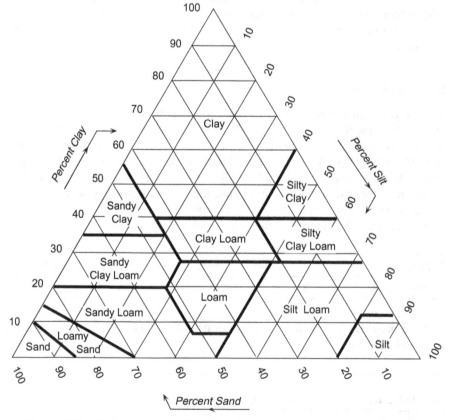

Figure 5.10   Soil texture classification triangle (USDA NRCS NSSH, 2003).

is plotted at 55 percent and a line is drawn down and to the left along the grid lines. The intersection of the two lines defines the classification. The clay line is added simply for completeness. The soil classification is found to be silt loam. The graphed solution is shown in Figure 5.11.

5.4.3 Water Storage and Infiltration

Texture is a good way to evaluate the water storage capacity and flow-through capacity of a soil. Gravelly sands, with larger diameter particles can store more water and infiltrate water faster than a silty-clay soil. As part of any USDA soil survey, the soil scientist evaluates the soil for capacity to store water by assigning a hydrologic capacity designation called *hydrologic soil group*. These groups of A, B, C, and D are used to categorize soils. The A soils are the sands and gravelly sands that have high infiltration rates and storage potential. The B soils are sandy loams that have moderate infiltration rates and storage potential. The C soils have a fine texture of clay loams that

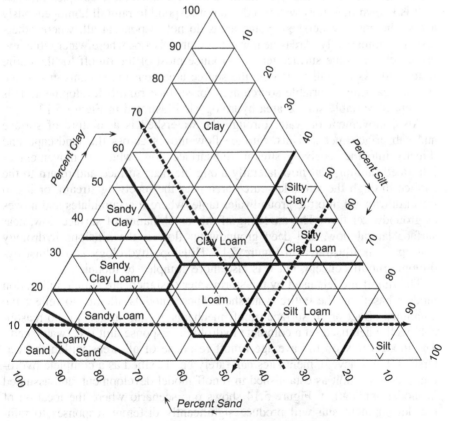

Figure 5.11 Solution to Example 5.4.

have low infiltration capacity. The D soils are the clays and silty clays that have very low infiltration capacity. These designations are used to support the selection of a curve number, which in turn is used to estimate runoff volumes for a specific rainfall event. The process is called the *hydrologic soil cover complex method* and is described in detail in Chapter 8.

5.5 WATERSHED VERSUS SITE HYDROLOGY

The methods presented in the following chapters are hydrologic modeling methods developed for watersheds. These methods include travel time, runoff depth, peak flows, and synthetic hydrographs. In general, watershed modeling methods are developed for an integral hydrologic response unit, with boundaries and drainage networks defined by natural topography. The hydrologic response of such a unit depends on many integrated factors, including soil, rock, geology, water table, and other factors. Most of the runoff models used in stormwater design are based on an infiltration loss model, where most losses of rainfall are due to infiltration into the entire watershed surface and subsurface. However, this is a simplification of a much more complex process.

It is known that most watersheds do not respond to rainfall homogeneously across the entire watershed. Some areas do not respond at all, where others respond dramatically. Areas nearer the stream network where water table levels are closer to the surface tend to produce most of the runoff for the entire watershed. As rainfall increases, the source area near the streams grows and shrinks, causing a variable source area for surface runoff development. This concept of variable source area hydrology is illustrated in Figure 5.12.

Also, movement of water through the watershed is a mixture of surface and subsurface mechanisms. Surface flow moves across the landscape and directly into the receiving stream. Subsurface flow, which is movement of infiltrated rainfall, can flow laterally along the near surface and return to the surface through the variable source area near the receiving stream, or it can travel downward into the groundwater table, where it accumulates and moves as groundwater flow. The modeling of this combination of surface flow, near surface lateral flow, and deep groundwater flow is the hillslope hydrology concept. It is illustrated in Figure 5.13. Hillslope hydrology is a robust hydrologic runoff concept, but it is also more complex to model.

The runoff models used by the stormwater designers are simple infiltration models based on the entire watershed. These models attempt to reflect the combined effect of all surface runoff mechanisms, and in general do reasonably well when used on a complete hydrologic response unit (i.e., watershed). The models rely on the average runoff response of all areas within the watershed. Land-development sites can rarely be classified as a complete hydrologic response unit as established in runoff model development, and assumed in model application. Figure 5.14 shows one scenario where the location of the development site will produce significantly different responses to rain-

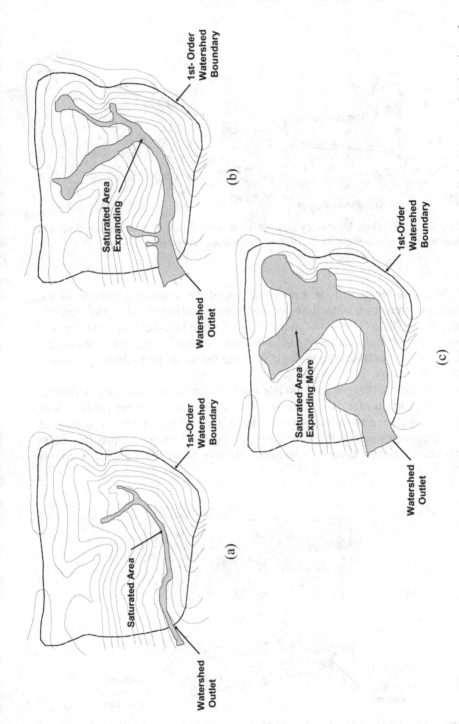

Figure 5.12 Variable source area hydrology concept where the area contributing to surface runoff changes over the duration of the rainfall event (courtesy of S. Brown, Penn State University).

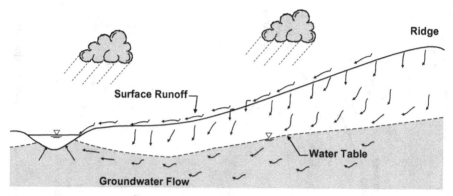

Figure 5.13 Hillslope hydrology concept with surface runoff, near surface flow, and groundwater flow (courtesy of S. Brown, Penn State University).

fall. Site 1 is located in the upper regions of the watershed outside of the variable source area. Site 2 is located almost entirely within the variable source area. There is no doubt that this exact same land-development site will produce significantly different runoff responses based on these two locations. This example illustrates the major difference between site hydrology and watershed hydrology.

Unfortunately, there are no models available to the stormwater practitioner that attempt to consider site location and site hydrology in the prediction of surface runoff. We must use what we have. One of the important aspects of the entire stormwater runoff modeling process is to recognize this limitation as the analysis and design progresses. Results from the standard methods

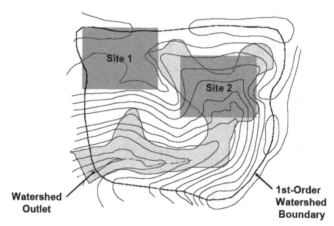

Figure 5.14 Effect of site location within a watershed on runoff potential (courtesy of S. Brown, Penn State University).

should be reviewed with caution and judgment, taking into account the general runoff characteristics of the surrounding watershed and the site location within the watershed. Often, we must ask simple questions like, "Does this answer make sense? How does the site location affect site hydrology within the modeling context of watershed hydrology? What is the best location for a detention facility, considering such characteristics as water table levels, near surface conditions for groundwater flow, proximity to groundwater recharge areas?" The good designer does more than crank out hydrographs and design structures to create a plan that works by the numbers to satisfy a land development regulation. The entire runoff process and the limitations of the tools available to the designer must be considered as well. The phrase "Think global before designing local" is appropriate. Understanding the runoff process and what is really happening in the surrounding watershed is important if good stormwater design is to be achieved. Additional discussion of this topic is presented by Brown et al. (2005).

As the methods of the following chapters are studied, it is important to keep in mind the assumptions and limitations of the models and the nature of the model application. Further study dealing with watershed processes and watershed modeling is suggested as a reasonable life-long education objective for any stormwater management designer.

REFERENCES

Brown, S. A., L. A. J. Fennessey, G. W. Petersen. 2005. "Understanding Hydrologic Process for Better Stormwater Management." *Proceedings of the 2005 Pennsylvania Stormwater Management Symposium.* Villanova University, Villanova, PA, October 11–13, 2005.

Bedient, P. B., and W. C. Huber. 2002. *Hydrology and Floodplain Analysis,* 3rd ed. Upper Saddle River, NJ: Prentice-Hall.

Chow, V. T. 1964. *Handbook of Applied Hydrology.* New York: McGraw-Hill.

McCuen, R. H. 2005. *Hydrologic Analysis and Design,* 3rd ed. Upper Saddle River, NJ: Prentice-Hall.

Singh, V. P. 1992. *Elementary Hydrology.* Englewood Cliffs, NJ: Prentice-Hall.

USDA NRCS. 2002. *National Engineering Handbook Part 630 Hydrology.* Washington, DC: ftp://ftp.wcc.nrcs.usda.gov/downloads/hydrology_hydraulics/neh630/.

USDA NRCS. 2003. *National Soil Survey Handbook,* title 430-VI. (http://soils.usda.gov/technical/handbook/).

USDA SCS. 1975. *Urban Hydrology for Small Watersheds.* Technical Release 55, U.S. Department of Agriculture, Washington, DC: Engineering Division.

USDA SCS. 1986. *Urban Hydrology for Small Watersheds.* Technical Release 55, U.S. Department of Agriculture, Washington, DC: Engineering Division.

CHAPTER 6

RAINFALL

6.1 INTRODUCTION

Rainfall is one of the most important inputs in hydrologic runoff models. Stormwater design deals with rainfall events that can be classified as rainfall intensities and rainfall depths. Rainfall intensities are flow rates. They are used in designing conveyance systems such as swales, gutters, channels, and sewers. Rainfall depths are volumes. They are used to design detention and retention storage facilities. In most cases, both intensities and volumes are needed to complete a stormwater management plan. A *hyetograph* is a plot of rainfall intensity or rainfall depth versus time for a given storm event. The graph provides both rainfall intensity information and rainfall volume information and is the most common input to hydrologic runoff models. The hyetograph will be discussed in detail after the characteristics of rainfall are presented.

Storm events can be classified as either actual or design. Actual storms are observed through field data collection. Traditionally, static and continuous rainfall gages have been used in the field to physically capture rain and measure rainfall volume over discrete periods of time. In recent times, digital event loggers are used to record rainfall events by capturing a discrete amount of rainfall and recording the event with a date/time stamp in a data logger. The typical recording interval is 0.01 inches, or 0.2 mm of rainfall. Figure 6.1 shows a rainfall logger manufactured by Onset Computer. The digital information in the logger is downloaded to a computer, where it can be transformed into a hyetograph like that shown in Figure 6.2. This figure shows hourly amounts of rainfall, yet the logger data can be transformed into rainfall amounts for many other time steps.

6.2 RAINFALL CHARACTERISTICS

Rainfall can be described according to four key characteristics: (1) volume, (2) duration, (3) intensity, and (4) frequency. Additionally, rainfall varies with time, space, and geographic location. All of these characteristics are important for defining and understanding rainfall and its effect on hydrologic runoff models.

6.2.1 Volume

The volume of rainfall is commonly provided in a length dimension, usually as depth in inches or centimeters. Volume of rainfall is implied in the depth

Figure 6.1 Recording rainfall logger is mounted beside a total rainfall gage. The picture on the right shows the tipping bucket and event recorder (*www.onsetcomputer.com*) (T. Seybert).

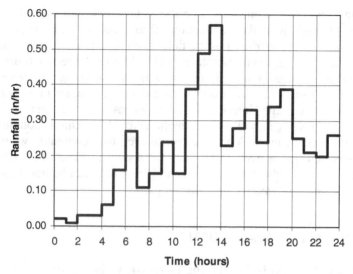

Figure 6.2 Hourly rainfall hyetograph for Crescent Lake Watershed, Auburn Township, Susquehanna County, PA, September 16–17, 2004.

dimension by associating the magnitude of the drainage area with the rainfall depth. This is why rainfall volumes are commonly reported in the units of acre-inches. For instance, if a 14-acre drainage area received 1.7 inches of rainfall, the rainfall volume would be $14 \times 1.7 = 23.8$ ac-in. In hydrologic analysis and design, rainfall volume is sometimes reported as a depth with the volume implied through the drainage area and other times it is explicitly reported as a volume. It is important to become comfortable with either method of expression. The volume of the storm shown in Figure 6.2 is the sum of all the ordinates times the time interval. In this case, the storm rainfall volume is 5.41 inches, as shown in Table 6.1.

6.2.2 Intensity

Rainfall intensity has the units of velocity. It is the rate at which rainfall falls from the sky. Like rainfall volume, intensity is associated with the magnitude of the surface runoff area. Intensity is expressed in dimensions of length per time (L/T), typically in the units of inches/hour or cm/hour. However, rainfall intensity can also be used to determine a volume flow rate because the rainfall is associated with the drainage area. For example, if a 1.5-acre parking lot is receiving rainfall at a rate of 5.0 inches per hour, the rainfall flow rate would be $(1.5 \text{ ac})(5.0 \text{ in/hr}) = 7.5$ ac-in/hr, which is equivalent to 7.5 ft^3/s, since 1 ac-in/hr = 1 ft^3/s. This explains why some peak volume runoff estimation methods require rainfall intensity as an input parameter.

**TABLE 6.1   Rainfall Amounts for Hour Intervals
for the Storm of Figure 6.2**

Hour	Rain (in/hr)	Hour	Rain (in/hr)
1	0.02	13	0.49
2	0.01	14	0.57
3	0.03	15	0.23
4	0.03	16	0.28
5	0.06	17	0.33
6	0.16	18	0.24
7	0.27	19	0.34
8	0.11	20	0.39
9	0.15	21	0.25
10	0.24	22	0.21
11	0.15	23	0.20
12	0.39	24	0.26
		Total	5.41

6.2.3 Duration

Duration is the time span over which rainfall occurs for a particular storm event. The duration of the storm in Figure 6.2 is 24 hours. Duration is often associated with standard storm lengths specified in a particular hydrologic method. In some methods, design storm durations are dictated by the time of concentration of the drainage area. See Chapter 7 for more on time of concentration. Longer-duration storms typically contain more rainfall volume. Shorter-duration storms typically have larger rainfall intensities.

6.2.4 Frequency

Rainfall frequency is commonly referred to as the *storm return period*. In statistical analysis, frequency of an event is expressed in terms of exceedence probability, which is the probability that the event (rainfall with specific depth and duration) will be exceeded in a specified time period. This time period is almost always one year. Return period T and exceedence probability p are related by

$$T = \frac{1}{p} \qquad (6.1)$$

For instance, if a storm has a 2 percent probability of being exceeded in any given year (one time period), then statistically we should expect this storm to occur (return) about once every $1/0.02 = 50$ years. The common return periods of storms used in stormwater management design have the exceedence probabilities shown in Table 6.2.

Care must be taken to not use the term *return period* incorrectly. Rainfall events are randomly occurring events that do not follow a deterministic pattern. Just because a storm is identified as having a return period of 50 years does not mean the storm can only occur once every 50 years. Although not highly probable, it is possible to have two or more 50-year storms occur in the same year.

6.2.5 Temporal Variation

Rainfall varies with time. For any given rainfall event of finite duration, the rainfall intensity varies with time. There could be periods of very light rainfall (low intensity) and other periods of very heavy rainfall (high intensity). There may even be short periods of no intensity. Sometimes the rainfall comes relatively uniform over the entire storm duration. A review of Table 6.1 shows that this particular 24-hour storm had time intervals where the rainfall intensity was as high as 0.57 in/hr and as low as 0.01 in/hr.

6.2.6 Spatial Variation

Rainfall varies with space. For watersheds of significant size, at any given time during a storm event, rainfall may be falling in a spatially nonuniform manner. For example, in a watershed of 30 square miles, it may be raining at a rate of 3.5 in/hr in the upper regions of the watershed and at the same time raining at a rate of 5.2 in/hr in the lower region. This is a case of spatially nonuniform rainfall. In stormwater design, it is rare that we concern ourselves with spatial variation. Land development sites are typically small enough to neglect the effects of spatial variation. The most popular hydrologic runoff methods used in stormwater management design do not have the capability to model spatial variation of rain.

6.2.7 Geographic Variation

It is common knowledge that rainfall varies with geographic location. Total annual rainfall varies significantly across the United States. Arizona may experience 7 to 10 inches of rain annually, whereas New York may experience 45 inches of rain in the same year. The intensity, duration, and frequency of these rainfall events also vary significantly. Figure 6.3 shows the geographic

TABLE 6.2 Exceedence Probabilities, *p*, for Common Return Periods in Stormwater Design

T (yr)	1	2	5	10	25	50	100
p	1.00	0.50	0.20	0.10	0.04	0.02	0.01

Figure 6.3 Geographic variation of total rainfall for the 10-year 24-hour rainfall (USDA, SCS TR-55, 1986).

variation of total rainfall depth in the United States for the 10-year, 24-hour storm. At the state level, rainfall data are often compiled to reflect local geographic variation. Figure 6.4 shows geographic variation of rainfall in Pennsylvania according to region. Each region has a common set of rainfall data. Region 1 is the least extreme region in terms of total volumes and intensities; Region 5 is the most extreme region.

6.3 VDF AND IDF CHARTS

Statistical analysis of observed rainfall records shows that the characteristics of volume, intensity, duration, and frequency are interrelated. For a specific geographic location and storm duration, as frequency decreases, volume and intensity increase. For the same geographic location with a given frequency, as duration increases, volume increases but intensity decreases. These characteristics are needed to adequately define a rainfall event for stormwater design. Figure 6.5 shows Intensity-Duration-Frequency (IDF) and Volume-Duration-Frequency (VDF) curves for rainfall Region 1 in Pennsylvania. Long-term rainfall records are used to define this interdependence using a statistical method called *frequency analysis.* In very general terms, records of many rainfall gaging stations are analyzed for rainfall depths above a specific threshold that defines an extreme event. The frequency of occurrence of events

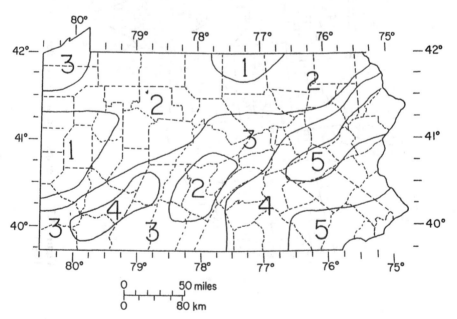

Figure 6.4 Rainfall regions in Pennsylvania (Pennsylvania Department of Transportation, 1986).

of similar volume, intensity, and duration is compiled and transformed into charts similar to Figure 6.5.

The most comprehensive rainfall data source in the United States is provided by the Hydro-meteorological Design Studies Center of the National Weather Service through its Precipitation Frequency Data Server. The data can be accessed through the Internet at *http://www.nws.noaa.gov/ohd/hdsc*. This site is a compilation of the most current rainfall data publications for the continental United States, Alaska, Hawaii, and Puerto Rico. The site contains data from many technical papers and documents. For stormwater design, the important documents include the following:

- **Technical Paper 40,** *Rainfall Frequency Atlas of the United States for Durations from 30 Minutes to 24 Hours and Return Periods from 1 to 100 Years (1961)*. This document includes a series of maps presenting rainfall-frequency values for selected durations from 30 minutes to 24 hours and return periods of 1 to 100 years. With a 1961 publication date the values are somewhat outdated, but still remain the best available data for many states.
- **Technical Memorandum NWS Hydro 35,** *Five to 60-minute Precipitation Frequency for Eastern and Central United States (1977)*. This document provides precipitation-frequency values for the central and eastern United States for return periods from 2 to 100 years, and for durations of 5 minutes to 1 hour using a series of maps and graphs. This material supersedes the similar material published in Technical Paper 40.
- **NOAA Atlas 2,** *Precipitation Frequency Atlas of the Western United States, (1973)*. This atlas provides generalized maps for 6- and 24-hour point precipitation for the return periods of 2, 5, 10, 25, 50, and 100 years. Equations and interpolation diagrams are provided for determining values for durations less than 24 hours and for intermediate return periods. Area reduction curves for adjusting point values for areas up to 400 square miles are included. Atlas 2 is published in separate volumes for each of the western states. This material supersedes the similar material published in Technical Paper 40.
- **NOAA Atlas 14,** *Precipitation Frequency Atlas for the United States,* includes Volume 1—The Semi-Arid Southwest (2003), and Volume 2—The Ohio River Basin and Surrounding States (2004). This publication is an Internet-based delivery of rainfall estimates based upon the most recent rainfall data. The Web site includes point-and-click selection for any geographic location to 30 arc-seconds resolution. Rainfall depths are provided for average return intervals ranging from 2 years to 1000 years, with durations ranging from 5 minutes to 60 days. Figure 6.6 shows typical tabulated rainfall results for a location in northern Virginia. In addition to the rainfall depths, 90 percent confidence intervals are provided for every rainfall estimate to give an indication of data precision.

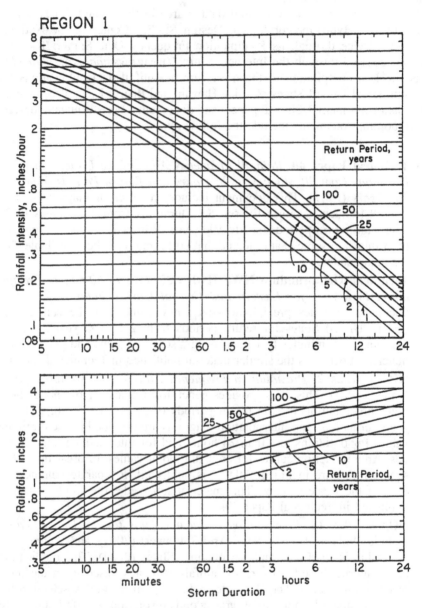

Figure 6.5 Intensity (IDF) and volume (VDF) curves for Pennsylvania Region 1 (Pennsylvania Department of Transportation, 1986).

Rainfall data specific to a rainfall gage site can also be obtained. Volume 1 covers Arizona, southeastern California, Nevada, New Mexico, and Utah. Volume 2 covers Illinois, Indiana, Ohio, Pennsylvania, New Jersey, Delaware, Maryland, District of Columbia, Virginia, West Virginia, Kentucky, Tennessee, North Carolina, and South Carolina. Other regions are planned for completion in the future. Atlas 14 rainfall data replace any comparable data available in TP 40, Hydro 35 and Atlas 2.

Atlas 14 estimates are available either as the result of an annual-maximum-series analysis or a partial-duration-series analysis. The two diverge up to 10 to 15 percent below the 25-year return period, so it is important to understand the difference. *Annual-maximum-series* analysis takes the maximum recorded rainfall event for each year in the total rainfall record and creates a data set of annual maximums. These rainfall amounts, and only these rainfall amounts, are used in the statistical analysis for return period. Annual series data are great for determining extreme rainfall amounts with frequencies greater than 5 to 10 years. In stormwater design, however, rainfall events with frequencies between 1 and 10 years, as well as those between 10 and 100 years, are routinely needed. For reliable rainfall data for the more frequent events, a frequency analysis must be based upon a partial-duration-series. A *partial-duration-series* analysis uses all measured rainfall amounts above some threshold value, irrespective of the rainfall year. A partial-duration-series data set can include several rainfall events from one year, and possibly no rainfall events from another year. This is the data used in the frequency analysis. Partial-duration-sets are almost always much larger than annual-maximum-duration data sets, making the frequency analysis much more involved. The bottom line of all this discussion about data series type is this—when using Atlas 14 data for stormwater design, it is usually more appropriate to select the partial-duration-series option over the annual-maximum-series option.

Atlas 14 does not provide rainfall intensities directly. However, the total rainfall depths provided in Atlas 14 can easily be transformed into rainfall intensities. The total rainfall depth is simply divided by the storm duration to transform rainfall inches into the average rainfall intensity for the duration.

Example 6.1 Using the Atlas 14 rainfall data provided in Figure 6.6, determine average rainfall intensities for the 10-year storms associated with durations of 5, 15, 30, 45, and 60 minutes.

Solution: The rainfall depths for the five storm durations are tabulated as shown below. Note that the 45-minute rainfall depth is linearly interpolated between the 30 and 60 minute values of Figure 6.6. Intensities are computed by dividing rainfall depth by duration in hours. For example, the 5-minute intensity is

POINT PRECIPITATION FREQUENCY
ESTIMATES
FROM NOAA ATLAS 14

Virginia 38.705 N 78.046 W 600 feet
from "Precipitation-Frequency Atlas of the United States" NOAA Atlas 14, Volume 2, Version 2
G.M. Bonnin, D. Todd, B. Lin, T. Parzybok, M. Yekta, and D. Riley
NOAA, National Weather Service, Silver Spring, Maryland, 2004
Extracted: Wed Mar 2 2005

| Confidence Limits || Seasonality || Location Maps || Other Info. || Grids || Maps || Help || Docs || U.S. Map |

Precipitation Frequency Estimates (inches)

ARI* (years)	5 min	10 min	15 min	30 min	60 min	120 min	3 lu	6 lu	12 lu	24 lu	48 lu	4 day	7 day	10 day	20 day	30 day	45 day	60 day
2	0.42	0.67	0.84	1.15	1.44	1.69	1.82	2.26	2.76	3.17	3.70	4.15	4.80	5.46	7.25	8.82	11.02	13.00
5	0.50	0.80	1.00	1.42	1.81	2.15	2.31	2.83	3.46	4.04	4.71	5.28	6.03	6.78	8.74	10.45	12.83	14.96
10	0.56	0.90	1.13	1.62	2.11	2.52	2.70	3.31	4.05	4.80	5.57	6.24	7.07	7.86	9.93	11.74	14.22	16.43
25	0.65	1.02	1.29	1.90	2.51	3.05	3.27	4.01	4.94	5.95	6.84	7.64	8.59	9.40	11.58	13.50	16.04	18.32
50	0.71	1.12	1.41	2.11	2.84	3.50	3.74	4.60	5.70	6.96	7.94	8.86	9.88	10.67	12.89	14.87	17.40	19.71
100	0.77	1.22	1.53	2.33	3.20	3.97	4.26	5.25	6.55	8.09	9.14	10.18	11.29	12.02	14.24	16.26	18.73	21.02
200	0.84	1.32	1.66	2.56	3.57	4.50	4.82	5.96	7.50	9.35	10.48	11.63	12.82	13.46	15.63	17.67	20.01	22.28
500	0.94	1.46	1.83	2.89	4.12	5.26	5.66	7.02	8.94	11.27	12.47	13.81	15.07	15.53	17.54	19.56	21.68	23.85
1000	1.01	1.57	1.97	3.15	4.57	5.92	6.38	7.93	10.19	12.95	14.17	15.66	16.98	17.24	19.05	21.03	22.91	24.98

| Text version of table | * These precipitation frequency estimates are based on a partial duration series. **ARI** is the Average Recurrence Interval.
Please refer to the documentation for more information. NOTE: Formatting forces estimates near zero to appear as zero.

Figure 6.6 Volume-Duration-Frequency point precipitation data for Virginia 38.705 N 78.046 W as provided through NOAA Atlas 14 (http://www.nws.noaa.gov/ohd/hdsc/).

$$i = \frac{P}{t} = \frac{0.56 \text{ in}}{5 \text{ min}} \times \frac{60 \text{ min}}{\text{hr}} = 6.72 \text{ in/hr}$$

All other intensities are computed in a similar fashion.

Duration (minutes)	5	15	30	45	60
Rainfall depth (in)	0.56	1.13	1.62	1.87	2.11
Rainfall intensity (in/hr)	6.72	4.52	3.24	2.49	2.11

6.4 DESIGN STORMS

A *design storm* is the time distribution of design rainfall, and it is typically generated mathematically based on VDF or IDF data for a specific region or design site. The simplest design storm can be a specific rainfall volume or intensity that is associated with a return period and storm duration. This simple information is read directly from a VDF or IDF chart and requires no further explanation. However, many hydrologic design methods require rainfall volumes or intensities expressed as a *hyetograph.*

In stormwater design, the most common uses of design storms are for estimates of a runoff peak flow or the creation of design runoff hydrographs. The use of design storms to create design runoff hydrographs is based on the simplified assumption that the *n*-year rainfall event causes the *n*-year runoff event, which is not necessarily true. This assumption overlooks the prestorm moisture condition of the site. For the same rainfall event, a prestorm dry site will create less runoff than a wet site. The assumption causes the design to be based on the return period of rainfall instead of the runoff. However, due to the difficulty of developing appropriate runoff-frequency curves for a site, this practice is accepted.

To create a design rainfall hyetograph, it is necessary to select the return period, duration, and time step. Return period and duration will determine the volume of rainfall contained in the distribution. The shape of the design storm will determine the time distribution of the rainfall volume. Shape can be created as needed, since the storm is synthetic. Three general shapes of early peaking, central peaking, and late peaking as shown in Figure 6.7 are usually considered. Runoff simulation studies by Kibler et al. (1982) have shown that the time distribution of rainfall has a significant impact on runoff flood peaks. The central- and late-peaking storms were found to create significantly larger peak flows than the early-peaking storm. This makes sense because the early portion of the central- and late-storms provides lighter rainfall, which has time to wet the earth surface and soak into the ground. When the most intense portion of the rainfall comes, the surface is saturated and the watershed responds similar to a paved surface. Computationally, the central-peaking storm is easier to construct, so most extreme-event modeling methods use a central peaking storm.

6.4.1 NRCS 24-Hour Rainfall Distributions

The most commonly used rainfall distributions in urban stormwater design is the NRCS 24-hour rainfall distributions defined through four types—namely,

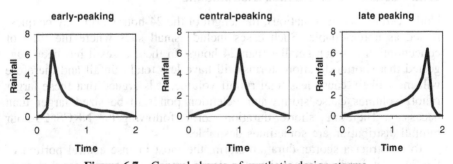

Figure 6.7 General shapes of synthetic design storms.

Type I, Type IA, Type II, and Type III. The distributions were developed from the analysis of U.S. Weather Bureau rainfall data for watersheds having drainage areas of 400 square miles or less, with durations up to 24 hours and return periods between 1 and 100 years. The approximate geographic boundaries for these four distributions are shown in Figure 6.8, while Figure 6.9 shows a graphical plot of each rainfall distribution. The distributions are expressed as dimensionless fractions of total rainfall for the storm. The S-curve shape of these storms reflects the central-peaking time distribution. Notice that the slope of the rainfall curves is steepest in the central portion of the chart. Since these curves are cumulative rainfall, the steep slopes indicate the most intense rate of rainfall during the event. Tabulated values of each of the SCS rainfall distributions are shown in Table 6.3.

To create a NRCS cumulative rainfall distribution, the 24-hour design rainfall depth is used as a multiplier to the dimensionless cumulative rainfall values in Table 6.3. If a rainfall intensity distribution is needed, differences between adjacent cumulative rainfall amounts are computed and plotted against time. An appropriate time step must be chosen before the design storm can be created.

Example 6.2   Create a NRCS 24-hour rainfall (inches) hyetograph for a site located in Pennsylvania, rainfall Region 1, for the 100-year event. Use a time step of 1 hour.

Solution: The hyetograph is best computed using a spreadsheet shown in Table 6.4. Time increments for 1-hour intervals are placed in column A. Using Figure 6.5, the 24-hour rainfall depth for a 100-year event is read as 4.55 inches. Pennsylvania is in the NRCS Type II region. Dimensionless values of P_t/P_{24} for time values from 0 to 24 hours in increments of 1 hour are read from Table 6.3 and placed in column B. Each of these values is multiplied by 4.55 inches to create cumulative precipitation in column C. Differences between successive precipitation amounts will give the hyetograph, and these values are shown in column D. The completed hyetograph is plotted in Figure 6.10.

6.4.2   Scaled NRCS Rainfall Distributions

Under certain design situations, the length of the 24-hour storm may be questioned as unreasonable. Such cases include small sites where the time of concentration is much smaller than 24 hours. In these cases it has been suggested that shorter-duration storms will have less total rainfall and therefore will most likely cause less total runoff volume. It is argued that these larger runoff volumes cause stormwater detention ponds to be sized larger than necessary. Therefore, shorter-duration storms following the NRCS 24-hour rainfall distribution are sometimes desirable.

To construct a shorter-duration storm, the most intense central portion of the 24-hour distribution equal to the desired storm duration is used to con-

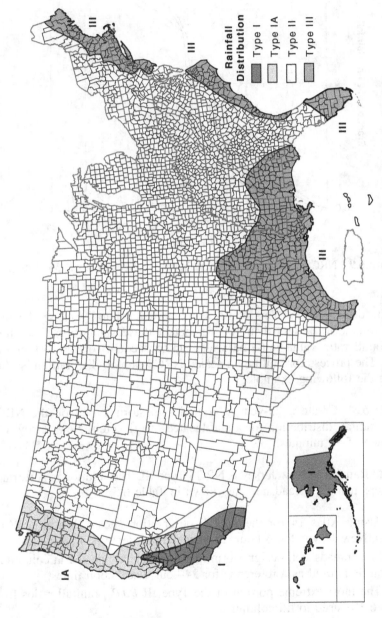

Figure 6.8 Approximate geographic boundaries for NRCS 24-hour rainfall distributions.

Rainfall Distribution

- Type I
- Type IA
- Type II
- Type III

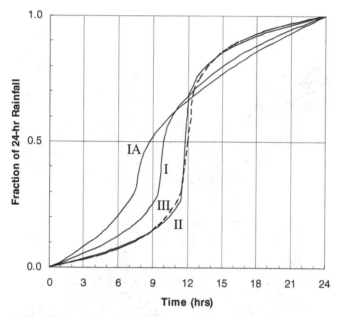

Figure 6.9   NRCS 24-hour rainfall distributions (USDA SCS TR-55, 1986).

struct the design storm. This storm segment will naturally cause the total rainfall volume to be less than 100 percent of the design storm. Therefore, each rainfall ratio value must be scaled up to account for the lost rainfall volume. The process for building a scaled NRCS rainfall distribution is illustrated in the following example.

Example 6.3   Create a 25-year, 6-hour design storm based on the NRCS 24-hour rainfall distribution for a site located in Princeton, New Jersey. Use a time step of 30 minutes.

Solution: Rainfall in New Jersey is NRCS Type III. The solution is performed in six steps using a spreadsheet, as shown in Table 6.5.

Step 1: Using Atlas 14 for the rainfall observation site at Princeton Water Works, New Jersey, the 6-hour, 25-year rainfall depth is 4.28 inches.

Step 2: In a spreadsheet, design storm time intervals are placed in column A. Column B is used as a reference for 24-hour distribution times.

Step 3: The most extreme portion of the Type III P_t/P_{24} rainfall ratios from Table 6.3 is used to fill column C.

Step 4: Rainfall ratio differences are calculated by subtracting successive P_t/P_{24} values of column C and placing them in column D. As an example, cell D4 = C4 − C3. Summation of column D shows that this 6-hour

TABLE 6.3 Tabulated Values Defining Cummulative NRCS 24-hour Rainfall Distributions (McCuen, 2005)

Time (hours)	P_t/P_{24}			
	Type I	Type IA	Type II	Type III
0.0	0.000	0.000	0.0000	0.0000
0.5	0.008	0.010	0.0053	0.0050
1.0	0.017	0.020	0.0108	0.0100
1.5	0.026	0.035	0.0164	0.0150
2.0	0.035	0.050	0.0223	0.0200
2.5	0.045	0.067	0.0284	0.0252
3.0	0.055	0.082	0.0347	0.0308
3.5	0.065	0.098	0.0414	0.0367
4.0	0.076	0.116	0.0483	0.0430
4.5	0.087	0.135	0.0555	0.0497
5.0	0.099	0.156	0.0632	0.0568
5.5	0.112	0.180	0.0712	0.0642
6.0	0.126	0.206	0.0797	0.0720
6.5	0.140	0.237	0.0887	0.0806
7.0	0.156	0.268	0.0984	0.0905
7.5	0.174	0.310	0.1089	0.1016
8.0	0.194	0.425	0.1203	0.1140
8.5	0.219	0.480	0.1328	0.1284
9.0	0.254	0.520	0.1467	0.1458
9.5	0.303	0.550	0.1625	0.1659
10.0	0.515	0.577	0.1808	0.1890
10.5	0.583	0.601	0.2042	0.2165
11.0	0.624	0.624	0.2351	0.2500
11.5	0.655	0.645	0.2833	0.2980
12.0	0.682	0.664	0.6632	0.5000
12.5	0.706	0.683	0.7351	0.7020
13.0	0.728	0.701	0.7724	0.7500
13.5	0.748	0.719	0.7989	0.7835
14.0	0.766	0.736	0.8197	0.8110
14.5	0.783	0.753	0.8380	0.8341
15.0	0.799	0.769	0.8538	0.8542
15.5	0.815	0.785	0.8676	0.8716
16.0	0.830	0.800	0.8801	0.8860
16.5	0.844	0.815	0.8914	0.8984
17.0	0.857	0.830	0.9019	0.9095
17.5	0.870	0.844	0.9115	0.9194
18.0	0.882	0.858	0.9206	0.9280
18.5	0.893	0.871	0.9291	0.9358
19.0	0.905	0.884	0.9371	0.9432
19.5	0.916	0.896	0.9446	0.9503
20.0	0.926	0.908	0.9519	0.9570
20.5	0.936	0.920	0.9588	0.9634
21.0	0.946	0.932	0.9653	0.9694

TABLE 6.3 (*Continued*)

Time	P_t/P_{24}			
(hours)	Type I	Type IA	Type II	Type III
21.5	0.956	0.944	0.9717	0.9752
22.0	0.965	0.956	0.9777	0.9808
22.5	0.974	0.967	0.9836	0.9860
23.0	0.983	0.978	0.9892	0.9909
23.5	0.992	0.989	0.9947	0.9959
24.0	1.000	1.000	1.0000	1.0000

TABLE 6.4 Hyetograph Calculations for Example 6.2

	A	B	C	D
1	Time (hrs)	P_t/P_{24}	P_t (in)	Rainfall (in)
2	0.0	0.0000	0.000	0.000
3	1.0	0.0108	0.049	0.049
4	2.0	0.0223	0.101	0.052
5	3.0	0.0347	0.158	0.056
6	4.0	0.0483	0.220	0.062
7	5.0	0.0632	0.288	0.068
8	6.0	0.0797	0.363	0.075
9	7.0	0.0984	0.448	0.085
10	8.0	0.1203	0.547	0.100
11	9.0	0.1467	0.667	0.120
12	10.0	0.1808	0.823	0.155
13	11.0	0.2351	1.070	0.247
14	12.0	0.6632	3.018	1.948
15	13.0	0.7724	3.514	0.497
16	14.0	0.8197	3.730	0.215
17	15.0	0.8538	3.885	0.155
18	16.0	0.8801	4.004	0.120
19	17.0	0.9019	4.104	0.099
20	18.0	0.9206	4.189	0.085
21	19.0	0.9371	4.264	0.075
22	20.0	0.9519	4.331	0.067
23	21.0	0.9653	4.392	0.061
24	22.0	0.9777	4.449	0.056
25	23.0	0.9892	4.501	0.052
26	24.0	1.0000	4.550	0.049

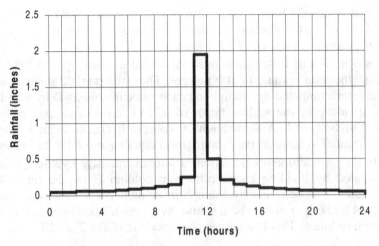

Figure 6.10 NRCS 24-hour hyetograph for Example 6.2.

TABLE 6.5 Calculations for the 6-hour NRCS Type III Design Storm of Example 6.3

	A	B	C	D	E	F
1	Storm Time (hrs)	24-hr Time (hrs)	Type III P_t/P_{24} (in)	P_t/P_{24} Difference (in)	Scaled Rainfall (in)	Rainfall Intensity (in/hr)
2	0.0	9.0	0.1458	0.0000	0.000	0.000
3	0.5	9.5	0.1659	0.0201	0.121	0.243
4	1.0	10.0	0.1890	0.0231	0.140	0.279
5	1.5	10.5	0.2165	0.0275	0.166	0.332
6	2.0	11.0	0.2500	0.0335	0.202	0.405
7	2.5	11.5	0.2980	0.0480	0.290	0.580
8	3.0	12.0	0.5000	0.2020	1.220	2.441
9	3.5	12.5	0.7020	0.2020	1.220	2.441
10	4.0	13.0	0.7500	0.0480	0.290	0.580
11	4.5	13.5	0.7835	0.0335	0.202	0.405
12	5.0	14.0	0.8110	0.0275	0.166	0.332
13	5.5	14.5	0.8341	0.0231	0.140	0.279
14	6.0	15.0	0.8542	0.0201	0.121	0.243
15			Sum:	0.7084	4.280	

portion of the 24-hour rainfall distribution contains 70.84 percent of the total rainfall. This fraction can also be computed by subtracting the first P_t/P_{24} ratio from the last P_t/P_{24} ratio.

Step 5: The 6-hour distribution must be scaled upward by $1/0.7084$ to increase the total volume to 100 percent. Thus, the rainfall amounts in column E are computed by multiplying each value in column D by 4.28 inches and dividing by the scaling factor of 0.7084. As an example, cell E4 = D4 * 4.28/0.7084. A summation on column E checks to make sure the total rainfall volume in the 6-hour storm equals the total 4.28 inches.

Step 6: As an additional calculation, a rainfall intensity hyetograph can be computed by dividing each ordinate in column E by the time step of 0.5 hours. The resulting hyetograph in column F shows a peak intensity of 2.44 inches per hour. The resulting hyetograph is symmetrical about the central ordinate. This is a unique characteristic of the Type III distribution.

It is interesting to note that a separate calculation of the full 24-hour rainfall distribution for the same site and time step of Example 6.3 creates a peak intensity of about 2.51 in/hr. This intensity is essentially the same as the 6-hour peak intensity of 2.44 in/hr. However the total rainfall volume for the 25-year 24-hour storm is 6.22 inches, which is about 45 percent higher than the 6-hour storm volume of 4.28 inches. By observation, then, one would expect both the 6-hour and the 24-hour design storms to create approximately the same peak flow, but the runoff volume should be significantly less with the 6-hour storm as compared to the 24-hour storm.

6.4.3 Design Storms from VDF/IDF Charts

Design storms are necessary for runoff modeling. For many watersheds, runoff modeling is done in parts. In these cases, the watershed is broken into subareas (sub-watersheds) and each subarea is analyzed independent from the whole. After each subarea analysis is complete, the runoff results of each subarea are hydrologically added together to create a composite runoff analysis for the watershed. In order to have compatible runoff results among the subareas, each subarea must experience the same rainfall event. This means that one design storm must be created that is appropriate for all subareas in the watershed. Time of concentration of the entire watershed typically drives the selection of the design storm duration. (See Chapter 7 for discussion on time of concentration.) Additionally, the design storm should include the critical design rainfall intensities for every subarea in the watershed. A central-peaking composite design storm should be constructed such that the maximum rain falling over any central time span equals the design storm depth indicated by the corresponding duration. Example 6.4 shows the alternating-block method for creating a design storm with these characteristics (ASCE, 1992).

Example 6.4 Create a 10-year central-peaking design storm for a site located in Pennsylvania rainfall region 1. Use a storm duration of 60 minutes and a time step of 5 minutes.

Solution: We can find the solution easily in five steps using a spreadsheet as shown in Table 6.6.

Step 1: Fill column A with time values in increments of 5 minutes, starting with 0 minutes and ending with 60 minutes.

Step 2: Using the VDF curve of Figure 6.5, read rainfall amounts for duration equal to the time value in column A and place these amounts in column B.

Step 3: Compute the incremental rainfall amounts between consecutive durations by subtracting successive rainfall values of column B and place the results in Column C.

Step 4: Rearrange the column C values into a central-peaking shape in column D by placing the largest value nearest the center of the storm duration, the next largest above the center, the third largest below, etc. until the rearrangement is completed by alternating the rainfall blocks around the center.

Step 5: Compute the rainfall intensities in column E by dividing each value in column D by the design storm time step, using a time step expressed in hours.

In Example 6.4, Column D represents a rainfall depth design storm and column E is a rainfall intensity design storm (see Figure 6.11). Either design

TABLE 6.6 Design Storm Calculations for Example 6.4

	A	B	C	D	E
1	Time	Rain	Rain Diff	Shifted Rain	Intensity
2	(min)	(in)	(in)	(in)	(in/hr)
3	0	0.00	0.00	0.00	0.00
4	5	0.42	0.42	0.04	0.48
5	10	0.65	0.23	0.05	0.60
6	15	0.81	0.16	0.07	0.84
7	20	0.93	0.12	0.09	1.08
8	25	1.02	0.09	0.16	1.92
9	30	1.10	0.08	0.42	5.04
10	35	1.17	0.07	0.23	2.76
11	40	1.23	0.06	0.12	1.44
12	45	1.28	0.05	0.08	0.96
13	50	1.32	0.04	0.06	0.72
14	55	1.36	0.04	0.04	0.48
15	60	1.39	0.03	0.03	0.36

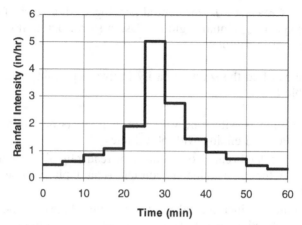

Figure 6.11   Rainfall intensity design storm for Example 6.4.

storm may be needed in runoff modeling, depending on the requirements of the hydrologic method used.

6.4.4   USWB/Yarnell Rainfall Distribution

When accessing precipitation data from ATLAS 14, the data tabulation is such that rainfall amounts are not provided in regular time intervals. Thus, when trying to develop a design storm, linear interpolation is necessary to use the data. Unfortunately, linear interpolation between tabulated rainfall values in ATLAS 14 oftentimes gives results that do not follow typical IDF curve relationships. This is mainly due to data precision and rounding in the displayed data. Therefore, as a substitute, we can use the standard rainfall distribution provided by the U.S. Weather Bureau. These curves are shown in Figure 6.12 and are attributed to David Yarnell (1935) of the USDA, since the equations are based on the data that he compiled on rainfall intensity-frequency data for the continental United States. These curves remove the need for return period as a parameter. The input to the curve requires a 1-hour rainfall depth and a storm duration. The user finds the curve that matches the 1-hour rainfall depth and follows that curve left or right to the desired storm duration. From that point, the user can read the intensity on the ordinate scale. The curves are good for storm durations ranging from 5 minutes to 90 minutes. Equations have been fitted to the curves (Aron et al., 1986) and are valid for storm durations of 5 to 120 minutes. The three equation set is

$$i = \frac{a}{(t + 15)^b} \qquad (6.2)$$

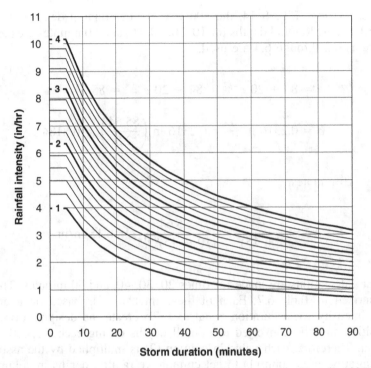

Figure 6.12 Standard USWB rainfall distribution curves (Yarnell, 1935).

$$a = 84 + 20\, e^{-i_{60}} \qquad (6.3)$$

$$b = 0.2316\, \ln \frac{a}{i_{60}} \qquad (6.4)$$

where i = rainfall intensity (in/hr)

$\quad i_{60}$ = 1-hour rainfall depth for the design return period (in)

$\quad t$ = duration (min)

$\quad e$ = the base of natural logarithms (2.718)

$\quad \ln$ = natural logarithm function

$\quad a$ = parameter defined by Equation (6.3)

$\quad b$ = parameter defined by Equation (6.4)

Example 6.5 Create a 100-year central-peaking design storm, in inches, for a site located in central Pennsylvania at latitude 40.72° and longitude −76.55°. Use a storm duration of 60 minutes, a time step of 10 minutes, and the USWB standard equations for the rainfall distribution.

Solution: Using ATLAS 14, the 100-year, 1-hour rainfall depth is found to be 2.50 inches. Rainfall depths for 10, 20, 30, 40, and 50 minutes are required. Equations 6.2 through 6.4 are used.

$$a = 84 + 20 \, e^{-i_{60}} = 84 + 20 \, e^{-2.5} = 85.64$$

$$b = 0.2316 \ln \frac{a}{i_{60}} = 0.2316 \ln \left(\frac{85.64}{2.5} \right) = 0.8184$$

For $t = 10$ minutes,

$$i = \frac{a}{(t + 15)^b} = \frac{85.64}{(10 + 15)^{0.8184}} = 6.15 \text{ in/hr}$$

Similar calculations are made for times 20, 30, 40, and 50 minutes. They are summarized in Table 6.7. Each of these intensities is based on a uniform storm intensity for a duration equal to t. To create the design storm, these intensities must be converted to rainfall depths during each respective time interval. Therefore, each value in column (2) is multiplied by the associated time duration in column (1) to get cumulative rainfall depths in column (3). Note that the 60-minute rainfall depth is 2.5 inches, which is expected. To get rainfall depths associated to each 10-minute time interval, we subtract successive rainfall depths in column (3). Results are shown in column (4). The sum of these increments in rainfall should equal 2.5 inches, which they do. Finally, these incremental rainfall depths are ordered into a central peaking storm, as shown in column (5).

TABLE 6.7   Tabulated Solution to Example 6.5

Time (min) (1)	Rainfall intensity (in/hr) (2)	Cumulative Rainfall (in) (3)	Rainfall Difference (in) (4)	Ordered Rainfall (in) (5)
0	0.000	0.000	0.000	0.000
10	6.145	1.024	1.024	0.158
20	4.666	1.555	0.531	0.250
30	3.799	1.899	0.344	0.531
40	3.223	2.149	0.250	1.024
50	2.811	2.343	0.194	0.344
60	2.501	2.501	0.158	0.194
Total			2.501	2.501

PROBLEMS

6.1 Using NOAA's Hydrologic Design Studies Center Web site, download Atlas 14 rainfall data for Roanoke, Virginia using the observation station ROANOKE VA 44-7275. Summarize the 24-hour rainfall depth data showing the 90 percent confidence limits for rainfall return periods (average reoccurrence intervals) of 2, 5, 10, 25, 50, and 100 years.

6.2 Extract NOAA Atlas 14 rainfall data for latitude 40.995° and longitude −79.574°. Summarize the 24-hour rainfall depth data showing the 90 percent confidence limits for rainfall return periods (average reoccurrence intervals) of 2, 5, 10, 25, 50, and 100 years.

6.3 Using the Atlas 14 rainfall data of problem 6.1, determine the 50-year rainfall intensities for storm durations ranging from 15 to 120 minutes in increments of 15 minutes. Use linear interpolation to determine rainfall amounts where necessary.

6.4 Using the Atlas 14 rainfall data of Problem 6.2, determine the 100-year rainfall intensities for storm durations ranging from 5 to 60 minutes in increments of 5 minutes. Use linear interpolation to determine rainfall amounts where necessary.

6.5 Create a 24-hour NRCS rainfall design storm for the 10-year event in Trenton, New Jersey. Use the NOAA Atlas 14 observation site TRENTON 2 NJ 28-8878 for your data. Use a 1-hour time step.

6.6 Create a 24-hour NRCS rainfall design storm for the 100-yr event in Clarksburg, West Virginia. Use the NOAA Atlas 14 observation site CLARKSBURG 1 WV 46-1677 for your data. Use a 1-hour time step.

6.7 Create a 12-hour central peaking storm for Annapolis, Maryland (latitude 38.9833° and longitude −76.4833°) using the 50-year rainfall event. Use Atlas 14 for your rainfall data and a 1-hour time step.

6.8 Create a 4-hour central peaking storm for Erie, Pennsylvania, using the 25-year rainfall event. Use NOAA Atlas 14 observation site ERIE WSO ARPT PA (36-2682) for your rainfall data and a time step of 0.25 hours. Use linear interpolation as necessary.

6.9 Using NOAA's Hydrologic Design Studies Center Web site, search for the TP-40 publication. Find the 24-hour rainfall maps for the United States. Compare the rainfall amounts presented in this publication to the same rainfall amounts provided in Atlas 14 for the shoreline of the most southerly tip of Lake Michigan. Examine the 2, 5, 10, 25, 50, and 100-year events.

6.10 Using the data of Problem 6.4, create a central-peaking design storm of 60-minute duration.

6.11   Create a 2-hour central-peaking design storm for the NOAA observation site at Columbus, Ohio, COLUMBUS VLY CROSSING OH (33-1783). Use the USWB rainfall distribution equations, a 15-minute time step, and a 25-year rainfall event.

6.12   Create a 2-hour central-peaking design storm for the NOAA observation site at Phoenix, Arizona, PHOENIX CITY AZ (02-6486). Use the USWB rainfall distribution equations, a 15-minute time step, and a 25-year rainfall event. Compare the results to Problem 6.11.

REFERENCES

American Society of Civil Engineers. 1992. *Design and Construction of Urban Stormwater Management Systems,* New York: ASCE.

Aron, G., D. J. Wall, E. L. White, C. N. Dunn, and D. M. Kotz. 1986. *Pennsylvania Department of Transportation Storm Intensity-Duration-Frequency Charts.* Institute for Research on Land and Water Resources. University Park, PA: The Pennsylvania State University.

Chin, D. A. 2000. *Water-Resources Engineering.* Upper Saddle River, NJ: Prentice-Hall.

Kibler, D. F., G. Aron, K. A. Riley, G. Osei-Kwadwo, and E. L. White. 1982. *Recommended Hydrologic Procedures for Computing Urban Runoff for Small Developing Watersheds in Pennsylvania.* Research Report to the Pennsylvania Department of Environmental Resources, Institute for Land and Water Resources. University Park, PA: Pennsylvania State University.

McCuen, R. H. 2005. *Hydrologic Analysis and Design,* 3rd ed., Upper Saddle River, NJ: Pearson Prentice-Hall.

National Weather Service. 1977. *Five to 60-minutes Precipitation Frequency for Eastern and Central United States.* Technical Memorandum NWS Hydro 35. Washington, DC: National Oceanic and Atmospheric Administration.

National Weather Service. 2003. *Precipitation Frequency Atlas for the United States,* ATLAS 14, Volume 1—The Semi-Arid Southwest (2003), National Oceanic and Atmospheric Administration, Silver Spring, MD (http://www.nws.noaa.gov/ohd/hdsc/).

National Weather Service. 2004. *Precipitation Frequency Atlas for the United States,* ATLAS 14, Volume 2—The Ohio River Basin and Surrounding States, National Oceanic and Atmospheric Administration, Silver Spring, MD (http://www.nws.noaa.gov/ohd/hdsc/).

National Weather Service. 1961. *Rainfall Frequency Atlas of the United States,* Technical Paper 40. Washington, DC: U.S. Department of Commerce.

USDA SCS. 1986. *Urban Hydrology for Small Watersheds.* Technical Release 55, U.S. Department of Agriculture. Washington, DC: Engineering Division.

Yarnell, D. L. 1935. *Rainfall Intensity-Frequency Data.* Miscellaneous Publication No. 204. Washington, D.C.: U.S. Dept. of Agriculture, 68 pp.

CHAPTER 7

TRAVEL TIME

7.1 INTRODUCTION

Most hydrologic design methods require the estimation of a parameter that represents the timing of runoff. *Travel time* is the most general term used to define hydraulic and hydrologic timing. In stormwater management, some common timing parameters are channel travel time, pipe travel time, time to inlet, watershed lag time, and watershed time of concentration. All of these parameters can be considered travel times in the most general sense. There are many methods for estimating travel times. Most are based on field studies where actual travel times were measured and used to create an empirical equation. A few others are based on theoretical analysis and then augmented with laboratory or field data. In any case, each method is usually developed for specific situations or conditions.

7.2 TIME OF CONCENTRATION

Time of concentration is probably the most important timing parameter in stormwater design. It characterizes the response time of a watershed to transform rainfall into runoff. There are two fundamental definitions of time of concentration. One is based on hydrograph analysis and the other on flow path analysis.

7.2.1 Hydrograph Analysis

Time of concentration from hydrograph analysis requires measured rainfall and runoff data. If a watershed is monitored for runoff via a stream gage (hydrograph) and rainfall via a continuous recording rain gage (hyetograph), the data can be plotted to compare the timing of runoff to the timing of rainfall. Figure 7.1 shows rainfall and runoff as recorded for a small undeveloped watershed in central Pennsylvania. The storm (upper graph) contains 3.4 inches of rainfall spread over 70 minutes. The event is compound, with rainfall coming in two distinct but very close time blocks. Looking at the stream hydrograph (lower graph), the first block of rain (0 to 30 min) appears to be absorbed by the watershed through abstractions, causing very little runoff. It appears that a very small local peak flow of 150 ft^3/s at 60 minutes is caused by the first block of rain. The second block of rain (45 to 70 min) falls on a watershed that is now saturated, causing this second block of rainfall to be entirely transformed into runoff. This second block of rainfall is essentially *rainfall excess*—that is, rainfall that could not be absorbed by the watershed and therefore transformed to surface runoff. The second block of rainfall creates a peak of about 880 ft^3/s at time 100 minutes. Since there was no runoff measured in the stream prior to the rainfall event, the stream hydrograph is essentially *direct runoff*—that is, entirely a direct response to the rainfall event without any flow coming from pre-storm flow in the stream. Comparing rainfall and runoff times, it appears that the peak flow (watershed outflow) lags the peak rainfall excess (watershed inflow) by about 40 minutes. Therefore, once the initial watershed abstractions are satisfied, it takes this watershed about 40 minutes to transform rainfall into runoff at the watershed outlet. This time is appropriately called watershed *lag time*.

From this type of analysis, *time of concentration* is defined as the time from the end of rainfall excess to the point of inflection on the receding limb of the direct runoff hydrograph. Schematically, this is shown in Figure 7.2. This definition is based on the theoretical assumption that the end of rainfall (watershed inflow returns to zero) will cause a rate of change of runoff with respect to time to move from positive to negative. In terms of calculus, rate of change with respect to time is the second derivative of the hydrograph. Whether we understand this mathematical definition or not, it is still intuitive that time of concentration reflects the general response time of a watershed to transform rainfall into runoff. This definition, although interesting, is not practical in stormwater management analysis because measured rainfall and runoff rarely exist for the design site. However, exposure to this definition helps in understanding the basic concept of time of concentration.

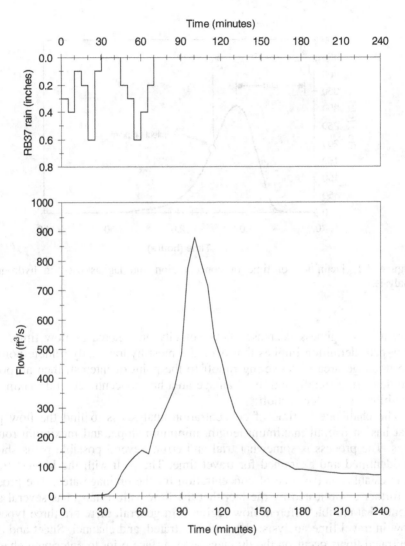

Figure 7.1   Rainfall and runoff for July 26, 1986 event for WE38 experimental watershed in central Pennsylvania.

7.2.2 Flow Path Analysis

In flow-path analysis, *time of concentration* is defined as the time required for runoff to travel from the most hydraulically remote point in the drainage area to the design point of interest. It is important to recognize that this path is not necessarily the most remote point based on distance. The term *most hydraulically remote* takes into account path distance, slope, and surface roughness. Increased slope increases flow velocity and reduces flow time.

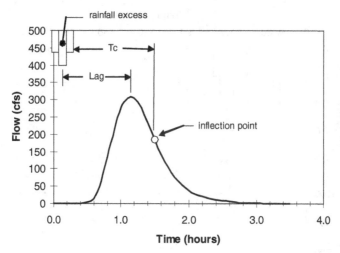

Figure 7.2 Definition of time of concentration and lag as used in hydrograph analysis.

Increased roughness decreases flow velocity and increases flow time. This flow-path definition implies that once the most hydraulically remote point in the drainage area is delivering runoff to the point of interest, then all points are delivering runoff, and the drainage area has concentrated and maximized its ability to produce runoff.

The challenge in time of concentration analysis is to find the flow path that has an overall maximum length, minimum slope, and maximum roughness. The process is somewhat trial and error. Several possible paths should be identified and examined for travel time. The path with the longest travel time establishes the time of concentration for the drainage area. The process is further complicated by the fact that the flow path usually has several segments that exhibit different flow regimes. In general, there are three types of flow in travel time analysis: sheet, concentrated, and channel. Sheet and concentrated flows occur on the drainage area surface prior to entering a channel such as a storm sewer, culvert, man-made channel, or natural channel. Sheet flow and concentrated flow are often called overland flows because they occur on the land surface as opposed to in a channel or stream. Figure 7.3 illustrates a watershed with varying flow regimes throughout the drainage area. Travel time calculation methods are commonly developed for specific flow types.

7.3 SHEET FLOW

Overland sheet flow is best described as very shallow where flow depths are on the same order of magnitude as the surface resistance. The flow is char-

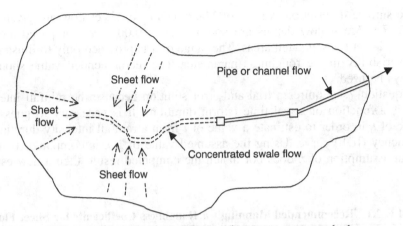

Figure 7.3 Variation of flow regime across a watershed.

acterized as generally shallow uniform depth over a uniform slope or plane surface. For instance, flow depths between zero and 0.02 feet or so may characterize sheet flow over a thick grassy area. The assumption is that the grass height is at least 0.1 feet or more. In reality, sheet flow "over" grass is better described as sheet flow "through" grass. The surface flow would slowly creep and meander around and through the surface cover. On average paved surfaces, the mean flow depth should be around 0.002 feet. Mean flow depths greater than this amount will most likely result in runoff concentrating at a larger depth in a pavement depression, curb gutter, or pavement swale. There are several sheet-flow methods, but only two will be presented here.

Morgali and Linsley (1965) developed a computer simulation of sheet flow and created a travel time equation for paved surfaces. The equation is based on Manning's equation and a kinematic wave assumption that the hydraulic radius of the flow path can be approximated by the product of rainfall intensity and travel time. The equation can be expressed as

$$t_t = \frac{0.94}{i^{0.4}} \left(\frac{nL}{S^{0.5}} \right)^{0.6} \tag{7.1}$$

where t_t = travel time in the flow path (min)
    L = length of overland flow path (ft)
    n = Manning roughness coefficient for sheet flow
    i = critical rainfall intensity of duration t_t (in/hr)
    S = average overland slope (ft/ft)

The roughness parameter is Manning's n for very shallow flow and must not be confused with Manning's n for open channel flow. The values are typically much larger for sheet flow than for open channel flow with the same surface description. Values of Manning's n for sheet flow are given in Table 7.1. Mean flow depths are approximately 0.002 feet for paved areas and 0.02 feet for vegetated areas. The range of n is provided only to illustrate the variability in the roughness parameter. The recommended value should always be used.

Equation 7.1 requires a trial-and-error solution because the rainfall intensity is a function of travel time (storm duration). It is necessary to guess a value of t_t in order to estimate a value of i from a rainfall intensity-duration-frequency (IDF) curve. Using the assumed value of i, t_t is computed. If the initial assumption of t_t does not match the computed result, then a new esti-

TABLE 7.1 Recommended Manning's n Roughness Coefficients for Sheet Flow

Cover or treatment	Recommended value[1]	Range[2]	Source[3]
Concrete or asphalt	0.011	0.01–0.013	b
Smooth surfaces[4]			
Bare soil	0.011	—	e
Gravel	0.011	—	e
Bare sand	0.01	0.010–0.016	b
Graveled surface	0.02	0.012–0.030	b
Bare clay-loam (eroded)	0.02	0.012–0.033	b
Fallow—no residue	0.05	0.006–0.16	c
Cultivated soils			
Residue cover $\leq$ 20%	0.06	—	e
Residue cover $>$ 20%	0.17	—	e
Range			
Clipped	0.10	0.02–0.24	d
Natural	0.13	0.01–0.32	c
Grass			
Short prairie	0.15	0.10–0.25	b
Dense[5]	0.24	0.17–0.30	a
Bermuda	0.41	0.30–0.48	a
Bluegrass sod	0.45	0.39–0.63	c
Woods[6]			
Light underbrush	0.40	—	d
Dense underbrush	0.80	—	d

[1]Range of mean flow depth is 0.002 feet for paved areas to 0.02 feet for vegetated areas.
[2]Range is shown only to illustrate the observed or expected variability in the roughness. The recommended value should always be used.
[3]Sources: (a) Palmer (1946), (b) Woolhiser (1975), (c) Engman (1986), (d) Welle and Woodward (1986), (e) USDA SCS (1986).
[4]These values are implied by the description provided in SCS TR-55 (1986) Table 3-1. Smooth surface is interpreted as a surface similar to a dirt or gravel road that has been compacted by vehicular traffic.
[5]Grass varieties include weeping lovegrass, bluegrass, buffalo grass, blue gamma grass, and native grass mixtures.
[6]When selecting n, consider cover to a height of about 0.1 feet. This is the only part of plant cover that will obstruct flow.

mate of i is taken from the IDF chart using the computed value of t_t. This process is repeated until a consistent solution t_t is obtained.

Example 7.1 A plane asphalt surface with a Manning's n value of 0.015 is 300 feet long, has a slope of 0.0025 ft/ft, and is located in Pennsylvania rainfall region 1. For the 10-year event, use the Morgali Equation 7.1 to determine the sheet flow travel time for this plane surface.

Solution: Since the drainage area is very small, we will assume a travel time (storm duration) of 5 minutes. From Figure 6.5, the IDF curves for Pennsylvania rainfall region 1 gives a rainfall intensity of 5.0 in/hr. The initial estimate of the travel time is

$$t_t = \frac{0.94}{(5.0)^{0.4}} \left(\frac{(0.015)(300)}{(0.0025)^{0.5}} \right)^{0.6} = 7.35 \text{ min}$$

This travel time is greater than the initial estimate, so a new rainfall intensity for a storm duration of 7.4 minutes is used for the second iteration. From Figure 6.5, i is found to be 4.4 in/hr. The new travel time is now

$$t_t = \frac{0.94}{(4.4)^{0.4}} \left(\frac{(0.015)(300)}{(0.0025)^{0.5}} \right)^{0.6} = 7.73 \text{ min}$$

With a new duration of 7.7 minutes, a new i is found to be 4.3 in/hr. One more iteration gives

$$t_t = \frac{0.94}{(4.3)^{0.4}} \left(\frac{(0.015)(300)}{(0.0025)^{0.5}} \right)^{0.6} = 7.80 \text{ min}$$

With a new duration of 7.8 minutes, the new i is found to be 4.3 in/hr, which is unchanged. Therefore, the solution converges on $t_t = 7.8$ minutes.

Welle and Woodward (1986) developed the *NRCS sheet-flow equation* specifically to avoid the iterative solution of Equation 7.1. In the development, they assumed a power-model relationship between rainfall intensity and rainfall duration to eliminate the need for the IDF curves in the solution. The rainfall intensity is replaced with P_2, a 2-year, 24-hour rainfall depth giving an alternative kinematic solution to Manning's equation as

$$t_t = \frac{0.007 \, L^{0.8} \, n^{0.8}}{P_2^{0.5} \, S^{0.4}} \quad \text{(hrs)} \tag{7.2}$$

where t_t is in hours and n, L, and S are as previously defined. This equation is the relation as presented in Chapter 3 of SCS TR-55, 1986. It is also used in the WinTR-55 computer program (USDA NRCS, 2002). The equation can be rewritten in a more convenient form as

$$t_t = \frac{0.42}{P_2^{0.5}} \left(\frac{nL}{S^{0.5}} \right)^{0.8} \text{ (min)} \tag{7.3}$$

where t_t is in minutes and n, L, and S are arranged into one compound term.

Sheet-flow length in Equation 7.2 and 7.3 was given a maximum limit of 300 feet (100 m) in the original SCS publication. However, in nature, sheet flow of 300 feet is very unlikely because the surface would have to be very planer and uniform. Welle and Woodward (1986) commented that the most likely maximum length for sheet flow is about 100 feet. Beyond 100 feet, sheet flow almost always transitions into concentrated flow. In practice, the best way to determine a reasonable value for this parameter is to visit the upper reaches of the watershed and estimate the average sheet flow length at the beginning of the flow path by simple observation. Merkel (2001) concluded that the practical limit of 100 feet for SCS sheet-flow length is reasonable until additional research is performed to show otherwise. The problem is rooted in the complexity of defining the transition point where sheet flow becomes shallow concentrated flow. Variables that make this difficult include soil type, vegetation, slope, and rainfall intensity. As a point of reference, McCuen and Spiess (1995) performed an empirical study that suggests the application of Equation 7.1 is valid if the term $nL/S^{1/2}$ is less than or equal to 100. A similar relation may exist for the SCS sheet-flow equation. With all this said, it is reasonable to suggest that for engineering practice, flow lengths greater than 100 feet in Equation 7.3 appear to be unusual, and special documentation would be necessary to justify such a length.

Example 7.2 The plane asphalt surface of Example 7.1 is an unusual case for sheet flow where the flow path is greater than 100 ft. Verify that Equation 7.1 is valid based on the McCuen–Spiess criteria. Use the NRCS sheet-flow equation to determine the sheet flow travel time for this plane surface surface and compare the difference.

Solution: The McCuen–Spiess criteria states that $nL/S^{1/2}$ must be less than 100 for Equation 7.1 to be valid.

$$\frac{nL}{S^{1/2}} = \frac{(0.015)(300)}{0.0025^{0.5}} = 90$$

Therefore, Equation 7.1 is valid. Solution of Equation 7.3 requires the 2-year 24-hour rainfall depth for PA region 1 (Figure 6.5), which is 2.3 inches.

$$t_t = \frac{0.42}{(2.3)^{0.5}} \left(\frac{(0.015)(300)}{(0.0025)^{0.5}} \right)^{0.8} = 10.1 \text{ min}$$

Equation 7.1 (Morgali) estimated t_t to be 7.8 minutes. If we assume Equation 7.1 to be more accurate, the percent difference is $(10.1 - 7.8)/7.8 \times 100 = 29$ percent. Therefore, for this example, Equation 7.3 gives a larger travel time as compared to Equation 7.1 by about 30 percent.

In the preceding example, the NRCS sheet-flow method is most likely in error, since the length limitation has been violated. A brief investigation of the effect of L on the two equations for this particular example is shown in Figure 7.4. The Welle/NRCS solution is within 13 percent of the Morgali solution through the range of 10 to 100 feet, but continues to diverge as L increases. This supports the notion that the NRCS sheet-flow equation works better when values of L are below 100 feet.

7.4 CONCENTRATED FLOW

At some point in the upper reaches of the watershed, sheet flow will transition to concentrated flow. This is where sheet flow gathers into well-defined gullies or swales to produce shallow depth overland flow. The runoff develops momentum due to increased flow depths that rise significantly above the surface resistance height. In the case of grass surfaces, flow is truly over the grass even if flow depth is 0.4 feet and grass height is 0.5 feet. The flow will lay the grass over on its side. Under dry conditions in the field, the transition point between sheet flow and concentrated flow can be estimated by identifying the location where a continuous surface depression begins, such that it

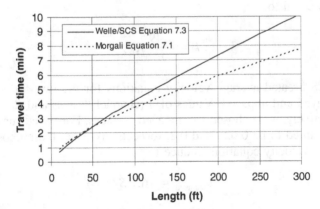

Figure 7.4 Comparison of Equations 7.1 and 7.3 for varying sheet flow lengths in Example 7.2.

will collect sheet flow from radial directions above the depression. The surface depression will direct the runoff downstream in a concentrated fashion.

The *average velocity method* is a common method used to compute concentrated flow. It is based on the constant velocity relationship of Newtonian mechanics, which states that time of travel is equal to distance traveled, divided by velocity. In hydrologic terms, travel time in a flow path is equal to

$$t_t = \frac{L}{60v} \tag{7.4}$$

where t_t = travel time in the flow path (min)
L = length of overland flow (ft)
v = average flow velocity (ft/s)

This equation applies to any path that has a relatively constant geometry, surface roughness, and slope. These conditions will provide a reasonably constant flow velocity. If the flow path has significantly different geometries, surface roughness, or slope, then the path should be broken into segments, with each segment analyzed separately.

The best-known average velocity method is probably that adopted by the USDA/SCS (1986) in TR-55. Average velocities for overland flow are based on a simplification of Manning's equation for open channel flow. A basic assumption is that the flow depth is small compared to the flow width, making the hydraulic radius equal to flow depth. Values were assumed for hydraulic radius and surface roughness, creating the simple relation between velocity and surface slope as

$$v = kS^{0.5} \tag{7.5}$$

where k is equal to

$$k = \frac{1.49}{n} R_h^{0.67} \tag{7.6}$$

The SCS created average velocity equations for the two surface descriptions of paved and unpaved. Values of n (channel flow n) and R_h of 0.05 and 0.4, respectively, were chosen for unpaved surfaces. For paved surfaces n and R_h was assumed to be 0.025 and 0.2, respectively. With these chosen values, the average velocity equations reduce to

$$v_{unpaved} = 16.1 \, S^{0.5} \tag{7.7}$$

$$v_{paved} = 20.3 \, S^{0.5} \tag{7.8}$$

These equations are plotted on logarithm scales to create the familiar chart from Chapter 3 of TR-55, 1986, which is shown in Figure 7.5. The method

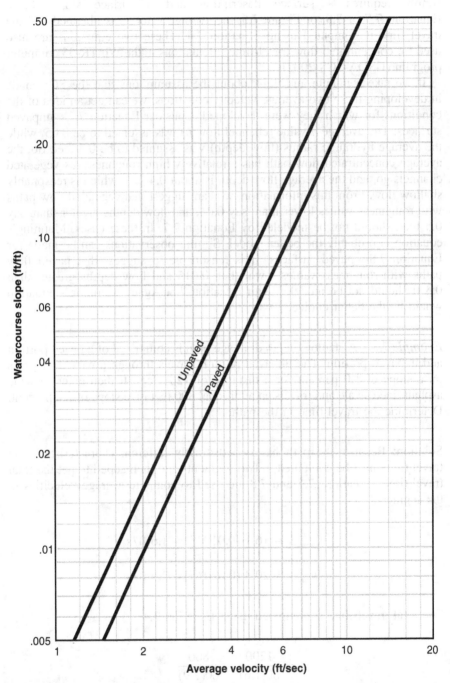

Figure 7.5 Average velocities for concentrated swale flow as provided in SCS TR-55 (1986).

simply requires a surface description and a surface slope. From Equations 7.7 or 7.8, or Figure 7.5, the average velocity is obtained and the travel time is computed using Equation 7.4. These two equations are also used for concentrated-flow travel-time calculations in the WinTR-55 computer program (USDA-SCS 2002).

If we take a minute and think about the assumptions that the SCS made in developing these two average velocity equations, we can get an idea of the conditions for which they were developed. Consider Equation 7.7—unpaved surfaces. The average n value (channel flow n) was assumed to be 0.05, while the average hydraulic radius (flow depth) was assumed to be 0.4 feet. So, the average concentrated flow path has a relatively high roughness, as vegetated channels go, and the average flow depth is about 0.4 feet, which is reasonably shallow flow. From this information, we can suggest that vegetated flow paths with roughness values lower than, say 0.04, and flow depths greater than, say 0.5 feet, should not be modeled by Equation 7.7. In these cases, Manning's equation is probably the better model. Similar observations can be made for Equation 7.8—paved surfaces. It is reasonable to suggest that paved flow paths with roughness values lower than 0.015 and flow depths greater than 0.3 ft should not be modeled with Equation 7.8. Again, Manning's equation would be the better choice.

Example 7.3   A shallow-depth drainage path is comprised of a paved portion and unpaved portion. The unpaved portion travels through a park over grass on a slope of 1.0 percent for a distance of 1200 feet. It then enters a wide asphalt lined swale and travels an additional 800 feet on a slope of 2.0 percent. Determine the travel time in the path.

Solution: Because the path has two distinctly different characteristics, the travel time must be computed in two segments and then added to get the total travel time. Equations 7.7 and 7.8 are used to compute average velocities in the segments.

$$v_{\text{unpaved}} = 16.1\,(0.010)^{0.5} = 1.6\ \text{ft/s}$$

$$v_{\text{paved}} = 20.3\,(0.020)^{0.5} = 2.9\ \text{ft/s}$$

The total travel time is computed using Equation 7.4.

$$t_t = \frac{1200}{60(1.6)} + \frac{800}{60(2.9)}$$

$$t_t = 12.5 + 4.6 = 17.1\ \text{min}$$

7.5 MIXED SHEET AND CONCENTRATED FLOW

There are several travel-time methods that do not necessarily model overland flow as either sheet or concentrated, but simply overland flow. These methods typically involve a single equation that was developed from data representing flow paths, beginning with sheet flow and transitioning to concentrated flow.

The *Federal Aviation Administration* (1970) presented an overland flow equation for travel time that was developed from airfield drainage data assembled by the U.S. Army Corps of Engineers. Travel time is computed by the relation

$$t_t = \frac{1.8(1.1 - C)L^{0.5}}{S^{0.333}} \tag{7.9}$$

where t_t = travel time in the flow path (min)
C = Rational method runoff coefficient
L = length of flow path (ft)
S = average overland slope in percent

The method has been popular in urban runoff calculations because of the inclusion of the Rational C runoff coefficient in the equation. Values of C as proposed by the FAA (1970) are in Table 7.2. Note that some of the values are limited to slopes for 1 to 2 percent. The ASCE Manual of Engineering Practice No. 77 (1992) offers additional values of C, as shown in Table 7.3. A C value in the middle of the range provided in Tables 7.2 and 7.3, should be chosen when using Equation 7.9.

Kirpich (1940) proposed an overland flow equation for mixed sheet and concentrated flow as

TABLE 7.2 Values of the Rational C Factor for the FAA Travel Time Equation (FAA, 1970)

Type of Surface	C
Watertight roof surfaces	0.75–0.95
Asphalt runway pavements	0.80–0.95
Concrete runway pavements	0.70–0.90
Gravel or macadam surfaces	0.35–0.70
Impervious soils (heavy)[1]	0.40–0.65
Impervious soils with turf[1]	0.30–0.55
Slightly pervious soils[1]	0.15–0.40
Slightly pervious soils with turf[1]	0.10–0.30
Moderately pervious soils[1]	0.05–0.20
Moderately pervious soils with turf[1]	0.00–0.10

[1] For slopes from 1 to 2 percent.

TABLE 7.3   Typical Rational Runoff Coefficients by Land Use for Return Periods of 2 to 10 Years (ASCE 1992)

Description of Area	C
Business	
Downtown	0.70–0.95
Neighborhood	0.50–0.70
Residential	
Single family	0.30–0.50
Multiunits, detached	0.40–0.60
Multiunits, attached	0.60–0.75
Residential (suburban)	0.25–0.40
Apartment	0.50–0.70
Industrial	
Light	0.50–0.80
Heavy	0.60–0.90
Parks, cemeteries	0.10–0.25
Playgrounds	0.20–0.35
Railroad yards	0.20–0.35
Unimproved	0.10–0.30

$$t_t = 0.0078 \, K \left(\frac{L^2}{S}\right)^{0.385} \tag{7.10}$$

where t_t = travel time in the flow path (min)
K = surface roughness adjustment factor
L = length of flow path from headwater to outlet (ft)
S = average slope of the flow path (ft/ft)

The definition of L clearly implies that this is a mixed-flow method. The equation was developed from data collected for the SCS by Ramser (1927) for seven rural/agricultural drainage areas in Tennessee, ranging in size from 1.25 to 112 acres, with well-defined divides and adequate channels. Average surface slopes were between 3 and 10 percent. The surface roughness adjustment factor is recommended as follows:

K = 1.0 for overland flow on bare soil or flow in roadside ditches
K = 0.4 for overland flow on concrete and asphalt surfaces
K = 0.2 for flow in concrete channels

The *Kerby–Hathaway* equation was developed by Kerby (1959) using drainage design charts developed by Hathaway (1945) for military airfields. The equation is

$$t_t = 0.83 \left(\frac{nL}{S^{0.5}}\right)^{0.47} \tag{7.11}$$

where t_t = travel time in the flow path (min)

n = Manning's roughness coefficient

L = length of overland flow path (ft)

S = average overland slope (ft/ft)

The equation is based on data for watersheds less than 10 acres in size, where sheet flow dominates the flow path. Watershed slopes are 1 percent or less, and Manning's roughness was 0.8 and less. Table 7.4 shows n values recommended by Kerby for several surface types. The overland flow length is further defined as the straight-line distance from the most distant point in the watershed to the outlet, parallel to the slope, until a well-defined channel is reached. Notice that the equation has the familiar compound term of $nL/S^{0.5}$, which is also present in the Morgali and SCS sheet-flow equations. Since Hathaway's data were for watersheds with flow paths containing both sheet flow and concentrated swale flow, the presence of the $nL/S^{0.5}$ term is reasonable.

The USDA-SCS (1975) offered the *SCS average velocity method* that is applicable to some sheet-flow paths, some concentrated-flow paths, and some paths that are a combination of both flow types. The method is based on the same assumptions as the average velocity method described earlier in this chapter. For six surface descriptions, assumed values of n and R_h were used to establish values of k to create average velocity equations according to the form of Equation 7.5. Table 7.5 summarizes estimated k values for these six curves. The resulting relations were plotted on logarithmic scales as straight

TABLE 7.4   Recommended Values of n for the Kerby–Hathaway Equation (Kerby 1959)

Type of Surface	n
Smooth, impervious surface	0.02
Smooth, bare, packed soil	0.10
Moderately rough, bare surfaces	0.20
Cultivated row crops	0.20
Pasture	0.40
Grass	
Poor	0.20
Average	0.40
Dense	0.80
Timberland	
Deciduous	0.60
Deciduous with deep forest litter	0.80
Conifer	0.80

TABLE 7.5   Values of k for Average Velocity Curves of Figure 7.6

Description	k
Paved area (sheet flow) and shallow gutter flow	20.3
Grassed waterway	16.1
Nearly bare ground	10*
Short grass, pasture, and lawns	7.0*
Fallow or minimum tillage cultivation	4.6*
Forest with heavy ground litter and meadow	2.5*

*Values are estimated by reading values of velocity from Figure 7.6, for slope equal to 1 percent, and solving Equation 7.4 for k.

lines, as shown in Figure 7.6. It is worth noting that the last two curves in Figure 7.6 are mathematically identical to the two curves of Figure 7.5. The two curves were renamed from *grassed waterway* and *paved area* to *unpaved surface* and *paved surface,* respectfully. In 1986, the SCS replaced the first four curves of Figure 7.6 with the SCS sheet-flow model of Equation 7.2. Thus, one may conclude that the first four curves of Figure 7.6 are mainly for sheet flow, and the last two curves are mainly for concentrated flow. This is true to some extent, but in reality all six curves are a very gray mixture of sheet flow and concentrated flow curves and should be used with care and critical judgment. As a matter of interest, McCuen (2005) reports additional values of n and R_h for several other upland surface descriptions, as shown in Table 7.6. These k values were created by selecting reasonable values of n and R_h for different land covers. The values of k in Table 7.6 should be used only if the values of n and R_h are reasonable for the flow path. Whether using Figures 7.5 or 7.6 or Table 7.6, this average velocity method is prone to significant errors because of its approximate nature. Yet, studies by Kibler (1982) have shown that this method gives reasonable results if applied appropriately and in a segmental fashion.

Example 7.4   A flow path in a residential subdivision begins at a watershed divide and ends 2500 feet later at the edge of a small stream. The path surface is best described as a turf or short grass surface with slightly pervious soils on a slope of 0.0175 ft/ft. Determine the travel time in the path using the (a) FAA equation, (b) Kirpich equation, (c) Kerby–Hathaway equation, and (d) the average velocity method of Figure 7.6.

Solution: For the FAA method a C value of 0.20 is chosen from Table 7.2 using the surface description of slightly pervious soils with turf.

$$t_t = \frac{1.8(1.1 - C)L^{0.5}}{S^{0.333}} = \frac{1.8(1.1 - 0.2)(2500)^{0.5}}{(1.75)^{0.333}} = 67.2 \text{ min}$$

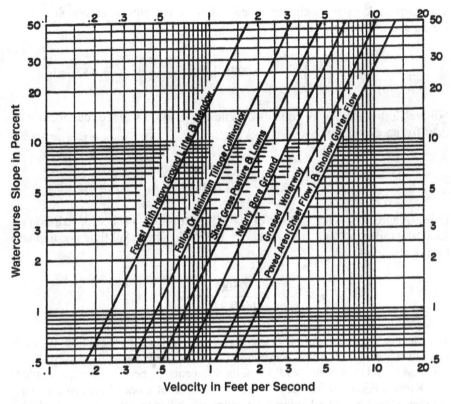

Figure 7.6 Average velocities for overland flow (sheet and swale) as provided in SCS TR-55 (1975).

TABLE 7.6 Values of k for the Average Velocity Method (McCuen, 2005)

Landuse/Flow Regime	n	R_{h}	k
Forest			
No underbrush	0.20	0.09	1.5
Light underbrush	0.40	0.15	1.0
Dense underbrush	0.80	0.21	0.7
Grass			
Short	0.15	0.08	1.8
Dense	0.24	0.10	1.3
Bermuda	0.41	0.14	1.0
Short grass pasture	0.08	0.04	2.2
Rangeland	0.13	0.04	1.3
Alluvial fans	0.017	0.04	10.3
Paved area (sheet flow)	0.012	0.02	9.1
Paved gutter	0.012	0.2	42.4

The Kirpich K value is chosen to be 1.0 since the path does not fit any of the adjustment descriptions.

$$t_t = 0.0078 \, K \left(\frac{L^2}{S}\right)^{0.385} = 0.0078(1.0) \left(\frac{2500^2}{0.0175}\right)^{0.385} = 15.3 \text{ min}$$

For the Kerby–Hathaway equation, Table 7.4 shows a surface roughness n of 0.40 for an average grass.

$$t_t = 0.83 \left(\frac{nL}{S^{0.5}}\right)^{0.47} = 0.83 \left(\frac{(0.40)(2500)}{0.0175^{0.5}}\right)^{0.47} = 55.2 \text{ min}$$

Using Figure 7.6, with a slope of 0.0175 ft/ft and a surface description of short grass, pasture, and lawn, read $v = 0.95$ ft/s. The travel time is computed by Equation 7.4.

$$t_t = \frac{L}{60v} = \frac{2500}{60(0.94)} = 44.0 \text{ min}$$

The results in this example vary significantly. Closer inspection of each method is warranted. The C value for the FAA equation was limited to slopes between 1 and 2 percent, so this method appears to be a reasonable choice. The Kirpich equation was developed for surfaces of slopes between 3 and 10 percent, plus a K value having a description similar to grass is not available, so it is not a good choice for this path. The Kerby–Hathaway equation was developed for slopes of 1 percent or less, so the equation is on the borderline of being a reasonable choice, but it is probably acceptable. The SCS average velocity method (Figure 7.6) is applicable but limited to the surface descriptions available. Without further information about the path, it is possible that the curve representing *forest with heavy ground litter and meadow* is equally applicable as *short grass pasture and lawn*. A travel time determined from a curve midway between these two (*fallow or minimum tillage cultivation*) results in a $t_t = 66.3$ minutes. This may be a more reasonable estimate of the path travel time. With this information it is reasonable to conclude that the travel time for this path is approximately 60 minutes.

7.6 CHANNEL OR PIPE FLOW

At some point, overland flow will enter a regular, well-defined channel or pipe. The travel time for flow in an open channel or pipe can be estimated using Manning's equation to compute average velocity, typically at the bank-full or pipe-full condition. Manning's general equation for U.S. standard units is Equation 4.5, repeated here for convenience.

$$v = \frac{1.49}{n} R_h^{2/3} S^{1/2}$$ (4.5)

where n is Manning's roughness for channel flow, R_h is the hydraulic radius of the channel in feet, and S is channel slope in ft/ft, as explained in Chapter 4. The flow is assumed to be uniform. With the computed velocity, the length of the conduit or channel is used to determine flow travel times according to Equation 7.4. The computation is essentially the same as done in the average velocity method, except actual channel roughness and geometry (n and R_h) are included in the calculation, giving improved results. Values of n for open channel flow are provided in Table 4.3 and are much different than values of n for sheet flow as shown in Table 7.1. Care must always be taken to make sure that the appropriate n value (sheet versus open channel) is being used in the equation.

The beginning of open channel flow in the watershed is typically defined at a point where a regular, well-defined channel exists on the surface. At this point, flow is no longer considered *over-the-land* but *in-the-channel,* thus more clearly defining the original intent of the term *overland flow.* The point where concentrated flow ends and channel flow begins can be defined by the location of the headwaters of a natural channel with perennial flow, or a natural channel well defined in size and shape but dry. Some people like to use the "blue-line" representation of streams on a USGS quadrangle map to define the beginning of channel flow, but it is better to locate the beginning of a channel by field inspection. There is no substitute for "walking the watershed." In the urban setting, a storm sewer inlet or the presence of a continuous stretch of storm sewer pipe will define the beginning of pipe or culvert flow.

The hydraulic radius of a natural channel section is typically estimated by approximating the channel section as rectangular or trapezoidal, and making the calculation from the associated channel area and wetted perimeter. Full channel flow is usually assumed. The average section geometry along the entire length of the open channel path must be considered. If the channel section geometry varies significantly for large sections of the path, then it may be prudent to break the channel into segments, calculating separate flow velocities for each section.

Example 7.5 A natural stream channel can be approximated by a rectangular section that is, on the average, 7 feet wide and 1.5 feet deep. The stream has a slope of 0.0085 ft/ft and a roughness coefficient of 0.035. Flow is assumed to be uniform. Determine the flow travel time for a path of one mile.

Solution: The hydraulic radius is the flow area divided by the wetted perimeter.

$$A = w \times d = 7.0 \times 1.5 = 10.5 \text{ ft}^2$$

$$P = w + 2d = 7.0 + 2(1.5) = 10.0 \text{ ft}$$

$$R_h = \frac{10.5}{10} = 1.05 \text{ ft}$$

The average velocity is computed using Manning's equation.

$$v = \frac{1.49}{n} R_h^{0.67} S^{0.5} = \frac{1.486}{0.035} 1.05^{0.67} \ 0.0085^{0.5} = 4.04 \text{ ft/s}$$

The travel time is

$$t_t = \frac{L}{60 \, v} = \frac{5280}{60(4.04)} = 21.8 \text{ min}$$

7.7   SEGMENTAL FLOW ANALYSIS

Watersheds typically vary significantly from top to bottom with regard to surface cover and surface slope. In these situations, the flow regime of the surface runoff will vary significantly, and thus a single travel-time calculation for the entire path will most likely give less reliable results. The reliability of any travel-time method depends on good estimates of surface roughness, slope, length, and flow type. For this reason, all travel-time calculations should follow a segmental analysis.

Segmental flow analysis breaks the flow path into segments, where each segment has distinctly different physical characteristics and flow regimes. Separate travel time calculations are performed on each segment, using the sum of the travel times to define the time of concentration.

$$t_c = \sum_{i=1}^{n} t_i \tag{7.12}$$

where t_c = time of concentration
  t_i = travel time of segment i
  n = number of segments in the path

In the segmental approach, the flow path used to determine the time of concentration may include several segments that are individually described as sheet flow, concentrated (swale or ditch) flow, mixed sheet and concentrated flow, or channel or pipe flow. A constant concern for the urban hydrologist in travel-time calculations is method selection. Which method is best suited for the condition of the path in question? The answer is to look at the assumptions and/or source data used in the method development and use the method that best models the conditions of the path. For convenience, Table 7.7 is provided as a quick reference summary of all of the travel-time methods discussed in this chapter.

Example 7.6 Three paths are candidates for the hydraulically longest flow path in a 62-acre watershed. Table 7.8 provides descriptive information on each segment of each path. Figure 7.7 shows a sketch of the drainage area. Use the SCS average velocity method (Figure 7.6) and Manning's equation in a segmental fashion to compute the time of concentration for the watershed.

Solution: Each path must be analyzed for travel time. The path with the longest travel time will establish the watershed time of concentration.

Path A-B-I: For segment A-B, Figure 7.6 (forest w/heavy ground litter, $S = 0.065$ ft/ft) gives $v = 0.64$ ft/s. Equation 7.4 gives

$$t_t = \frac{L}{60v} = \frac{350}{60(0.64)} = 9.1 \text{ min}$$

Segment B–I, Figure 7.6 (grassed waterway, $S = 0.029$ ft/ft) gives $v = 2.7$ ft/s. Thus,

$$t_t = \frac{L}{60v} = \frac{1100}{60(2.7)} = 6.8 \text{ min}$$

Travel time in path A–B–I is

$$t_c = \sum_{i=1}^{n} t_i = 9.1 + 6.8 = 15.9 \text{ min}$$

Path C–D–E–I: For segment C-D, Figure 7.6 (forest w/heavy ground litter, $S = 0.070$ ft/ft) gives $v = 0.65$ ft/s.

$$t_t = \frac{270}{60(0.65)} = 6.9 \text{ min}$$

Segment D–E, Figure 7.6 (grassed waterway, $S = 0.042$ ft/ft) gives $v = 3.3$ ft/s.

$$t_t = \frac{610}{60(3.3)} = 3.1 \text{ min}$$

TABLE 7.7   Reference Summary of Travel Time and Time of Concentration Methods

Method	Formula for t_t or t_c (minutes)	Remarks
Morgali and Linsley (1965) Sheet Flow	$$t = \frac{0.94}{i^{0.4}} \left(\frac{nL}{S^{0.5}} \right)^{0.6}$$ L = length of flow path (ft) n = Manning's sheet flow roughness i = rainfall intensity (in/hr) S = average overland slope (ft/ft)	This is an overland (sheet) flow equation developed from a kinematic wave analysis of surface runoff from developed (paved) surfaces. The method requires iteration since rainfall intensity is a function of travel time.
SCS TR-55 (1986) Sheet Flow	$$t = \frac{0.42}{P_2^{0.5}} \left(\frac{nL}{S^{0.5}} \right)^{0.8}$$ P_2 = 2-yr, 24-hr rainfall depth (in) n = Manning's sheet flow roughness L = length of flow path (ft) S = average overland slope (ft/ft)	This simplified version of the Morgali and Linsley equation was developed for the SCS by Welle and Woodward (1986). It has the advantage of a rainfall parameter that is independent of travel time, and therefore an iterative solution is not required.
FAA (1970) Sheet and Concentrated Flow	$$t = \frac{1.8(1.1 - C)\, L^{0.5}}{S^{0.333}}$$ C = Rational runoff coefficient L = length of flow path (ft) S = average overland slope (%)	This equation was developed from airfield drainage data assembled by the U.S. Army Corps of Engineers. The method was intended for use on airfield drainage problems but has been frequently used for overland flow in urban watersheds.
Kirpich (1940) Sheet and Concentrated Flow	$$t = 0.0078\, K \left(\frac{L^2}{S} \right)^{0.385}$$ K = surface roughness factor L = length of flow path from headwater to outlet (ft) S = average slope of flow path (ft/ft)	Developed for seven rural/ agricultural basins in Tennessee, 1.25 to 112 acres, well-defined channels, slopes between 3% and 10%. Surface roughness factors: $K = 1.0$ for overland flow on bare soil; or for flow in roadside ditches; $K = 0.4$ for overland flow on concrete and asphalt surfaces; $K = 0.2$ for flow in concrete channels.

TABLE 7.7 (*Continued*)

Method	Formula for t_t or t_c (minutes)	Remarks
Kerby–Hathaway (1959) Sheet and Concentrated Flow	$t = 0.83 \left(\dfrac{nL}{S^{0.5}} \right)^{0.47}$ L = length of flow path (ft) n = Manning's roughness coefficient S = average overland slope (ft/ft)	Developed on watersheds less than 10 acres, sheet flow dominated, watershed slopes of 1% or less, Manning's roughness 0.8 and less. Length is straight-line distance from most distant point in watershed to outlet, parallel to slope until a well defined channel is reached.
SCS Average Velocity Method Sheet and Concentrated Flow	$t = \dfrac{L}{60v}$ L = length of flow path (ft) v = velocity from Figure 7.4 or 7.5	Computation of an average runoff velocity. It assumes Manning's equation simplifies to $v = kS^{0.5}$ by replacing the R_h, n, and constant 1.49 with a coefficient, k.
Manning's Equation Channel or Pipe Flow	$t = \dfrac{L}{60v}$, $v = \dfrac{1.486}{n} R_h^{0.67} S^{0.5}$ L = length of flow path (ft) n = roughness coefficient R = hydraulic radius (ft) S = channel or pipe slope (ft/ft)	This method requires the computation of a runoff flow velocity, using Manning's equation, and then computing a travel time based on the channel/pipe length. This method is suitable for well-defined channels, either man-made or natural, and storm sewer pipes.

TABLE 7.8   Flow Path Characteristics for Example 7.6

Path	L (ft)	S (ft/ft)	Surface Description/Path Geometry
A–B	350	0.065	forest with heavy ground litter
B–I	1100	0.029	grassed waterway
C–D	270	0.070	forest with heavy ground litter
D–E	610	0.042	grassed waterway
E–I	850	0.021	rectangular channel, 1.5 ft wide, 1.0 ft deep, $n = 0.035$
F–G	230	0.072	forest with heavy ground litter
G–H	1590	0.035	grassed waterway
H–I	840	0.065	grassed waterway

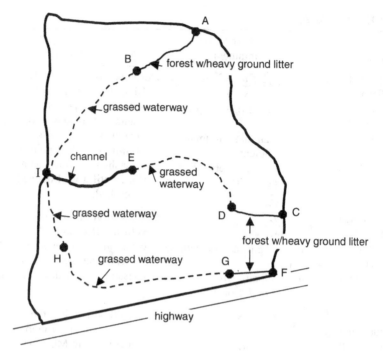

Figure 7.7   Time of concentration flow path for watershed in Example 7.6.

Segment E–I, Manning's, $A = 1.5 \times 1.0 = 1.5$ ft^2, $P = 1 + 1.5 + 1 = 3.5$ ft, $R_h = 1.5/3.5 = 0.43$ ft.

$$v = \frac{1.49}{0.035} \, 0.43^{0.67} 0.021^{0.5} = 3.50 \text{ ft/s}$$

$$t_t = \frac{850}{60(3.5)} = 4.0 \text{ min}$$

Travel time in path C–D–E–I is

$$t_c = \sum_{i=1}^{n} t_i = 6.9 + 3.1 + 4.0 = 14.0 \text{ min}$$

Path F–G–H–I: For segment F–G, Figure 7.6 (forest w/heavy ground litter, $S = 0.072$ ft/ft) gives $v = 0.66$ ft/s.

$$t_t = \frac{L}{60v} = \frac{230}{60(0.66)} = 5.8 \text{ min}$$

Segment G–H, Figure 7.6 (grassed waterway, $S = 0.035$ ft/ft) gives $v = 2.9$ ft/s.

$$t_t = \frac{1590}{60(2.9)} = 9.1 \text{ min}$$

Segment H–I, Figure 7.6 (grassed waterway, $S = 0.065$ ft/ft) gives $v = 3.9$ ft/s.

$$t_t = \frac{840}{60(3.9)} = 4.0 \text{ min}$$

Travel time in path F–G–H–I is

$$t_c = \sum_{i=1}^{n} t_i = 5.8 + 9.1 + 4.0 = 18.9 \text{ min}$$

The watershed time of concentration is the longest travel time of the three paths (15.9, 14.0, 18.9). Therefore, the time of concentration is 18.9 minutes.

7.8 NRCS SEGMENTAL METHOD

In 1986, the NRCS (SCS) adopted a segmental method for calculating watershed time of concentration, and it was illustrated in Chapter 3 of TR-55 (1986). The method identifies flow in the watershed as either sheet, concentrated, or channel. Field inspection is recommended for identifying the transition points of each flow type. Two or more segments of each type of flow are possible. The three equations modeling each flow type are covered in previous sections. Sheet flow follows Equation 7.2 or 7.3. Concentrated flow follows Equation 7.4 in conjunction with Equation 7.7 or Equation 7.8. Channel flow follows Equation 7.4 in conjunction with Equation 4.5. The sum of the travel times of all the path segments equals the time of concentration, assuming the path is the hydraulically longest path in the watershed. Be aware that the SCS methodology uses the standard SCS units of hours for travel time and time of concentration, while the equations in this text use units of minutes.

Example 7.7 The flow path in a 147-acre watershed located in Greene County, Tennessee is broken into four segments. The characteristics of each flow segment are shown in Table 7.9 and illustrated in Figure 7.8. Use the SCS segmental method to determine the travel time in the path. The 2-year, 24-hour rainfall depth for this county is 3.1 inches.

TABLE 7.9 Flow Path Characteristics for Example 7.7

Path	Flow type	L (ft)	S (ft/ft)	Surface Description/Path Geometry
1–2	Sheet	50	0.015	Forest with heavy undercover
2–3	Concentrated	1500	0.055	Unpaved through forest area
3–4	Concentrated	1280	0.031	Unpaved through meadow area
4–5	Natural channel	750	0.025	Rectangular section, 2.0 ft wide, 1.0 ft deep, $n = 0.040$

Solution: Segment 1–2: Equation 7.3 is used for SCS sheet flow. From Table 7.1, the best cover description to match the path surface is woods with dense underbrush, $n = 0.80$.

$$t_t = \frac{0.42}{P_2^{0.5}}\left(\frac{nL}{S^{0.5}}\right)^{0.8} = \frac{0.42}{3.1^{0.5}}\left(\frac{(0.80)(50)}{(0.045)^{0.5}}\right)^{0.8} = 15.8 \text{ min}$$

Segment 2–3: Equation 7.7 is used to compute the average velocity in the forest swale.

$$v_{\text{unpaved}} = 16.1\,S^{0.5} = 16.1(0.055)^{0.5} = 3.78 \text{ ft/s}$$

Equation 7.4 is used to compute the segment travel time.

$$t_t = \frac{L}{60v} = \frac{1500}{60(3.78)} = 6.6 \text{ min}$$

Segment 3–4: Again, Equations 7.7 and 7.4 are used to compute the average velocity and travel time in the flatter-sloped meadow swale.

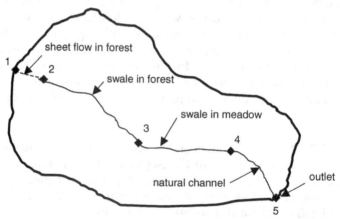

Figure 7.8 Time of concentration flow path for watershed in Example 7.7.

$$v_{\text{unpaved}} = 16.1 \, S^{0.5} = 16.1(0.031)^{0.5} = 2.83 \text{ ft/s}$$

$$t_t = \frac{L}{60v} = \frac{1280}{60(2.83)} = 7.5 \text{ min}$$

Segment 4–5: Assuming bank-full flow conditions, the natural channel has an approximate flow area $A = (2)(1) = 2$ ft^2 and a wetted perimeter of $P = 1 + 2 + 1 = 4$ ft. The hydraulic radius is $R_h = 2/4 = 0.5$ ft. Manning's equation and Equation 7.4 are used to compute travel time.

$$v = \frac{1.49}{0.040} \, 0.5^{0.67} 0.025^{0.5} = 3.69 \text{ ft/s}$$

$$t_t = \frac{L}{60v} = \frac{750}{60(3.69)} = 3.4 \text{ min}$$

The total travel time in the path is

$$t_c = \sum_{i=1}^{n} t_i = 15.8 + 6.6 + 7.5 + 3.4 = 33.3 \text{ min}$$

The several steps necessary to complete the solution of this example are easily managed in the NRCS computer program WinTR-55 (USDA NRCS 2002). The program includes all of the computational techniques documented in TR-55 (USDA SCS 1986), except for Chapter 5—Tabular Hydrograph Method, which has been replaced with the NRCS unit-hydrograph method and Muskingum-Cunge channel routing method. Figure 7.9 shows the WinTR-55 *Main Window* and the *Time of Concentration Details* window with the data input and computational results of Example 7.7. Note that the WinTR-55 solution is expressed in hours.

Notice that the shortest segment in the flow path provides the longest travel time in the overall path. This is the nature of the kinematic wave sheet-flow equation. In general, the sheet-flow equation will give large travel times. It is very important to accurately estimate the flow path length, slope, and surface roughness of this segment to get a reasonable result. Arbitrary assignment of a length equal to the maximum allowable (100 ft) is poor engineering analysis. In predevelopment analysis, the designer should walk the site and estimate the path length. In postdevelopment design close examination of the grading plan may be needed instead of walking the site.

7.9 NRCS LAG EQUATION

The NRCS (SCS) defines watershed lag as the time between a brief heavy rain and the peak discharge. For a given watershed, lag can be estimated

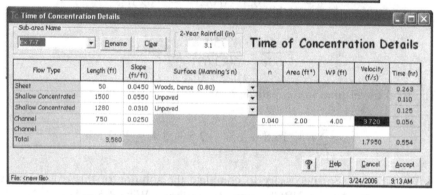

Figure 7.9   Using WinTR-55 to solve Example 7.7.

based on the analysis of recorded rainfall and hydrographs, as explained earlier in this chapter. Lag is affected by the watershed parameters of length, slope, and surface roughness. Considering the hydrograph definition of time of concentration, it is clear that lag is a related parameter. The SCS analyzed many storm events from a range of watershed conditions and determined watershed lag to be 60 percent of watershed time of concentration. Using this relation, and relating watershed parameters to lag, the NRCS lag equation for estimating time of concentration was established as

$$t_c = \frac{L^{0.8} \left[\dfrac{1000}{CN} - 9 \right]^{0.7}}{190 \, S^{0.5}} \tag{7.13}$$

where t_c = time of concentration (min)

L = the hydraulic length of the watershed (longest flow path) (ft)

CN = runoff curve number (see Chapter 8)

S = average watershed slope (ft/ft)

This equation is often called a lumped-flow equation because it was developed considering the time of concentration path as one, unsegmented path, with all flow regimes along the path lumped into one calculation.

The method was developed for rural, agricultural watersheds where overland flow is the dominate flow regime along the flow path. In the 1975 publication of TR-55, the equation is recommended for homogenous watersheds under natural conditions up to 2000 acres. Curiously, the method is not mentioned in the 1986 publication of TR-55. However, independent studies have shown the method to work reasonably well for its intended purpose. Based on field studies at Penn State University by Kibler et al. (1982), this method was found to work best in the upper reaches of a basin where development is limited or nonexistent and flow is predominately overland and concentrated. McCuen et al. (1984) found the method to give accurate estimates for watersheds up to 4000 acres. The use of the equation is illustrated in Example 8.7.

7.10 COMPARISON OF METHODS

The various methods presented in the previous sections are all developed for specific flow types and flow conditions. Some methods are more robust than others, but all are used in one way or another to support stormwater management design. The following example takes a look at the variability of results of travel time methods, and their effect on the size of a stormwater drain pipe. All methods were applied in a segmental fashion.

Example 7.8 Consider the three-segment flow path shown in Figure 7.10. The watershed area is 200 acres with an average watershed surface slope of 0.030 ft/ft. The impervious cover is 5%, with a *CN* value of 70 and a Rational *C* value of 0.20. The watershed is located in Pennsylvania rainfall region 1 (Figure 6.5). The channel segments are described as follows.

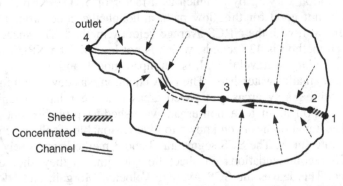

Figure 7.10 Schematic of watershed flow path of Example 7.8.

Segment 1–2: Sheet-length = 70 feet, slope = 0.037 ft/ft, meadow cover with dense grass (n = 0.24)

Segment 2–3: Concentrated-length = 1250 feet, slope = 0.042 ft/ft, cover is grass swale (unpaved)

Segment 3–4: Channel-length = 2300 feet, slope = 0.025 ft/ft, n = 0.040 (natural channel), bank-full flow area = 10 ft², wetted perimeter = 8.47 feet

Compute the watershed time of concentration using the following methods with the noted assumptions.

Kirpich—Use sheet and swale K values equal to 1.0.

SCS Average Velocity Figure 7.6 (1975)—Use the meadow curve for sheet flow and the grassed waterway curve for swale flow.

Morgali—Use the IDF curves developed by Yarnel (USWB), with the 1-hour, 25-year rainfall depth equal to 1.6 in/hr. For swale time, use the average velocity method of TR-55 1986.

NRCS Segmental 1—Use the sheet and swale lengths as described in the problem.

NRCS Segmental 2—Increase the sheet path to 150 feet, and decrease the swale path to 1170 feet.

NRCS Segmental 3—Increase the sheet path to 300 feet (not recommended), and decrease the swale path to 1020 feet.

FAA—Assume the sheet C to be 0.075 and use the watershed C of 0.2 for the swale.

NRCS Lag—Be sure to use average watershed slope and not average channel slope.

Calculations are left to the reader. The results are summarized in Table 7.10 and they show a wide variation in results, with the estimated time of concentration varying by as much as a factor of 5. The Kirpich equation is probably not good for this flow path, although the concentrated segment agrees very well with the NRCS average velocity method. The sheet time for the Kirpich method is 42 seconds, which is not logical. The NRCS lag equation gives the largest travel time. It is a lumped-model, and this may not work real well for smaller watersheds. The FAA equation was developed for airport runways, with grassy areas and paved areas that are relatively uniform in slope. The application to a non-urban watershed is probably not the best choice. The equation has been known to give reasonable results when applied to urban watersheds. The SCS segmental 2 and 3 methods purposely violated the NRCS recommendations on sheet flow length, so they should not be considered. This leaves the SCS Average Velocity, Morgali, and NRCS segmental 1 solutions. The results of these three are reasonably close with the maximum variation being about 50%. The watershed time of concentration is probably around 20 minutes.

TABLE 7.10 Comparison of Time of Concentration Results Using Eight Different Methods

| Method | t_t (min) | | | t_c (min) | i^B (in/hr) | q_{25}^C (ft³/s) | D_{pipe}^D (in) |
	Sheet	Concentrated	Channel[A]				
Kirpich	0.7	6.4	5.8	12.9	3.9	156	42
SCS Avg. Vel. (1975)	2.4	6.3	5.8	14.5	3.7	148	42
Morgali	7.3	6.3	5.8	19.4	3.2	128	42
NRCS Segmental 1	9.9	6.3	5.8	22.0	3.0	120	42
NRCS Segmental 2	18.2	5.9	5.8	29.9	2.5	100	36
NRCS Segmental 3	31.7	5.1	5.8	42.6	2.0	80	36
FAA	10.0	35.5	5.8	51.3	1.8	72	36
NRCS Lag	—	—	—	68.5	1.5	60	30

General computation notes:
A—Channel time is computed using Manning's equation under bank-full conditions.
B—The Pennsylvania DOT IDF curves are used to estimate intensity, i, for Region 1, 25-yr event.
C—The peak flow q_{25} is computed using the Rational formula, $q = CiA$, with $C = 0.2$ and $A = 200$ ac. The Rational formula is covered in Chapter 8.
D—Pize size based upon Manning's equation, full flow, $S = 0.030$ ft/ft, $n = 0.014$.

Results like these are typical of time of concentration calculations when methods are applied indiscriminately. Such variation does not offer confidence in any particular calculation method. However, if one takes some time to understand the intended use of each method, the results will not diverge as much as in this example. Another aspect of variability of time of concentration results is the effect they have on a calculated flow rate, and the associated design of a stormwater structure. The last three columns of Table 7.10 show the results of a design pipe size that is based on a peak flow computed by the Rational peak flow method (see Chapter 8). The peak flow calculation depends on the critical rainfall intensity that is determined through an IDF curve using a storm duration equal to the calculated time of concentration. The critical rainfall intensity is shown in column (6) and the resulting peak flow is shown in column (7). The final design pipe size is shown in the last column. As can be seen, the design diameter varies by only one pipe size (36 inch to 42 inch) for all of the flows, except the one dependent on the NRCS lag equation. This is the saving grace, so to speak, of the pipe sizing calculation. In this particular case, a wide variation in time of concentration did not significantly affect the final design of the stormwater structure.

PROBLEMS

7.1 Consider a rectangular, asphalt-paved parking lot that is 265 feet long and 130 feet wide with contours as shown in Figure 7.11. The surface is in excellent condition, with no cracks or surface undulations. The lot

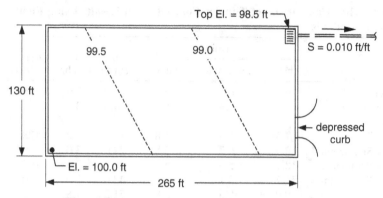

Figure 7.11   Parking lot of Problem 7.1 and 7.2.

is curbed all around and acts as a single drainage area; that is, only the paved area contributes runoff to the inlet. Use Morgali's kinematic wave equation to determine the sheet-flow travel time from elevation 100.0 feet to the outlet at elevation 98.5 feet. Use Figure 6.5 to select rainfall intensities, using a return period of 10 years.

7.2   Use the NRCS sheet-flow equation (Equation 7.2 or 7.3) to determine the travel time of Problem 7.1. Compare the results and suggest reasons for any differences.

7.3   Consider a football field in southern Florida that is 100 yards long and 40 yards wide. The geometric center of the field is elevated 0.48 feet with respect to the field perimeter. All runoff from the field travels along lines that emanate radially from the field center to the perimeter. The field surface condition is excellent. Surface slopes are uniform along the radial flow lines. Using the NRCS sheet-flow equation, determine the overland flow travel time for the path starting at the field center point and ending at the midpoint of the goal line. The 2-year, 24-hour rainfall depth for this location is 5.0 inches.

7.4   A small drainage area has a flow path that is composed of a sheet-flow segment followed by a concentrated swale-flow segment. The sheet-flow segment is covered with dense grass at a surface slope of 0.015 ft/ft and length of 50 feet. The swale flow segment is over a lawn/meadow area that has a slope of 0.012 ft/ft and length of 850 feet. Compute the travel time in this flow path using the NRCS segmental method. Use a 2-year, 24-hour rainfall depth of 2.5 inches.

7.5   Use the FAA equation to determine overland flow time for the flow path described in Problem 7.4, using a single computation for the entire path. Compare the results and suggest reasons for the differences.

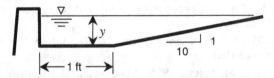

Figure 7.12 Concrete curb gutter of Problem 7.7.

7.6 A flow path in an agricultural watershed begins at a watershed divide and ends 1850 feet later, creating a confluence with an intermittent stream. The flow path travels through woods with moderate to heavy underbrush at an average slope of 3.50 percent. The watershed drained by the flow path has a runoff curve number *CN* of 55 and Rational *C* of 0.10. Determine the travel time of the path using (a) the FAA equation, (b) the SCS 1975 average velocity method (Figure 7.6), and (c) the NRCS lag equation. Compare the results and comment on any differences.

7.7 The concrete curb gutter of Figure 7.12 has a flow depth of $y = 0.3$ feet and slope of 0.025 ft/ft. If the gutter length is 350 feet, determine the travel time for flow along the gutter path.

7.8 A natural stream channel that is 1760 feet long can be approximated by a trapezoidal section that has an average bottom width of 5 feet, average side slopes left and right of 1H:1V, and average channel slope of 0.0080 ft/ft. The bank-full flow depth is approximately 1.5 feet and the channel roughness is approximately 0.040. Flow is assumed to be uniform. Determine the flow travel time for the stream.

REFERENCES

ASCE. 1992. *Design and Construction of Urban Stormwater Management Systems.* ASCE Manuals and Reports of Engineering Practice No. 77.

Engman, E. T. 1986. "Roughness Coefficients for Routing Surface Runoff." *Journal of Irrigation and Drainage Engineering,* 112(1): 39–53.

Federal Aviation Agency. 1970. *Airport Drainage,* A/C 150-5320-5B. Washington, DC: Department of Transportation Advisory Circular.

Hathaway, G. A. 1945. "Design of Drainage Facilities." *ASCE Transactions,* 30: 697–730.

Kerby, W. S. 1959. "Time of Concentration for Overland Flow." *Civil Engineering,* 29(3): 174.

Kibler, D. F., G. Aron, K. A. Riley, G. Osei-Kwadwo, and E. L. White 1982. *Recommended Hydrologic Procedures for Computing Urban Runoff from Small Watersheds in Pennsylvania.* PA-DER Bureau of Dams and Waterways, Division of Stormwater Management, Harrisburg, PA.

Kirpich, Z. P. 1940. "Time of Concentration of Small Agricultural Watersheds." *Civil Engineering,* (10)6: 362.

McCuen, R. H. 2005. *Hydrologic Analysis and Design,* 3rd ed. Upper Saddle River, NJ: Pearson Prentice-Hall.

McCuen, R. H., and J. M. Spiess. 1995. "Assessment of Kinematic Wave Time of Concentration." *Journal of Hydraulic Engineering,* 121 (256).

McCuen, R. H., S. L. Wong, and W. J. Rawls. 1984. "Estimating Urban Time of Concentration." *Journal of Hydraulic Engineering,* ASCE, 110(7): 887–904.

Merkel, W. 2001. *References on Time of Concentration with Respect to Sheet Flow.* USDA National Resource Conservation Service, National Weather and Climate Center, Beltsville, MD (http://www.wcc.nrcs.usda.gov/hydro/hydro-tools-models-wintr55.html).

Morgali, J. R., and R. K. Linsley. 1965. "Computer Simulation of Overland Flow." *Journal of Hydraulics Division,* ASCE 91(HY3): 81–100.

Palmer, V. J. 1946. "Retardance Coefficients for Low Flow in Channels Lined with Vegetation. Transactions." *American Geophysical Union,* 27(II): 187–197.

Ramser, C. E. 1927. "Runoff from Small Agricultural Areas." *Journal of Agricultural Research,* 34(9): 797–823.

USDA SCS. 1975. *Urban Hydrology for Small Watersheds.* Technical Release 55, Engineering Division, Washington, DC.

USDA SCS. 1986. *Urban Hydrology for Small Watersheds.* Technical Release 55, Engineering Division, Washington, DC.

USDA NRCS. 2002. *WinTR-55 Small Watershed Hydrology,* computer program, Engineering Division, Washington, DC. (http://www.wcc.nrcs.usda.gov/hydro/hydro-tools-models-wintr55.html).

Welle, P., and D. Woodward. 1986. *Time of Concentration.* Hydrology Technical Note No. 4, USDA Soil Conservation Service, Northeast NTC, Chester, PA (http://www.wcc.nrcs.usda.gov/hydro/hydro-tools-models-wintr55.html).

Woolhiser, D. A. 1975. *Simulation of Unsteady Overland Flow.* Chapter 12, Institute on Unsteady Flow, Water Resources Pub., Colorado State University, Fort Collins, CO.

CHAPTER 8

RUNOFF DEPTH AND PEAK FLOW

8.1 INTRODUCTION

Before any type of stormwater management design can begin, estimates of surface runoff are necessary. Runoff occurs during a storm event after certain initial losses are satisfied. Rainfall initially wets the surface of the Earth, including trees, grass, rooftops, and pavement. After surface and vegetation wetting, the soil absorbs and infiltrates rainfall as long as the soil infiltration capacity is not exceeded by the rainfall intensity. As the soil saturates, the soil infiltration capacity reduces, and rainfall that cannot infiltrate transforms into surface water. The water gathers on the watershed surface, collecting in small depressions and surface undulations. As the water accumulates on the surface, it eventually finds a flow path, following linear depressions, concentrating in small swales and creating overland runoff flow. The surface runoff eventually travels downslope and collects in the major drainage way in the watershed. In the urban watershed, the drainage way may be a natural stream, a man-made storm sewer, a concrete-lined channel, or some combination of these. Whatever the path characteristics, the elements make up the stormwater drainage network that collects and transports surface runoff from the extremities of the watershed to the outlet. Good estimates of surface runoff volumes and rates are necessary to analyze and design these drainage ways and other elements of a stormwater management plan.

Runoff estimates are made for specific design purposes. Peak runoff rates are required when sizing stormwater conveyance structures, and runoff volumes are required when designing stormwater storage facilities. There are many methods available for estimating surface runoff. Peak flow methods give a single flow rate, usually for design of conveyance systems such as swales, channels, gutters, pipes, or culverts. Volume methods give total runoff volume during an event and are usually needed for retention, detention, or infiltration basin design. Hydrograph methods give both peak flow rates and runoff volumes and provide enough information for both conveyance and storage design. All three methods are represented here and in Chapter 9, through the discussion of the several common methods used in stormwater management.

8.2   RUNOFF CURVE NUMBER METHOD

The Natural Resources Conservation Service (NRCS), previously known as the Soil Conservation Service (SCS), developed the curve number (CN) methodology for estimating runoff. The method was originally developed for agricultural watersheds, but later adapted to developing watersheds. The method is based on a hydrologic soil-cover classification system for selection of curve numbers, a watershed abstraction and infiltration relationship, and a simplified form of the conservation of mass equation.

8.2.1   Runoff Equations

Three equations are the basis of the curve number method for estimating runoff:

$$Q = \frac{(P - I_a)^2}{(P - I_a + S)} \tag{8.1}$$

$$I_a = 0.2S \tag{8.2}$$

$$S = \frac{1000}{CN} - 10 \tag{8.3}$$

where Q = direct runoff (in)
$\quad P$ = precipitation (in)
$\quad I_a$ = initial abstraction (in)
$\quad S$ = potential maximum retention (in)
$\quad CN$ = curve number

Very briefly stated, direct runoff Q, is a volume since the depth is associated with the watershed drainage area. The precipitation P, also known as the total rainfall depth, is determined from design rainfall data, or possibly an event of record. The method requires information about land use, hydrologic condition, and hydrologic soil type of the drainage area. Using this information, a CN value is determined, typically from tabulated data. With P and CN estimated, S, I_a, and finally Q are computed.

Equations 8.1 through 8.3 can be combined to create a single relation between Q, P, and CN, negating the need to compute S and I_a. The result is

$$Q = \frac{\left(P - \dfrac{200}{CN} + 2\right)^2}{\left(P + \dfrac{800}{CN} - 8\right)} \tag{8.4}$$

A graphical representation of Equations 8.1 and 8.4 is shown in Figure 8.1. It is worth noting that a mathematical constraint of these equations is that P must be greater than I_a. When P is less than I_a, direct runoff Q is defined as zero.

This is the curve number method in a nutshell. In order to apply the method with confidence, it is important to understand hydrologic soil groups, the hydrologic soil cover classification system, and the development of the runoff equations.

8.2.2 Hydrologic Soil Groups

Approximately 14,000 soils in the United States have been classified by NRCS soil scientists. Initially, classifications were based on rainfall-runoff

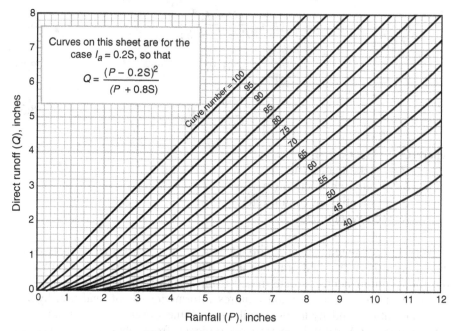

Curves on this sheet are for the case $I_a = 0.2S$, so that

$$Q = \frac{(P - 0.2S)^2}{(P + 0.8S)}$$

Figure 8.1   Solution of the NRCS (SCS) runoff equation (Equations 8.1 and 8.4).

data from small watersheds or infiltrometer plots. However, the majority of the soils were classified hydrologically, based on the judgment of the soil scientists, using physical properties of the soil to assign a hydrologic classification. Soils are classified to indicate the minimum infiltration of bare soil that is thoroughly wetted. The classifications are A, B, C, or D, and the four hydrologic soil groups (HSG) are defined by the NRCS according to Table 8.1.

Determining hydrologic soil classification is typically done by using county soil survey maps, which can be obtained from a local NRCS or county conservation district office. An example of a county soil survey is shown in Figure 8.2. The soil survey maps contain aerial photographs of the entire county with soils delineated by boundary with a two- or three-character symbol. The symbol is used to cross-reference to the soil name and eventually to the HSG. The HSG tables are presented in TR-55 (USDA SCS, 1986) Exhibit A or the NRCS National Engineering Handbook 630 (NEH 630) (USDA, 2002) (hydro_soil_group.pdf). Both can be found on the Internet at http://www.wcc.nrcs.usda.gov/hydro.

The minimum infiltration rates specified in Table 8.1 were based on in-situ soils that have undisturbed soil profiles. In the urbanized watershed, soils are often disturbed, leaving profiles completely mixed and causing the HSG classification of the disturbed soil to be no longer valid. For these cases, the texture of the disturbed soil as described in Table 8.2 and presented by Brak-

TABLE 8.1   Characteristics and Minimum Infiltration Rates for Hydrologic Soil Groups (USDA SCS TR-55, 1986)

Group	Characteristics	Minimum Infiltration Rate (in/hr)
A	High infiltration rates (low runoff potential); well to excessively drained deep sands or gravel; deep loess; aggregated silts	greater than 0.30
B	Moderate infiltration rates when thoroughly wetted; moderately deep to deep; moderately well to well drained; moderately fine to moderately course textures; shallow loess; sandy loam	0.15 to 0.30
C	Low infiltration rates when thoroughly wetted; soils with a layer that impedes downward water movement; moderately fine to fine texture; clay loams; shallow sandy loams; soils low in organic content; soils usually high in clay	0.05 to 0.15
D	Very low infiltration rates (high runoff potential) when thoroughly wetted; clay soils with high swelling potential; permanent high water table; claypan or clay layer at or near the surface; heavy plastic clays; certain saline soils	0 to 0.05

ensiek and Rawls (1983) can be used to determine the new HSG. The method assumes that significant compaction of the soil has not occurred.

8.2.3 Hydrologic Soil Cover Complex and Curve Numbers

The hydrologic soil cover classification system developed by the SCS is used to describe the runoff potential of land use and soil combinations. Hydrologic soil group, land use, and hydrologic condition combine to create a hydrologic soil cover complex (HSCC). Each unique HSCC is assigned a curve number that indicates runoff potential during unfrozen ground conditions. A curve number (CN) is a dimensionless number ranging between 0 and 100 and is an indicator of the ability of a land surface to produce runoff. As a variable, CN is related to maximum possible retention, S, through the empirical relation given in Equation 8.3.

The practical range of CN is 40 to 98. Using the limits of the practical range, a quick examination of Equation 8.3 shows that S will be 15 inches when CN is 40. This is the condition of very low runoff potential, where the watershed can absorb up to 15 inches of rainfall. Similarly, S will be 0.2 inches when CN is 98. This is the condition of very high runoff potential, where the watershed can absorb only 0.2 inches of rainfall during an event. Therefore, as CN increases, S decreases, and as S decreases, Q will increase.

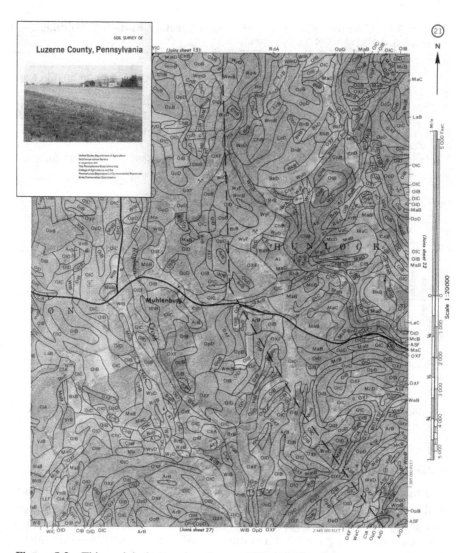

Figure 8.2 This aerial photo, taken from a USDA SCS soil survey, is marked with soil delineations for a portion of Luzerne County, Pennsylvania.

TABLE 8.2 **Texture Descriptions for HSG Classification of Soils Significantly Altered in Profile Due to Land-Development Activities (Brakensiek and Rawls, 1983)**

Group	Texture Description
A	Sand, loamy sand, or sandy loam
B	Silt loam or silt
C	Sandy clay or loam
D	Clay loam, silty clay loam, sandy clay, silty clay, or clay.

Inspection of Equation 8.4 and Figure 8.1 show that with $CN = 100$, $Q = P$, which means the rainfall–runoff relation is linear, with an intercept of 0 and a slope of 1. This models the case where all rainfall is converted into runoff. With $CN = 40$, the relation is nonlinear, reflecting significant losses prior to runoff. The watershed produces very little runoff, even for the most extreme rainfall events.

Table 8.3 shows runoff curve numbers for selected HSCC classifications under average antecedent runoff conditions (ARC). The ARC is explained in section 8.2.4. These data come from NEH 630 Chapter 9, Table 9.1. The land-use descriptions in Table 8.3 are those most likely to be encountered in a land development situation. Other CN values are given in NEH 630, but they are mainly related to agricultural and conservation practices. These agricultural classifications are also found in TR-55 1986.

8.2.4   Antecedent Runoff/Antecedent Moisture Conditions

Watershed conditions prior to a storm event affect runoff. The antecedent runoff condition (ARC) is an index of runoff potential for a watershed or site before a storm occurs. It is a condition that is used to account for variations in CN from storm to storm, based on watershed prestorm conditions. The ARC is affected by several possible factors, including soil moisture, season, and temperature. ARC is a term that appears in more recent NRCS publications, and is used in place of the term *antecedent moisture condition* (AMC), which was used in earlier SCS literature. The original SCS literature focused mainly on soil moisture conditions, thus the reason for AMC. In either case (ARC or AMC), it is a condition that affects curve number and it is commonly thought to be based mainly on soil moisture conditions prior to the event.

If soil moisture conditions are wet prior to a certain rainfall event, more runoff should be expected than for the prestorm condition of very dry soils. Table 8.4 provides definition of AMC classes I through III, based on a moisture condition description and reported by McCuen (2005). Although the table supplies information directed toward the agricultural watershed, it provides reasonable insight into the nature of CN values as they vary with ARC/AMC.

The majority of CN values presented in the professional literature were developed for the average prestorm watershed condition, ARC/AMC II. If modeling runoff for either conditions I or III, the CN values must be adjusted according to Table 8.5.

Example 8.1   A 10-acre site has a land use of quarter-acre residential lots. The county soil survey shows the site to be underlain by soils that are hydrologic soil type C. The hydrologic condition of the site is good. For a rainfall of 3.5 inches, estimate the total runoff in ac-ft caused by the event, assuming the pre-storm antecedent runoff condition is II.

TABLE 8.3 Runoff Curve Numbers for Select Land Uses for Antecedent Runoff Condition II (USDA NRCS NEH 630, 2002)

Cover Description		Curve Numbers for Hydrologic Soil Group			
Land Use and Hydrologic Condition		A	B	C	D
Fully developed urban areas (*vegetation established*)					
Open space (lawn, park, golf course, cemetery, etc.)[1]					
Poor: < 50% grass cover		68	79	86	89
Fair: 50% to 75% grass cover		49	69	79	84
Good: > 75% grass cover		39	61	74	80
Impervious areas					
Paved parking lots, roofs, driveways, etc. (exclude right-of-way)		98	98	98	98
Streets and roads					
Paved; curbs and storm sewers (exclude right-of-way)		98	98	98	98
Paved; open ditches (include right-of-way)		83	89	92	93
Gravel (include right-of-way)		76	85	89	91
Dirt (include right-of-way)		72	82	87	89
Western desert urban areas					
Natural desert landscaping (pervious areas only)[2]		63	77	85	88
Artificial desert landscaping (impervious weed barrier, desert shrub with 1- to 2-inch sand or gravel mulch and basin borders)		96	96	96	96
Urban districts	(average % impervious)[3]				
Commercial and business	(85)	89	92	94	95
Industrial	(72)	81	88	91	93
Residential districts by average lot size					
1/8 acre or less (townhouses)	(65)	77	85	90	92
1/4 acre	(38)	61	75	83	87
1/3 acre	(30)	57	72	81	86
1/2 acre	(25)	54	70	80	85
1 acre	(20)	51	68	79	84
2 acre	(12)	46	65	77	82
Developing urban areas					
Newly graded areas (pervious areas only, no vegetation)[4]		77	86	91	94
Idle lands (*CN*s are determined using cover types similar to pasture, meadow, brush and woods.)					

[1] *CN*s shown are equivalent to those of pasture. Composite *CN*s may be computed for other combinations of open space cover type.

[2] Composite *CN*s for natural desert landscaping should be computed using Figure 8.3 or 8.4 based on the impervious area percentage (*CN* = 98) and the pervious area *CN*. The pervious area *CN*s are assumed equivalent to desert shrub in poor hydrologic condition.

[3] The average percent impervious area shown was used to develop the composite *CN*s. Other assumptions are as follows: impervious areas are directly connected to the drainage system, impervious areas have a *CN* of 98, and pervious areas are considered equivalent to open space in good hydrologic condition. *CN*s for other combinations of conditions may be computed using Figure 8.3 or 8.4.

[4] Composite *CN*s to use for the design of temporary measures during grading and construction should be computed using Figure 8.3 or 8.4 based on the degree of development (impervious area percentage) and the *CN*s for the newly graded pervious areas.

TABLE 8.3 (*Continued*)

Cover Description	Curve Numbers for Hydrologic Soil Group			
Land Use and Hydrologic Condition	A	B	C	D
Undeveloped rural areas				
Farmsteads—buildings, lanes, driveways, and surrounding lots	59	74	82	86
Pasture, grassland, or range—continuous forage for grazing				
Poor: < 50% ground cover or heavily grazed with no mulch	68	79	86	89
Fair: 50 to 75% ground cover and not heavily grazed	49	69	79	84
Good: 75% ground cover, lightly or only occasionally grazed	39	61	74	80
Meadow—continuous grass, protected from grazing and generally mowed for hay, good condition	30	58	71	78
Brush-weed-grass mixture (brush the major element)[5]				
Poor: < 50% ground cover	48	67	77	83
Fair: 50 to 75% ground cover	35	56	70	77
Good: 75% ground cover	30[5]	48	65	73
Woods-grass combination (orchard or tree farm)				
Poor:	57	73	82	86
Fair:	43	65	76	82
Good:	32	58	72	79
Woods				
Poor: Forest litter, small trees, and brush grazed or burned	45	66	77	83
Fair: Grazed but not burned; some forest litter covers the soil	36	60	73	79
Good: Protected from grazing; soil covered by litter and brush	30[6]	55	70	77
Forest-Range				
Herbaceous—mixture of grass, weeds, and low-growing brush, with brush the minor element				
Poor: < 30% ground cover (litter, grass, and brush overstory)		80	87	93
Fair: 30 to 70% ground cover	[7]	71	81	89
Good: > 70% ground cover		62	74	85
Oak-aspen—mountain brush mixture of oak brush, aspen, mountain mahogany, bitter brush, maple and other brush				
Poor: < 30% ground cover (litter, grass, and brush overstory)		66	74	79
Fair: 30 to 70% ground cover	[7]	48	57	63
Good: > 70% ground cover		30	41	48
Pinyon and/or juniper with grass understory				
Poor: < 30% ground cover (litter, grass, and brush overstory)		75	85	89
Fair: 30 to 70% ground cover	[7]	58	73	80
Good: > 70% ground cover		41	61	71
Sagebrush with grass understory				
Poor: < 30% ground cover (litter, grass, and brush overstory)		67	80	85
Fair: 30 to 70% ground cover	[7]	51	63	70
Good: > 70% ground cover		35	47	55
Desert shrub—major plants include saltbush, greasewood, creosotebush, blackbrush, bursage, palo verde, mesquite, cactus				
Poor: < 30% ground cover (litter, grass, and brush overstory)	63	77	85	88
Fair: 30 to 70% ground cover	55	72	81	86
Good: > 70% ground cover	49	68	79	84

[5] *CN*s shown are for areas with 50% woods and 50% grass (pasture). Other combinations may be computed from *CN*s for woods and pasture.

[6] Actual curve number is less than 30. Use *CN* = 30 for runoff computations.

[7] Curve numbers for soil group A have not been developed.

TABLE 8.4   Watershed Moisture Condition for Estimating Antecedent Moisture Condition (McCuen 2005)

AMC Class	Moisture Condition
I	Soils are dry but not to the wilting point; satisfactory cultivation has taken place.
II	Average conditions.
III	Heavy rainfall or light rainfall with low temperatures have occurred within the last 5 days; saturated soil

Solution: From Table 8.3 for a residential district of average quarter-acre lot size and soil type C, *CN* is chosen as 83. Using Equation 8.4 the runoff depth *Q* is determined as

$$Q = \frac{\left(3.5 - \dfrac{200}{83} + 2\right)^2}{\left(3.5 + \dfrac{800}{83} - 8\right)} = 1.86 \text{ inches}$$

Total runoff volume is computed by multiplying *Q* by the drainage area.

$$V = \frac{(1.86 \text{ in})(10 \text{ ac})}{12 \text{ in/ft}} = 1.55 \text{ ac-ft}$$

TABLE 8.5   *CN* Adjustment for ARC I (dry) and ARC III (wet) Based on the *CN* for ARC II (USDA NEH 630, 2002)

CN for ARC II	Adjusted CN for	
	ARC I	ARC III
100	100	100
95	87	98
90	78	96
85	70	94
80	63	91
75	57	88
70	51	85
65	45	82
60	40	78
55	35	74
50	31	70
45	26	65
40	22	60

Example 8.2 For the 10-acre site of Example 8.1, determine the runoff from the same rainfall event, but assume the pre-storm condition to be (a) ARC I and (b) ARC III.

Solution: Using interpolation in Table 8.5, the *CN* value of 83 (ARC II) is used to establish the AMC I *CN* = 67 and the AMC III *CN* = 93. Using Equation 8.4 for these *CN* values gives

$$Q_I = \frac{\left(3.5 - \dfrac{200}{67} + 2\right)^2}{\left(3.5 + \dfrac{800}{67} - 8\right)} = 0.85 \text{ in}$$

$$Q_{III} = \frac{\left(3.5 - \dfrac{200}{93} + 2\right)^2}{\left(3.5 + \dfrac{800}{93} - 8\right)} = 2.73 \text{ in}$$

The runoff model suggests that the effect of AMC can vary the total runoff volume from 0.85 inches to 2.73 inches for the 10-acre site. This is a range of 1.88 inches, which is a wide range when compared to the average moisture condition runoff of 1.86 inches.

8.2.5 Impervious Areas and Unconnected Impervious Areas

The *CN* values for urban and residential districts listed in Table 8.3 were computed by performing a simple area based weighting of pervious and impervious areas. Each land use is assumed to contain a specific percentage of impervious cover directly connected to a storm drain system. The pervious area is assumed to have a CN_p value equal to open space in good hydrologic condition and the impervious area is assumed to have a *CN* value of paved parking lots, roofs, and driveways (98 for all HSGs). The composite CN_c calculation for urban land uses that have different percent impervious can be easily computed using the equation

$$CN_c = CN_p + f(98 - CN_p) \tag{8.5}$$

where CN_c = composite *CN*
CN_p = pervious *CN*
f = fraction of impervious area

Example 8.3 Determine the composite CN_c value for an urban land use that is 45 percent impervious and has a hydrologic soil group B.

Solution: From Table 8.3, the pervious *CN* for B soils is 61 (open space in good condition). Using Equation 8.5 gives

$$CN_c = 61 + 0.45(98 - 61) = 78$$

Graphically, the weighting method of Equation 8.5 is represented by Figure 8.3, which was first presented in the 1975 printing of TR-55 and retained in TR-55 1986. This graph can be used to verify all of the urban *CN* values associated with a percent impervious as presented in Table 8.3, or used to compute urban *CN* values for other impervious percentages.

A second graph related to *CN* and impervious cover, as shown in Figure 8.4, was proposed by the SCS in the 1986 TR-55 publication. The graph was established to give credit to stormwater designs that disconnected impervious areas from the stormwater drainage system. The idea behind disconnected impervious area is that runoff from impervious surfaces is directed to pervious surfaces that are essentially planar, causing the flow regime to be sheet flow and thus slowing the runoff. This gives the runoff significant opportunity to infiltrate into the ground through the pervious surface. The equation representing Figure 8.4 is

$$CN_c = CN_p + f(98 - CN_p)(1 - 0.5R) \tag{8.6}$$

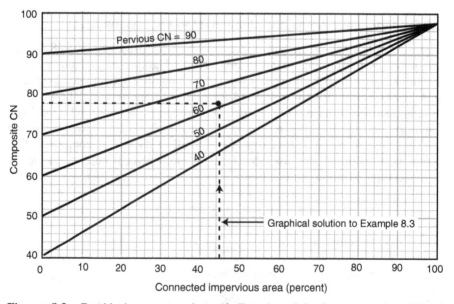

Figure 8.3 Graphical representation of Equation 8.5, for composite *CN* of impervious-pervious land-use mixture with all impervious surfaces directly connected to the storm drainage system (USDA SCS TR-55, 1986).

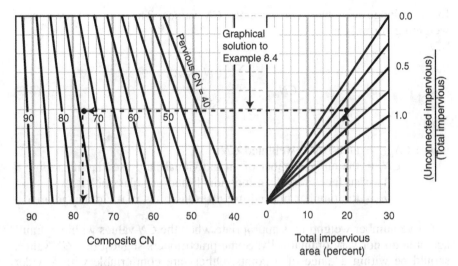

Figure 8.4 Graphical representation of Equation 8.6, for composite *CN* of impervious-pervious land use mixture, with total impervious surfaces less than 30%, not directly connected to the drainage system (USDA SCS TR-55, 1986).

where *R* is the ratio of unconnected impervious area to total impervious area. This adjustment can be made for cases where the impervious area is 30 percent or lower. This implies that for drainage areas with higher percentages of impervious cover, the effect of pervious cover on slowing or infiltrating surface runoff is not significant.

Example 8.4   Consider an urban land use that is 20 percent impervious and contains *C* soils. Approximately 50 percent of the impervious area is not directly connected to the site's storm drainage system. Determine the composite *CN* value for this land use.

Solution: From Table 8.3, the pervious *CN* for C soils is 74 (open space in good condition). Using Equation 8.6 gives

$$CN_c = 74 + 0.20(98 - 74)(1 - 0.5(0.50)) = 77.6$$

In this example, if the adjustment for disconnected impervious area was not taken, the *CN* value would have been 79. The graphical solution is shown by dashed lines in Figure 8.4. Other typical situations can provide a drop in *CN* in the range of 1 to 10 points.

8.2.6 Curve Number and Runoff Averaging

It is common for a drainage area to have more than one cover description. Therefore, it is routine practice to compute weighted average values of *CN* for a drainage area with two or more *CN* values. The standard area-based weighting formula is

$$CN_{avg} = \frac{\sum\limits_{i=1}^{n} (CN_i \times A_i)}{\sum\limits_{i=1}^{n} A_i} \tag{8.7}$$

where CN_{avg} = area-based weighted *CN*
CN_i = the curve number of an individual land use classification
A_i = surface area of an individual land use classification
n = the number of land-use classifications in the drainage area

Curve number weighting is appropriate when the *CN* values within a drainage area do not vary dramatically. Some practitioners suggest that *CN* values should be within a range of 5 points. Others are comfortable with a wider range, sometimes as wide as 12 to 15 points. Equation 8.4 clearly shows that *Q* varies in a nonlinear fashion with *CN*. Therefore, the wider the range of *CN* values incorporated into a weighted average, the less accurate will be the resulting *Q*.

Example 8.5 Using a weighted *CN*, determine the runoff depth for a rainfall of 4.2 inches, antecedent moisture condition II, for a 62-acre site comprised of four land-use and soil-group combinations, as shown in the following table.

Cover Description	Soil Group	Area (acres)
Wooded, good condition	B	15.5
Wooded, good condition	C	13.9
Meadow, good condition	B	14.2
Meadow, good condition	C	18.4

Solution: From Table 8.3, values of *CN* are determined to be 55, 70, 58, and 71, respectively, for each cover description. Using Equation 8.7, the weighted *CN* is determined.

$$CN_{avg} = \frac{(55 \times 15.5) + (70 \times 13.9) + (58 \times 14.2) + (71 \times 18.4)}{62} = 63.8$$

And thus *Q* is computed as

$$Q = \frac{\left(4.2 - \dfrac{200}{63.8} + 2\right)^2}{\left(4.2 + \dfrac{800}{63.8} - 8\right)} = 1.075 \text{ in}$$

Example 8.5 contains *CN* values in a single drainage area that vary within a range of 16 points (55 to 71). Computing runoff depth for each cover description, then computing the area-based average of runoff, will give a more accurate estimate.

Example 8.6 For the data provided in Example 8.5, determine the site runoff depth by computing runoff depths for each cover description, and then determining an area-based average runoff depth.

Solution: Using Equation 8.4, the runoff depths are determined for each cover description.

Cover Description	Soil Group	Area (acres)	*CN*	*Q*
Wooded, good condition	B	15.5	55	0.612
Wooded, good condition	C	13.9	70	1.465
Meadow, good condition	B	14.2	58	0.758
Meadow, good condition	C	18.4	71	1.533

The area-based average value of *Q* is

$$Q = \frac{(0.612 \times 15.5) + (1.465 \times 13.9) + (0.758 \times 14.2) + (1.533 \times 18.4)}{62}$$

$$Q = 1.110 \text{ in}$$

Example 8.6 shows one case where, using *CN* values ranging in 16 points, the *CN* averaging method provides essentially the same direct runoff result as the *Q* averaging method (3.2 percent difference). Examination of Equation 8.4 and Figure 8.1 implies that differences in *Q* estimates will increase as precipitation gets smaller. Computations of *Q* for storms ranging from 4 inches to 1.5 inches, using the two methods are summarized in Table 8.6. The results show an increase in discrepancy as rainfall decreases.

TABLE 8.6 Disparities between *CN* Averaging versus *Q* Averaging for Estimating Runoff from Varying Rainfall Depth for Example 8.6

P (inches)	*Q* (inches)		% difference
	CN averaging	*Q* averaging	
4.0	0.961	0.997	3.5
3.5	0.696	0.732	4.9
3.0	0.461	0.497	7.2
2.5	0.265	0.299	11.4
2.0	0.114	0.146	21.4
1.5	0.022	0.049	54.5

8.2.7   Runoff Equation Development

If one is to use a set of equations, it is a good idea to know how the equations were developed. In a complete rainfall-runoff event, it is known that runoff begins some time after rainfall begins. The delay is attributed to losses caused by initial abstractions. The SCS started the development of Equation 8.1 with a simplified rainfall event where rainfall and runoff begin at the same time. This simplified storm removes the need to be concerned about the initial losses of the early portion of the event where the initial abstraction of rainfall occurs (rainfall with no runoff). To create the simplified event, the initial abstraction, I_a, is subtracted from the total rainfall to create the term $P - I_a$, which is rainfall while runoff occurs. In this simple event, it is assumed that the ratio of rainfall losses during runoff (F) to potential maximum retention (S), is the same as the ratio of direct runoff (Q) to precipitation while runoff occurs ($P - I_a$). In equation form, this relation is

$$\frac{F}{S} = \frac{Q}{P - I_a} \tag{8.8}$$

A second assumption is based on conservation of mass. The hydrologic budget equation, in its classical surface hydrology form can be expressed as

$$P - I - R - E - T = \Delta S_w \tag{8.9}$$

where P = precipitation (in)
  I = infiltration (in)
  R = runoff (in)
  E = evaporation (in)
  T = transpiration (in)
  ΔS_w = change in watershed storage (in)

The terms are all expressed in inches, which really imply volumes. Watershed storage, S_w, is a combination of surface depression storage (small-scale surface undulations capturing and storing water for short periods of time) and surface water storage (streams, ponds, and lakes).

The SCS simplified this hydrologic budget equation by assuming that inflow (precipitation or rainfall) is transformed into three outflow components; direct runoff, Q, which is equivalent to R in Equation 8.9, infiltration during runoff, F, sometimes also called actual retention which is a portion of I in Equation 8.9, and initial abstraction, I_a, which includes E, T, the remaining portion of I, and part of ΔS_w in Equation 8.9. The conversion of rainfall into these three components is graphically represented in Figure 8.5.

With these assumptions, Equation 8.9 is transformed into

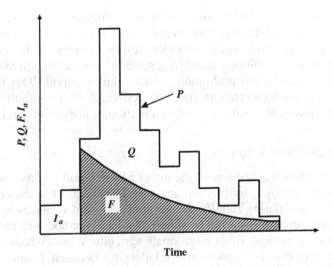

Figure 8.5   Graphic representation of the SCS simplified hydrologic budget transforming precipitation (P) into initial abstraction (I_a), infiltration during runoff (F), and direct runoff (Q) (USDA NRCS NEH 630, 2002).

$$P - I_a - Q - F = 0 \tag{8.10}$$

which is rearranged as

$$F = P - I_a - Q \tag{8.11}$$

Substituting Equation 8.11 into 8.8 gives

$$\frac{P - I_a - Q}{S} = \frac{Q}{P - I_a} \tag{8.12}$$

Solving for Q gives

$$Q = \frac{(P - I_a)^2}{(P - I_a + S)} \tag{8.1}$$

The parameters of Q and P are pretty easy to understand and are left with no further explanation. More explanation of S and I_a is helpful.

8.2.8   Potential Maximum Retention

The potential maximum retention S represents the potential maximum amount of water that the watershed can store (retain) *after* runoff begins. It consists

mainly of infiltration and is affected by soil infiltration capacity, which is
controlled by one of three factors: infiltration at the soil surface, water trans-
mission rate in the soil profile, or water storage capacity of the soil. A wet
antecedent runoff condition caused by a series of storms prior to the modeled
event will affect the soil infiltration capacity during runoff. This is because
the soil may not have enough time to recover to its pre-runoff condition
through the physical mechanisms of evaporation, transpiration, and drainage.

8.2.9 Initial Abstraction

Initial abstraction is defined as all the losses before runoff begins, and consists
mainly of interception, infiltration, and surface storage. It is the counterpart
to F, total losses during runoff, and the sum of I_a and F makes up the total
rainfall losses during a storm. To simplify the CN method and the determination of I_a, empirical studies on small agricultural watersheds were performed to establish an approximate relationship between I_a and maximum
potential retention, S. A subset of the original data to determine this relationship is plotted in Figure 8.6. The data subset was chosen to simply show the
range of data points accumulated in the study. From this data, Equation 8.2

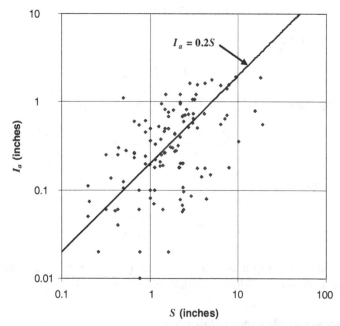

Figure 8.6 Relationship of I_a and S. Plotted points are a subset of the original data
derived from experimental watershed data (adapted from USDA NRCS NEH 630,
2002).

was established, stating that initial abstraction is 20 percent of potential maximum retention.

Equation 8.2 was not a least squares fit of the data. There has been recent discussion among hydrologists suggesting a change in the relation to $I_a = 0.05\ S$. The suggestion comes from a more analytical evaluation of the original data. However, CN values as presented in the majority of the literature were developed based upon the assumption that initial abstraction is 20 percent of the potential maximum retention. Using something other than Equation 8.2 to compute initial abstraction would require the development of new CN values based on the new I_a relation. Such a change may make the model more appropriate, but the potential for confusion in using correct CN values is a significant concern. Presently in professional practice, it is not recommended that a relation other than Equation 8.2 be used.

8.3 NRCS GRAPHICAL PEAK DISCHARGE METHOD

The SCS developed a peak flow method that was introduced in TR-55 (USDA, 1975) and later improved in the 1986 update of the same publication. The method uses unit discharge graphs and a peak flow equation. The graphs are shown in Figures 8.7 through 8.10 and were developed from hydrograph analyses using the NRCS computer program TR-20. This computer program is based on the NRCS unit hydrograph method for runoff modeling, which will be discussed in Chapter 9. The graphs are used to determine peak discharges for a one-square-mile watershed with one inch of runoff, thus the reason they are called "unit" discharges. The discharges are expressed in the units of cubic feet per second, per square mile, per inch, abbreviated as csm/in. The unit discharges are modified to fit a given site and runoff event by multiplying them by drainage area and runoff depth.

8.3.1 Equation and Parameters

The peak discharge equation is

$$q_p = q_u A_m Q F_p \qquad (8.13)$$

where q_p = peak discharge (ft^3/s)
  q_u = unit peak discharge (csm/in)
  A_m = watershed drainage area (mi^2)
  Q = runoff depth (in)
  F_p = pond or swamp adjustment factor

The following parameters must be determined to use the method: (1) drainage area, (2) time of concentration, (3) NRCS rainfall distribution, (4) 24-

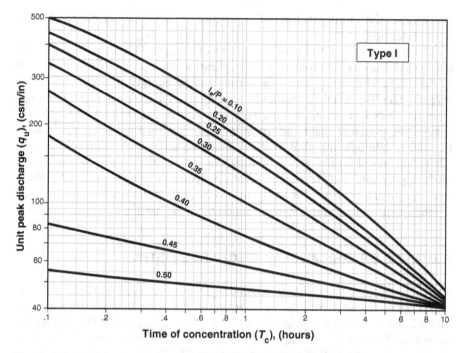

Figure 8.7 Unit peak discharge (q_u) for NRCS type I rainfall (USDA SCS TR-55, 1986).

hour rainfall depth in inches, (5) curve number, and (6) the percentage of watershed that is covered with ponds or swamp. Time of concentration is typically computed using the NRCS segmental approach, but any method discussed in Chapter 7 could be used if deemed appropriate. The NRCS rainfall distribution is determined using Figure 6.8. The 24-hour rainfall depth is best determined by using NOAA Atlas 14 or the best available data provided on the NOAA Web site, as discussed in Chapter 6. The curve number is determined using methods presented in Section 8.2.3 through 8.2.6.

8.3.2 Graphs and I_a/P Ratio

To select the correct curve on the graphs, the ratio of I_a/P must be determined. This ratio represents the fraction of the storm rainfall lost to initial abstraction before runoff begins. With a known CN and design rainfall P, the ratio is computed as

$$\frac{I_a}{P} = \frac{0.2}{P}\left(\frac{1000}{CN} - 10\right) \tag{8.14}$$

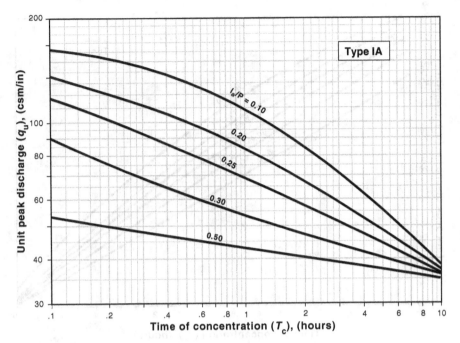

Figure 8.8 Unit peak discharge (q_u) for NRCS type IA rainfall (USDA SCS TR-55, 1986).

Instead of using Equation 8.14, the ratio can be determined by using the values in Table 8.7. Note from the table that if I_a/P is greater than 0.5, then 0.5 must be used, and if I_a/P is less than 0.1, then 0.1 must be used. This reflects a limitation of the method and shows that extrapolation beyond the limit of the upper or lower bound is not recommended. Interpolation between I_a/P curves in Figures 8.7 through 8.10 is acceptable.

If there are swamps or ponds spread throughout the watershed, and the time of concentration path does not pass through a significant portion of the swamp or pond area, then an adjustment factor is used to reduce the peak flow. The pond and swamp adjustment factor is shown in Table 8.8. Significant amounts of pond water will increase the runoff response time of a watershed. These adjustment factors attempt to reflect this delay.

8.3.3 Limitations

To use the graphical peak method, the watershed must be homogeneous and represented by one curve number. This means that CN weighting is acceptable as long as the variation in CN values is around 5 to 10 units. Additionally, CN should be greater than 40. The design rainfall must be a 24-hour event that follows one of the four NRCS rainfall distributions (I, IA, II, or III). The

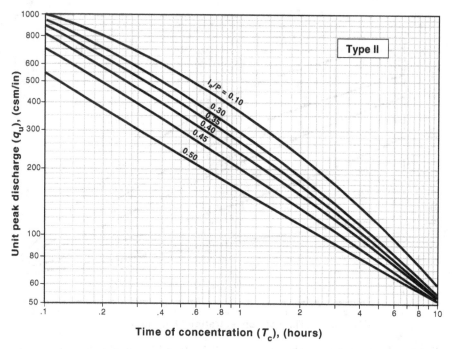

Figure 8.9 Unit peak discharge (q_u) for NRCS type II rainfall (USDA SCS TR-55, 1986).

watershed should have only one main stream channel. If it has more than one, then the travel time in each channel to the watershed outlet should be very similar. The F_p factor can be used only for swamp and pond areas outside the main stream channel. The graphs limit the method in two ways. First, the ratio of I_a/P must be greater than 0.1 and less than 0.5 (see Table 8.7). Second, the value of t_c must be greater than 0.1 hours and less than 10 hours.

Example 8.7 The Simms Pond watershed of Figure 8.11 contains 1350 acres of rural drainage area in Pennsylvania. The site is 65 percent wooded in good condition, 31 percent meadow in good condition, and 4 percent rural residential. All watershed soils are classified as HSG group C. The watershed has an average surface slope of 0.048 percent and the main drainage path is 13,100 feet in length. The watershed is free of significant pond or swamp area, and its location is approximately 41° 20′ 00″ N and 76° 02′ 30″ W. Use the NRCS graphical peak discharge method to determine the peak discharge from the watershed for the 2-, 10-, and 25-year events.

Solution: The steps for solution include determining design rainfall, curve number, time of concentration, and peak flow.

Using Atlas 14 (*http://www.nws.noaa.gov/ohd/hdsc/*) for latitude 41.3333°, longitude −76.0417°, the 2-, 10-, and 25-year, 24-hour rainfall

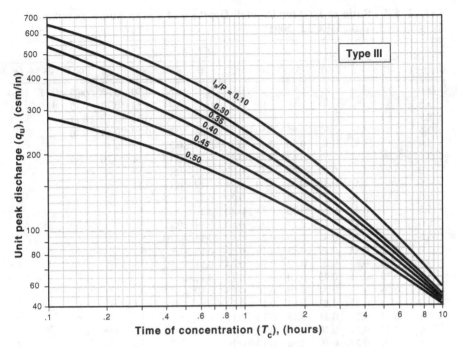

Figure 8.10 Unit peak discharge (q_u) for NRCS type III rainfall (USDA SCS TR-55, 1986).

depths are found to be 2.83, 4.09, and 5.00 inches, respectively. The watershed is located in a Type II rainfall region, as shown in Figure 6.8.

Curve number weighting is used to get an average watershed curve number. CN values are taken from Table 8.3. The residential land use is assumed to have 2-acre lots on the average. Calculations are shown in the following table. As a matter of standard practice, the weighted CN is rounded to the nearest whole unit.

Land use	Condition	HSG	CN	Area Fraction	$CN \times$ Area Fraction
Wooded	good	C	70	0.65	45.50
Meadow	good	C	71	0.31	22.01
Residential	good	C	77	0.04	3.08
Total/average			71	1.00	70.59

Since the watershed is nonurban, relatively homogeneous, and under 2,000 acres, the NRCS Lag equation is chosen as a reasonable time of concentration method.

TABLE 8.7   Ratio of I_a/P for Rainfall Depths and Curve Numbers (adapted from Brown et al., HEC22, 2001)

Rainfall (inches)	CN 40	45	50	55	60	65	70	75	80	85	90	95	98
1.0	1	1	1	1	1	1	1	0.50	0.50	0.35	0.22	0.11	0.10
1.5	1	1	1	1	1	1	0.50	0.44	0.33	0.24	0.15	0.10	2
2.0	1	1	1	1	1	0.50	0.43	0.33	0.25	0.18	0.11	2	2
2.5	1	1	1	1	0.50	0.43	0.34	0.27	0.20	0.14	0.10	2	2
3.0	1	1	1	0.50	0.44	0.36	0.29	0.22	0.17	0.12	2	2	2
3.5	1	1	1	0.47	0.38	0.31	0.24	0.19	0.14	0.10	2	2	2
4.0	1	1	0.50	0.41	0.33	0.27	0.21	0.17	0.13	2	2	2	2
4.5	1	0.50	0.44	0.36	0.30	0.24	0.19	0.15	0.11	2	2	2	2
5.0	1	0.49	0.40	0.33	0.27	0.22	0.17	0.13	0.10	2	2	2	2
5.5	1	0.44	0.36	0.30	0.24	0.20	0.16	0.12	2	2	2	2	2
6.0	0.50	0.41	0.33	0.27	0.22	0.18	0.14	0.11	2	2	2	2	2
6.5	0.46	0.38	0.31	0.25	0.21	0.17	0.13	0.10	2	2	2	2	2
7.0	0.43	0.35	0.29	0.23	0.19	0.15	0.12	2	2	2	2	2	2
7.5	0.40	0.33	0.27	0.22	0.18	0.14	0.11	2	2	2	2	2	2
8.0	0.38	0.31	0.25	0.20	0.17	0.13	0.11	2	2	2	2	2	2
8.5	0.35	0.29	0.24	0.19	0.16	0.13	0.10	2	2	2	2	2	2
9.0	0.33	0.27	0.22	0.18	0.15	0.12	2	2	2	2	2	2	2
9.5	0.32	0.26	0.21	0.17	0.14	0.11	2	2	2	2	2	2	2
10.0	0.30	0.24	0.20	0.16	0.13	0.11	2	2	2	2	2	2	2
10.5	0.29	0.23	0.19	0.16	0.13	0.10	2	2	2	2	2	2	2
11.0	0.27	0.22	0.18	0.15	0.12	2	2	2	2	2	2	2	2
11.5	0.26	0.21	0.17	0.14	0.12	2	2	2	2	2	2	2	2
12.0	0.25	0.20	0.17	0.14	0.11	2	2	2	2	2	2	2	2
12.5	0.24	0.20	0.16	0.13	0.11	2	2	2	2	2	2	2	2
13.0	0.23	0.19	0.15	0.13	0.10	2	2	2	2	2	2	2	2
13.5	0.22	0.18	0.15	0.12	2	2	2	2	2	2	2	2	2
14.0	0.21	0.17	0.14	0.12	2	2	2	2	2	2	2	2	2
14.5	0.21	0.17	0.14	0.11	2	2	2	2	2	2	2	2	2
15.0	0.20	0.16	0.13	0.11	2	2	2	2	2	2	2	2	2
15.5	0.19	0.16	0.13	0.11	2	2	2	2	2	2	2	2	2
16.0	0.19	0.15	0.13	0.10	2	2	2	2	2	2	2	2	2

[1] The ratio of I_a/P is greater than 0.5; therefore, use 0.5.
[2] The ratio of I_a/P is less than 0.1; therefore, use 0.1.

$$t_c = \frac{L^{0.8}\left[\dfrac{1000}{CN} - 9\right]^{0.7}}{190\, S^{0.5}} = \frac{(13,100)^{0.8}\left[\dfrac{1000}{71} - 9\right]^{0.7}}{190\,(0.048)^{0.5}}$$

$$t_c = 148 \text{ minutes} = 2.46 \text{ hours}$$

Values of I_a/P and Q are determined using Equations 8.14 and 8.4, respectively. For the 2-year event:

TABLE 8.8 Adjustment Factor for Pond and Swamp Areas for the NRCS Graphical Peak Method (USDA SCS TR-55, 1986)

Percentage of Pond and Swamp Areas	F_p
0	1.00
0.2	0.97
1.0	0.87
3.0	0.75
5.0	0.72

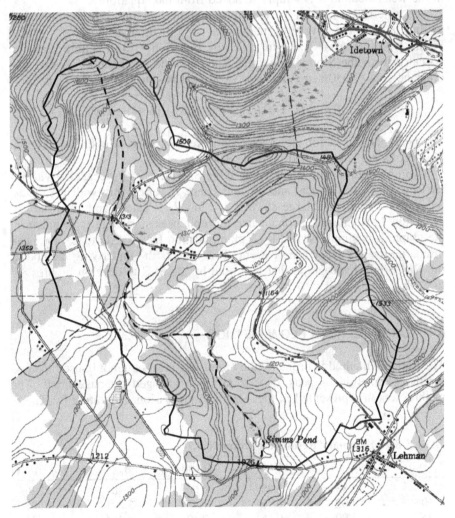

Figure 8.11 Simms Pond watershed of Example 8.7.

$$\frac{I_a}{P} = \frac{0.2}{P}\left(\frac{1000}{CN} - 10\right) = \frac{0.2}{2.83}\left(\frac{1000}{71} - 10\right) = 0.29$$

$$Q = \frac{\left(P - \frac{200}{CN} + 2\right)^2}{\left(P + \frac{800}{CN} - 8\right)} = \frac{\left(2.83 - \frac{200}{71} + 2\right)^2}{\left(2.83 + \frac{800}{71} - 8\right)} = 0.66 \text{ in}$$

The watershed pond factor is 1.0 because there is no significant swamp area in the watershed, so it is simply removed from the equation.

The watershed is in a Type II rainfall region; therefore, Figure 8.9 is used to find q_u. For the 2-year event, with $t_c = 2.46$ hours, and $I_a/P = 0.29$, Figure 8.9 gives $q_u = 165$ csm/in. Using Equation 8.13, this unit discharge is scaled to fit the Simms Pond watershed and the 2-year runoff event. The drainage area (1,350 acres) must be expressed in square miles (2.11 mi²).

$$q_p = q_u A_m Q F_p = (165)(2.11)(0.66)(1.0) = 230 \text{ ft}^3/\text{s}$$

The peak discharges for the other events are computed in a similar fashion. The results are summarized in Table 8.9.

Two observations are made from Table 8.9. First, I_a/P decreases with increasing P. This is logical and obvious, since I_a varies only with CN. Thus, for a given watershed, large storms give low I_a/P values and small storms give high I_a/P values. Second, once the unit peak discharge is found from the graph, it is simply scaled by a multiplication factor $A_m Q$ to get the peak discharge for any other runoff event. This reflects the underlying method of the NRCS unit hydrograph that was used by the SCS to develop Figures 8.7 through 8.10.

8.4 RATIONAL PEAK FLOW METHOD

The Rational method is probably the oldest and most commonly used method for the calculation of peak flow from small ungaged drainage areas. The method was first presented in the American professional literature by Kuich-

TABLE 8.9 Summary Results for Example 8.7

T_r (yrs)	P (in)	I_a/P	Q (in)	$A_m Q$	q_p (ft³/s)
2	2.83	0.29	0.66	1.402	230
10	4.09	0.20	1.45	3.071	505
25	5.00	0.16	2.12	4.464	734

ling (1889) as a method for estimating peak runoff in sewers in Rochester, New York. In the United Kingdom, the method is often referred to as the Lloyd-Davies method after a paper presented by Lloyd-Davies in 1906.

8.4.1 Formula and Methodology

In its most common form, the Rational formula is given as

$$q_p = CiA \qquad (8.15)$$

where q_p = peak flow (ft^3/s)
C = runoff coefficient
i = rainfall intensity (in/hr)
A = drainage area (ac)

The assumptions in the Rational formula are as follows:

- *The rainfall intensity is uniform over the watershed.* For small catchments this is a reasonable assumption. This assumption becomes more questionable as the drainage area increases in size. Therefore, it is often suggested that use of the formula be restricted to small watersheds. There is little agreement on a numerical value to define a small watershed size limit. The limit varies widely from one expert to the next, ranging from 20 acres for the very conservative, to a few square miles for the most liberal. In practical terms, a drainage area size of 100 acres is probably a good compromise.
- *The duration of the design rainfall intensity is equal to the time of concentration of the drainage area.* This condition supports the idea that the peak flow occurs when the entire watershed is contributing runoff to the drainage area outlet.
- *The return period of the peak flow is equal to the return period of the rainfall intensity.* In other words, the *n*-year rainfall intensity, *i*, is assumed to produce the *n*-year flood. This assumption is not necessarily true, particularly for catchments that are undeveloped and highly pervious. Runoff is affected by the prestorm conditions of soil moisture and storage. As the amount of pervious area is decreased, the effect of prestorm conditions on rainfall abstractions and rainfall excess becomes less pronounced. Therefore, the rational formula will give better results for catchments with larger impervious areas.

At first glance, the units in the formula appear to be dimensionally non-homogeneous. However, analysis of the right side units shows that one ac-in/hr is equal to 1.008 ft^3/s, as follows:

$$(ac)\left(\frac{in}{hr}\right) \times \left(\frac{43{,}560 \text{ ft}^2}{ac}\right) \times \left(\frac{ft}{12 \text{ in}}\right) \times \left(\frac{hr}{3600 \text{ s}}\right) = 1.008 \frac{\text{ft}^3}{\text{s}}$$

The unit conversion coefficient of 1.008 is sufficiently close to 1.0 that it is dropped from Equation 8.15 and the units of ft^3/s are retained.

The rainfall intensity is defined by a storm duration equal to the time of concentration of the drainage area. This criteria establishes a condition of equilibrium where all points in the watershed are contributing runoff to the watershed outlet, thus establishing flow at the outlet that is a maximum value for the given rainfall intensity. The rainfall intensity is typically obtained from IDF curves for the region—an example of which is shown in Figure 6.5. NOAA Atlas 14 data (see Chapter 6) is also reasonable IDF information, however, interpolation between tabulated intensities to obtain an estimated intensity for the required storm duration may be required.

The runoff coefficient, C, is a number between 0 and 1 that reflects the ability of the drainage area to convert rainfall to runoff. The coefficient was originally considered to be a function of ground cover only, independent of rainfall intensity and other watershed factors. Some typical values of C based on a land-use description are given in Table 8.10, as provided by ASCE (1992).

The values of C provided in Table 8.10 are difficult to apply with consistency since they are given as a relatively broad range for each land use. The common recommendation for selection of a C value from tables like Table 8.10 is to use the mid-value of the range, unless there is strong data to suggest otherwise. In reality, C is a composite runoff factor representing the combined effect of ground cover, soil type, soil moisture condition, surface slope, rainfall intensity, storm return period, and other hydrologic factors. Rawls et al. (1981) tried to remove some of the uncertainty in selecting C by providing a set of values that are based on NRCS hydrologic soil group, average surface slope, and storm return period. These values are summarized in Table 8.11.

8.4.2 Nonhomogeneous Areas

Should the drainage area contain varying amounts of different land use, the runoff coefficients can be determined for individual land use areas, and a weighted runoff coefficient for the entire basin can be computed as

$$C_w = \frac{\Sigma C_i A_i}{\Sigma A_i} \tag{8.16}$$

where C_w = weighted runoff coefficient
C_i = runoff coefficient of each individual land use
A_i = drainage area of each individual land use

TABLE 8.10   Rational Formula Runoff Coefficients (adapted from ASCE, 1992)

Description	Coefficient*
Composite areas by land use	
Unimproved	0.10–0.30
Parks, cemeteries	0.10–0.25
Playgrounds	0.20–0.35
Railroad yards	0.20–0.35
Residential	
Suburban	0.25–0.40
Single family	0.30–0.50
Multiunits detached	0.40–0.60
Apartment	0.50–0.75
Multiunits attached	0.60–0.75
Industrial	
Light	0.50–0.80
Heavy	0.60–0.90
Business	
Neighborhood	0.50–0.70
Downtown	0.70–0.95
Homogeneous areas	
Lawns, sandy soil	
Flat (2%)	0.05–0.10
Average (2 to 7%)	0.10–0.15
Steep (>7%)	0.15–0.20
Lawns, heavy soil	
Flat (2%)	0.13–0.17
Average (2 to 7%)	0.18–0.22
Steep (>7%)	0.25–0.35
Pavement	
Porous	0.05–0.10
Brick	0.70–0.85
Asphalt and concrete	0.70–0.95

*Range of C values presented are typical for return periods of 2 to 10 years. Higher values are appropriate for larger design storms.

Example 8.8.   The 62.7-acre watershed of Example 7.6 has a time of concentration of 19 minutes and is located in rainfall region 1 in Pennsylvania (Figure 6.5). The watershed is primarily undeveloped, with 10.5 acres in forest and the remainder in meadow. The underlying soil is classified as hydrologic soil group C and the average watershed slope is 5 percent. Determine the peak flow from this site for a 10-year runoff event using the Rational formula.

Solution: From Figure 6.5, the design rainfall intensity for a watershed in Pennsylvania rainfall region 1 with storm duration of 19 minutes is 2.7 in/hr.

TABLE 8.11 Rational Formula Runoff Coefficients Based on Soil Type, Surface Slope, and Return Period (Rawls et al. 1981)

Hydrologic Soil Group and Average Surface Slope

Values shown as [a]/[b], where the first value applies to storm-recurrence intervals less than 25 years and the second to intervals of 25 years or longer.

Land Use	A 0–2%	A 2–6%	A 6%+	B 0–2%	B 2–6%	B 6%+	C 0–2%	C 2–6%	C 6%+	D 0–2%	D 2–6%	D 6%+
Forest	0.05/0.08	0.08/0.11	0.11/0.14	0.08/0.10	0.11/0.14	0.14/0.18	0.10/0.12	0.13/0.16	0.16/0.20	0.12/0.15	0.16/0.20	0.20/0.25
Open space	0.05/0.11	0.10/0.16	0.14/0.20	0.08/0.14	0.13/0.19	0.19/0.26	0.12/0.18	0.17/0.23	0.24/0.32	0.16/0.22	0.21/0.27	0.28/0.39
Cultivated	0.08/0.14	0.13/0.18	0.16/0.22	0.11/0.16	0.15/0.21	0.21/0.28	0.14/0.20	0.19/0.25	0.26/0.34	0.18/0.24	0.23/0.29	0.31/0.41
Meadow	0.10/0.14	0.16/0.22	0.25/0.30	0.14/0.20	0.22/0.28	0.30/0.37	0.20/0.26	0.28/0.35	0.36/0.44	0.24/0.30	0.30/0.40	0.40/0.50
Pasture	0.12/0.15	0.20/0.25	0.30/0.37	0.18/0.23	0.28/0.34	0.37/0.45	0.24/0.30	0.34/0.42	0.44/0.52	0.30/0.37	0.40/0.50	0.50/0.62
Residential 1 acre lot	0.14/0.22	0.19/0.26	0.22/0.29	0.17/0.24	0.21/0.28	0.26/0.34	0.20/0.28	0.25/0.32	0.31/0.40	0.24/0.31	0.29/0.35	0.35/0.46
Residential 1/2 acre lot	0.16/0.25	0.20/0.29	0.24/0.32	0.19/0.28	0.23/0.32	0.28/0.36	0.22/0.31	0.27/0.35	0.32/0.42	0.26/0.34	0.30/0.38	0.37/0.48
Residential 1/3 acre lot	0.19/0.28	0.23/0.32	0.26/0.35	0.22/0.30	0.26/0.35	0.30/0.39	0.25/0.33	0.29/0.38	0.34/0.45	0.28/0.36	0.32/0.40	0.39/0.50
Residential 1/4 acre lot	0.22/0.30	0.26/0.34	0.29/0.37	0.24/0.33	0.29/0.37	0.33/0.42	0.27/0.36	0.31/0.40	0.36/0.47	0.30/0.38	0.34/0.42	0.40/0.52
Residential 1/8 acre lot	0.25/0.33	0.28/0.37	0.31/0.40	0.27/0.35	0.30/0.39	0.35/0.44	0.30/0.38	0.33/0.42	0.38/0.49	0.33/0.41	0.36/0.45	0.42/0.54
Industrial	0.67/0.85	0.68/0.85	0.68/0.86	0.68/0.85	0.68/0.86	0.69/0.86	0.68/0.86	0.69/0.86	0.69/0.87	0.68/0.86	0.69/0.86	0.70/0.88
Streets	0.70/0.76	0.71/0.77	0.72/0.79	0.71/0.80	0.72/0.82	0.74/0.84	0.72/0.84	0.73/0.85	0.76/0.89	0.73/0.89	0.75/0.91	0.78/0.95
Commercial	0.71/0.88	0.71/0.88	0.72/0.79	0.72/0.89	0.72/0.89	0.72/0.89	0.72/0.89	0.72/0.89	0.72/0.90	0.72/0.89	0.72/0.89	0.72/0.90
Parking	0.85/0.95	0.86/0.96	0.87/0.97	0.85/0.95	0.86/0.96	0.87/0.97	0.85/0.95	0.86/0.96	0.87/0.97	0.85/0.95	0.86/0.96	0.87/0.97

[a] Runoff coefficients for storm-recurrence intervals less than 25 years
[b] Runoff coefficients for storm-recurrence intervals of 25 years or longer

From Table 8.11, with soil type C, surface slope 5 percent, and a 10-year event, the runoff coefficients for meadow and forest are 0.28 and 0.13, respectively. The weighted C value is

$$C_w = \frac{\Sigma\, C_i A_i}{\Sigma\, A_i} = \frac{(0.28 \times 52.5) + (0.13 \times 10.5)}{62.7} = 0.256$$

The peak runoff is computed as

$$q_p = CiA = (0.256)(2.7)(62.7) = 43 \text{ ft}^3/\text{s}$$

8.4.3 Peak Flows for Subareas

There are times in stormwater analysis where it is desirable to compute peak flows at various locations in the drainage network of a small watershed. Hydrograph analysis is typically used to perform such calculations. However, the Rational method can be used in place of hydrograph analysis for small drainage networks. For each point of interest in the watershed, the drainage area and associated time of concentration to the point of interest is used to compute the peak flow. For points of interest where drainage is collecting from two or more subareas, the longest time of concentration of these composite subareas is used to establish the rainfall intensity. A weighted runoff coefficient is computed, and the total drainage area of the combined subareas is used to compute the peak flow. The process is illustrated by example.

Example 8.9 A small urban drainage area is shown schematically in Figure 8.12. It is divided into three areas connected by a straight run of storm sewer. Drainage area characteristics are shown in Table 8.12. The associated storm sewer flow times are shown in Table 8.13. Use the Rational formula to compute peak flows to each inlet, and peak flow in pipes 1–2, 2–3, and 3–4. Use the 25-year event. Use Figure 6.5 as the IDF curves for the region.

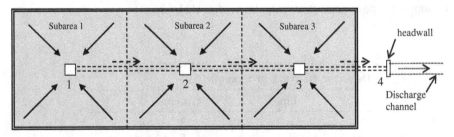

Figure 8.12   Drainage area of Example 8.9.

TABLE 8.12   Subarea Characteristics for the Drainage Area of Example 8.9

Subarea	Area (ac)	C	t_c (min)
1	5.8	0.25	11
2	6.1	0.40	12
3	5.5	0.85	6

Solution: The peak flows to each inlet in the watershed can be simply computed by applying the Rational formula for each area. The drainage area to inlet 1 is 5.8 acres, with a C value of 0.25. The rainfall intensity associated with a storm duration of 11 minutes for the 25-year event is taken from Figure 6.5 as 4.1 in/hr. The peak flow to inlet 1 is

$$q_{p(1)} = CiA = (0.25)(4.1)(5.8) = 5.9 \text{ ft}^3/\text{s}$$

Peak flows to the other two inlets are computed in a similar fashion. The design rainfall intensities for storm durations of 12 and 6 minutes are read from Figure 6.5 to yield values of 4.0 and 5.1, respectively. Peak flows for each inlet are computed using the Rational formula and the results for all three inlets are summarized as follows.

Inlet	Area (ac)	C	t_c (min)	Intensity (in/hr)	Peak Flow ft^3/s
1	5.8	0.25	11	4.1	5.9
2	6.1	0.40	12	4.0	9.8
3	5.5	0.85	6	5.1	23.8

The inlets can be sized based on these flows. However, summing of these flows for sizing of the pipes is not recommended. Instead, the drainage area, associated time of concentration, and weighted C value should be determined to support a new peak-flow calculation for each pipe.

TABLE 8.13   Storm Sewer Characteristics for Drainage Network of Example 8.9

Pipe	t_t (min)
1–2	3
2–3	5
3–4	2

The peak flow for pipe 1–2 is identical to the peak flow for inlet 1 since there is no change in drainage area contributing flow to the pipe.

The drainage area to pipe 2–3 includes the drainage area to inlet 2 and the drainage area to inlet 1, which equals 11.9 acres. The weighted C value for this drainage area is

$$C_{w(2-3)} = \frac{\Sigma\, C_i A_i}{\Sigma\, A_i} = \frac{(0.25 \times 5.8) + (0.40 \times 6.1)}{11.9} = 0.327$$

The time of concentration to pipe 2–3 is the larger of two values: (1) time of concentration of subarea 2 (12 min) or (2) time of concentration of subarea 1 plus the pipe travel time from inlet 1 to inlet 2 (11 + 3 = 14 min). The latter controls, so the rainfall intensity of duration 14 minutes is read from Figure 6.5 to be 3.6 in/hr. The peak flow to inlet 2 becomes

$$q_{p(2-3)} = CiA = (0.327)(3.6)(11.9) = 14.0 \text{ ft}^3/\text{s}$$

The drainage area to pipe 3–4 includes subareas 1, 2, and 3 and equals 17.4 acres. The weighted C value for this drainage area is

$$C_{w(3-4)} = \frac{\Sigma\, C_i A_i}{\Sigma\, A_i} = \frac{(0.25 \times 5.8) + (0.40 \times 6.1) + (0.85 \times 5.5)}{17.4} = 0.492$$

The time of concentration to pipe 3–4 is the larger of three values: (1) time of concentration of subarea 3 (6 min), (2) time of concentration of subarea 2 plus the travel time of pipe 2–3 (12 + 5 = 17 min), or (3) time of concentration of subarea 1 plus the travel time of pipes 1–2 and 2–3 (11 + 3 + 5 = 19 min). The third time controls, so the rainfall intensity of duration 19 minutes is read from Figure 6.5 and found to be 2.8 in/hr. The peak flow to pipe 3–4 becomes

$$q_{p(3-4)} = CiA = (0.492)(2.8)(17.4) = 24.0 \text{ ft}^3/\text{s}$$

As a point of comparison, the sum of the three independently computed inlet peak flows (5.9 + 9.8 + 23.8 = 39.5 ft³/s) exceeds the peak flow computed for the composite drainage area draining to pipe 3–4 (24.0 ft³/s). Again, the summing of peak flows from several independent subareas to create a peak flow for a composite area is not appropriate.

The composite method of subarea analysis using the Rational method is accepted as a reasonable approach to computing peak flows for design points in a watershed. It is believed to provide a reasonable level of protection with respect to flood risk for each design point. The method is logical, yet a better and probably more accurate methodology would be to use full hydrograph analysis procedures, as explained in Chapter 9.

PROBLEMS

8.1   A 44-acre site has a land use of 1-acre residential lots. The county soil survey document shows the site to be underlain by soils that are hydrologic soil type C. The hydrologic condition of the site is good. For a rainfall of 6.5 inches, estimate the total runoff in ac-ft caused by the event, assuming the pre-storm antecedent runoff condition is II.

8.2   An industrial park contains six commercial lots, each containing 22 acres. Seventy-five percent of the site is underlain by NRCS type C soils, while the remainder has type B. The site is in good hydrologic condition. For a rainfall of 4.35 inches, estimate the total runoff in ac-ft caused by the event, assuming the prestorm antecedent runoff condition is II.

8.3   Repeat Problem 8.2, except assume that the prestorm runoff condition is III.

8.4   Determine the composite *CN* value for an urban land use that is 52 percent impervious and has a hydrologic soil group B.

8.5   An urban drainage area is 30 percent impervious and contains B soils. Seventy-five percent of the impervious area is not directly connected to the site's storm drainage system. For a rainfall depth of 5 inches, determine the *CN* value and runoff depth for this land use by (a) taking into account the disconnected nature of the impervious area and (b) neglecting the effect of the disconnected nature of the impervious area.

8.6   Determine the runoff depth for a 24-hour, 10-year rainfall of 2.9 inches for antecedent runoff condition II, for a 245-acre site composed of the land use and soil group combinations in Table 8.14. Use the *CN* weighting method.

8.7   For the data provided in Problem 8.6, determine the runoff depth by computing runoff depths for each cover description, and then determine the area-based average runoff depth.

TABLE 8.14   Land Use Information for Problem 8.6

Cover Description	Soil Type	Area (ac)
Forest	A	37
Forest	B	109
Meadow	B	27
Commerical	C	21
Residential 0.5 acre lots	B	41
Residential 0.5 acre lots	C	9

TABLE 8.15 Subarea Characteristics for the Drainage Area of Problem 8.10

Subarea	Area (ac)	C	t_c (min)
1	13.1	0.4	10
2	6.5	0.2	9
3	9.2	0.6	7

8.8   A watershed contains 740 acres of drainage area. The site is 21 percent wooded in fair condition, 54 percent meadow in good condition, and 25 percent residential with average lot sizes of 2 acres. All watershed soils are classified as HSG group B. The watershed has an average surface slope of 0.024 percent and the main drainage path is 8700 feet in length. The watershed is free of significant pond or swamp area, and its location is approximately 38.285° N and 88.821° W. Use the NRCS graphical peak discharge method to determine the peak discharge from the watershed for the 2-, 10-, and 100-year events. Use the NRCS lag equation to compute the watershed time of concentration.

8.9   Use the Rational method to estimate the 25-year peak flow from a rectangular paved parking lot that is 310 feet by 1200 feet. The pavement is in average condition. The drainage path is overland flow on a paved surface for the 1,200 feet distance with a slope of 0.015 ft/ft. Use Figure 6.5 for the rainfall IDF information. Use the average velocity method to compute the time of concentration.

8.10 A small drainage area is shown schematically in Figure 8.12. It is divided into three areas connected by a straight run of storm sewer. Drainage area characteristics are shown in Table 8.15 and the associated storm sewer flow times are shown in Table 8.16. Use the Rational formula to compute peak flows to each inlet, and for pipes 1–2, 2–3, and 3–4. Use the 10-year event and Figure 6.5 as the IDF curves representing the region.

TABLE 8.16   Storm Sewer Characteristics for Drainage Network of Problem 8.10

Line	t_t (min)
1–2	5
2–3	2
3–4	3

REFERENCES

American Society of Civil Engineers. 1992. "Design and Construction of Urban Stormwater Management Systems." *Manual and Report of Engineering Practice 77*, New York.

Brakensiek, D. L., and W. J. Rawls. 1983. "Green-Ampt Infiltration Model Parameters for Hydrologic Classification of Soils." In J. Borrelli, V. R. Hasfurther, and R. D. Burman, eds., *Advances in Irrigation and Drainage Surviving External Pressures.* Proceedings of the American Society of Civil Engineers Specialty Conference, New York, p. 226–233.

Kuchling, E. 1889. "The Relation between the Rainfall and the Discharge of Sewers in Populous Districts." *ASCE Transactions,* 20: 1–56.

Lloyd-Davies, D. E. 1906. "The Elimination of Storm Water From Sewerage Systems." *Proceedings of the Institute of Civil Engineering,* 164: 41–67.

McCuen, R. H. 2005. *Hydrologic Analysis and Design,* 3rd ed. Upper Saddle River, NJ: Prentice-Hall.

Rallison, R. E. 1981. "Past, Present, and Future SCS Runoff Procedure," *Rainfall-Runoff Relationship: Proceedings of the International Symposium on Rainfall-Runoff Modeling.* V. J. Singh, ed. Mississippi State University, May 18–21, 1981.

Rawls, W. J., A. Shalaby, and R. H. McCuen. 1981. "Evaluation of Methods for Determining Urban Runoff Curve Numbers." *Transactions of the American Society of Agricultural Engineers,* 24(6): 1562–1566.

Rawls, W. J., S. L. Long, and R. H. McCuen. 1981. *Comparison of Urban Flood Frequency Procedures.* Preliminary draft report prepared for the Soil Conservation Service, Beltsville, Maryland.

Brown, S. A., S. M. Stein, and J. C. Warner. 2001. *Urban Drainage Design Manual,* HEC 22, 2nd ed., Federal Highway Administration, Report No. FHWA-NHI-01-021.

USDA NRCS. 2002. *National Engineering Handbook 630 Hydrology.* Washington, DC, *http://www.wcc.nrcs.usda.gov/hydro,* downloadable PDF file.

USDA NRCS. 2003. *Supplement to the New Jersey Bulletin,* No. NJ210-3-1. September 8, 2003.

USDA SCS. 1972. *Soil Survey of Luzerne County, Pennsylvania.*

USDA SCS. 1975. *Urban Hydrology for Small Watersheds,* Technical Release 55, Engineering Division, Washington, DC.

USDA SCS. 1986. *Urban Hydrology for Small Watersheds,* Technical Release 55, Engineering Division, Washington, DC.

CHAPTER 9

HYDROGRAPHS

9.1 INTRODUCTION

Many times in stormwater management analysis, runoff volumes or peak flow rates as described in Chapter 8 are not sufficient to meet the needs of the design. Instead, a hydrograph is required. A hydrograph is nothing more than a graphical plot of surface runoff flow against time. Hydrographs provide runoff rates, peak rate, runoff volume, and the time distribution of the runoff volume. With observed hydrographs and measured rainfall, watershed timing parameters such as time of concentration or lag can be estimated. For stormwater design, hydrographs are needed for routing surface runoff over the landscape and through stormwater-detention facilities. In very broad and general terms, there are four types of hydrographs: observed, synthetic, unit, and dimensionless unit.

Observed, or natural, hydrographs are those that are recorded by use of stream gages and flow records. Figure 9.1 shows an observed hydrograph for an experimental watershed in central Pennsylvania. The gage flow is in response to the rainfall, also recorded and plotted along with the hydrograph. This is the best hydrograph data because it directly reflects the response characteristics of the watershed.

However, very few watersheds are gaged, so *synthetic hydrographs* are used to simulate the response of ungaged watersheds to rainfall events. Synthetic hydrographs are created based on watershed and storm parameters.

Unit hydrographs are commonly used to create synthetic hydrographs. They are natural or synthetic hydrographs that contain a runoff volume equal

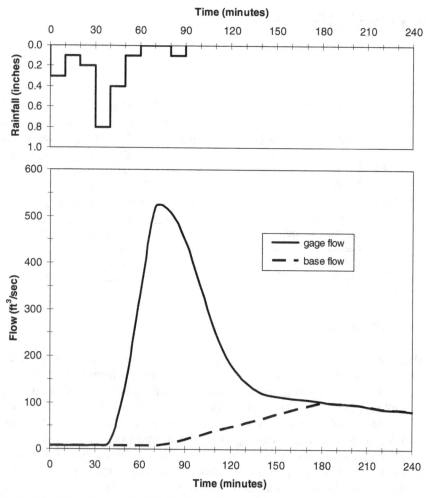

Figure 9.1   Gage flow and rainfall of June 23, 1976, in the Mahantango Experimental Watershed, WE38.

to one inch. They are for specific watersheds and specific unit durations. The unit graph is typically used for gaged watersheds when it is desirable to create synthetic runoff events of larger or smaller runoff volumes, and shorter or longer runoff durations.

Dimensionless unit hydrographs are special unit hydrographs that are transferable from one watershed to another as long as the watersheds are similar in hydrologic characteristics. They are also adjustable to different storm durations. They are commonly used for design purposes to create synthetic hydrographs for land development sites under several different storm conditions.

9.2 UNIT HYDROGRAPH CONCEPTS

The unit hydrograph is a tool used in watershed analysis to create hydrographs for ungaged watersheds. Two basic assumptions of the method are: (1) at any given time, surface runoff is proportional to rainfall excess, and (2) hydrograph shape as affected by time parameters remains constant.

The unit hydrograph has five primary characteristics:

1. It is associated with a specific watershed.
2. It contains one unit (inch or cm) of direct runoff.
3. It has an associated unit duration of rainfall excess.
4. The rainfall excess is generated uniformly over the watershed.
5. Rainfall excess is constant over the duration of the storm.

Unit duration is defined as an optimal duration for occurrence of rainfall excess. The NRCS suggests that unit duration can be estimated by evaluating runoff from a short-duration, high-intensity storm. From this data, unit duration is estimated to be about 20 percent of the time interval between the beginning of runoff and the peak runoff. There are more complex methods to estimate unit duration. However, for the purpose of this text, this simple method is adequate. Unit duration is different than storm duration. Storm duration is the actual duration of rainfall excess that varies from storm to storm.

Unit hydrographs can be created using a method called the *rainfall-excess reciprocal method*. This method requires an observed hydrograph, with associated observed rainfall, and watershed drainage area. The method starts with estimating rainfall excess (direct runoff) for the recorded runoff event. This is done by removing base flow from the stream-flow hydrograph. Base flow is that portion of stream flow that comes from groundwater. There are several methods available for base-flow separation; one such method is illustrated in Example 9.1. Once base flow is removed, the total runoff volume under the hydrograph is computed, which is declared rainfall excess for the associated rainfall event. The process is completed by taking the rainfall-excess hydrograph and converting it into a hydrograph containing one unit of runoff, dividing every ordinate in the rainfall-excess graph by the rainfall-excess total. This is the reciprocal part of the process. Example 9.1 is used to illustrate this method.

Example 9.1 The hydrograph of Figure 9.1 was observed at a stream-flow gage located at the outlet of experimental watershed WE38, which contains 1778 acres. The associated rainfall was also captured and totals 2.0 inches over a span of 90 minutes, with 70 percent of the rain falling during a period of 30 minutes. The storm is classified as a relatively short-duration, high-intensity storm. The watershed is a relatively even mix of agricultural and wooded land use. Using this rainfall-runoff data, create a unit hydrograph for the watershed and make an estimate of unit duration.

Solution: The data of Figure 9.1 is tabulated in Table 9.1. The first step in the solution is to remove base flow from the stream flow hydrograph to get

TABLE 9.1 Unit Hydrograph Calculation for WE38 Watershed Using the June 23, 1976, Runoff Event

Time (min)	Rainfall (in)	Stream Flow (ft³/s)	Base Flow (ft³/s)	Surface Runoff (ft³/s)	Unit Graph Time (min)	Unit Graph Flow (ft³/s)
0	0.0	7	7	0		
10	0.3	7	7	0		
20	0.1	7	7	0	0	0
30	0.2	8	7	1	10	4
40	0.8	15	7	8	20	32
50	0.4	131	7	124	30	478
60	0.1	331	7	324	40	1250
70	0.0	520	7	513	50	1979
80	0.0	510	11	499	60	1923
90	0.1	448	20	428	70	1648
100		350	29	321	80	1235
110		252	38	214	90	826
120		181	47	134	100	516
130		144	56	88	110	340
140		121	65	56	120	215
150		114	74	40	130	154
160		109	83	26	140	100
170		106	92	14	150	54
180		102	101	1	160	5
190		97	97	0	170	0
200	—	96	96	0		
Totals	2.0			0.2593*		1.000*

*These totals are expressed in inches. See Example 9.1 solution for conversion process.

a hydrograph that contains only runoff caused by the rainfall. A very simple method is used here. First, it is assumed that base flow is unaffected until the peak of the hydrograph occurs, at which point the base flow increases linearly to some point on the falling limb of the hydrograph, where it is assumed that stream flow returns to a condition where it is totally supplied by groundwater. In this case, judgment is used to establish this point at 101 ft^3/s.

Once base flow is removed, the hydrograph reflects total rainfall excess, which is all the rainfall that transformed into runoff. From the surface runoff hydrograph, the total volume of runoff in inches is computed, which is shown as 0.2593 inches in the table. This value is determined in four steps—(1) sum the surface runoff ordinates (2789 ft^3/s), (2) multiply the sum of surface runoff ordinates by the time step (600 seconds) to get total runoff volume in ft^3, (3) convert the total runoff volume to ac-in by changing ft^2 to acres (43,560 ft^2/acre) and feet to inches (12 in/ft), and (4) express the total runoff volume as a runoff depth by dividing it by watershed area (1778 acres). The summary calculation is

$$Q_{\text{total}} = \frac{(2789 \text{ ft}^3/\text{s})(600 \text{ s})(12 \text{ in/ft})}{(1778 \text{ acres})(43,560 \text{ ft}^2/\text{ac})} = 0.2593 \text{ in}$$

Thus, the surface runoff hydrograph in Table 9.1 contains 0.2593 inches of direct runoff. To create a similar hydrograph that contains 1.000 inch of direct runoff, the ordinates of the surface runoff graph are divided by 0.2593 inches, which results in the unit hydrograph.

Since the storm is relatively short (for all practical purposes, 60 minutes) with high intensities (4.8 in/hr and 2.4 in/hr for time steps 40 and 50 minutes), the unit duration is estimated using the NRCS 20 percent rule. The time to unit hydrograph peak is 50 minutes, and therefore unit duration, based on the observations of this single unit hydrograph is 0.2 × 50 = 10 minutes.

9.2.1 Application of the Unit Hydrograph

Once a unit hydrograph is developed, it can be used to create synthetic hydrographs for other rainfall events that create larger or smaller runoff amounts. The principle of invariance and superposition are used. These two principles, as related to unit hydrograph application, can be summarized as follows. A given distribution of rainfall over a watershed will create the same surface runoff hydrograph over and over again—that is, it does not vary. This invariance principle is assumed to be correct, yet field data show that it is not exactly true. However, if the rainfall excess duration is short, this principle is a reasonably good assumption. The second principle assumes that a given time distribution of rainfall excess can be used to build a surface runoff hydrograph by superimposing *unit-duration* runoff hydrographs generated from unit durations of rainfall excess. This method utilizes the principle of proportionality mentioned earlier, where hydrograph flows are assumed proportional to rainfall excess. The method is illustrated by example.

Example 9.2   Determine the surface runoff hydrograph for the WE38 watershed of Example 9.1, when it responds to the 100-year, 1-hour duration storm as determined by NOAA ATLAS 14. Use a central-peaking storm with a time step (unit duration) of 10 minutes. The average CN value for the watershed is 75. The watershed location is latitude 40.72° and longitude −76.55°.

Solution: A 100-yr, 1-hour design storm created for latitude 40.72° and longitude −76.55°, using ATLAS 14 data, is given in Example 6.5 and is shown in column (2) of Table 9.2. The time step is 10 minutes.

The curve number method is applied to this rainfall to create a time distribution of rainfall excess. To do so, it is necessary to transform the design storm of column (2) to cumulative rainfall by accumulating rainfall with time, as shown in column (3). This cumulative rainfall is then converted into cumulative runoff by applying the NRCS runoff method (Equation 8.4) to each cumulative rainfall amount, as shown in column (4). The first three values in this column are zero because the initial abstraction, I_a, is greater than the cumulative rainfall, P. Runoff begins at time interval 30 minutes and continues to the end of the event. A total of 0.651 inches of rainfall excess (runoff) results from this design storm. The cumulative runoff is then parsed out in increments of the rainfall time step (unit duration) as shown in column (5). This last column represents the time distribution of rainfall excess for the 100-yr, 1-hour design storm for watershed WE38. These are the rainfall-excess data that are used to create the synthetic runoff hydrograph.

TABLE 9.2   Incremental Runoff Calculations using the CN Method for Example 9.2

(1)	(2)	(3)	(4)	(5)
Time (min)	Design Storm (in)	Cumulative Rainfall (in)	Cumulative Runoff (in)	Incremental Runoff (in)
0	0.000	0.000	0.000	—
10	0.158	0.158	0.000	0.000
20	0.250	0.408	0.000	0.000
30	0.531	0.939	0.021	0.021
40	1.024	1.963	0.363	0.342
50	0.344	2.307	0.541	0.178
60	0.194	2.501	0.651	0.110
Totals	2.501	—	—	0.651

With the incremental runoff, unit-duration hydrographs are created for each incremental runoff depth. In this example, four unit-duration hydrographs are created as shown in Table 9.3. The mathematics of the convolution process is simple. Each rainfall-excess amount is used to create a synthetic runoff hydrograph by multiplying the watershed unit hydrograph ordinates by the rainfall excess. These synthetic hydrographs of unit duration must be oriented properly in time. Each synthetic hydrograph that creates runoff starts at a time equal to the rainfall excess time that generated the runoff. For example, the runoff values for Hyd(3) in Table 9.3 begin at 30 minutes. For Hyd(4), runoff ordinates begin at 40 minutes. Once the four unit-duration hydrographs are created and correctly superimposed over the time scale, they are added together along table rows to create the composite hydrograph in the last column. This is the synthetic surface runoff hydrograph of WE38 watershed for a 100-year, 1-hour duration design storm.

9.2.2 Dimensionless Unit Hydrograph

The unit hydrograph is for a single watershed and an associated unit duration of rainfall excess. Although very useful within the gaged watershed, it has little value to any other watershed. In stormwater design, the dimensionless unit hydrograph is used to create runoff hydrographs for ungaged watersheds, covering a wide range of sizes. To make a unit hydrograph dimensionless, the flow ordinates are divided by the peak flow, and the time ordinates are divided by the time to peak. To have a reasonably reliable dimensionless unit hydrograph, a large set of individual unit hydrographs derived from runoff events for watersheds of similar hydrologic response characteristics are analyzed and converted to make dimensionless unit hydrographs. The entire set of dimensionless unit hydrographs are then averaged to create a generalized dimensionless unit hydrograph. The resulting graph is used to create unit hydrographs for different watersheds of similar characteristics by multiplying the dimensionless time ratios by time to peak, and the dimensionless flow ratios by peak flow. Obviously, a method for computing time to peak and peak flow must also be a part of the method. The process for creating a dimensionless unit hydrograph is illustrated by example.

Example 9.3 Transform the unit hydrograph of Example 9.1 into a dimensionless unit hydrograph.

Solution: The unit hydrograph of Example 9.1 has a peak flow of 1979 ft³/s and a time to peak of 50 minutes. The dimensionless graph is created by dividing all time ordinates in the unit hydrograph by 50 minutes and all flow ordinates by 1979 ft³/s. Results are shown in Figure 9.2 and Table 9.4.

The dimensionless unit hydrograph of Example 9.3 could be one of many dimensionless unit hydrographs necessary to establish a generalized (average) dimensionless unit hydrograph.

TABLE 9.3 Convolution of Unit Hydrograph and Rainfall Excess to Create the Composite Hydrograph of Example 9.2

Time (min)	UH (ft³/s)	Runoff (in)	Hyd(1) (ft³/s)	Hyd(2) (ft³/s)	Hyd(3) (ft³/s)	Hyd(4) (ft³/s)	Hyd(5) (ft³/s)	Hyd(6) (ft³/s)	Composite Hydrograph (ft³/s)
0	0		0.0						0
10	4	0.000	0.0	0.0					0
20	32	0.000	0.0	0.0	0.0[1]	[2]	[3]		0
30	478	0.021	0.0	0.0	0.1	0.0		[4]	0
40	1250	0.342	0.0	0.0	0.6	1.4	0.0		2
50	1979	0.178	0.0	0.0	9.8	10.8	0.7	0.0	21
60	1923	0.110	0.0	0.0	25.7	163.6	5.6	0.4	195
70	1648		0.0	0.0	40.7	427.9	85.1	3.5	557
80	1235		0.0	0.0	39.6	677.5	222.5	52.6	992
90	826		0.0	0.0	33.9	658.4	352.2	137.6	1182
100	516		0.0	0.0	25.4	564.3	342.3	217.9	1150
110	340		0.0	0.0	17.0	422.8	293.4	211.8	945
120	215		0.0	0.0	10.6	282.8	219.8	181.5	695
130	154		0.0	0.0	7.0	176.7	147.0	136.0	467
140	100		0.0	0.0	4.4	116.4	91.8	91.0	304
150	54		0.0	0.0	3.2	73.5	60.5	56.8	194
160	5		0.0	0.0	2.0	52.6	38.2	37.4	130
170	0		0.0	0.0	1.1	34.1	27.3	23.6	86
180				0.0	0.1	18.5	17.7	16.9	53
190					0.0	1.6	9.6	11.0	22
200						0.0	0.8	6.0	7
210							0.0	0.5	1
220								0.0	0

[1] Hyd(3) values computed by multiplying the unit hydrograph ordinates by 0.021.
[2] Hyd(4) values computed by multiplying the unit hydrograph ordinates by 0.342.
[3] Hyd(5) values computed by multiplying the unit hydrograph ordinates by 0.178.
[4] Hyd(6) values computed by multiplying the unit hydrograph ordinates by 0.110.

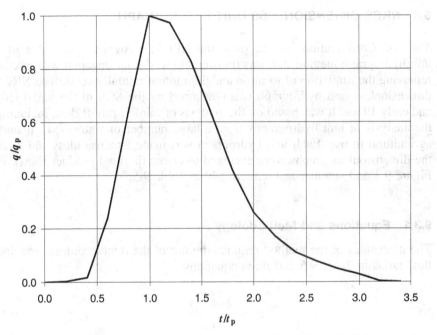

Figure 9.2 Dimensionless unit hydrograph for Example 9.3.

TABLE 9.4   Dimensionless Unit Hydrograph of Example 9.3

Time (min)	Unit Graph Flow (ft³/s)	t/t_p	q/q_p
0	0	0.000	0.000
10	4	0.200	0.002
20	32	0.400	0.016
30	478	0.600	0.241
40	1250	0.800	0.632
50	1979	1.000	1.000
60	1923	1.200	0.972
70	1648	1.400	0.833
80	1235	1.600	0.624
90	826	1.800	0.417
100	516	2.000	0.261
110	340	2.200	0.172
120	215	2.400	0.108
130	154	2.600	0.078
140	100	2.800	0.050
150	54	3.000	0.027
160	5	3.200	0.002
170	0	3.400	0.000

9.3   NRCS DIMENSIONLESS UNIT HYDROGRAPH

The Soil Conservation Service (now the NRCS) recognized the value of a unit hydrograph method that was transferable to similar ungaged watersheds, removing the limitation of location and duration of rainfall excess. The NRCS dimensionless unit hydrograph was developed by the SCS in the mid-1950s and early 1960s. It was based on the analysis of rainfall-runoff data, including the analysis of unit hydrographs from a large number of watersheds, mainly agricultural in use. Each unit hydrograph was made dimensionless, and then the dimensionless graphs were averaged to create the final product shown in Figure 9.3 and summarized numerically in Table 9.5.

9.3.1   Equations and Methodology

The mechanics of the method requires the use of the dimensionless time and flow ratios in Table 9.5 and three equations:

$$q_p = \frac{484 \, AQ}{t_p} \tag{9.1}$$

$$t_p = \frac{\Delta D}{2} + 0.6 \, t_c \tag{9.2}$$

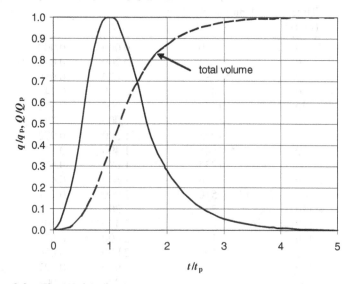

Figure 9.3   The NRCS dimensionless unit hydrograph and total volume curve.

TABLE 9.5   Ratios for Dimensionless Unit Hydrograph and Mass Curve (USDA NRCS NEH 630 2002)

Time Ratio (t/t_p)	Discharge Ratio (q/q_p)	Mass Curve Ratio (Q_a/Q)	Time Ratio (t/t_p)	Discharge Ratio (q/q_p)	Mass Curve Ratio (Q_a/Q)
0	0.000	0.000	1.7	0.460	0.790
0.1	0.030	0.001	1.8	0.390	0.822
0.2	0.100	0.006	1.9	0.330	0.849
0.3	0.190	0.012	2.0	0.280	0.871
0.4	0.310	0.035	2.2	0.207	0.908
0.5	0.470	0.065	2.4	0.147	0.934
0.6	0.660	0.107	2.6	0.107	0.953
0.7	0.820	0.163	2.8	0.077	0.967
0.8	0.930	0.228	3.0	0.055	0.977
0.9	0.990	0.300	3.2	0.040	0.984
1.0	1.000	0.375	3.4	0.029	0.989
1.1	0.990	0.450	3.6	0.021	0.993
1.2	0.930	0.522	3.8	0.015	0.995
1.3	0.860	0.589	4.0	0.011	0.997
1.4	0.780	0.650	4.5	0.005	0.999
1.5	0.680	0.700	5.0	0.000	1.000
1.6	0.560	0.751			

$$\Delta D \le \frac{2}{15} t_c \qquad (9.3)$$

where t_p = hydrograph time to peak (hrs)

t_c = watershed time of concentration (hrs)

q_p = peak flow (ft^3/s)

A = watershed area (mi^2)

Q = direct runoff depth (in)

ΔD = unit duration of rainfall and hydrograph time step (hrs)

There are nine steps in creating a composite hydrograph:

1. Determine the watershed characteristics of A, CN, and t_c.
2. Compute and select a convenient value of ΔD using Equation 9.3.
3. Compute t_p using Equation 9.2 and the chosen value of ΔD.
4. Compute q_p using Equation 9.1 and setting Q equal to one inch.
5. Create the watershed unit hydrograph by multiplying all time ratios in Table 9.5 by t_p and all discharge ratios by q_p.

6. Construct a working unit hydrograph by selecting and/or interpolating watershed unit hydrograph values at time intervals equal to ΔD.
7. Create a design storm of appropriate duration and discretize it into time steps equal to ΔD. See Chapter 6 methods.
8. Compute the incremental runoff coming from the design storm for the watershed. See Example 9.2.
9. Create a composite runoff hydrograph using superposition and convolution by using the incremental runoff results and the working unit hydrograph. See Example 9.2.

This process is illustrated by example.

Example 9.4 A 240-acre developing watershed has a curve number of 85 and a time of concentration of 0.75 hours. Using the 1-hour design storm provided in Table 9.6, create a synthetic hydrograph using the NRCS dimensionless unit hydrograph.

Solution: The unit hydrograph parameters are computed using Equations 9.1 through 9.3.

$$\Delta D \leq \frac{2}{15} t_c \leq \frac{2}{15} (0.75 \text{ hr}) \leq 0.1 \text{ hr}$$

The unit duration will be set to 0.1 hour for convenience of calculation.

TABLE 9.6   Design Storm for Example 9.4

Time (hr)	Design Storm (in)
0.0	0.0000
0.1	0.1325
0.2	0.1724
0.3	0.2397
0.4	0.3731
0.5	0.7894
0.6	0.5112
0.7	0.2931
0.8	0.2013
0.9	0.1502
1.0	0.1171
Total	2.9800

$$t_p = \frac{\Delta D}{2} + 0.6 \, t_c = \frac{0.1}{2} + 0.6(0.75) = 0.5 \text{ hr}$$

$$q_p = \frac{484 \, AQ}{t_p} = \frac{(484)(0.375 \text{ mi}^2) \, (1 \text{ in})}{0.5 \text{ hr}} = 363 \text{ ft}^3/\text{s}$$

Using Table 9.5 data, the unit hydrograph is created by multiplying all time ratios by 0.5 hours and all discharge ratios by 363 ft³/sec. Time ratios are chosen such that the time values have a time step equal to the unit duration of 0.1 hours. Between t/t_p of 4 and 5, interpolation is performed at 0.1-hour intervals to create approximate values of q/q_p. The calculations are summarized in Table 9.7.

TABLE 9.7 Unit Hydrograph Calculations for Example 9.4

Time Ratio (t/t_p)	Time (hrs)	Discharge Ratio (q/q_p)	Unit Discharge (ft^3/s)
0.00	0.000	0.000	0.0
0.20	0.100	0.100	36.3
0.40	0.200	0.310	112.5
0.60	0.300	0.660	239.6
0.80	0.400	0.930	337.6
1.00	0.500	1.000	363.0
1.20	0.600	0.930	337.6
1.40	0.700	0.780	283.1
1.60	0.800	0.560	203.3
1.80	0.900	0.390	141.6
2.00	1.000	0.280	101.6
2.20	1.100	0.207	75.1
2.40	1.200	0.147	53.4
2.60	1.300	0.107	38.8
2.80	1.400	0.077	28.0
3.00	1.500	0.055	20.0
3.20	1.600	0.040	14.5
3.40	1.700	0.029	10.5
3.60	1.800	0.021	7.6
3.80	1.900	0.015	5.4
4.00	2.000	0.011	4.0
4.20*	2.100	0.009*	3.3
4.40*	2.200	0.006*	2.2
4.60*	2.300	0.004*	1.4
4.80*	2.400	0.002*	0.7
5.00	2.500	0.000	0.0

*Values are interpolated from Table 9.5.

Using the design storm provided in Table 9.6, incremental runoff is computed using the methods of Example 9.2, Table 9.3. Results are shown in Table 9.8.

Using the results of Tables 9.7 and 9.8, the hydrograph is created using the principles of superposition and convolution. The calculations and resulting hydrograph are shown in Table 9.9. Figure 9.4 is a plot of the hydrograph and graphically shows the individual hydrographs resulting from unit durations of rainfall excess. Note the time shift of unit-duration between peak flows of each unit-duration hydrograph.

9.3.2 Derivation of the Equations

The geometry of the curvilinear dimensionless unit hydrograph is shown in Figure 9.5. Characteristics of the graph are as follows: (1) the time base is five times t_p, (2) 37.5 percent, or $3/8^{th}$ of the runoff takes place before the peak, (3) 62.5 percent, or $5/8^{th}$ of the runoff takes place after the peak, and (4) the inflection point on the falling limb occurs at 1.7 times t_p.

Figure 9.5 shows a second dimensionless unit hydrograph that is triangular. It is geometrically equivalent to the curvilinear graph in terms of area under the curve. Using right triangle geometry, a relationship between the two time parameters defining the base dimension of the triangular unit hydrograph can be established by proportion as follows:

$$\frac{t_p}{0.375} = \frac{t_r}{0.625} \tag{9.4}$$

$$t_r = \frac{5}{3} t_p \tag{9.5}$$

TABLE 9.8 Incremental Runoff Calculations for Example 9.4

Time (hrs)	Design Storm (in)	Cumulative Rainfall (in)	Cumulative Runoff (in)	Incremental Runoff (in)
0.0	0.0000	0.0000	0.0000	—
0.1	0.1325	0.1325	0.0000	0.0000
0.2	0.1724	0.3049	0.0000	0.0000
0.3	0.2397	0.5446	0.0188	0.0188
0.4	0.3731	0.9177	0.1369	0.1181
0.5	0.7894	1.7071	0.5880	0.4510
0.6	0.5112	2.2183	0.9585	0.3706
0.7	0.2931	2.5114	1.1875	0.2290
0.8	0.2013	2.7127	1.3501	0.1626
0.9	0.1502	2.8629	1.4738	0.1237
1.0	0.1171	2.9800	1.5714	0.0977
Totals	2.9800			1.5714

TABLE 9.9 Hydrograph Computations for the NRCS Unit Hydrograph of Example 9.4

Time (hrs)	UH (ft³/s)	Runoff (in)	H3 (ft³/s)	H4 (ft³/s)	H5 (ft³/s)	H6 (ft³/s)	H7 (ft³/s)	H8 (ft³/s)	H9 (ft³/s)	H10 (ft³/s)	Composite (ft³/s)
0.0	0.0	0.0000									0.0
0.1	36.3	0.0000									0.0
0.2	112.5	0.0000	0.0								0.0
0.3	239.6	0.0188	0.7	0.0							0.7
0.4	337.6	0.1188	2.1	4.3	0.0						6.4
0.5	363.0	0.4510	4.5	13.3	16.4	0.0					34.1
0.6	337.6	0.3706	6.3	28.3	50.7	13.4	0.0				98.8
0.7	283.1	0.2290	6.8	39.9	108.1	41.7	8.3	0.0			204.7
0.8	203.3	0.1626	6.3	42.9	152.3	88.8	25.8	5.9	0.0		321.9
0.9	141.6	0.1237	5.3	39.9	163.7	125.1	54.8	18.3	4.5	0.0	411.6
1.0	101.6	0.0977	3.8	33.5	152.3	134.5	77.3	39.0	13.9	3.6	457.7
1.1	75.1		2.7	24.0	127.7	125.1	83.1	54.9	29.6	11.0	458.1
1.2	53.4		1.9	16.7	91.7	104.9	77.3	59.0	41.7	23.5	416.7
1.3	38.8		1.4	12.0	63.9	75.3	64.8	54.9	44.9	33.1	350.3
1.4	28.0		1.0	8.9	45.8	52.5	46.5	46.0	41.7	35.5	278.0
1.5	20.0		0.7	6.3	33.9	37.6	32.4	33.1	35.0	33.1	212.1
1.6	14.5		0.5	4.6	24.1	27.8	23.3	23.0	25.1	27.7	156.2
1.7	10.5		0.4	3.3	17.5	19.8	17.2	16.5	17.5	19.9	112.1
1.8	7.6		0.3	2.4	12.6	14.4	12.2	12.2	12.6	13.9	80.5
1.9	5.4		0.2	1.7	9.0	10.4	8.9	8.7	9.3	9.9	58.1
2.0	4.0		0.1	1.2	6.5	7.4	6.4	6.3	6.6	7.4	42.0
2.1	3.3		0.1	0.9	4.7	5.4	4.6	4.6	4.8	5.2	30.3
2.2	2.2		0.1	0.6	3.4	3.9	3.3	3.3	3.5	3.8	21.9
2.3	1.4		0.1	0.5	2.4	2.8	2.4	2.4	2.5	2.7	15.8
2.4	0.7		0.0	0.4	1.8	2.0	1.7	1.7	1.8	2.0	11.4
2.5	0.0		0.0	0.3	1.5	1.5	1.2	1.2	1.3	1.4	8.4

TABLE 9.9 (*Continued*)

Time (hrs)	UH (ft³/s)	Runoff (in)	H3 (ft³/s)	H4 (ft³/s)	H5 (ft³/s)	H6 (ft³/s)	H7 (ft³/s)	H8 (ft³/s)	H9 (ft³/s)	H10 (ft³/s)	Composite (ft³/s)
2.6			0.0	0.2	1.0	1.2	0.9	0.9	0.9	1.0	6.2
2.7			0.0	0.1	0.6	0.8	0.8	0.7	0.7	0.7	4.3
2.8				0.0	0.3	0.5	0.5	0.5	0.5	0.5	2.9
2.9					0.0	0.3	0.3	0.4	0.4	0.4	1.7
3.0						0.0	0.2	0.2	0.3	0.3	1.0
3.1							0.0	0.1	0.2	0.2	0.5
3.2								0.0	0.1	0.1	0.2
3.3									0.0	0.1	0.1
3.4										0.0	0.0

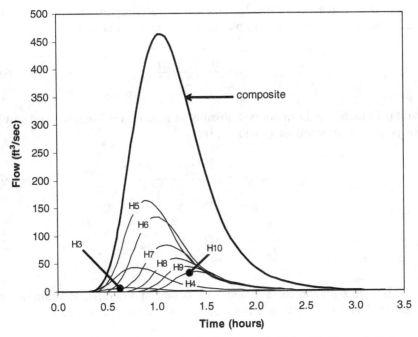

Figure 9.4 Graph of composite hydrograph of Table 9.9, Example 9.4.

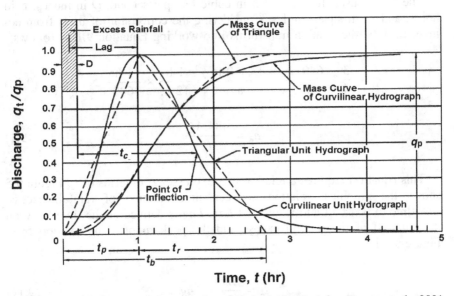

Figure 9.5 NRCS (SCS) dimensionless unit hydrograph (after Brown et al., 2001, HEC 22)

The area under the triangular unit hydrograph represents runoff volume, and it can be computed by simple triangle area formula as

$$Q = \frac{q_p (t_p + t_r)}{2}$$
(9.6)

with Q in inches and t in hours. Substituting Equation 9.5 into 9.6 and solving for peak flow in terms of Q and t_p gives

$$q_p = \frac{2Q}{\left(t_p + \frac{5}{3} t_p\right)}$$
(9.7)

$$q_p = \frac{3Q}{4t_p}$$
(9.8)

This is an equation for a dimensionless unit hydrograph, so drainage area is implied as a unit area, and the area parameter, A, can be added.

$$q_p = \frac{3 AQ}{4t_p}$$
(9.9)

The NRCS uses the units of q in cubic feet per second, Q in inches, t_p in hours, and A, in square miles. Considering the conversion of units from ac-in/hr to ft^3/s, the relation transforms into working Equation 9.1 as follows:

$$q_p = \frac{3}{4} \times \frac{640 \text{ ac}}{\text{mi}^2} \times \frac{43{,}560 \text{ ft}^2}{\text{ac}} \times \frac{1 \text{ ft}}{12 \text{ in}} \times \frac{1 \text{ hr}}{3600 \text{ s}} \times \frac{AQ}{t_p}$$
(9.10)

$$q_p = \frac{484 \, AQ}{t_p}$$
(9.1)

This equation requires a relation that expresses t_p in terms of t_c. Figure 9.5 shows the graphical relation between unit duration of rainfall excess, ΔD, time to peak, t_p, and watershed *Lag*. *Lag* is defined as the time between the centroid of the rainfall excess and the peak runoff. The relation from Figure 9.5 is

$$t_p = \frac{\Delta D}{2} + Lag$$
(9.11)

The SCS analyzed many storm events from a range of watershed conditions and determined watershed lag to be 60 percent of watershed time of concentration (i.e., *Lag* = $0.6t_c$). Substituting this empirical relation into Equation 9.11, give the relation between t_p and t_c as

$$t_p = \frac{\Delta D}{2} + 0.6t_c \tag{9.2}$$

Additionally, the NRCS recommends that unit duration be 20 percent of t_p or smaller (i.e., $\Delta D = t_p/5$ or smaller). Substituting this recommendation into Equation 9.2 and solving for t_c gives

$$\Delta D \leq \frac{2}{15} t_c \tag{9.3}$$

Equations 9.1, 9.2, and 9.3 make up the original equations used in the SCS unit hydrograph calculation as documented in NEH 630. These equations can be simplified somewhat if the user is not too concerned about the convenient selection of ΔD, which is often the case when using an electronic spreadsheet or writing a computer program. If Equation 9.3 is modified to

$$\Delta D = \frac{2}{15} t_c \tag{9.12}$$

then Equations 9.1 and 9.2 can be directly expressed in terms of t_c. Substituting Equation 9.12 into Equation 9.2 gives

$$t_p = \frac{2}{3} t_c \tag{9.13}$$

Substituting Equation 9.13 into 9.1 gives

$$q_p = \frac{726 \, AQ}{t_c} \tag{9.14}$$

Equations 9.12, 9.13, and 9.14 become the simplified set that replaces Equations 9.1, 9.2, and 9.3.

9.3.3 Peak Rate Factor

The constant 484 in Equation 9.1 results from the geometric characteristic of the dimensionless unit hydrograph specifying that 3/8th of the runoff volume is contained under the rising side of the graph. This constant is known as the peak rate factor (*PRF*), and Equation 9.1 can be rewritten in more general terms as

$$q_p = \frac{(PRF)\, AQ}{t_p} \tag{9.15}$$

Considering that the shape of the standard NRCS dimensionless unit hydrograph is based on the average runoff response of many watersheds of varying surface slope, it is reasonable to expect the *PRF* to be different for watersheds with extreme surface slopes. In the original SCS document NEH-4 (now NEH 630), Chapter 16, it was suggested that the *PRF* might be as high as 600 for mountainous (very steep) watersheds and as low as 300 for coastal (very flat) watersheds. This information suggests that regionally created dimensionless unit hydrographs might give improved results over the standard NRCS dimensionless unit hydrograph.

9.4 DELMARVA UNIT HYDROGRAPH

The Delmarva unit hydrograph is a regional hydrograph method based on the structure of the standard NRCS dimensionless unit hydrograph, where the *PRF* is established as 284. This special unit hydrograph was created by Welle et al. (1980) for use in the Delaware–Maryland–Virginia peninsula on the Atlantic coast of the United States. It has been also approved for use in New Jersey for coastal regions that have flat topography (average watershed slope less than 5 percent), low relief, and significant surface storage in swales and depressions (USDA NRCS 2003). The dimensionless ratios of the Delmarva UH are necessarily different, due to the definition of the geometry of the NRCS standard UH, and these ratios are shown in Table 9.10.

To get an idea of the differences between the standard and Delmarva unit graphs, a simple hypothetical watershed having a drainage area of one square mile, with a time to peak of one hour, and direct runoff of one inch is used to create contrasting unit hydrographs. The results are shown in Figure 9.6. Recognize that both hydrographs have the same volume of runoff, but the way the runoff is distributed is different. The Delmarva unit graph has a peak that is about one-half that of the standard NRCS unit graph, but its time base is almost twice as long. Also, in Table 9.10, note that at $t/t_p = 1$, the mass curve ratio is 0.220, which means 22 percent of the runoff under the unit hydrograph falls under the rising limb, as compared to 37.5 percent for the standard UH. This change in shape of the Delmarva UH from the standard UH is a reasonable representation of the effect that flatter surface slope, low relief terrain, and additional surface depression storage has on the transformation of rainfall excess into a runoff hydrograph.

TABLE 9.10   Ratios for the Delmarva Dimensionless Unit Hydrograph and Mass Curve (USDA NRCS WinTR-55, 2002)

Time Ratio (t/t_p)	Discharge Ratio (q/q_p)	Mass Curve Ratio (Q_a/Q)	Time Ratio (t/t_p)	Discharge Ratio (q/q_p)	Mass Curve Ratio (Q_a/Q)
0.0	0.000	0.000	5.0	0.109	0.935
0.2	0.111	0.005	5.2	0.097	0.944
0.4	0.356	0.025	5.4	0.086	0.952
0.6	0.655	0.069	5.6	0.076	0.959
0.8	0.896	0.137	5.8	0.066	0.965
1.0	1.000	0.220	6.0	0.057	0.970
1.2	0.929	0.304	6.2	0.049	0.975
1.4	0.828	0.381	6.4	0.041	0.979
1.6	0.737	0.450	6.6	0.033	0.982
1.8	0.656	0.510	6.8	0.027	0.985
2.0	0.584	0.565	7.0	0.024	0.987
2.2	0.521	0.613	7.2	0.021	0.989
2.4	0.465	0.656	7.4	0.018	0.991
2.6	0.415	0.694	7.6	0.015	0.992
2.8	0.371	0.729	7.8	0.013	0.993
3.0	0.331	0.760	8.0	0.012	0.994
3.2	0.296	0.787	8.2	0.011	0.995
3.4	0.265	0.811	8.4	0.009	0.996
3.6	0.237	0.833	8.6	0.008	0.997
3.8	0.212	0.853	8.8	0.008	0.998
4.0	0.190	0.871	9.0	0.006	0.998
4.2	0.170	0.886	9.2	0.006	0.999
4.4	0.153	0.900	9.4	0.005	0.999
4.6	0.138	0.913	9.6	0.005	1.000
4.8	0.123	0.925	9.8	0.000	1.000

Several other PRFs exist for regions of south Florida and Georgia. Sheridan et al. (2002) studied several flatland watersheds in the southeastern United States and found that the *PRF* varied significantly (174 to 476) for these watersheds. He proposed a relation that predicted the PRF in terms of watershed channel slope and watershed drainage area.

$$PRF = 631.7 \times CS^{0.882} \times DA^{0.264} \qquad (9.16)$$

In this equation, *CS* is the main channel slope in percent, measured at 10 percent and 85 percent of the total main channel, and *DA* is the watershed drainage area in mi^2. It is reasonable to speculate that future development of the NRCS dimensionless unit hydrograph method will most likely include the determination of regional PRFs with associated dimensionless unit hydro-

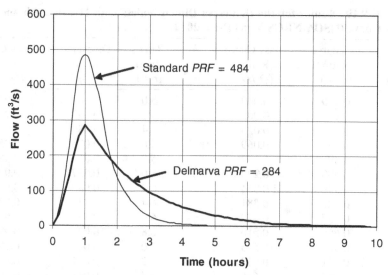

Figure 9.6 Comparison of the standard NRCS UH and the Delmarva UH for a hypothetical watershed.

graph ratios. Clearly, Sheridan's study shows this to be a practical approach to runoff analysis if watershed modeling is to be improved.

9.5 NRCS TABULAR HYDROGRAPH

The NRCS standard unit hydrograph method was used to create part of the SCS Technical Release 20, a computer program that contains several hydrologic procedures to perform watershed modeling. This program originally required the use of a mainframe computer, which was very expensive and not readily available to many of the SCS field offices. To fill the need for an inexpensive and relatively easy method for obtaining peak runoff rates and partial hydrographs, the tabular hydrograph method was developed in 1975, and subsequently improved in 1986, through the publication *Urban Hydrology for Small Watersheds,* TR-55. In 2002, the NRCS replaced the tabular hydrograph method with a personal computer program *WinTR-55* that utilizes TR-20 calculation routines, removing the need for the tabular method. However, the tabular method remains very popular today and is widely accepted in professional practice as a valid method.

9.5.1 Equations, Tables, and Methodology

The tabular method is a method for estimating peak flows from rural and urban areas through the construction of partial composite hydrographs. The peak flows can be determined for any location in the watershed, based on the delineation of the watershed into hydrologically homogeneous subareas. The method is an approximation of the more detailed procedures in TR-20. The method was created to handle drainage areas with time of concentrations between 0.1 hours and 2 hours, and reach travel times between 0 and 3 hours. Reach travel time is defined as the time required for a subarea's discharge to arrive at a downstream point through a channel outside of the subarea, but still inside the watershed.

Hydrologic data necessary to use the tabular method include the 24-hour design rainfall depth (P) in inches and the NRCS rainfall type (I, IA, II, or III). Additionally, the method requires watershed information for each subarea of curve number (CN), time of concentration (t_c) in hours, travel time (t_t) outside the subarea in hours, and drainage area (A) in square miles.

The travel time parameter requires explanation. This parameter is the time required for runoff to flow in a stream channel immediately below a subarea that connects the subarea outlet to the watershed outlet. This travel time is used to account for channel storage effects on the subarea hydrograph. A hydrologic routing procedure called the Modified Att-Kin method was used by the SCS to evaluate the storage and timing effects of downstream channels on discharge rates from subarea hydrographs. The results were incorporated into the method in such a fashion that the user only needs to provide t_t to account for the effects of channel storage. Chapter 10 provides a more detailed explanation of channel routing and its affect on hydrographs.

The tabular method relies on tabulated hydrographs with varying conditions of rainfall distribution, time of concentration t_c, the ratio of initial abstraction to precipitation (I_a/P), and channel travel time, t_t. Each tabulated hydrograph represents runoff for a 1-square-mile drainage area, with 1 inch of rainfall excess. Therefore, each tabulated hydrograph is a unit hydrograph for a unit drainage area. Tables 9.11 and 9.12 are 2 of 40 exhibits created for the method. The exhibits come in four groups of ten sheets, with each group representing a standard NRCS rainfall distribution (I, IA, II, or III). The ten sheets of each group provide tabulated hydrographs for ten different times of concentration ranging from 0.1 to 2.0 hours.

Table 9.11 is Exhibit 5-II, sheet 5 of 10 in TR-55 (1986), for a unit drainage area having a rainfall Type II and a t_c of 0.5 hours. Close inspection of the table reveals that it is really three tables on one sheet, with each table reflecting different ratios of I_a/P, namely 0.1, 0.3, and 0.5. Each table contains 12 rows of tabulated hydrographs, each with a different associated t_t value. The t_t values range from 0.0 to 3.0 in nonuniform time steps. Therefore, on this single sheet, there are 36 different tabulated hydrographs presented, each for a different combination of t_c, I_a/P, and t_t. In all, there are 1440 tabulated unit hydrographs in TR-55 (1986) that can be modified to fit a specific drainage area size and specific rainfall excess depth.

Hydrograph times that run across the top of Table 9.11 range from 11.0 hours to 26.0 hours, with nonuniform time intervals. The 11.0 hour time is

TABLE 9.11 Tabular Hydrograph Unit Discharges (csm/in) for Type II Rainfall Distribution, t_c = 0.5 hours (USDA SCS TR-55, 1986)

HYDROGRAPH TIME (HOURS). The marker * * * TC = 0.5 HR * * * falls between columns 12.7 and 12.8.

TRVL TIME (hr)	11.0	11.3	11.6	11.9	12.0	12.1	12.2	12.3	12.4	12.5	12.6	12.7	12.8	13.0	13.2	13.4	13.6	13.8	14.0	14.3	14.6	15.0	15.5	16.0	16.5	17.0	17.5	18.0	19.0	20.0	22.0	26.0
IA/P = 0.10																																
0.0	17	23	32	57	94	170	308	467	529	507	402	297	226	140	96	74	61	53	47	41	36	32	29	26	23	21	20	19	16	14	12	0
.10	16	22	30	51	80	140	252	395	484	499	434	343	265	162	108	80	65	55	49	42	36	33	29	26	23	21	20	19	16	14	12	0
.20	14	19	25	38	47	69	116	207	332	434	477	449	378	207	149	101	77	62	53	45	39	34	30	27	24	22	20	19	17	14	12	0
.30	13	18	24	35	43	60	97	170	278	382	446	448	401	270	171	114	83	66	56	46	40	34	31	27	24	22	20	19	17	15	12	0
.40	12	15	21	29	33	40	53	83	141	233	332	408	434	361	243	157	107	79	64	51	43	36	32	28	25	22	21	20	17	15	12	0
.50	11	15	20	28	31	37	48	71	118	194	286	367	412	378	271	178	119	86	68	53	44	37	32	29	25	23	21	20	17	15	12	0
.75	9	11	14	16	21	24	27	31	37	49	74	118	182	319	374	328	244	169	117	76	56	43	35	31	28	25	23	21	18	16	12	1
1.0	7	9	12	17	17	21	24	32	40	55	83	117	188	309	359	322	245	172	102	68	49	38	32	32	31	29	26	23	19	16	12	1
1.5	5	7	8	11	13	14	15	17	19	21	23	27	43	89	175	269	322	309	280	225	140	77	49	38	32	29	25	23	20	17	10	5
2.0	3	4	6	7	8	8	10	10	11	11	12	14	15	18	23	35	65	181	202	297	280	198	88	52	39	33	29	26	21	19	14	10
2.5	2	3	4	5	6	6	7	7	7	8	9	9	10	12	15	18	24	66	87	150	244	278	171	87	52	39	33	29	23	20	15	11
3.0	1	1	2	3	3	4	4	4	5	5	6	7	8	11	13	16	20	37	86	102	198	263	182	96	56	40	33	29	21	16	11	11
IA/P = 0.30																																
0.0	0	0	0	0	9	53	157	314	433	439	379	299	237	159	118	95	81	71	65	56	50	46	42	38	34	31	30	28	25	22	20	0
.10	0	0	0	1	6	37	117	248	372	416	391	330	237	218	150	113	96	79	70	60	53	47	43	39	35	32	30	29	26	22	20	0
.20	0	0	0	1	4	26	87	194	313	382	416	388	349	244	167	122	97	82	72	62	54	48	43	39	36	33	31	29	26	22	20	0
.30	0	0	0	0	3	19	64	151	259	316	341	372	330	316	171	114	83	94	80	67	58	50	45	41	38	34	31	31	26	23	20	0
.40	0	0	0	0	0	2	13	47	116	211	298	354	328	245	172	113	83	71	65	59	53	47	42	38	34	31	30	28	25	22	20	0
.50	0	0	0	0	0	0	9	34	89	170	255	303	341	316	225	152	96	76	70	60	53	47	43	39	35	32	30	29	26	22	20	0
.75	0	0	0	0	0	0	1	4	14	41	89	152	270	305	268	181	118	87	70	57	48	44	39	36	33	31	30	27	24	21	20	0
1.0	0	0	0	0	0	0	0	0	2	7	22	98	212	295	285	207	120	88	67	53	46	41	38	34	31	31	28	25	23	20	20	2
1.5	0	0	0	0	0	0	0	0	0	0	0	0	0	5	30	95	183	265	269	221	152	96	66	53	46	41	37	34	30	26	20	8
2.0	0	0	0	0	0	0	0	0	0	0	0	0	0	0	0	3	18	21	59	125	245	182	105	69	54	47	42	38	32	28	22	16
2.5	0	0	0	0	0	0	0	0	0	0	0	0	0	0	0	0	1	5	21	84	174	230	172	103	69	54	46	42	34	30	23	18
3.0	0	0	0	0	0	0	0	0	0	0	0	0	0	0	0	0	0	1	1	21	56	157	217	163	101	68	53	46	37	31	25	18

TABLE 9.11 (Continued)

IA/P = 0.50   * * * TC = 0.5 HR * * *   IA/P = 0.50

0.0	0	0	0	2	26	89	170	217	229	200	179	144	119	104	93	85	78	70	64	59	55	51	46	43	41	40	36	32	28	0
.10	0	0	0	0	1	18	65	135	190	216	205	170	137	115	101	91	83	74	67	61	56	52	47	44	42	40	36	32	28	0
.20	0	0	0	0	1	12	47	106	162	198	203	178	145	121	105	94	85	76	68	61	57	52	48	44	42	40	37	32	28	0
.30	0	0	0	0	0	1	8	34	82	135	177	194	168	139	117	102	92	80	71	63	58	54	49	45	43	41	37	33	28	0
.40	0	0	0	0	0	0	6	25	63	111	155	189	174	146	122	106	94	82	73	64	58	54	50	45	43	41	37	33	28	0
.50	0	0	0	0	0	0	4	18	48	90	133	184	177	152	128	110	97	84	74	65	59	55	50	45	43	41	38	33	28	0
.75	0	0	0	0	0	0	1	7	22	47	80	142	169	164	144	124	108	91	79	68	61	56	51	47	44	42	38	34	28	0
1.0	0	0	0	0	0	0	0	0	1	3	11	51	112	155	166	154	134	109	91	76	65	59	54	49	45	43	39	35	28	2
1.5	0	0	0	0	0	0	0	0	0	0	0	2	16	50	97	136	154	145	121	95	75	64	58	54	49	45	41	37	29	10
2.0	0	0	0	0	0	0	0	0	0	0	0	0	0	4	18	47	86	134	146	125	94	75	64	58	53	49	42	39	31	21
2.5	0	0	0	0	0	0	0	0	0	0	0	0	0	0	0	3	11	44	95	140	127	97	77	65	58	54	45	41	33	26
3.3	0	0	0	0	0	0	0	0	0	0	0	0	0	0	0	0	1	7	29	86	122	135	95	76	58	58	49	43	35	27

RAINFALL TYPE = II   * * * TC = 0.5 HR * * *   SHEET 5 OF 10

TABLE 9.12 Tabular Hydrograph Unit Discharges (csm/in) for Type II Rainfall Distribution, $t_c = 0.75$ hours (USDA SCS TR-55, 1986)

HYDROGRAPH TIME (HOURS)

IA/P = 0.10   * * * TC = 0.75 HR * * *

TRVL TIME (hr)	11.0	11.3	11.6	11.9	12.0	12.1	12.2	12.3	12.4	12.5	12.6	12.7	12.8	13.0	13.2	13.4	13.6	13.8	14.0	14.3	14.6	15.0	15.5	16.0	16.5	17.0	17.5	18.0	19.0	20.0	22.0	26.0
0.0	13	18	24	36	46	68	115	194	294	380	424	410	369	252	172	123	93	74	61	49	41	35	31	27	24	22	20	19	17	15	12	0
.10	13	17	23	34	42	59	97	162	250	337	395	405	381	279	191	135	100	79	65	51	42	36	31	28	25	22	21	19	17	15	12	0
.20	11	15	20	28	32	39	52	82	135	211	295	362	391	351	255	178	127	95	75	57	46	38	32	29	26	23	21	20	18	15	12	0
.30	11	14	19	26	30	36	47	70	113	179	256	326	379	360	277	196	140	103	80	60	48	38	33	29	26	23	21	20	18	15	12	0
.40	10	12	16	22	25	28	33	42	61	96	151	221	291	367	336	255	182	131	98	69	54	42	34	30	27	24	22	20	18	16	12	0
.50	9	12	16	21	24	27	31	39	53	82	128	190	258	358	343	274	200	144	106	74	56	43	35	30	27	24	22	20	18	16	12	1
.75	8	10	13	17	18	21	23	26	31	39	55	82	122	230	314	329	281	217	161	104	72	51	38	33	29	26	23	21	19	16	12	1
1.0	6	8	11	13	14	15	17	19	21	23	27	32	42	89	177	272	319	303	249	163	105	66	45	36	31	27	24	22	19	17	13	3
1.5	4	6	7	9	10	10	11	12	14	15	16	18	20	46	90	163	241	295	275	204	170	119	66	45	35	31	27	24	20	18	13	7
2.0	3	4	5	6	7	7	8	9	11	15	16	20	28	48	89	151	245	274	219	170	115	65	44	36	30	26	22	19	18	16	14	10
2.5	1	1	2	3	4	5	6	7	8	10	14	24	37	86	170	219	260	247	157	105	71	47	36	31	26	22	20	17	16	14	11	11
3.0	1	1	2	3	4	4	5	6	7	8	9	11	14	17	30	64	105	157	247	260	219	127	84	53	40	33	28	24	20	18	16	12

IA/P = 0.30   * * * TC = 0.75 HR * * *

TRVL TIME (hr)	11.0	11.3	11.6	11.9	12.0	12.1	12.2	12.3	12.4	12.5	12.6	12.7	12.8	13.0	13.2	13.4	13.6	13.8	14.0	14.3	14.6	15.0	15.5	16.0	16.5	17.0	17.5	18.0	19.0	20.0	22.0	26.0
0.0	0	0	0	0	1	6	30	86	174	266	326	348	328	246	181	138	110	92	79	66	57	49	44	40	36	32	29	26	23	21	19	0
.10	0	0	0	0	0	4	22	65	137	223	292	329	303	254	228	170	131	106	89	73	61	52	46	41	37	33	30	27	24	22	19	0
.20	0	0	0	0	0	3	15	48	108	185	256	305	321	245	184	141	112	93	75	63	53	46	42	37	34	30	27	24	21	19	18	0
.30	0	0	0	0	2	11	36	84	151	221	277	308	289	260	199	152	120	98	78	65	54	47	42	38	34	31	30	27	24	20	19	0
.40	0	0	0	0	0	0	1	8	27	65	122	188	246	286	301	243	187	144	114	87	71	57	48	43	39	35	32	30	27	24	21	1
.50	0	0	0	0	0	0	6	20	50	98	158	254	292	263	243	200	155	122	91	74	59	48	42	38	34	30	27	24	21	19	18	1
.75	0	0	0	0	0	0	2	8	23	51	82	140	231	269	253	211	167	119	90	68	53	46	42	37	34	31	28	25	22	19	18	2
1.0	0	0	0	0	0	0	0	1	4	29	96	186	249	261	231	169	120	84	61	50	44	40	36	33	31	28	26	24	21	19	18	5
1.5	0	0	0	0	0	0	0	0	1	8	34	91	163	220	241	197	131	83	61	50	44	40	35	31	27	24	21	19	18	16	14	12
2.0	0	0	0	0	0	0	0	0	0	2	11	36	85	174	226	241	196	135	96	61	50	44	39	35	31	27	24	21	19	18	16	17
2.5	0	0	0	0	0	0	0	0	0	1	6	37	105	196	214	196	135	87	62	51	44	36	31	28	26	24	21	19	18	18	18	18
3.0	0	0	0	0	0	0	0	0	0	0	1	6	24	96	196	214	196	127	84	53	40	33	28	24	21	19	18	18	19	24	26	18

TABLE 9.12 (Continued)

IA/P = 0.50   * * * TC = 0.75 HR * * *   IA/P = 0.50

0.0	0	0	0	0	2	16	45	92	137	166	185	170	146	125	110	98	89	79	70	63	58	53	48	44	42	41	37	33	28	+
.10	0	0	0	0	0	1	11	34	73	115	149	180	163	141	122	107	96	84	74	65	59	54	50	45	43	41	38	33	28	0
.20	0	0	0	0	0	1	8	25	57	96	131	173	166	146	126	111	99	86	76	66	59	55	50	46	43	41	38	34	28	0
.30	0	0	0	0	0	0	1	5	18	44	79	143	170	160	141	122	108	92	81	69	61	56	52	47	44	42	38	34	28	1
.40	0	0	0	0	0	0	0	4	14	34	64	127	166	162	145	127	111	95	82	70	62	57	52	47	44	42	38	34	28	1
.50	0	0	0	0	0	0	0	0	2	10	26	82	138	162	157	140	123	103	88	75	64	58	53	49	45	43	39	35	28	2
.75	0	0	0	0	0	0	0	0	1	4	12	47	98	139	154	148	135	113	96	80	67	60	55	50	46	43	39	36	29	3
1.0	0	0	0	0	0	0	0	0	0	0	6	30	73	119	146	151	134	113	91	74	63	58	53	48	45	41	37	33	29	7
1.5	0	0	0	0	0	0	0	0	0	0	0	0	1	9	30	66	105	143	143	117	90	73	63	52	48	44	42	39	30	18
2.0	0	0	0	0	0	0	0	0	0	0	0	0	0	0	2	30	77	121	137	114	88	72	57	52	48	44	40	32	25	
2.5	0	0	0	0	0	0	0	0	0	0	0	0	0	1	3	19	55	111	132	111	87	71	62	56	47	42	34	27		
3.0	0	0	0	0	0	0	0	0	0	0	0	0	0	2	12	51	112	128	108	86	71	62	51	44	36	27			

RAINFALL TYPE = II   * * * TC = 0.75 HR * * *

SHEET 6 OF 10

241

the eleventh hour of the 24-hour storm. The column provides the runoff rate that the drainage area is generating 11 hours after the rainfall begins. The 26.0 time occurs 2 hours after the rainfall ends. Because of these time limits, the composite hydrograph developed from this method is necessarily a partial hydrograph. However, when the method is applied to small watersheds like those typically encountered in stormwater management design, the partial hydrographs end up being complete hydrographs because the flow ordinates at 11.0 hours and 26.0 hours are zero or very nearly zero.

The ratio of I_a/P is used to reflect the ability of the watershed to absorb rainfall and therefore delay the beginning of runoff as well as reduce the magnitude of the flows. Its magnitude depends on the severity of the design rainfall (P) and the soil-cover complex (CN) of the drainage area. For $I_a/P = 0.1$, only 10 percent of the design rainfall is lost to the initial abstraction, which allows runoff to begin early in the storm and leaves plenty of rainfall excess. For $I_a/P = 0.5$, one-half of the rainfall is lost to the initial abstraction and much less runoff can be expected to move across the landscape.

To create the hydrograph for a particular drainage area, the rainfall type and t_c are first determined. From this, the correct matching exhibit is chosen. The ratio of I_a/P is computed (or read from Table 8.7) using the value of CN and the design rainfall. Based on this value of I_a/P, the table in the exhibit that is closest to this computed value is chosen (upper table for 0.1, middle table for 0.3, or lower table for 0.5). Within the chosen table, the value of t_t is used to select the appropriate row of unit discharge values. The values are multiplied by the product of drainage area in square miles, A_m and the rainfall excess Q to create hydrograph flows for specific hydrograph times. The working relation is

$$q = q_t A_m Q, \tag{9.20}$$

where q = the hydrograph ordinate (ft^3/s)
  q_t = tabulated unit discharge from Exhibit 5 (TR-55) (ft^3/s/mi^2/in, csm/in)
  A_m = drainage area (mi^2)
  Q = direct runoff depth (in)

The multiplier $A_m Q$ acts like a scaling factor that increases or decreases the tabular unit discharge rates to match the characteristics of the drainage area and the rainfall event.

Example 9.5   A watershed containing 182 acres is divided into two subareas, as shown in Figure 9.7. Both subareas are relatively homogeneous in land use, with the lower subarea mostly developed having a CN of 82 and the upper subarea completely undeveloped with a CN of 68. Other subarea characteristics are given in Table 9.13. Using the tabular hydrograph method, create a partial composite hydrograph for this watershed, using a NRCS Type II 24-hour storm containing 5.0 inches of rainfall.

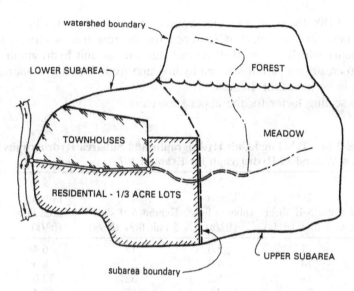

Figure 9.7 Two subarea watersheds of Example 9.5.

Solution: The upper subarea is analyzed first. With a *CN* of 68, the direct runoff and initial abstraction are computed, along with the ratio of I_a/P.

$$Q = \frac{\left(P - \dfrac{200}{CN} + 2\right)^2}{\left(P + \dfrac{800}{CN} - 8\right)} = \frac{\left(P - \dfrac{200}{68} + 2\right)^2}{\left(P + \dfrac{800}{68} - 8\right)} = 1.88 \text{ inches}$$

$$I_a = 0.2\,S = 0.2\left(\frac{1000}{CN} - 10\right) = 0.2\left(\frac{1000}{68} - 10\right) = 0.941$$

$$\frac{I_a}{P} = \frac{0.941}{5} = 0.188$$

The upper subarea has a t_c of 0.75 hours, so Exhibit 5-II (sheet 6 of 10) of TR-55, Chapter 5 (1986) is chosen, which is shown in Table 9.12. With

TABLE 9.13 Subarea Characteristics for Example 9.5

Subarea	Area, ac (mi²)	CN	t_c, min (hrs)	t_t, min (hrs)
Upper	104 (0.162)	68	45 (0.75)	17 (0.28)
Lower	78 (0.122)	82	30 (0.50)	—

$I_a/P = 0.188$, the nearest tabulated value of I_a/P is chosen, which is 0.1. The upper table in Table 9.11 is searched for the row that is closest to a t_t of 0.28 hours which is $t_t = 0.30$ hours. This row of unit hydrograph values is used to create the partial subarea hydrograph from hour 11 to hour 26 and is shown in column 2 of Table 9.14.

The scaling factor for the upper subarea is

TABLE 9.14   Tabulated Unit Hydrographs and Subarea Hydrographs to Create a Watershed Hydrograph for Example 9.7

1 Time (hrs)	2 Exhibit 5-II sheet 6 unit flow (ft³/s)	3 Upper subarea flow (ft³/s)	4 Exhibit 5-II sheet 5 unit flow (ft³/s)	5 Lower subarea flow (ft³/s)	6 Composite flow (ft³/s)
11.0	11	3.3	17	6.4	9.8
11.3	14	4.3	23	8.6	12.9
11.6	19	5.8	32	12.0	17.8
11.9	26	7.9	57	21.4	29.3
12.0	30	9.1	94	35.3	44.4
12.1	36	10.9	170	63.9	74.8
12.2	47	14.3	308	115.8	130.1
12.3	70	21.3	467	175.6	196.9
12.4	113	34.4	529	198.9	233.3
12.5	179	54.4	507	190.6	245.0
12.6	256	77.8	402	151.2	229.0
12.7	326	99.1	297	111.7	210.8
12.8	379	115.2	226	85.0	200.2
13.0	360	109.4	140	52.6	162.0
13.2	277	84.2	96	36.1	120.3
13.4	196	59.6	74	27.8	87.4
13.6	140	42.6	61	22.9	65.5
13.8	103	31.3	53	19.9	51.2
14.0	80	24.2	47	17.7	42.0
14.3	60	18.2	41	15.4	33.6
14.6	48	14.6	36	13.5	28.1
15.0	38	11.6	32	12.0	23.6
15.5	33	10.0	29	10.9	20.9
16.0	29	8.8	26	9.8	18.6
16.5	26	7.9	23	8.6	16.5
17.0	23	7.0	21	7.9	14.9
17.5	21	6.4	20	7.5	13.9
18.0	20	6.1	19	7.1	13.2
19.0	18	5.5	16	6.0	11.5
20.0	15	4.6	14	5.3	9.9
22.0	12	3.6	12	4.5	8.1
26.0	0	0.0	0	0.0	0.0

$$A_m Q = (0.162 \text{ mi}^2)(1.88 \text{ in}) = 0.304 \text{ mi}^2\text{-in}$$

The unit discharges of column 2 are scaled by 0.304, resulting in the values of column 3. This gives an upper subarea hydrograph with a peak flow of 115.2 ft³/s at 12.8 hours.

The lower subarea is analyzed in the same manner.

$$Q = \frac{\left(P - \dfrac{200}{82} + 2\right)^2}{\left(P + \dfrac{800}{82} - 8\right)} = 3.08 \text{ inches}$$

$$I_a = 0.2\left(\frac{1000}{CN} - 10\right) = 0.2\left(\frac{1000}{82} - 10\right) = 0.439$$

$$\frac{I_a}{P} = \frac{0.439}{5} = 0.088$$

The scaling factor for the lower subarea is

$$A_m Q = (0.122 \text{ mi}^2)(3.08 \text{ in}) = 0.376 \text{ mi}^2\text{-in}$$

Since the rainfall type is II and t_c is 0.5 hours, Exhibit 5-II (sheet 5 of 10) of TR-55 Chapter 5 (1986) is chosen, and it is shown in Table 9.11. The first row ($t_t = 0.0$ hrs) of the upper table ($I_a/P = 0.1$) is chosen and placed in column 4 of Table 9.14. The scaling factor of 0.376 is applied to each value in column 4 to create the lower subarea discharge values in column 5. Note that the lower subarea has a peak of 198.9 ft³/s at 12.4 hours.

Finally, the flows from the upper subarea (column 3) are combined with the flows from the lower subarea (column 5) to create the composite hydrograph for the two-subarea watershed as shown in column 6. The resulting peak flow is 245.0 ft³/s at 12.5 hours.

The three hydrographs of columns 3, 5, and 6 are plotted in Figure 9.8 for comparison. Note that all three hydrographs start at a nonzero value, which means these hydrographs are truly partial hydrographs, but the leading flows are so small compared to the peak that the hydrographs could be used as full hydrographs without interjecting much error, and this is often done in practice. Notice that simply adding the peaks of the upper subarea and the lower subarea for the estimate of the peak flow for the entire watershed would result in a peak flow of 314 ft³/s, which is significantly larger than the peak of the composite hydrograph, which is 245 ft³/s. Timing of flows from one subarea to the other is the reason, and timing is always very important in watershed

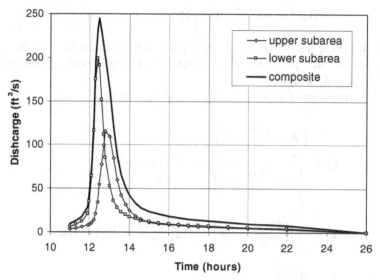

Figure 9.8 Plot of hydrographs for Example 9.5.

analysis and modeling. Chapter 10 will explain some of the methods used to account for channel flow timing and the effects that a channel has on a hydrograph peak, time to peak, and shape.

9.5.2 Limitations

The tabular hydrograph method has a few limitations. It does not have a limitation of use for drainage area. Instead, the method is limited by timing parameters. The method should not be used if any of these conditions apply:

- t_c is less than 0.1 hours and greater than 2.0 hours.
- t_t is greater than 3 hours.
- A complete hydrograph is needed for evaluation of storage effects such as stormwater basin design.

The first and second limitations are limits of the tabulated unit hydrographs of TR-55 Exhibit 5 (Tables 9.11 and 9.12), and values should not be extrapolated from this data. It is worth noting that interpolation between t_c or t_t values in these exhibits is acceptable, but the effort necessary to do so is probably not worth the gain in accuracy. The third limitation is violated somewhat regularly, as discussed earlier. A good rule of thumb for accepting the tabular hydrograph as a complete hydrograph is to look at the beginning and ending discharge values. If they are less than 5 percent of the peak flow, then the hydrograph is probably adequate for storage design. The better test is to evaluate the total runoff volume under the tabular hydrograph. If this volume is 95 percent or more of the direct runoff volume (A_mQ), then the hydrograph is more than adequate. The NRCS recommends the use of the TR-20 computer program in place of the tabular hydrograph method if any of these limitations exist.

Other aspects of the method are discussed further in the TR-55 (1986) publication. Particularly, the selection of t_c, t_t, and I_a/P is discussed since the drainage area values are not always equal to the values provided in the tables. Rules for rounding and interpolation are presented. Users who wish to know more should read the 1986 publication, which also includes discussion of runoff, travel time, peak flow, and storage detention estimates. The publication is available from the NRCS Internet Web site as a downloadable PDF file.

9.6 RATIONAL HYDROGRAPH

Several simplistic hydrograph methods exist that are based on the Rational peak-flow formula presented in Chapter 8. As mentioned in that chapter, there are three assumptions of the peak flow method:

1. Rainfall intensity is uniform over the watershed.
2. Duration of the design rainfall intensity is equal to the time of concentration of the drainage area.
3. The return period of the peak flow is equal to the return period of the rainfall intensity.

These assumptions can be extended to transform the peak flow formula into a hydrograph method.

9.6.1 Rational Triangular Hydrograph

The simplest transformation of the Rational peak-flow method to a hydrograph method is the Rational triangular hydrograph. It is based on the following assumptions:

- The peak discharge of the hydrograph is found using the Rational formula, $q_p = CiA$.
- The time to peak is equal to the drainage area time of concentration, t_c.
- The time base of the hydrograph is equal to two times t_c.
- The shape of the hydrograph is an isosceles triangle, with the rising limb having a slope of $+q_p/t_c$ and the falling limb having a slope of $-q_p/t_c$.

The hydrograph is easy to construct. We just need peak flow and time base. The construction is illustrated in Figure 9.9, showing a Rational triangular

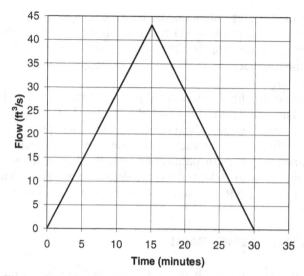

Figure 9.9 Shape of the Rational triangular hydrograph.

hydrograph for a drainage area having a t_c = 15 minutes, C = 0.5, i = 4.8 in/hr, and A = 18 acres, making the time base equal to 30 minutes and the peak flow equal to 43.2 ft^3/s.

The volume of runoff under the hydrograph is the area of an isosceles triangle.

$$V_R = \frac{1}{2}(CiA)(2t_c) = CiAt_c \qquad (9.21)$$

This triangular shape guarantees that the runoff volume, V_R, of the hydrograph is equal to the total rainfall excess, V_{RFE}. The assumption of constant, uniform rainfall over the entire drainage area for a storm duration equal to t_c, establishes the total rainfall volume, V_P, as

$$V_P = iAt_c \qquad (9.22)$$

Rainfall excess is established by reducing the rainfall by a fraction defined through the runoff coefficient, C. Thus the volume of rainfall excess is

$$V_{RFE} = CiAt_c \qquad (9.23)$$

The triangular shape of the hydrograph is realistic for only those watersheds that respond quickly to rainfall both in rising and falling runoff rates. Because of this characteristic shape, the Rational triangular hydrograph is probably reasonable only for small urban drainage areas that are relatively homogeneous hydrologically, and with medium to high levels of impervious area.

The triangular hydrograph is probably not a good hydrograph method when trying to estimate storage requirements for stormwater detention. In these cases, a modified method is used where the triangular hydrograph is stretched into a trapezoidal hydrograph by increasing the duration of the design rainfall intensity to some critical duration where storage requirements are maximized. This is discussed further in Chapter 12.

9.6.2 Application of the Rational Triangular Hydrograph

The Rational Triangular hydrograph can be used for subarea modeling when the watershed subareas are small and urban. Consider the three-subarea watershed of Example 8.9. This watershed was analyzed for peak flow for each subarea, independent of the entire watershed, to determine peak flows to the subarea inlets. Additionally, it was analyzed for flow in the pipe system, where the characteristics of the cumulative area above the pipe segment were used to compute a peak flow. An alternate approach to the method of Example 8.9 is to use Rational triangular hydrographs in combination with simple pipe routing. A reasonable hydrograph routing assumption for short pipes and culverts is that the pipe or culvert stores very little runoff during conveyance and the hydrograph is only changed by a delay in pipe travel time. This causes a pure translation, or shift, of the hydrograph with no attenuation (reduction) of the peak. For example, if the hydrograph of Figure 9.9 was to travel through a pipe that had a flow travel time of 10 minutes, it would look like the dashed hydrograph in Figure 9.10 as it exited the pipe. Using this assumption, Example 8.9 can be analyzed in a bit more sophisticated fashion, hydrologically speaking.

Example 9.6 For the small urban watershed of Example 8.9, determine the pipe design flows for pipe segments 2–3 and 3–4, using the Rational triangular hydrograph for subarea runoff calculation and simple pipe translation for routing the flows through the pipes. Use Figure 6.5 for the rainfall IDF data of the 25-year event.

Solution: Timing information for each subarea (SA) is summarized in Table 9.15. The largest time of concentration of all the subareas is 12 minutes, so the storm duration for modeling the entire watershed is set to 12 minutes, which will ensure that all three subareas have a chance to concentrate. This simply means that all portions of each subarea will contribute runoff to the watershed outlet.

Figure 6.5 gives a rainfall intensity of 4.0 in/hr for a storm duration of 12 minutes. Thus, the design storm is a simple constant intensity storm of 12 minutes, which is the design storm for the entire watershed. This storm is used on all subareas to compute hydrographs.

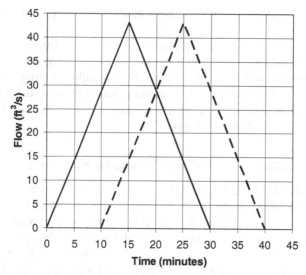

Figure 9.10   Hydrograph translated through 10 minutes due to pipe travel time.

An adjustment to the triangular hydrograph must be made for subareas 1 and 3, since they both have a t_c less than 12 minutes. One assumption of the hydrograph method is that the peak flow occurs at t_c under constant rainfall intensity. Since the rainfall intensity does not end at t_c for these subareas, the rainfall must continue to generate the peak flow until the rainfall ends, which is at time equal 12 minutes. Thus, the triangular hydrographs gets stretched into trapezoidal hydrographs for subareas 1 and 3. The new time base turns out to be t_c plus storm duration. Once the subarea hydrographs are computed, pipe travel times are used to translate the subarea hydrographs to inlets 2 and 3 as appropriate.

The peak flow and time base for each subarea are computed using $q_p = CiA$, and $t_b = 2t_c$ or $t_b = t_c +$ storm duration. The results are shown in Table 9.16. Figure 9.11 shows the shapes of the three hydrographs.

Table 9.17 shows the procedure used to estimate the design flow for pipe 2–3. The time scale is divided into time steps of 1 minute to facilitate hy-

TABLE 9.15   Timing Summary for Subareas of Example 8.9

Subarea	Time of Concentration (min)	Pipe Travel Time (min)
1	11	3
2	12	5
3	6	0

TABLE 9.16 **Triangular Hydrograph Dimensions for Each Subarea in Example 9.6**

Subarea	C	i (in/hr)	A (ac)	q_p (ft³/s)	t_c (min)	t_b (min)
1	0.25	4.0	5.8	5.8	11	23
2	0.40	4.0	6.1	9.8	12	24
3	0.85	4.0	5.5	18.7	6	18

drograph addition. Column 2 shows the hydrograph for SA1 as it enters inlet 1. Note that the peak of 5.8 ft³/s is stretched for an extra minute to match the time base to the storm duration. Once the rainfall ends, the flow begins to recede. This hydrograph is routed to the mouth of pipe 2–3 by using pure translation through pipe 1–2. The translation time is 3 minutes and the resulting hydrograph is shown in Column 3. Column 4 shows the hydrograph for SA2 as it enters inlet 2. Notice that it is a triangular graph because the subarea t_c is equal to the storm duration. Finally, Column 5 shows the sum of the hydrographs of columns 3 and 4 to give the hydrograph entering pipe 2–3. The resulting design flow for pipe 2–3 is 14.5 ft³/s.

A similar procedure is used to estimate the design flow for pipe 3–4, and the results are shown in Table 9.18. Column 2 shows the hydrograph at the mouth of pipe 2–3, which is column 5 of Table 9.17. This hydrograph is routed to the mouth of pipe 3–4 by using translation through pipe 2–3. The translation time is 5 minutes, and the resulting hydrograph is shown in column 3. Column 4 shows the trapezoidal hydrograph for SA3 as it enters inlet 3. Note that the peak flow of 18.7 ft³/s continues from time 6 to 12

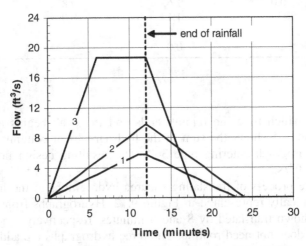

Figure 9.11 Triangular and trapezoidal subarea hydrographs reflect length of rainfall duration for the entire drainage area in Example 9.6.

TABLE 9.17 Rational Triangular Hydrographs Used to Find Design Flow for Pipe 2–3 in Example 9.6

(1) Time (min)	(2) SA1 Flow to Inlet 1 (ft³/s)	(3) SA1 Flow trans. to Inlet 2 (ft³/s)	(4) SA2 Flow to Inlet 2 (ft³/s)	(5) Total Flow into Pipe 2–3 (ft³/s)
0	0.0		0.0	0.0
1	0.5		0.8	0.8
2	1.1		1.6	1.6
3	1.6	0.0	2.5	2.5
4	2.1	0.5	3.3	3.8
5	2.6	1.1	4.1	5.2
6	3.2	1.6	4.9	6.5
7	3.7	2.1	5.7	7.8
8	4.2	2.6	6.5	9.1
9	4.7	3.2	7.4	10.6
10	5.3	3.7	8.2	11.9
11	5.8	4.2	9.0	13.2
12	5.8	4.7	9.8	14.5
13	5.3	5.3	9.0	14.3
14	4.7	5.8	8.2	14.0
15	4.2	5.8	7.4	13.2
16	3.7	5.3	6.5	11.8
17	3.2	4.7	5.7	10.4
18	2.6	4.2	4.9	9.1
19	2.1	3.7	4.1	7.8
20	1.6	3.2	3.3	6.5
21	1.1	2.6	2.5	5.1
22	0.5	2.1	1.6	3.7
23	0.0	1.6	0.8	2.4
24		1.1	0.0	1.1
25		0.5		0.5
26		0.0		0.0

minutes, at which time the rainfall ends and the peak begins to decrease. Finally, column 5 shows the sum of the hydrographs of columns 3 and 4 to give the hydrograph entering pipe 3–4. The resulting design flow for pipe 3–4 is 26.5 ft³/s.

The entire process of translating subarea hydrographs to the inlet of pipe 3–4 is graphically represented in Figure 9.12. Hydrographs from subareas 1 and 2 are shown translated by 8 and 5 minutes, respectively. The subarea 3 hydrograph does not need routing. The three hydrographs are added together to create the composite hydrograph for the flow in pipe 3–4.

TABLE 9.18 Rational Triangular Hydrographs Used to Find Design Flow for Pipe 3–4 in Example 9.6

(1) Time (min)	(2) Total Flow into Pipe 2–3 (ft³/s)	(3) Pipe 2–3 Flow trans. to Inlet 3 (ft³/s)	(4) SA3 Flow to Inlet 3 (ft³/s)	(5) Total Flow into Pipe 3–4 (ft³/s)
0	0.0		0.0	0.0
1	0.8		3.1	3.1
2	1.6		6.2	6.2
3	2.5		9.4	9.4
4	3.8		12.5	12.5
5	5.1	0.0	15.6	15.6
6	6.5	0.8	18.7	19.5
7	7.8	1.6	18.7	20.3
8	9.2	2.5	18.7	21.2
9	10.5	3.8	18.7	22.5
10	11.9	5.1	18.7	23.8
11	13.2	6.5	18.7	25.2
12	14.5	7.8	18.7	26.5
13	14.3	9.2	15.6	24.8
14	14.0	10.5	12.5	23.0
15	13.2	11.9	9.4	21.3
16	11.8	13.2	6.2	19.4
17	10.5	14.5	3.1	17.6
18	9.1	14.3	0.0	14.3
19	7.8	14.0		14.0
20	6.4	13.2		13.2
21	5.1	11.8		11.8
22	3.7	10.5		10.5
23	2.4	9.1		9.1
24	1.1	7.8		7.8
25	0.5	6.4		6.4
26	0.0	5.1		5.1
27		3.7		3.7
28		2.4		2.4
29		1.1		1.1
30		0.5		0.5
31		0.0		0.0

The results of Example 9.6 can be compared to the results obtained from the peak flow method of Example 8.9. In that solution, the design flow for pipe 2–3 was 14.0 ft³/s as compared to 14.5 ft³/s from the hydrograph method (3.4% increase). The design flow for pipe 3–4 was 24.0 ft³/s using the peak flow method as compared to 26.5 ft³/s using the hydrograph method (9.4% increase). From this single example, it might be concluded that the two

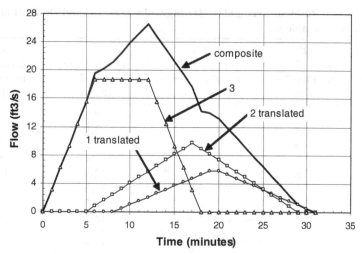

Figure 9.12   Example 9.6 composite hydrograph entering pipe 3–4. Three subarea hydrographs are translated to the pipe inlet then added.

methods give similar results, with the hydrograph method giving slightly larger values. Of course, it would be premature to conclude which method gives better results based on one example. Both methods are based on logical and practical assumptions. The peak-flow method lumps the C value into one and therefore "blurs" the model a little bit through averaging. The hydrograph method uses pure translation in the pipe routing scheme, which is not quite true, but frankly, not that bad. In the end, it is up to the practitioner to select the method for analysis.

PROBLEMS

9.1   Using the standard NRCS dimensionless unit hydrograph method, create a unit hydrograph for a watershed that contains 160 acres and has a time of concentration of 45 minutes.

9.2   For the unit hydrograph created in Problem 9.1, mathematically show that the volume of runoff under the curve is equal to 1 inch.

9.3   Using the Delmarva dimensionless unit hydrograph, create a unit hydrograph for the watershed described in Problem 9.1. Plot the Delmarva hydrograph against the standard NRCS hydrograph and compare the differences.

9.4   A watershed contains 78 acres and has a curve number of 82 and time of concentration of 30 minutes. Use the 10-year, 1-hour design storm

TABLE 9.19 Watershed Data for Problem 9.7

Subarea	Area (ac)	CN	t_c (min)	t_t (min)
1	65	77	23	30
2	88	81	32	18
3	45	73	24	0

created in Example 6.4. Perform the steps necessary to create a design hydrograph using the NRCS dimensionless unit hydrograph method.

9.5 Using the design hydrograph created in Problem 9.4, verify that the runoff under the graph equals the total rainfall excess used to create the hydrograph.

9.6 Create an NRCS tabular hydrograph for a 200-acre watershed that experiences 1.5 inches of direct runoff. Assume the watershed has a time of concentration of 0.5 hours.

9.7 The data provided in Table 9.19 is watershed information for a three-subarea drainage area located in Ohio. The subareas are connected in series with subarea 1 draining directly into subarea 2 which drains directly into subarea 3. Use the tabular hydrograph method to create a composite hydrograph for a 24-hour storm that totals 4.8 inches.

9.8 Create hydrographs using the Rational triangular method for the three subareas detailed in Table 9.20. Use Figure 6.5 to obtain the design rainfall intensities.

9.9 Assume that the subareas of Table 9.20 are connected in a linear fashion like that shown in Figure 8.12. Pipe travel times are provided in Table 9.21. Use the results of Problem 9.8 and simple time translation of pipe flow to create a composite hydrograph for pipe 3–4. Use Figure 6.5 for rainfall data.

9.10 Use the Rational peak-flow method and compute a peak flow for the entire drainage area defined in Tables 9.20 and 9.21. Compare this peak flow to the peak flow of the composite hydrograph of Problem 9.9. Are the two peak flows similar? Which method is better?

TABLE 9.20 Watershed Data for Problem 9.8

Subarea	Area (ac)	CN	t_c (min)
1	17.2	0.31	13
2	14.3	0.40	17
3	9.5	0.28	11

TABLE 9.21 Pipe Timing Data for Problem 9.9

Pipe	t_t (min)
1–2	13
2–3	9
3–4	–

REFERENCES

Brakensiek, D. L., and W. J. Rawls. 1983. "Green-Ampt Infiltration Model Parameters for Hydrologic Classification of Soils." In J. Borrelli, V. R. Hasfurther, and R. D. Burman (ed.). Advances in Irrigation and Drainage Surviving External Pressures, Proceedings of the American Society of Civil Engineers Specialty Conference, New York, p. 226–233.

Brown, S. A., S. M. Stein, and J. C. Warner. 2001. *Urban Drainage Design Manual, Hydraulic Engineering Circular 22,* 2nd ed., Federal Highway Administration, Report No. FHWA-NHI-01-021.

Chow, V. T. 1964. *Handbook of Applied Hydrology.* New York: McGraw-Hill.

Haan, C. T., H. P. Johnson, and D. L. Brakensiek, eds. 1982. *Hydrologic Modeling of Small Watersheds.* St. Joseph, MI: American Society of Agricultural Engineers.

McCuen, R. H. 2005. *Hydrologic Analysis and Design,* 3rd ed. Upper Saddle River, NJ: Prentice-Hall.

Rallison, R. E. 1981. "Past, Present, and Future SCS Runoff Procedure." Rainfall-Runoff Relationship: Proceedings of the International Symposium on Rainfall-Runoff Modeling. V. J. Singh, ed. Mississippi State University, May 18–21, 1981.

Rawls, W. J., A. Shalaby, and R. H. McCuen. 1981. "Evaluation of Methods for Determining Urban Runoff Curve Numbers." *Transactions of the American Society of Agricultural Engineers,* 24(6): 1562–1566.

Sheridan, J. M., W. H. Merkel, and D. D. Bosch. 2002. "Peak Rate Factors for Flatland Watersheds." *Applied Engineering in Agriculture,* 18(1): 65–69.

Singh, V. P. 1992. *Elementary Hydrology.* Englewood Cliffs, NJ: Prentice-Hall.

USDA NRCS, 1975. *Urban Hydrology for Small Watersheds,* TR-55, Engineering Division, Washington, DC.

USDA NRCS, 1986. *Urban Hydrology for Small Watersheds,* TR-55, Engineering Divsion, Washington, DC.

USDA NRCS, 2002. *National Engineering Handbook,* Part 630, Hydrology. Washington, DC.

USDA NRCS, 2003. *Supplement to the New Jersey Bulletin* No. NJ210-3-1, dated September 8, 2003.

Welle, P. I., D. E. Woodward and Moody H. Fox. "A Dimensionless Unit Hydrograph for the Delmarva Peninsula, 1980." Paper No. 80-2013, ASAE 1980 summer meeting, 18 pp.

ROUTING METHODS

10.1 INTRODUCTION

Flood routing is a mathematical technique used to estimate the change in characteristics of a hydrograph as it travels through a reach of river or a storage detention facility. In watershed modeling, channel routing and reservoir routing are often performed through different methods, yet the fundamental concepts behind the flood routing problem are the same.

As a flood wave passes down a channel, flow depth and channel storage increase, causing attenuation of the peak and flattening of the hydrograph. Additionally, it takes time for the flood wave to pass through the channel, which causes a translation of the hydrograph. A similar scenario is posed if a hydrograph is passed through a storage detention facility. Initially, the detention facility contains a large amount of storage capacity. As the inflow enters the detention facility, the water depth increases. The increased water depth places energy head on the outlet structure, causing the structure to release flow but at a reduced rate and delayed in time as compared to the inflow.

Typically, detention storage is much larger than channel storage, so the effects on the hydrograph are much more dramatic in detention facilities, as compared to channels. In either case, the key characteristics of a hydrograph that are of interest in routing are (1) peak flow, (2) time to peak flow, and (3) shape (time distribution of runoff volume).

10.2 CHANNEL ROUTING

Figure 10.1 shows a schematic drawing of a channel network in a watershed. If the hydrograph for a particular event is known at point B, channel routing estimates the change in shape of the hydrograph as it travels down the channel from B to A. Figure 10.2 shows the general affect that channel storage and travel time have on a hydrograph as it travels through a reach. Notice that the hydrograph shape has been "squashed" and "stretched," causing the peak flows to be reduced in magnitude and delayed in time. Routing methods can be categorized as either hydraulic or hydrologic. Both have advantages and disadvantages with appropriate applications. Both are briefly explained here.

10.2.1 Hydraulic Routing

Hydraulic routing of a flood wave relies on the simultaneous solution of the continuity and momentum equations for unsteady, gradually varied (nonuniform) flow. If lateral inflow to the channel is significant, the continuity (conservation of mass) relation in differential form is

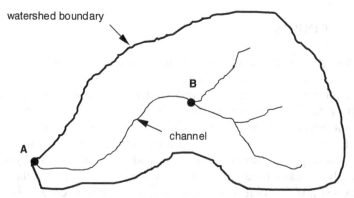

Figure 10.1 Watershed and channel network with points of interest B and A.

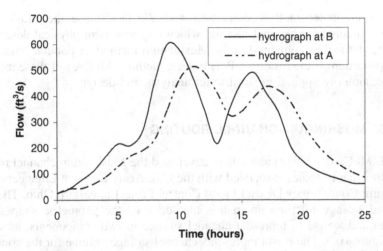

Figure 10.2 Effect of storage and travel time on a hydrograph routed through channel B-A of Figure 10.1.

$$A \frac{\partial v}{\partial x} + v B \frac{\partial y}{\partial x} + B \frac{\partial y}{\partial t} = q \tag{10.1}$$

where A = channel flow area, v = velocity, x = channel segment length, B = channel top width, y = flow depth, t = time, and q = lateral inflow. This equation is augmented with a conservation of momentum equation as presented by Henderson (1966) for unsteady flow in a river channel

$$S_f = S_o - \frac{\partial y}{\partial x} - \frac{v}{g} \frac{\partial v}{\partial x} - \frac{1}{g} \frac{\partial v}{\partial t} \tag{10.2}$$

where S_f = friction slope, S_o = bed slope, and g = gravitational constant. These equations are nonlinear partial differential equations that require sophisticated numerical techniques for solution. The use of these equations are well beyond the scope of this text. They are worth presenting here simply because they are the fundamental equations used in the river analysis computer model HEC-RAS developed by the U.S. Army Corp of Engineers (USACE, 2002). Simpler hydrologic methods are typically used in stormwater runoff modeling.

10.2.2 Hydrologic Routing

Hydrologic methods of channel routing do not attempt a direct solution of Equations 10.1 and 10.2. Instead, these methods solve the conservation of mass equation with the aid of a simplified storage-outflow relationship. A popular hydrologic channel routing method is the Muskingum method. The

NRCS computer models WinTR-55 and WinTR-20 use the Muskingum-Cunge method for channel routing, which requires more physical description of the channel as compared to the Muskingum method. A popular basin routing procedure is the Modified-Puls routing method. All three of these methods are commonly applied in stormwater analysis and design.

10.3 MUSKINGUM CHANNEL ROUTING

G. T. McCarthy (1938) and others developed the Muskingum channel routing method using studies associated with the U.S. Army Corps of Engineers Muskingum Conservancy District Flood Control Project in eastern Ohio. The simplified storage relationship in this method uses the geometric shapes of a prism and wedge to represent channel storage in two components, as shown in Figure 10.3. The prism represents channel storage volume for the condition where flow is steady—that is, inflow equals outflow. The wedge represents the channel storage volume above the prism that is caused by the passing of the flood wave. An assumption in this method is that channel section geometry is relatively constant throughout the reach.

10.3.1 Equations for Muskingum Method

The Muskingum method uses two basic equations. The first is a storage relationship based upon the geometry of Figure 10.3 and some assumptions about the characteristics of channel inflow, outflow, and storage.

$$S = K[XI + (1 - X)O] \qquad (10.3)$$

where S = channel storage (ft³)
$\quad I$ = channel inflow (ft³/s)
$\quad O$ = channel outflow (ft³/s)
$\quad K$ = storage time parameter (s)
$\quad X$ = storage prism parameter also known as the weighting factor

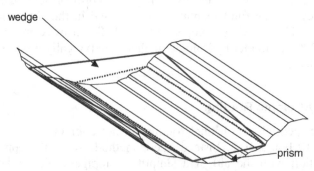

Figure 10.3 Channel storage of a flood wave is represented by a prism and a wedge.

This equation states that channel storage is a function of channel inflow, I, and channel outflow, O. The effects of each flow are weighted by the prism parameter X.

The second equation is conservation of mass.

$$I - O = \frac{\Delta S}{\Delta t} \tag{10.4}$$

where Δt = the routing time interval (s)

This equation states that all water entering the channel must either exit the channel, or cause a change in channel storage. The development of these two equations into a set of working equations is provided in Appendix B. The working equations are summarized as follows:

$$O_{n+1} = C_0 I_{n+1} + C_1 I_n + C_2 O_n \tag{10.5}$$

where the routing coefficients C_0, C_1, and C_2 are defined as follows:

$$C_0 = \left(\frac{-KX + 0.5\Delta t}{K - KX + 0.5\Delta t} \right) \tag{10.6}$$

$$C_1 = \left(\frac{KX + 0.5\Delta t}{K - KX + 0.5\Delta t} \right) \tag{10.7}$$

$$C_2 = \left(\frac{K - KX - 0.5\Delta t}{K - KX + 0.5\Delta t} \right) \tag{10.8}$$

These three routing coefficients, C_0, C_1, and C_2, are dimensionless. Therefore the time units of K and Δt must be the same. Also, mathematical integrity requires the sum of the three coefficients to be equal to unity.

The method requires examining flow into and out of the channel over very short time steps. Equation 10.5 has subscripts $n+1$ and n. The solution requires looking at flows at the beginning of a time interval (n) and at the end of the time interval ($n+1$). With the predetermined values of K, X, and Δt, the routing coefficients are computed and a general routing equation in the form of Equation 10.5 is created. The solution begins by identifying the initial inflow and outflow conditions in the channel. We usually assume uniform flow in the channel prior to passing a flood wave. Therefore, these two initial flow values are typically the same and the inflow and outflow of the beginning of the time step are known. Additionally, the inflow at the end of the time step is known. Therefore, the outflow at the end of the time step can be solved directly using Equation 10.5. This process is repeated for each subsequent overlapping pair of hydrograph ordinates until the entire hydrograph is routed through the channel.

10.3.2 Routing Parameters

The challenge in the application of this method is determining reasonable estimates of parameters K and X. In order to use the method with confidence, K and X should be determined through the analysis of stream gauge information, where both upstream and downstream hydrographs are known. With this information, K and X can be determined through a statistical process that is explained by McCuen (2005) or a graphical process that is explained by Bedient and Huber (2002). However, in practice this kind of data is rarely available. Therefore, the practical application of this method requires the adoption of some guiding rules of thumb that have some logical meaning attached to the rules.

Storage Time Parameter K. K is the *storage time parameter* for the channel reach. It can be assumed to be approximately equal to the travel time within the reach. Often, Manning's equation is used to estimate an average velocity in the channel for bank-full conditions, and this velocity is used to compute a travel time based on reach length. Care must be taken to verify that bank-full conditions are reasonable in the representation of the channel section geometry for the flood wave being routed. The effect of out-of-bank flow resistance to the flood wave velocity may need consideration, depending on the geometry of the channel and flood plain section.

Prism Parameter X. X is the weighting factor that proportions the relative effect of the upstream and downstream sections on the ability of the channel to store water. X is often referred to as the *prism parameter,* reflecting its ability to affect channel storage capacity in the relation. Since the method assumes the upstream and downstream sections to be similar in geometry and hydraulic characteristics, the reasonable range of X is 0.0 to 0.5.

If 0.0 is chosen for X, this causes the downstream channel section to act like a flow control device, similar to a dam or flow obstruction, and negates any effect that the upstream section has on channel storage. In this case the channel section has a very large amount of storage capacity and acts like a storage detention facility. This is the extreme case for channel sections that have very, very, wide flood plain areas that provide very large volumes for out-of-bank storage.

If 0.5 is chosen for X, this causes the upstream and downstream channel sections to have equal weighting in the storage relationship. The channel has very little capacity for storage, and acts mainly as a conveyance device. This is the case for highly prismatic channels such as a designed trapezoidal channel or a closed storm sewer.

Effect of K and X on Routing. Figure 10.4 shows the effect that K and X have on the routing process. When X is chosen to be 0.5, the channel has little or no storage. Therefore, the hydrograph goes through a simple *translation* in time based on the value of K. The hydrograph peak experiences little or no *attenuation*. When the value of X is chosen to be 0.1, the channel has large amounts of storage available, and therefore the hydrograph peak is attenuated significantly and also translated in time based on K.

In practical terms, X is rarely chosen to be lower than 0.1. For natural streams it is generally accepted that the range of X is between 0.2 and 0.3, with typical values being 0.2 or 0.25. A flat-sloped stream with huge flood plains might have an X value as low as 0.1. A steep sloped, narrow stream with no flood plain in a mountainous region could possibly have an X value as high as 0.4. For the prismatic, regular section channel (no overbank storage area) or the closed conduit, the choice of X equal to 0.5 is reasonable.

An additional criteria for selecting X is the magnitude of flows that will be routed through the channel. For high-probability events (low return periods) the flows will probably remain in-bank, and therefore the storage characteristics of the channel itself should be considered in choosing X. However, for low-probability events (high return periods) flow will undoubtedly spill over bank into the channel flood plain. For these events, the value of X may be significantly different than the in-bank X value, depending on the storage capability of the floodplain.

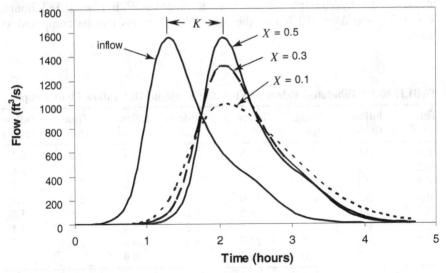

Figure 10.4 The effect of varying X in the Muskingum routing procedure.

10.3.3 Routing Interval

The routing interval should be chosen such that the shape of the routed hydrograph can be adequately captured in the step-by-step solution. The general rule of thumb for selecting the routing interval is to choose Δt such that five or six ordinates on the inflow hydrograph are captured in the routing before the peak flow is reached. When using a computer or spreadsheet solution, it is easiest to choose a routing interval that equals the time step of the inflow hydrograph, which almost always ensures that five or six ordinates exist before the peak flow. Choosing the timestep of the inflow hydrograph also guarantees that the peak of the inflow graph will appear in the routing output in the computer solution.

Once the routing coefficients are determined, the method reduces to solving Equation 10.5 in a tabulated format. The inflows are known from the inflow hydrograph for all time steps. The initial outflow in the routing is assumed to be equal to the initial inflow, suggesting that steady uniform flow is present in the channel prior to the passing of the flood wave.

Example 10.1   A computer-generated inflow hydrograph to a stream channel in a small watershed is shown in Table 10.1. The travel time through the channel is approximately 20 minutes. The prism storage parameter, X is assumed to be 0.25. Use the Muskingum method to estimate the shape of the outflow hydrograph after it passes through the reach.

Solution: A review of the inflow hydrograph shows that seven hydrograph ordinates occur prior to the peak inflow. Thus, a routing time interval equal to the inflow hydrograph time step is acceptable. With K = 0.333 hours, X = 0.25, and Δt = 0.2 hours, the routing coefficients can be computed as follows:

TABLE 10.1   Tabulated Values of Flow for Example 10.1 Inflow Hydrograph

Time (hrs)	Inflow (ft³/s)	Time (hrs)	Inflow (ft³/s)	Time (hrs)	Inflow (ft³/s)	Time (hrs)	Inflow (ft³/s)
0.0	0.0	1.6	70.5	3.2	18.4	4.8	9.1
0.2	1.2	1.8	55.3	3.4	16.6	5.0	8.6
0.4	2.1	2.0	43.2	3.6	15.0	5.2	8.1
0.6	3.2	2.2	37.0	3.8	13.6	5.4	7.7
0.8	5.0	2.4	31.6	4.0	12.4	5.6	7.4
1.0	9.3	2.6	27.1	4.2	11.4	5.8	7.1
1.2	20.8	2.8	23.5	4.4	10.6	6.0	6.8
1.4	60.7	3.0	20.7	4.6	9.9		

$$C_0 = \left(\frac{-0.333(0.25) + 0.5(0.2)}{0.333 - 0.333(0.25) + 0.5(0.2)} \right) = 0.0479$$

$$C_1 = \left(\frac{0.333(0.25) + 0.5(0.2)}{0.333 - 0.333(0.25) + 0.5(0.2)} \right) = 0.5239$$

$$C_2 = \left(\frac{0.333 - 0.333(0.25) - 0.5(0.2)}{0.333 - 0.333(0.25) + 0.5(0.2)} \right) = 0.4282$$

The routing can be done in a table or spreadsheet as shown in Table 10.2. The table is started by establishing the columns of time, inflow I, $C_0 I_{n+1}$, $C_1 I_n$, $C_2 O_n$, and outflow O_2. The inflow hydrograph with associated times is entered into column 2. The initial condition of the routing requires the initial outflow, O_1, to be set equal to the initial inflow, I_1, of zero.

The first routing interval of $\Delta t = 0.0$ to $\Delta t = 0.2$ hours is solved using Equation 10.5.

$$O_{n+1} = C_0 I_{n+1} + C_1 I_n + C_2 O_n$$

$$O_2 = (0.0479)(1.2) + (0.5239)(0) + (0.4282)(0) = 0.1 \text{ ft}^3/\text{s}$$

The solution continues by solving the remaining rows in a similar fashion.

$$O_3 = (0.0479)(2.1) + (0.5239)(1.2) + (0.4282)(0.1) = 0.8 \text{ ft}^3/\text{s}$$

$$O_4 = (0.0479)(3.2) + (0.5239)(2.1) + (0.4282)(0.8) = 1.6 \text{ ft}^2/\text{s}$$

$$O_5 = (0.0479)(5.0) + (0.5239)(3.2) + (0.4282)(1.6) = 2.6 \text{ ft}^3/\text{s}$$

. . . and so forth

The complete routing is shown in Table 10.2. The hydrographs are plotted in Figure 10.5.

A review of the solution shows the effect of the routing. The peak inflow of 70.5 ft³/s at $t = 1.6$ hrs is attenuated to 57.8 ft³/s and translated to $t = 1.8$ hrs. The translation is reasonable because it is similar in magnitude to the channel storage time parameter. In Figure 10.5, note the attenuation and translation of the peak and the tendency toward smoothing of the hydrograph curve. This is the expected effect of channel storage on a flood wave.

TABLE 10.2 Tabulated Solution to Example 10.1

Channel ID: Example Channel

Routing Interval = 0.2 hours $C_0 = 0.0479$

$K = 0.333$ hours $C_1 = 0.5239$

$X = 0.25$ $C_2 = 0.4282$

n	Time (hrs) (1)	Inflow (ft³/s) (2)	$C_0 \times I_{n+1}$ (ft³/s) (3)	$C_1 \times I_n$ (ft³/s) (4)	$C_2 \times O_n$ (ft³/s) (5)	Outflow (ft³/s) (6)
1	0.0	0.0	—	—	—	0.0
2	0.2	1.2	0.1	0.0	0.0	0.1
3	0.4	2.1	0.1	0.6	0.0	0.8
4	0.6	3.2	0.2	1.1	0.3	1.6
5	0.8	5.0	0.2	1.7	0.7	2.6
6	1.0	9.3	0.4	2.6	1.1	4.1
7	1.2	20.8	1.0	4.9	1.8	7.7
8	1.4	60.7	2.9	10.9	3.3	17.1
9	1.6	70.5	3.4	31.8	7.3	42.5
10	1.8	55.3	2.6	36.9	18.2	57.7
11	2.0	43.2	2.1	29.0	24.7	55.8
12	2.2	37.0	1.8	22.6	23.9	48.3
13	2.4	31.6	1.5	19.4	20.7	41.6
14	2.6	27.1	1.3	16.6	17.8	35.7
15	2.8	23.5	1.1	14.2	15.3	30.6
16	3.0	20.7	1.0	12.3	13.1	26.4
17	3.2	18.4	0.9	10.8	11.3	23.0
18	3.4	16.6	0.8	9.6	9.9	20.3
19	3.6	15.0	0.7	8.7	8.7	18.1
20	3.8	13.6	0.7	7.9	7.8	16.4
21	4.0	12.4	0.6	7.1	7.0	14.7
22	4.2	11.4	0.5	6.5	6.3	13.3
23	4.4	10.6	0.5	6.0	5.7	12.2
24	4.6	9.9	0.5	5.6	5.2	11.3
25	4.8	9.1	0.4	5.2	4.8	10.4
26	5.0	8.6	0.4	4.8	4.5	9.7
27	5.2	8.1	0.4	4.5	4.1	9.0
28	5.4	7.7	0.4	4.2	3.9	8.5
29	5.6	7.4	0.4	4.1	3.6	8.1
30	5.8	7.1	0.3	3.9	3.4	7.6
31	6.0	6.8	0.3	3.7	3.3	7.3

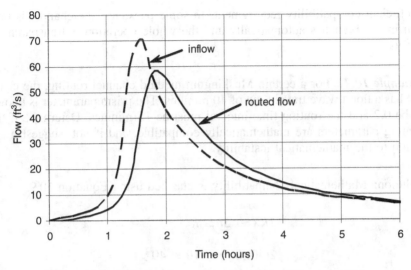

Figure 10.5 Inflow and routed hydrographs of Example 10.1.

10.3.4 Routing with Subreaches

In certain channel routing problems, it is possible that the selection of reasonable values of K, X, and Δt will cause one or two routing coefficients to be negative. Such coefficients could cause the routing procedure to create negative outflows, which is physically unreasonable. This condition of incompatible routing parameters causes a mathematical instability in the routing procedure. Mathematical stability is ensured by satisfying the following conditions:

$$2KX \leq \Delta t \leq K \tag{10.9}$$

These conditions can be met by breaking the channel into two or more subreaches and performing a series of routings through each subreach. The inflow to any given subreach is the routed outflow from the subreach immediately above. The following relation can be used to determine the minimum number of subreaches required to resolve the instability.

$$N = \frac{K}{\Delta t} \tag{10.10}$$

By breaking the channel into subreaches, the value of K for each subreach routing is obviously reduced. The reduction of K will cause the routing coefficients C_0, C_1, and C_2 to be computed as positive, allowing a valid routing. Some hydrologic software packages provide the user with the option of breaking the channel into subreaches. Some allow simple violation of the routing coefficient compatibility requirement. In some packages, the channel is broken into subreaches automatically and the whole operation is transparent to the user.

Example 10.2   For a certain Muskingum method channel routing, the channel has a flood wave travel time of 40 minutes. The prism parameter is known to be 0.2 and the routing time interval must be 15 minutes. Determine if the routing parameters are mathematically compatible, and if not, suggest a solution to the mathematical instability.

Solution: Mathematical compatibility is checked using Equation 10.9.

$$2KX \leq \Delta t \leq K$$

$$2(40)(0.2) \leq 10 \leq 40$$

$$16 \leq 10 \leq 40: \quad FALSE$$

Therefore, the routing parameters are NOT mathematically compatible. One of the parameters need changed. Since X and Δt should not be changed, K must be changed by breaking the channel into several subreaches. Using Equation 10.10 yields

$$N = \frac{K}{\Delta t} = \frac{40}{15} = 2.67 \text{ subreaches}$$

The result must be rounded up to the nearest whole, so the channel must be broken into three subreaches. This makes K equal to 13.33 minutes for each subreach and mathematical compatibility should be good.

$$2KX \leq \Delta t \leq K$$

$$2(13.33)(0.2) \leq 10 \leq 40$$

$$5.33 \leq 10 \leq 40: \quad TRUE$$

In Example 10.2 the routing is completed by routing the hydrograph through the first subreach. The outflow from the first subreach routing is then used as the inflow for the second subreach routing. Finally the outflow from the second subreach routing is used as the inflow for the third subreach routing, and this outflow is the final routed hydrograph through the entire reach.

10.4 MUSKINGUM-CUNGE CHANNEL ROUTING

In many software packages the Muskingum-Cunge channel routing method is used instead of the Muskingum method. Cunge (1969) developed a channel routing method, which uses hydraulic routing techniques. In certain simplified conditions, the method is identical to the Muskingum, thus the reason for the name Muskingum-Cunge. A complete treatment of the Cunge method is not given here, yet it is worth discussing since it is used in public domain software such as WinTR-55 and WinTR-20.

The big advantage Muskingum-Cunge has over Muskingum is that it allows better definition of the physical characteristics of the channel. Parameters such as length, roughness, slope, and geometry are required as input. This allows the computation of K and X for each routing interval. Specifically, Cunge proposed that K and X be computed using

$$K = \frac{L}{c}$$ (10.11)

and

$$X = 0.5\left(12 - \frac{q_u}{cSL}\right)$$ (10.12)

where L = reach length (ft)
c = kinematic wave celerity (ft/s)
q_u = characteristic unit discharge (ft^3/s/ft)
S = friction slope (ft/ft)

The kinematic wave celerity, c, is a velocity based on kinematic wave theory. A discharge rating curve for the channel is necessary to compute c, and a common approach to approximate the curve is using Manning's equation. With this assumption, c can be computed as

$$c = \frac{5}{3}v$$ (10.13)

where v is the average velocity in the channel. One possible approach to creating this rating table is to assume that the channel section is trapezoidal in shape, which includes the special cases of triangular and rectangular. This is the approach used in WinTR-55 (USDA, 2002), the Windows based computer model created by the NRCS to replace the desktop methods presented in TR-55 (1986). Using this assumption, the geometric characteristics of the channel are defined by the following equations:

$$T = B + 2zy \tag{10.14}$$

$$A_{xs} = \frac{(B + T)y}{2} \tag{10.15}$$

$$P = B + 2\sqrt{\left(\frac{T - B}{2}\right)^2 + y^2} \tag{10.16}$$

$$q = \frac{1.49}{n} \frac{A^{5/3}}{P^{2/3}} S^{1/2} \tag{10.17}$$

where A_{xs} = cross-section area (ft²)
  q = flow (ft³/s)
  T = top width (ft)
  B = bottom width (ft)
  y = flow depth (ft)
  P = wetted perimeter (ft)
  z = side slope, dimensionless
  S = friction (bottom) slope (ft/ft)

With these equations, a rating table is created by selecting flow depths ranging from 0 to the maximum expected value during the routing. For each flow depth the parameters of T, A, and P are computed and used to estimate q, resulting in the rating table.

Figure 10.6 shows the data input screen for reach data in WinTR-55. The physical data needed for routing is reach length, roughness, slope, bottom width, and average side slope. These data are used to create the rating table at the bottom of the window, in this case for Reach 1. Note that the NRCS uses standard flow depths of 0.5, 1, 2, 5, 10, and 20 feet to create the rating table. Using the rating table and channel characteristics, Equations 10.11 and 10.12 are used to compute K and X for every flow in the channel routing procedure. The method removes the guesswork in estimating K and X as in the Muskingum method. Logically, the Muskingum-Cunge method should provide more accurate results.

When using the trapezoidal geometry to approximate the channel section, it is important to select channel parameters that reflect the section shape during the anticipated routing. As was suggested with the selection of X in the Muskingum method, high-probability events flow at depths much lower than low-probability events. Therefore, the section geometry parameters for the same channel could be significantly different if a routing was being performed for significantly different events. It would be reasonable that the same channel would have a larger bottom width and flatter side slopes when routing the 100-year event, as compared to the 2-year or 5-year event.

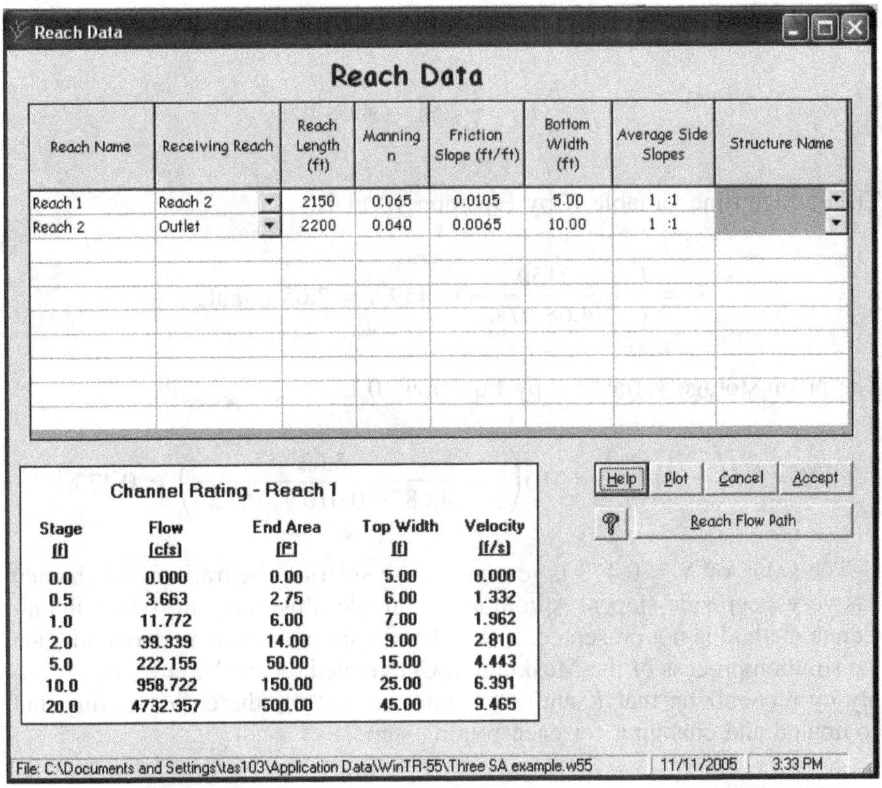
Reach Data
Reach Data
Reach Name | Receiving Reach | Reach Length (ft) | Manning n | Friction Slope (ft/ft) | Bottom Width (ft) | Average Side Slopes | Structure Name
Reach 1 | Reach 2 | 2150 | 0.065 | 0.0105 | 5.00 | 1 :1
Reach 2 | Outlet | 2200 | 0.040 | 0.0065 | 10.00 | 1 :1
Help
Plot
Cancel
Accept
Reach Flow Path
Channel Rating - Reach 1
Stage [ft] | Flow [cfs] | End Area [ft²] | Top Width [ft] | Velocity [ft/s]
0.0 | 0.000 | 0.00 | 5.00 | 0.000
0.5 | 3.663 | 2.75 | 6.00 | 1.332
1.0 | 11.772 | 6.00 | 7.00 | 1.962
2.0 | 39.339 | 14.00 | 9.00 | 2.810
5.0 | 222.155 | 50.00 | 15.00 | 4.443
10.0 | 958.722 | 150.00 | 25.00 | 6.391
20.0 | 4732.357 | 500.00 | 45.00 | 9.465
File: C:\Documents and Settings\tas103\Application Data\WinTR-55\Three SA example.w55
11/11/2005
3:33 PM

Figure 10.6 Reach data input screen supports Muskingum-Cunge channel routing in WinTR-55.

Example 10.3 For Reach 1 in Figure 10.6, compute the storage time variable K and the prism variable X for the condition where flow depth (stage) is equal to 2.0 feet.

Solution: From the channel-reach rating table in Figure 10.6, the flow is noted to be 39.34 ft^3/s and the velocity is 2.81 ft/s. The channel flow must be converted to flow per unit width in the channel, and this is done by computing an average channel width and dividing this into q. The bottom width is given as $B = 5$ feet and the top width is given as $T = 9$ feet.

Flow per unit foot is channel flow divided by average channel width.

$$q_u = \frac{2q}{(T + B)} = \frac{2(39.34\ \text{ft}^3/\text{s})}{(5 + 9)\text{ft}} = 5.62\ \text{ft}^3/\text{s}$$

Wave celerity c is computed using Equation 10.13.

$$c = \frac{5}{3}v = \frac{5}{3}2.81 = 4.68 \text{ ft/s}$$

The storage time variable K by Equation 10.11 is

$$K = \frac{L}{c} = \frac{2150 \text{ ft}}{4.68 \text{ ft/sec}} = 459 \text{ s} = 7.65 \text{ minutes}$$

The prism storage variable X by Equation 10.12 is

$$X = 0.5\left(1 - \frac{q_u}{cSL}\right) = 0.5\left(1 - \frac{5.62}{4.68 \times 0.0105 \times 2150}\right) = 0.473$$

The value of $X = 0.473$ is reasonable considering the trapezoidal channel has very steep side-slopes. A complete example illustrating the Muskingum-Cunge method is not presented. If the Muskingum method is understood, then the solution process of the Muskingum-Cunge method can be envisioned simply by recognizing that K and X are not constant for the entire routing, but computed and changing for each routing step.

10.5   MODIFIED PULS BASIN ROUTING

The effect of a detention structure on a flood hydrograph is most often modeled using the Modified Puls basin routing method, which is also known as the storage indication method. The method was developed by L. G. Puls (1928) and modified later within the U.S. Bureau of Reclamation (1949). The process models the effect of a storage facility on an inflow hydrograph. Figure 10.7 schematically depicts the situation of a detention basin. Initially, inflow to the basin causes the water surface to rise. As water surface rises, static head is placed on the outlet structure, which, in turn, causes the structure to gradually release outflow. As the water surface continues to increase, so does static head, and outflow. At some point, the inflow reduces to a level lower than the outflow and the water surface begins to fall, until some point where inflow stops and the basin simply drains empty. Through the process, the shape of the hydrograph is changed significantly with a reduction in peak and delay in peak timing.

The Modified Puls method solves the difference form of the conservation of mass Equation 10.4 in conjunction with a storage-indication chart. Storage

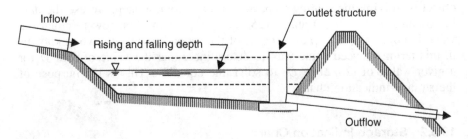

Figure 10.7 Sketch of a detention facility with inflow, rising and falling depth, and outflow.

in this case is detention basin storage. The storage indication chart is developed from the detention basin storage characteristics and the outlet structure flow capability.

10.5.1 Conservation of Mass

In difference form the conservation of mass equation becomes

$$\left(\frac{I_n + I_{n+1}}{2}\right) - \left(\frac{O_n + O_{n+1}}{2}\right) = \left(\frac{S_{n+1} - S_n}{\Delta t}\right) \tag{10.18}$$

In order to solve this equation, the initial storage (S_1) and outflow (O_1) of the detention facility must be known, as well as the ordinates of the inflow hydrograph (I_1, I_2, I_3, etc.). Thus for the routing interval between $n = 1$ and $n+1 = 2$, S_1, O_1, I_1, and I_2 are known. Conversely, S_2 and O_2 are unknown. It is convenient to rearrange Equation 10.18 by placing all known quantities on the left side and all unknown quantities on the right side. The resulting equation becomes

$$(I_n + I_{n+1}) + \left(\frac{2S_n}{\Delta t} - O_n +\right) = \left(\frac{2S_{n+1}}{\Delta t} + O_{n+1}\right) \tag{10.19}$$

A routing table, like that shown in Table 10.6, is used to solve Equation 10.19. The routing is performed by using the data in adjacent row pairs in the routing table, starting with the first and second rows. Note the structure of Equation 10.19. The first term is known for all rows of the routing table since all inflow values are known. The second term contains the storage and outflow terms associated with the first row in the pair. These terms are always known, either from the initial conditions in the pond or from a previously completed routing step. The third term contains storage and outflow terms associated with the second row in the pair. These terms are always unknown and are the object of solving the routing step. So, for each routing step, we use the data in columns 3 $(I_n + I_{n+1})$ and 4 $(2S_n/\Delta t - O_n)$ of the first row to equal the value in column 5 $(2S_{n+1}/\Delta t + O_{n+1})$ of the second row. With two unknowns in this term, we need some way to determine either the value of S or O for a given value of $(2S/\Delta t + O)$ to solve the equation. This is the purpose of the storage-indication chart.

10.5.2 Storage Indication Chart

From the geometric shape of the detention basin, a chart is created expressing detention storage as a function of water surface elevation. In addition, from the configuration of the outlet structure, a rating chart of the outlet structure can be created and expressed as outflow versus water surface elevation. With some manipulation, the two charts can be used to create a third chart that displays detention pond storage S as a function of detention pond outflow O. To simplify the solution of Equation 10.19, the storage-outflow function is developed into a chart that expresses the quantity $(2S/\Delta t) + O$ as a function of O. The time step, Δt must be set before creating the chart. The rule of thumb is to select a time step smaller than one-fifth the inflow hydrograph time to peak. Most times, the time step of the inflow hydrograph is used by default since it is almost always smaller than one-fifth time to peak. In the final analysis we will have a chart that allows us to determine pond outflow at the end of a routing time interval as long as we know inflow, storage, and outflow at the beginning of the routing interval.

As a side note, the term $2S/\Delta t + O$ does not seem to have any tangible meaning in a direct physical sense. It is a term that *indicates* storage (in an odd form) as a function of outflow. We should consider this as a convenience term that allows us to solve the continuity relation expressed in Equation 10.19 in a clever fashion. In a mathematical sense, the $2S/\Delta t + O$ vs. O chart is a graphical tool that acts as the second equation paired with Equation 10.19 to solve for the two unknowns of S and O.

10.5.3 General Routing Procedure

The general procedure for routing a hydrograph through a detention facility is summarized in the following steps. It is assumed that the inflow hydrograph, detention storage geometry, and outlet geometry are already known.

1. Create a chart showing the relation between water surface elevation and storage in the detention facility (elevation-storage, or ES curve).
2. Create a chart showing the relation between water surface elevation and flow through the detention facility outlet structure (elevation-outflow, or EO curve).

3. Select a routing time interval suitable for the routing. A time step smaller than 1/5 the time to peak of the inflow hydrograph is usually acceptable.
4. Construct a storage indication curve of $2S/\Delta t + O$ vs. O based on the ES and EO curves.
5. Create a routing table with columns of (1) time, (2) I_n, (3) $I_n + I_{n+1}$, (4) $2S_n/\Delta t - O_n$, (5) $2S_{n+1}/\Delta t + O_{n+1}$, and (6) O_{n+1}.
6. Initiate the routing process by filling columns 1, 2, and 3 with known values, and also filling in initial values of S and O for the first row.
7. Perform the routing using pairs of rows (1–2, 2–3, 3–4, etc.) beginning with the first row pair.
8. In the row pair, compute $2S/\Delta t - O$ for the first row using the values of S and O.
9. Use Equation 10.19 to solve for $2S/\Delta t + O$ in the second row.
10. Use the storage indication chart to solve for O in the second row.
11. Working with every successive row pair, repeat steps 8 through 10 until the hydrograph is completely routed.

Example 10.4 The hydrograph shown in Table 10.3 is to be routed through a rectangular basin with storage and outflow characteristics, as shown in Table 10.4. The basin is initially empty. Route the hydrograph through the basin using the Modified Puls routing method.

Solution: Table 10.4 provides the E-S and E-O curves necessary for the routing. The routing time interval is chosen to be 0.2 hours, which is the hydrograph time step. This time interval provides six hydrograph ordinates prior to

TABLE 10.3 Inflow Hydrograph of Example 10.4

Time (hours)	Flow (ft³/s)	Time (hours)	Flow (ft³/s)	Time (hours)	Flow (ft³/s)
0.0	0.4	2.2	5.2	4.2	2.3
0.2	1.0	2.4	4.5	4.4	2.3
0.4	2.0	2.6	4.0	4.6	2.1
0.6	3.0	2.8	3.6	4.8	2.0
0.8	6.7	3.0	3.3	5.0	1.9
1.0	17.3	3.2	3.0	5.2	1.8
1.2	51.4	3.4	2.8	5.4	1.8
1.4	35.3	3.6	2.6	5.6	1.7
1.6	15.2	3.8	2.5	5.8	1.6
1.8	8.9	4.0	2.4	6.0	1.6
2.0	6.3				

TABLE 10.4 Elevation-Storage and Elevation-Outflow Data for the Basin of Example 10.4

Elevation (ft)	Storage (ft³)	Outflow (ft³/s)	Elevation (ft)	Storage (ft³)	Outflow (ft³/s)
100.0	0	0.00	104.5	32,420	20.98
100.5	2,522	1.64	105.0	37,508	22.33
101.0	5,294	4.65	105.5	42,925	23.61
101.5	8,323	8.54	106.0	48,681	24.82
102.0	11,619	12.11	106.5	54,785	25.98
102.5	15,191	14.33	107.0	61,247	27.08
103.0	19,049	16.25	107.5	68,074	28.15
103.5	23,200	17.97	108.0	75,276	29.17
104.0	27,654	19.53			

the peak flow, which is adequate. The storage indication chart is computed as follows:

For elevation 100.0 ft, $S = 0$, $O = 0$, and therefore $2S/\Delta t + O = 0$.

For elevation 100.5 ft, $S = 2,522$ ft³, $O = 1.64$ ft³/sec, and $\Delta t = 0.2$ hours, or 720 seconds. Thus

$$\frac{2S}{\Delta t} + O = \frac{2(2,522 \text{ ft}^3/\text{s})}{720 \text{ s}} + 1.64 = 8.65 \text{ ft}^3/\text{s}$$

For elevation 101.0 ft, $S = 5,294$ ft³ and $O = 4.65$ ft³/sec.

$$\frac{2S}{\Delta t} + O = \frac{2(5,294 \text{ ft}^3/\text{sec})}{720 \text{ sec}} + 4.65 = 19.35 \text{ ft}^3/\text{sec}$$

Similar calculations are repeated for each elevation resulting in Table 10.5 and plotted in Figure 10.8.

The routing table is used to perform the routing as shown in Table 10.6. The time, inflow, and $I_n + I_{n+1}$ columns are filled using the inflow hydrograph information. The first row is seeded using the initial condition of $S_1 = 0$ and $O_1 = 0$. The calculations are performed as follows.

The routing process requires the use of two adjacent rows in the table that define a time interval. Values on the left side of Equation 10.19 are for the beginning of the time interval, and values on the right side are for the end of the time interval.

Routing Interval 1: Rows 1 and 2 for $t_1 = 0$ and $t_2 = 0.2$ hrs are used. The $2S_1/\Delta t - O_1$ of column 4 is zero due to the initial condition. Using Equation 10.19, $2S_2/\Delta t + O_2$ in column 5 in row 2 is the sum of columns 3 and 4 in row 1.

TABLE 10.5   Storage Indication Table for Example 10.4

Elevation (ft)	Storage (ft³)	Outflow (ft³/s)	$2S/\Delta t + O$ (ft³/s)
100.0	0	0.00	0.00
100.5	2,522	1.64	8.65
101.0	5,294	4.65	19.35
101.5	8,323	8.54	31.66
102.0	11,619	12.11	44.39
102.5	15,191	14.33	56.53
103.0	19,049	16.25	69.16
103.5	23,200	17.97	82.41
104.0	27,654	19.53	96.35
104.5	32,420	20.98	111.04
105.0	37,508	22.33	126.52
105.5	42,925	23.61	142.85
106.0	48,681	24.82	160.05
106.5	54,785	25.98	178.16
107.0	61,247	27.08	197.21
107.5	68,074	28.15	217.24
108.0	75,276	29.17	238.27

$$\frac{2S_2}{\Delta t} + O_2 = 1.0 + 0 = 1.0 \text{ ft}^3/\text{s}$$

Using the value of 1.0 ft³/s for $2S_2/\Delta t + O_2$, Figure 10.8 or Table 10.6 is used to estimate O_2 as 0.2 ft³/s.

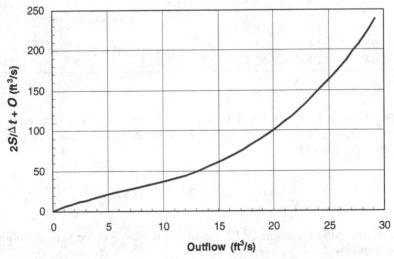

Figure 10.8   Plot of the storage indication curve for Example 10.4.

TABLE 10.6 Routing Table for Example 10.4

n	Time (hrs) (1)	I_n (ft^3/s) (2)	$I_n + I_{n+1}$ (ft^3/s) (3)	$2S_n/\Delta t - O_n$ (ft^3/s) (4)	$2S_{n+1}/\Delta t + O_{n+1}$ (ft^3/s) (5)	O_{n+1} (ft^3/s) (6)
1	0.0	0.0	1.0	0.0	—	0.0
2	0.2	1.0	3.2	0.6	1.0	0.2
3	0.4	2.2	5.7	2.4	3.8	0.7
4	0.6	3.5	10.2	4.9	8.1	1.6
5	0.8	6.7	24.0	8.2	15.1	3.5
6	1.0	17.3	68.7	14.9	32.2	8.7
7	1.2	51.4	86.7	47.4	83.6	18.1
8	1.4	35.3	50.5	88.3	134.1	22.9
9	1.6	15.2	24.1	92.2	138.8	23.3
10	1.8	8.9	15.2	73.4	116.3	21.4
11	2.0	6.3	11.5	51.3	88.6	18.7
12	2.2	5.2	9.7	32.2	62.8	15.3
13	2.4	4.5	8.5	19.1	41.9	11.4
14	2.6	4.0	7.6	13.1	27.6	7.3
15	2.8	3.6	6.9	10.6	20.7	5.1
16	3.0	3.3	6.3	9.2	17.5	4.1
17	3.2	3.0	5.8	8.4	15.5	3.6
18	3.4	2.8	5.4	7.8	14.2	3.2
19	3.6	2.6	5.1	7.4	13.2	2.9
20	3.8	2.5	4.9	7.1	12.5	2.7
21	4.0	2.4	4.7	6.8	12.0	2.6
22	4.2	2.3	4.6	6.7	11.5	2.4
23	4.4	2.3	4.4	6.5	11.3	2.4
24	4.6	2.1	4.1	6.4	10.9	2.3
25	4.8	2.0	3.9	6.2	10.5	2.2
26	5.0	1.9	3.7	6.0	10.1	2.1
27	5.2	1.8	3.6	5.7	9.7	2.0
28	5.4	1.8	3.5	5.6	9.3	1.9
29	5.6	1.7	3.3	5.6	9.1	1.8
30	5.8	1.6	3.2	5.6	8.9	1.7
31	6.0	1.6	3.2	5.5	8.8	1.7

Routing Interval 2: Rows 2 and 3 for $t_1 = 0.2$ and $t_2 = 0.4$ hrs are used. The $2S_2/\Delta t - O_2$ of column 4 is computed by subtracting two values of O_2 from $2S_2/\Delta t + O_2$, thus giving

$$\frac{2S_2}{\Delta t} - O_2 = 1.0 - 2(0.2) = 0.6 \text{ ft}^3/\text{s}$$

Once again, using Equation 10.19, column 5 in row 3 is the sum of columns 3 and 4 in row 2.

$$\frac{2S_3}{\Delta t} + O_3 = 3.2 + 0.6 = 3.8 \text{ ft}^3/\text{s}$$

Using the value of 3.8 ft³/s for $2S_3/\Delta t + O_3$, Figure 10.8 or Table 10.5 is used to estimate O_3 as 0.7 ft³/s.

Routing Interval 3: Rows 3 and 4 for $t_3 = 0.4$ and $t_4 = 0.6$ hrs are used. The $2S_3/\Delta t - O_3$ of column 4 is computed by subtracting two values of O_3 from $2S_3/\Delta t + O_3$, thus giving

$$\frac{2S_3}{\Delta t} - O_3 = 3.8 - 2(0.7) = 2.4 \text{ ft}^3/\text{s}$$

Once again using Equation 10.19, column 5 in row 4 is the sum of columns 3 and 4 in row 3.

$$\frac{2S_4}{\Delta t} + O_4 = 5.7 + 2.4 = 8.1 \text{ ft}^3/\text{s}$$

Using the value of 8.1 ft³/s for $2S_4/\Delta t + O_4$, Figure 10.8 or Table 10.5 is used to estimate O_4 as 1.6 ft³/s.

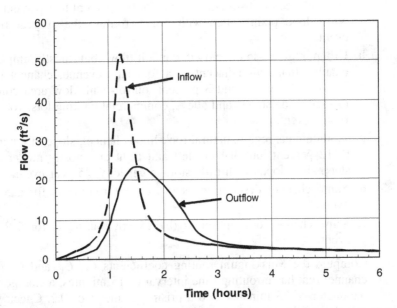

Figure 10.9 Inflow and outflow hydrographs of detention basin routing in Example 10.4.

This process is repeated for all succeeding row combinations until the entire hydrograph is routed. The results are shown in Table 10.6 and Figure 10.9.

The routed hydrograph has a peak flow of 23.3 ft³/s occurring at 1.6 hours. Thus, this detention pond reduced the peak by more than one-half.

The detention routing procedure is computationally involved, as illustrated in the previous example. This example was a simple analysis of an existing facility. In design, the elevation-storage relation must be created by making preliminary estimates of storage requirements. Additionally, the elevation-outflow relation must be created. This requires the preliminary design of the outlet structure to meet the stormwater management requirements. Routing of the hydrograph must be performed to determine if the preliminary design is controlling flow properly. If it is not, then a new design must be tried. Design of detention facilities is covered in Chapter 12.

PROBLEMS

10.1   Explain why the routing interval for either channel routing or basin routing should be one-fifth the time to peak flow, or smaller.

10.2   For the following channel descriptions, select a routing prism parameter X. Justify your selection.

   a. Coastal region, natural meandering stream with a well defined channel free of obstructions, slope of 0.2 percent to 1 percent, flat, wide flood plains filled with brush, routing the 50-year runoff event.

   b. Urban region, some closed conduit flow but mostly improved channel that runs adjacent to a four-lane avenue, channel slope between 1 percent and 3 percent, out-of-bank flow area consists of many side streets and alleys, commercial parking lots, 100-year runoff event.

   c. Mountainous region, natural rock-lined channel, slope of 4 percent to 12 percent, out-of-bank left and right are mostly moderate to steep side slopes with little storage capacity, 25-year event.

   d. Same channel description as (a), except routing is for a 5-year event.

   e. Same channel description as (b), except routing is for a 2-year event.

10.3   Compute the Muskingum routing coefficients C_0, C_1, and C_2 for a channel that has a routing time interval of 15 minutes, a storage time parameter of 25 minutes, and a prism parameter of 0.2. Check your calculations by comparing the sum of the coefficients to unity.

10.4   In a Muskingum channel routing, at routing time 80 minutes the inflow is 382 ft³/s and the outflow is 81 ft³/s. In the next routing time 100 minutes, the inflow is 614 ft³/s. If the channel $K = 0.42$ hrs, and X is 0.25, calculate the channel outflow for routing time 100 minutes.

10.5   A channel reach is 2,700 feet in length. It has an average section shape approximating a trapezoidal channel, with slope of 0.0058 ft/ft, bottom width of 10 feet, side slopes of 2:1, and Manning's roughness of 0.045. If the Muskingum-Cunge method is used to route a flood wave through this channel, determine the K and X values for a flow depth of 3.1 feet.

10.6   Route the hydrograph in Table 10.7 through a channel that has the routing parameters of $K = 8$ minutes and $X = 0.25$. Use a time step equal to 5 minutes.

10.7   For the elevation, storage, and outflow data shown in Table 10.8, create the associated $2S/\Delta t + O$ chart. Plot the chart using $2S/\Delta t + O$ as the ordinate, and O as the abscissa. Use a routing interval of 0.2 hours.

10.8   Route the hydrograph of Table 10.9 using the elevation-outflow-storage data of Table 10.8. Use a routing time interval of 0.2 hours.

10.9   Using a computer spreadsheet, set up the equations necessary to route a hydrograph through a channel using the Muskingum channel-routing method. Allow the spreadsheet to be flexible enough to handle cell locations for the input of parameters K, X, Δt and the inflow

TABLE 10.7   Hydrograph for Problem 10.6

Time (min)	Inflow (ft³/s)	Time (min)	Inflow (ft³/s)
0	0.0	65	19.0
5	1.3	70	16.5
10	1.9	75	14.5
15	2.5	80	12.9
20	3.5	85	11.6
25	6.3	90	10.5
30	14.6	95	9.5
35	42.5	100	8.7
40	49.4	105	8.0
45	38.7	110	7.4
50	30.2	115	6.9
55	25.9	120	6.4
60	22.1	125	6.0

TABLE 10.8 Elevation-Storage-Outflow Data for Problem 10.7

Elevation (ft)	Storage (ft³)	Outflow (ft³/s)
1297	0	0.0
1298	958	5.6
1299	3,833	17.6
1300	7,013	24.5
1301	10,498	29.7
1302	14,288	36.5
1303	18,382	42.4
1304	22,782	47.3
1305	27,486	51.6
1306	32,539	59.0
1307	37,897	100.0

hydrograph. Check the correctness of your spreadsheet by solving Example 10.1.

10.10 For the data provided in Example 10.3 and Figure 10.6, compute the storage time variable K and the prism variable X for all flow depths provided in Figure 10.6. Plot the variation of K and X against flow depth and explain the variability or lack of variability of each parameter.

10.11 Use a computer spreadsheet to set up a tabulated routine for the interactive solution of a basin routing using Modified Puls. Check your spreadsheet by solving Example 10.3.

TABLE 10.9 Inflow Hydrograph for Problem 10.8

Time (hrs)	Inflow ft³/s	Time (hrs)	Inflow ft³/s
0.0	0.0	2.6	14.2
0.2	2.5	2.8	11.0
0.4	5.0	3.0	9.6
0.6	7.5	3.2	9.0
0.8	9.4	3.4	8.4
1.0	11.4	3.6	7.7
1.2	18.8	3.8	7.0
1.4	39.8	4.0	6.3
1.6	60.8	4.2	6.1
1.8	64.9	4.4	5.9
2.0	46.2	4.6	5.7
2.2	27.5	4.8	5.5
2.4	17.5	5.0	5.3

REFERENCES

Bedient, P. B., and W. C. Huber. 2002. *Hydrology and Floodplain Analysis,* 3rd ed. Reading, MA: Addison-Wesley.

Chow, V. T. 1964. *Handbook of Applied Hydrology.* New York: McGraw-Hill.

Henderson, F. M. 1966. *Open Channel Flow.* New York: MacMillen.

McCarthy, G. T. 1938. "The Unit Hydrograph and Flood Routing." Conf. North Atlantic Div., U.S. Corps of Engineers, New London, CT, 1938.

Cunge, J. A. 1969. "On the Subject of a Flood Propagation Method (Muskingum Method)," *J. Hydraul. Res.,* 7(2): 205–230.

McCuen, R. H. 2005. *Hydrologic Analysis and Design,* 3rd ed. Upper Saddle River, NJ: Prentice-Hall.

Puls, L. G. 1928. *Flood Regulation in the Tennessee River,* 70th Congr., 1st Session, H.D. 185, Part 2, Appendix B.

U.S. Bureau of Reclamation. 1949. *Flood Routing,* Chapter 6.10, in Flood Hydrology, Part. 6, in Water Studies, Vol. IV of USBR Manual.

USDA NRCS. 2002. WinTR-55 computer program, downloadable program, http://www.wcc.nrcs.usda.gov/hydro/.

USACE. 2002. *HEC-RAS River Analysis System User's Manual,* Hydrologic Engineering Center, Davis, CA (http://www.hec.usace.army.mil).

CHAPTER 11

DRAINAGE CONVEYANCE AND CONTROL

11.1   INTRODUCTION

Drainage conveyance is a broad term that is used to describe any natural path or man-made structure that carries runoff from one point to the next. Traditionally, these conveyance systems have been surface flow paths or subsurface piping systems. They commonly include natural gullies, streams, rivers, swales, open channels, storm sewers, and culverts. For the typical stormwater management plan, one or several of these man-made conveyance structures must be designed to transport surface runoff away from buildings and streets, and toward a management structure like a detention pond or infiltration trench. In common land development design, storm sewer systems and open channels are typically small and reasonably simple in layout. This chapter covers common methods for designing these systems. More complex systems require more rigorous hydraulic methods and should be handled by an experienced hydraulic engineer.

11.2 SWALES AND OPEN CHANNELS

The design of open channel flow commonly includes a regular prismatic section on a uniform slope with uniform surface roughness. Under these conditions, the Manning equation is a reasonable model for designing the channel. Swales and diversion channels are typically smaller channels that carry stormwater around structures and through a land-development project, directing runoff either to a curb gutter, storm sewer inlet, receiving stream, detention pond, or some other stormwater management structure.

11.2.1 Channel Sizing

The procedure for sizing a channel is covered in Chapter 4. The fundamental relation used in sizing is the re-arranged form of the Manning's equation provided in Equation 4.13 which is repeated here as a matter of convenience

$$AR_{\mathrm{h}}^{2/3} = \frac{qn}{1.49\ S^{1/2}} \qquad (4.13)$$

As explained in Chapter 4, the sizing process is trial and error, where a guess at the section geometry is made and a flow depth is assumed. From the assumed depth, geometric properties are computed and the magnitude of the left side of Equation 4.13 is determined and compared to the magnitude of the right side. The process is repeated until both sides of the equation agree. This process is illustrated in Example 4.8.

There are certain design situations that do not require a solution on depth, but rather a solution on a different channel dimension. Example 11.1 illustrates one such situation.

Example 11.1   A concrete lined rectangular channel is proposed as an alternative section geometry for the channel sized in Example 4.8. The design flow is the same at 19 ft^3/s, but the maximum flow depth is adjusted to 1.0 ft and the channel width is to be reduced to the smallest possible dimension due to a change in site conditions. Channel slope remains at 0.0185 ft/ft but the roughness coefficient is changed to 0.018 to reflect a rough concrete finish.

In this design, we determine the smallest channel width by setting flow depth equal to 1.0 ft. The flow area and hydraulic radius are expressed in terms of b.

$$A = by = b(1.0) = b$$

$$P = b + 2y = b + 2(1.0) = b + 2$$

$$R_h = \frac{A}{P} = \frac{b}{b + 2}$$

With flow, roughness, and slope established, Equation 4.13 is simplified to

$$AR_h^{2/3} = \frac{qn}{1.49 \ S^{1/2}} = \frac{(19)(0.018)}{1.49(0.0185)^{1/2}}$$

$$AR_h^{2/3} = 1.688$$

Area and hydraulic radius are expressed in terms of channel width b giving the working equation

$$b\left(\frac{b}{b + 2}\right)^{2/3} = 1.688$$

$$\frac{b^{5/2}}{(b + 2)} = 2.193$$

This equation is now solved by trial and error to find the minimum channel width b. We arbitrarily start with a width of 1 foot.

This solution offers another channel section geometry that will handle the flow and site conditions of Example 4.8. This design will save plenty of surface area since its total width is 2.5 feet as compared to the first solution of Example 4.8 where the top width was 15.2 feet, and the second solution where the top width was 7.86 feet. The results of Example 11.1 and Example 4.8 show that a particular flow rate on a specified slope can be handled in many different ways. This same channel with a smooth concrete finish ($n = 0.011$) will reduce the top width of the channel further to 1.72 feet, providing yet one more possible channel to carry the design flow.

TABLE 11.1   Trial and Error Solution for Example 11.1

Trial	b (ft)	$b^{5/2}/(b + 2)$	Comment
1	1	0.333	low
2	3	3.118	high
3	2	1.414	low
4	2.5	2.196	OK!

11.2.2 Freeboard

Freeboard is depth above the maximum expected water surface elevation in the channel. A common default freeboard depth is often given as 1 foot. Many times the amount of freeboard is specified in the local municipal stormwater ordinance, and other times it is left to the discretion of the design engineer. In the absence of any specification, it is generally accepted that height of freeboard, H_{FB}, should be equal to 1 velocity head plus 0.5 ft. Simply stated, in U.S. standard units,

$$H_{FB} = 0.5 + \frac{v^2}{2g} \qquad (11.1)$$

For very shallow channels, such as roadside channels and minor stormwater diversions, flow depths are often 1 foot or less. In these cases, a reasonable freeboard depth is one-half of the maximum flow depth.

Example 11.2 Determine the freeboard for the channel of Example 11.1. Assume that the minimum allowable freeboard is defined by Equation 11.1.

Solution: The velocity in the channel is computed using continuity, converted to velocity head, and inserted into Equation 11.1.

$$v = \frac{q}{A} = \frac{19}{2.5} = 7.6 \text{ ft/s}$$

$$\frac{v^2}{2g} = \frac{7.6^2}{2(32.2)} = 0.897 \text{ ft}$$

$$H_{FB} = 0.5 + \frac{v^2}{2g} = 0.5 + 0.897 = 1.40 \text{ ft}$$

Equation 11.1 provides a freeboard depth of 1.40 ft, which is larger than the design flow depth. As a matter of comparison, the one-half maximum flow depth rule provides freeboard equal to 0.5 ft. A possible compromise between these two might be to set freeboard to the velocity head of 0.9 ft, or 1.0 ft to be a little more conservative.

11.2.3 Grass-Lined Channels

Grass-lined channels are desirable in stormwater plans. They have the ability to convey flow during large runoff events while providing filtration of runoff pollutants during lower runoff events. Grass linings can reduce flow velocity and the flash-like response of urban runoff. Larger channels with flat bottom slopes provide some storage detention benefit as well. Additionally, they provide some capability for groundwater recharge. In order to maintain healthy, vegetated cover in the channel bottom, the channels are designed to flow only during surface runoff events.

Manning's roughness coefficient for grass lining is a function of flow velocity, hydraulic radius, and vegetation type. Table 11.2 provides classifications of vegetal covers as to degree of retardance based on cover type and condition. In cases where the vegetation density is well established, the height of the vegetation controls the degree of retardance. For most cases, except for very sparse coverage, the simpler Table 11.3 can be used to estimate retardance. In either case, the retardance taken from the table is used in conjunction with the product of velocity times hydraulic radius (vR_h) to estimate Manning's roughness by using Figure 11.1. The selection process is trial and error in the design, since hydraulic radius and velocity depend on channel roughness.

Channel section geometry is commonly triangular or trapezoidal. The parabolic section is probably the best geometry for the grass-lined channel. It provides a low flow region but spreads out rapidly with increasing depth. The triangular section may be susceptible to erosion at the invert and the trapezoidal section may experience sedimentation across the horizontal bottom. However, since the parabolic section is more difficult to construct, most designs are either triangular or trapezoidal. In the field, both triangular and trapezoidal sections usually transform into a parabolic section over time if the channel is poorly maintained or simply left alone.

Grass-lined channels require extra design attention, particularly in terms of lining stability and maintenance issues. Side slopes are usually 2H:1V and flatter to guarantee side-slope stability. For safe mowing and easier maintenance, side slopes of 4H or 5H to 1V are recommended. Channel bottom slope and flow depth should be kept to a minimum to prevent erosion problems. In general, wide and shallow vegetated channels are preferred over deep and narrow. Yet, very flat channels may be prone to sedimentation problems, which can cause channel capacity loss after several years of use. Periodic sediment removal and reseeding may be necessary as part of a long-term channel maintenance plan.

The best way to prevent channel erosion is to keep the flow velocity as low as possible. Nonerosive velocities were proposed by the Soil Conservation Service based on studies performed in Stillwater, Oklahoma (USDA, SCS TP-61, 1947; revised 1954). Guidelines for permissible velocities are shown in Table 11.4. Additional restrictions for site specific conditions are as follows:

TABLE 11.2   Classification of Vegetal Covers as to Degree of Retardance in Grass-lined Channels (Source USDA TP-61, 1947)

Retardance	Cover	Condition	Height (inches)
A	Reed canarygrass or yellow bluestem ischaemum	Excellent stand, tall	36
	Weeping lovegrass	Excellent stand, tall	30
B	Smooth bromegrass	Good stand, mowed	12–15
	Bermudagrass	Good stand, tall	12
	Native grass mixture (little bluestem, blue grama, and other midwest grasses)	Good stand, unmowed	
	Tall fescue	Good stand, unmowed	18
	Sericea lespedeza	Good stand, not woody	19
	Grass legume mixture— timothy, smooth bromegrass, orchard grass	Good stand, uncut	20
	Reed canarygrass	Good stand, uncut	12–15
	Tall fescue with birdsfoot trefoil or ladino clover	Good stand, uncut	18
	Blue grama	Good stand, uncut	13
C	Bahiagrass	Good stand, uncut	6–8
	Bermudagrass	Good stand, mowed	6
	Redtop	Good stand, headed	15–20
	Grass-legme mixture— summer (orchardgrass, redtop, Italian ryegrass, and common lespedeza)	Good stand, uncut	6–8
	Centipedegrass	Very dense cover	6
	Kentucky bluegrass	Good stand, headed	6–12
D	Bermudagrass	Good stand, cut	2.5
	Red fescue	Good stand, headed	12–18
	Buffalograss	Good stand, uncut	3–6
	Grass-legume mixture—fall, spring (orchardgrass, redtop, Italian ryegrass, and common lespedeza)	Good stand, uncut	4–5
	Sericea lespedeza or Kentucky bluegrass	Good stand, cut. Very good stand before cutting	2
E	Bermudagrass	Good stand, cut	1.5
	Burmudagrass	Burned stubble	

TABLE 11.3   Retardance Based on Length of Vegetation (Source USDA TP-61, 1947)

Average Length of Vegetation (inches)	Degree of Retardance	
	Good Stand	Fair Stand
Longer than 30	A	B
11 to 24	B	C
6 to 10	C	D
2 to 6	D	D
Less than 2	E	E

- When only sparse cover can be maintained, the channel velocity should not exceed 3 ft/s.
- If vegetation is to be established by seeding, a velocity of 3 to 4 ft/s should be used under normal conditions.
- When dense sod is established quickly or if water can be diverted out of the channel while vegetation is being established, then a velocity of 4 to 5 ft/s is acceptable.

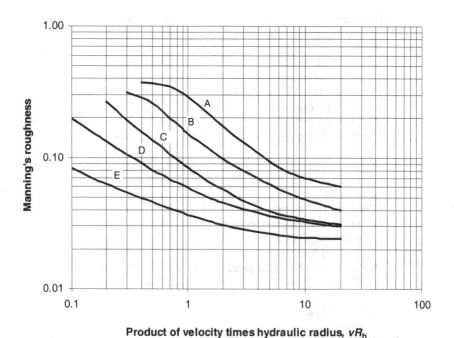

Figure 11.1   Manning's roughness for grass-lined channels (USDA TP-61, 1947).

TABLE 11.4 Permissible Velocities for Channels Lined with Vegetation (USDA TP-61, 1947)

| Cover | Slope Range[2] (%) | Permissible Velocity[1] | |
		Erosion Resistant Soils[3] (ft/s)	Easily Eroded Soils[4] (ft/s)
Bermudagrass	< 5	8	6
	5–10	7	5
	> 10	6	4
Bahiagrass, buffalograss,	< 5	7	5
Kentucky bluegrass,	5–10	6	4
smooth bromegrass,	> 10	5	3
blue grama, tall fescue			
Grass mixture, reed	< 5	5	4
canarygrass	5–10	4	3
Sericea lespedeza, weeping	< 5[5]	3.5	2.5
lovegrass, yellow			
bluestem redtop, alfalfa,			
red fescue			
Common lespedeza[6] or	< 5[7]	3.5	2.5
Sudan grass[6]			

[1] Use velocities exceeding 5 ft/s only where good covers and proper maintenance can be obtained.
[2] Do not use on slopes steeper than 10 percent except for vegetated side slopes in combination with a stone, concrete, or highly resistant vegetative center section.
[3] Cohesive (clayey) fine-grain soils and coarse-grain soils with cohesive fines with a plasticity index of 10 to 40 (CL, CH, SC and CG)
[4] Soils that do not meet requirements for erosion-resistant soils.
[5] Do not use on slopes steeper than 5% except for vegetated side slopes in combination with a stone concrete or highly resistant vegetative center section.
[6] Annuals—use on mild slope or as temporary protection until permanent covers are established.
[7] Use on slopes steeper than 5% is not recommended.

- On a well-established, good-quality sod a velocity of 5 to 6 ft/s can be used.
- On an established, excellent quality sod when flow cannot be handled at a lower velocity, a velocity of 6 to 8 ft/s is permitted as long as special maintenance provisions and appurtenant structures are in place.

The design procedure for channels with vegetated lining is typically a dual design process. The channel is first sized for stability based on the expected retardance for the period when the channel is just constructed and vegetation is beginning to establish. This period typically presents lower retardance and higher velocities. The channel is then checked for conveyance using the expected retardance, which will occur once the vegetation is fully developed. The second condition typically presents a higher retardance and thus a lower velocity. French (1985) and Chin (2000) provide a very structured approach to the design of vegetated channels. Their methods are very good, yet for certain section shapes, it is often easiest to take an educated guess at the section geometry and see how it performs.

Example 11.3   Stormwater on a commercial site is to be diverted around a building. The channel is to be trapezoidal and lined with Kentucky bluegrass. It must carry 10.2 ft³/s on a slope of 1.5 percent through an easily eroded soil. Side slopes of 4H to 1V minimum are required to accommodate machine mowing. During early stages of channel use, vegetation will have a fair stand with a height of 2 inches or less. Once fully developed, the vegetation is expected to be a good stand, cut periodically to a height of 6 to 8 inches. The stormwater right of way for the channel is limited to 20 feet. Determine the required flow depth and bottom width. Check that the top width, based on flow depth and required freeboard, is within the bounds of the right of way.

First Design Condition-Early Stage of Use: To begin the design, a permissible velocity to protect against erosion must be determined. From Table 11.4, with Kentucky bluegrass, 1.5 percent slope, easily eroded soil, the recommended permissible velocity is 5 ft/s. Using this value the estimated flow area becomes

$$A_{est} = \frac{q}{v} = \frac{10.2 \text{ ft}^3/\text{s}}{5 \text{ ft/s}} = 2.0 \text{ ft}^2$$

From this value, a first guess at channel dimensions is made. A bottom width of the channel is arbitrarily chosen to be 2 feet. Side slopes are set to 4H: 1V. The area equation for a trapezoidal section is solved for y.

$$A = (b + zy)y = by + zy^2$$

$$zy^2 + by - A = 0$$

$$4y^2 + 2y - 2.1 = 0$$

Solving this equation with the binomial formula gives two answers, one of which is logical.

$$y = \frac{-2 \pm \sqrt{2^2 - 4(4)(-2.1)}}{2(4)} = 0.517, \ -1.02 \text{ ft}$$

Therefore, we will assume a flow depth of about 0.52 feet, for a channel having a bottom width of 2 feet and side slopes of 4H:1V.

Roughness must also be estimated. Figure 11.1 clearly shows that Manning's n for vegetated channels varies with velocity and hydraulic radius; thus, an educated guess at the value is required. Table 11.3 reveals that the channel retardance rating of E is appropriate for early-stage conditions. If depth in the channel is assumed to be 0.52 feet, then the hydraulic radius is computed using wetted perimeter and flow area.

$$P = b + 2y\sqrt{1 + z^2} = 2 + 2(0.52)\sqrt{1 + 4^2} = 6.29 \text{ ft}$$

$$R_h = \frac{A}{P} = \frac{2.1 \text{ ft}^2}{6.29 \text{ ft}} = 0.334 \text{ ft}$$

The product of vR_h is 5×0.334, which equals 1.67 ft²/s. From Figure 11.1, with retardance E, Manning's n is estimated as 0.032.

With this first estimate of channel properties, Equation 4.13 is used to calculate the conveyance term $AR^{2/3}$.

$$AR_h^{2/3} = \frac{qn}{1.49 \ S^{1/2}} = \frac{(10.2)(0.032)}{1.49(0.015)^{1/2}} = 1.789$$

The flow depth is solved by trial and error and the solution is summarized in Table 11.5.

With this flow depth, the Manning's roughness and flow velocity must be checked to make sure it is appropriate. The actual channel velocity is

$$y = \frac{q}{A} = \frac{10.2}{3.210} = 3.18 \text{ ft/s}$$

TABLE 11.5   First Iteration of Flow-depth Solution for the First Design Condition of Example 11.3

Trial	y (ft)	A (ft²)	P (ft)	R (ft)	$AR^{2/3}$	Check
1	0.50	2.000	6.123	0.327	0.949	low
2	0.60	2.640	6.948	0.380	1.385	low
3	0.70	3.360	7.772	0.432	1.921	high
4	0.68	3.210	7.607	0.422	1.805	OK

The permissible velocity of 5 ft/s has not been exceeded. The product of vR_h is 3.18 times 0.422, which is 1.34 ft²/s. With this value of vR_h, Figure 11.1 shows that the originally assumed n value is incorrect and a new suggestion is $n = 0.035$. A second flow-depth calculation must be done based on this value. A new conveyance term $AR^{2/3}$ is computed.

$$AR_h^{2/3} = \frac{qn}{1.49\ S^{1/23}} = \frac{(10.2)(0.035)}{1.49(0.015)^{1/2}} = 1.956$$

Flow depth is solved once again by trial and error, as shown in Table 11.6. The new channel velocity is

$$v = \frac{q}{A} = \frac{10.2}{3.436} = 2.97\ \text{ft/s}$$

The new product of vR is 2.97 times 0.437 which is 1.30 ft²/s. With this value of vR, Figure 11.1 shows that the assumed n value is essentially unchanged, so the flow depth of 0.71 feet is accepted as close enough.

Required freeboard for this part of the design is

$$H_{FB} = 0.5 + \frac{(2.97\ \text{ft/s})^2}{2(32.2\ \text{ft/s}^2)} = 0.5 + 0.14 = 0.64\ \text{ft}$$

Constructed top width of the channel is based on flow depth plus freeboard, and is computed as

$$T = b + 2zy = 2 + 2(4)(0.71 + 0.64) = 12.8\ \text{ft}$$

This is well within the limits of the 20-feet drainage path right of way.

Thus, for the first design condition, the geometry of $b = 2$ feet, side slopes of 4H:1V, $S = 0.015$ ft/ft, $y = 0.71$ feet, $H_{FB} = 0.640$ feet, and $T = 12.8$ feet is accepted as a workable channel section.

TABLE 11.6 Second Iteration of Flow-depth Solution for the First Design Condition of Example 11.3

Trial	y (ft)	A (ft²)	P (ft)	R (ft)	$AR^{2/3}$	Check
1	0.65	2.990	7.360	0.406	1.640	low
2	0.68	3.210	7.607	0.422	1.805	low
3	0.71	3.436	7.855	0.437	1.980	OK

Second Design Condition: Established Vegetated Cover: After the vegetation has established itself and developed into full height grass, the retardance condition will change. With a good stand of 6 to 8 inches, Table 11.3 is used to assign a retardance rating of C. The process of the first design is repeated here to determine depth of flow with the higher retardance. The product of vR_h found in the first design condition (1.33 ft^2/s) is used as an estimate of vR_h for the second condition, giving $n = 0.070$ from Figure 11.1. The conveyance term $AR_h^{2/3}$ is computed.

$$AR_h^{2/3} = \frac{qn}{1.49 \ S^{1/2}} = \frac{(10.2)(0.070)}{1.49(0.015)^{1/2}} = 3.913$$

Since an increase in retardance will increase flow depth as compared to the first condition solution, an initial flow depth of 1.0 feet is assumed. The trial-and-error process for flow-depth solution is shown in Table 11.7.

The channel velocity is

$$v = \frac{q}{A} = \frac{10.2}{5.704} = 1.79 \text{ ft/s}$$

A check on the assumed channel roughness is again required. The product of vR_h is 1.79 times 0.570, which is 1.02 ft^2/s. The originally assumed n value was low. A more correct value is 0.084. The conveyance term $AR_h^{2/3}$ is computed again, based on the new n value.

$$AR_h^{2/3} = \frac{qn}{1.49 \ S^{1/2}} = \frac{(10.2)(0.084)}{1.49(0.015)^{1/2}} = 4.695$$

An initial flow depth of 1.0 foot is assumed again to start the trial and error process. Results are shown in Table 11.8.

Channel velocity is once again computed as

$$v = \frac{q}{A} = \frac{10.2}{6.510} = 1.57 \text{ ft/s}$$

TABLE 11.7 First Iteration of Flow-depth Solution for the Second Design Condition of Example 11.3

Trial	y (ft)	A (ft^2)	P (ft)	R (ft)	$AR^{2/3}$	Check
1	1.00	6.000	10.246	0.586	4.200	high
2	0.97	5.704	9.999	0.570	3.923	OK

TABLE 11.8 Second Iteration of Flow-depth Solution for the Second Design Condition of Example 11.3

Trial	y (ft)	A (ft^2)	P (ft)	R (ft)	$AR^{2/3}$	Check
1	1.00	6.000	10.246	0.586	4.200	low
2	1.10	7.040	11.071	0.636	5.206	high
3	1.05	6.510	10.659	0.611	4.686	OK

Channel roughness is again checked. The product of vR_h is 1.57 times 0.611, which is 0.957 ft^2/s. The originally assumed n value (0.084) was correct (0.085) for all practical purposes, so the flow depth of 1.05 feet is accepted as correct. As expected, the permissible velocity of 5 ft/s is not exceeded for the second design condition. Required freeboard for this second part of the design is

$$H_{FB} = 0.5 + \frac{(1.57 \text{ ft/s})^2}{2(32.2 \text{ ft/s}^2)} = 0.5 + 0.04 = 0.54 \text{ ft}$$

A check on top width of the constructed channel gives

$$T = b + 2zy = 2 + 2(4)(1.05 + 0.54) = 14.7 \text{ ft}$$

Again, this is well within the maximum width of 20 feet. The final design for the channel is as follows

Design flow = 10.2 ft^3/s
Design flow velocity = 1.57 ft/s
Slope = 0.015 ft/ft
Bottom width = 2 ft
Side slopes = 4H:1V
Kentucky bluegrass, good stand, cut to 6″ to 8″ height, roughness = 0.085
Flow depth = 1.05 ft
Freeboard = 0.54 ft
Construction depth = 1.59 ft
Construction top width = 14.7 ft

11.3 STORM SEWER DESIGN

Minor storm sewer systems are underground piping systems that collect, transport, and discharge stormwater runoff to a downstream facility or receiving channel. There are no specific criteria for designating a sewer collection system as minor, but a good rule of thumb can be any branched system of pipes (no loops) where pipe diameters are less than 4 to 5 feet, slopes are less than 8 to 10 percent, and junctions are relatively simple in geometry.

The design is typically performed using the Rational method for peak-flow estimation and the Manning equation for pipe sizing. The fundamental equations for the two methods are repeated here as a matter of convenience.

$$q_p = CiA \tag{8.15}$$

$$D_{min} = 16\left(\frac{qn}{S^{1/2}}\right)^{3/8} \text{ (inches)} \tag{4.16}$$

The use of these two common methods place certain limitations on the system in terms of size and complexity. The Rational method requires uniform rainfall over the drainage area, thus requiring the design area to be reasonably small—certainly less than 1 square mile and probably less than 300 acres. The Manning equation assumes that flow is uniform. This is a reasonably good assumption for closed conduits flowing full or partially full that are straight, regular in section, with constant slope. At the transition points, mainly inlets and manholes, the Manning equation does not necessarily apply. Uniform flow can be disturbed by the geometry of the entrance and exit conditions and change of direction through the structure. Calculation of the hydraulic and energy grade lines for the entire sewer system will verify if there is need for concern at these junction points. The hydraulic and energy grade lines are discussed in Section 11.3.3.

11.3.1 Pipe Sizing

The design process begins with system layout. Locations for inlets are determined based on the site topography, street alignments, and other proposed construction. Typically, storm sewer inlets are located along streets in the curb gutter or in swales parallel to the street. Local ordinances often dictate where inlets must be located, particularly at street intersections. Many states and municipalities require the space between inlets to be no more than 300 to 400 feet. Other state or municipal design requirements might be applicable, and it is up to the designer to research these requirements before design begins. Each inlet is a design point in the storm sewer system. Once the system layout is complete, basic information is collected for each inlet and each pipe segment between inlets.

For inlets, the data and analysis are primarily related to hydrology and peak-flow analysis. The steps required follow:

1. Delineate and calculate the drainage area contributing to each design point.
2. Determine the approximate top elevation of each inlet.

3. Determine the Rational runoff coefficient for each drainage area.

4. Calculate the time of concentration for each drainage area.

For pipe segments, the data and analysis are related to hydrologic and hydraulic flow analysis. The Manning equation for normal-depth pipe flow is assumed to be valid. The data collection includes the following:

- Determine the distance between successive design points along the drainage network.
- Determine the elevation change between successive design points.
- Select a pipe material and establish a Manning's roughness coefficient.

With this information, the design begins at the uppermost portion of the drainage network. The design process is best illustrated by example.

Example 11.4 Consider the schematic diagram of a drainage network in a small development shown in Figure 11.2. A preliminary design of pipe sizes is required. The watershed contains 15.22 acres and is divided into seven subareas, identified by drainage inlet. Subareas 1, 2, 4, 5, and 7 will be developed into quarter-acre residential lots, while subareas 3 and 6 will remain undisturbed woods in good hydrologic condition.

The streets do not have curbs. Instead, the developer is using grass-lined swales along both sides of all streets. The runoff enters inlets as shown, and then is carried to the discharge point 8 through the storm sewers. The entire site contains hydrologic soil group C, with average surface slopes ranging

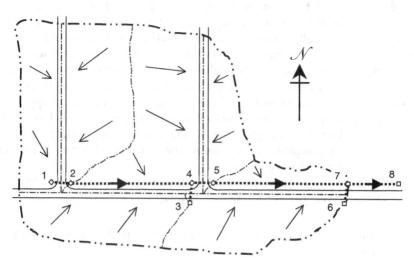

Figure 11.2 Schematic diagram of the drainage area of Example 11.4.

from 0 to 2 percent. The east–west roadway is a state road, and the state department of transportation requires all drainage pipes to carry the 25-year event. The minimum pipe diameter is 15 inches. The minimum pipe velocity is 2 ft/s to provide scour and keep the pipes clean. Based on this information, Table 8.11 was used to select runoff coefficients. Also, the NRCS segmental method was used to compute time of concentrations. Basic hydrologic data are summarized in Table 11.9.

Pipe lengths between inlets and grade elevations for the inlet tops have been established through the grading plan. For the preliminary design, pipe slopes are assumed to be parallel to surface slopes between inlets. This hydraulic information is summarized in Table 11.10.

Using the IDF rainfall curves given in Figure 6.5, determine (1) the design flows for each inlet in the system, (2) pipe diameters for each segment assuming that N-12 smooth-bore plastic pipe will be used, and (3) invert elevations for each pipe segment at each inlet.

Solution. Part 1: The inlet design flow is the runoff peak that flows directly to and through the surface opening of the inlet. In this problem, the analysis reduces to seven applications of the Rational method. Table 11.11 summarizes the results. The rainfall intensity is read from Figure 6.5 using the time of concentration of each subarea as the storm duration. These flows are used to make sure the inlet flow capacity is not exceeded for the critical rainfall event.

Solution. Part 2: Pipes are sized using Manning's equation. The Web site of the plastic pipe manufacturer is searched and reveals that $n = 0.012$ is the recommended design value. The process for design begins with the estimation of the design flow, which is the runoff that drains to the pipe, both on the surface and through the pipe network above the pipe.

Pipe 1–2. The design flow of this pipe is identical to the design flow of inlet 1. The slope is 0.0083 ft/ft. Thus, the minimum diameter is

TABLE 11.9 Hydrologic Data for the Subareas of Example 11.4

Subarea	Area (ac)	Rational C	Inlet Time of Concentration (min)
1	1.98	0.36	8.9
2	2.82	0.36	10.0
3	2.12	0.12	17.0
4	3.85	0.36	11.9
5	1.22	0.36	8.1
6	2.18	0.12	15.4
7	1.05	0.36	7.7

TABLE 11.10   Hydraulic Information for the Sewer System of Example 11.4

Inlet	Pipe Segment	Length (ft)	Grade Elev. (ft)	Slope (ft/ft)
1			393.7	
	1–2	36		0.00833
2			393.4	
	2–4	250		0.01080
4			390.7	
	4–5	38		0.01053
5			390.3	
	5–7	240		0.00500
7			389.1	
	7–8	100		0.00700
8			388.4	
3	—	—	391.0	—
	3–4	45		0.00667
6			389.5	
	6–7	45		0.00889

$$D_{min} = 16\left(\frac{qn}{S^{1/2}}\right)^{3/8} = 16\left[\frac{(3.21)(0.012)}{0.0083^{1/2}}\right]^{3/8} = 11.57 \text{ inches}$$

Hydraulically, the minimum pipe diameter is 12 inches, yet the state requires all drainage pipes to be 15 inches or larger, so a 15-inch pipe is used. The pipe full capacity is computed using Equation 8.15, modified to solve directly for q.

$$q_f = \left(\frac{D}{16}\right)^{8/3}\left(\frac{S^{1/2}}{n}\right) = \left(\frac{15}{16}\right)^{8/3}\left(\frac{0.0083^{1/2}}{0.012}\right) = 6.40 \text{ ft}^3/\text{s}$$

TABLE 11.11   Inlet Design Flows Using Rational Method for Example 11.4

Inlet	Area Direct to Inlet (ac)	C	Inlet t_c (min)	i (in/hr)	Inlet Design Flow ft³/s
1	1.98	0.36	8.9	4.5	3.21
2	2.82	0.36	10.0	4.3	4.37
3	2.12	0.12	17.0	3.4	0.86
4	3.85	0.36	11.9	4.0	5.54
5	1.23	0.36	8.1	4.7	2.06
6	2.18	0.12	15.4	3.6	0.94
7	1.05	0.36	7.7	4.8	1.81

With this, the ratio of q/q_f is $3.21/6.40$, which is 0.50. The hydraulic elements graph in Figure 4.10 gives $y/D = 0.50$, giving the design flow depth, $y = (0.50)(1.25 \text{ ft}) = 0.63$ ft. This flow depth can be used in the development of a hydraulic grade line in the final design.

Scour velocity must be checked. The design flow velocity is computed using the hydraulic elements chart to determine the design flow area, A. From Figure 4.10, based on $y/D = 0.50$, the ratio $A/A_f = 0.50$. The pipe full area is

$$A_{15} = \frac{\pi(D^2)}{4} = \frac{\pi(1.25^2)}{4} = 1.227 \text{ ft}^2$$

The design flow area is $0.50(1.227) = 0.614$ ft². The design flow velocity in the pipe is

$$v = \frac{q}{A} = \frac{3.21}{0.614} = 5.23 \text{ ft/s}$$

This velocity is greater than 2 ft/s and is acceptable in terms of scour.

The flow travel time in the pipe is needed for the design of the next downstream pipe segment. Travel time in a pipe is pipe length divided by design flow velocity, which is divided again by 60 to convert seconds to minutes.

$$t_{1-2} = \frac{L}{60v} = \frac{36}{60(5.23)} = 0.1 \text{ min}$$

Pipe 2–4. The total drainage area for this pipe is the sum of subarea 1 and 2, which is 4.80 acres. The critical time of concentration for this pipe is either (1) the overland flow time to inlet 1 plus the pipe travel time through pipe segment 1–2 or (2) the overland flow time to inlet 2.

$$t_1 = 8.9 + 0.1 = 9.0 \text{ min}$$

$$t_2 = 10.0 \text{ min}$$

The longer time controls, therefore $t_c = 10$ minutes. From Figure 6.5, the design rainfall intensity is 4.3 in/hr. The runoff coefficient for the combined subareas still remains 0.36 since both have the same C value. The design flow for pipe 2–4 becomes

$$q = (0.36)(4.3)(4.80) = 7.43 \text{ ft}^3/s$$

The minimum pipe diameter is

$$D_{min} = 16 \left[\frac{(7.43)(0.012)}{0.0108^{1/2}} \right]^{3/8} = 15.11 \text{ inches}$$

The next larger pipe diameter is 18 inches. Again, pipe full capacity is computed.

$$q_f = \left(\frac{18}{16} \right)^{8/3} \left(\frac{0.0108^{1/2}}{0.012} \right) = 11.86 \text{ ft}^3/\text{s}$$

From this the ratio of $q/q_f = 0.63$, and from the hydraulic elements graph $y/D = 0.58$ and $A/A_f = 0.60$. From this information, $y = 0.87$ ft. Pipe full area is

$$A_{18} = \frac{\pi(1.5^2)}{4} = 1.767 \text{ ft}^2$$

and $A = 0.60(1.767) = 1.060$ ft². Design velocity is computed as

$$v = \frac{7.43}{1.060} = 7.01 \text{ ft/s}$$

Scour velocity is OK. Pipe travel time is

$$t_{2-4} = \frac{250}{60(7.01)} = 0.6 \text{ min}$$

Pipe 3–4. This segment is a pipe spur, so the design of this pipe segment is solely based on the design flow of inlet 3, which is 0.86 ft³/s. This pipe diameter is almost certainly the minimum allowable of 15 inches, but the calculations are done as a matter of completeness.

$$D_{min} = 16 \left[\frac{(0.86)(0.012)}{0.0067^{1/2}} \right]^{3/8} = 7.38 \text{ inches}$$

The minimum diameter needed is indeed 15 inches. Pipe full capacity is

$$q_f = \left(\frac{15}{16} \right)^{8/3} \left(\frac{0.0067^{1/2}}{0.012} \right) = 5.73 \text{ ft}^3/\text{s}$$

The hydraulic elements graph is used once again with $q/q_f = 0.15$, to establish that $y/D = 0.26$, and thus $y = (0.26)(1.25) = 0.33$ ft; $A/A_f = 0.21$, and thus $A = (0.21)(1.227) = 0.258$ ft². From this, $v = 0.86/0.258 = 3.33$ ft/s, and flow time in the pipe is

$$t_{3-4} = \frac{45}{60(3.33)} = 0.2 \text{ min}$$

Pipe 4–5. The contributing area for this pipe segment is the sum of subareas 1, 2, 3, and 4, which is 10.77 acres. The controlling t_c for this pipe segment is the largest of four choices: (1) overland flow time to inlet 1 plus pipe travel time through pipe segments 1–2 and 2–4; (2) overland flow time to inlet 2 plus pipe travel time through pipe segment 2–4; (3) overland flow time to inlet 3 plus pipe travel time through segment 3–4; and (4) overland flow time to inlet 4. These values are

$$t_1 = 8.9 + 0.1 + 0.6 = 9.6 \text{ min}$$

$$t_2 = 10 + 0.6 = 10.6 \text{ min}$$

$$t_3 = 17.0 + 0.2 = 17.2 \text{ min}$$

$$t_4 = 11.9 \text{ min}$$

The controlling time is 17.2 min. With this t_c, the design rainfall intensity from Figure 6.5 is 3.4 in/hr. The runoff coefficient is the weighted value for the four contributing subareas. Using equation 8.16, the weighted C value is

$$C_w = \left[\frac{(1.98)(0.36) + (2.82)(0.36) + (2.12)(0.12) + (3.85)(0.36)}{10.77} \right] = 0.313$$

The peak flow is computed as

$$q = (0.313)(3.4)(10.77) = 11.46 \text{ ft}^3/\text{s}$$

The minimum pipe diameter is

$$D_{\min} = 16\left(\frac{qn}{S^{1/2}}\right)^{3/8} = 16\left[\frac{(11.46)(0.012)}{0.0105^{1/2}}\right]^{3/8} = 17.85 \text{ inches}$$

An 18-inch diameter pipe is adequate. As in other pipe-segment design steps, the pipe full flow is computed and found to be 11.70 ft³/s. The hydraulic elements chart is used with $q/q_f = 0.98$, to give $y/D = 0.80$, $y = 1.20$ ft, $A/A_f = 0.86$, $A = 1.520$ ft², $v = 7.54$ ft/s, and $t_{4-5} = 0.1$ min. The velocity is above the minimum for scour.

Similar calculations are made for pipe segments 5–7, 6–7, and 7–8. The detailed calculations are provided in Appendix C. The results are summarized in Table 11.12 along with the results of the previous segment calculations.

TABLE 11.12 Summary Calculations of Preliminary Pipe Sizing for Example 11.4

Segment	t_c (min)	C_w	q_{design} (ft³/s)	D_{min} (in)	D (in)	y (ft)	A_{design} (ft²)	v (ft/s)	$\dfrac{v^2}{2g}$ (ft)	t_{pipe} (min)
1–2	8.9	0.36	3.21	11.57	15	0.63	0.614	5.23	0.424	0.1
2–4	10.0	0.36	7.43	15.11	18	0.87	1.060	7.01	0.763	0.6
3–4	17.0	0.12	0.86	7.38	15	0.33	0.258	3.33	0.172	0.2
4–5	17.2	0.313	11.46	17.85	18	1.20	1.520	7.54	0.882	0.1
5–7	17.3	0.318	12.96	21.50	24	1.30	2.231	5.81	0.524	0.7
6–7	15.4	0.12	0.94	7.22	15	0.31	0.245	3.84	0.229	0.2
7–8	18.0	0.292	14.67	21.15	24	1.26	2.073	7.08	0.778	0.2

11.3.2 Invert Elevations

Sewer pipe inverts must be set at each junction in the sewer system. Most junctions are either a surface water inlet (also called a catch-basin) or a manhole. Inverts are set based on friction losses in the pipes, energy losses at the junctions, minimum cover requirements, and possibly frost protection requirements. Figure 11.3 shows a schematic detail of a typical catch basin illustrating energy, cover, and frost issues.

Friction losses are relatively easy to compute by simply multiplying the pipe slope by the pipe length. This is based on the assumption that the pipe flow is uniform and the energy friction slope is equal to the pipe slope.

Energy losses at junctions are a bit more complex. These losses are minor losses that depend on many factors. Exact evaluation requires detailed calculation of minor losses through each pipe junction. Many times simple rules of thumb are used in place of detailed calculations when the sewer systems

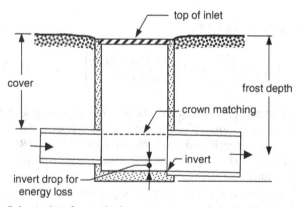

Figure 11.3 Schematic of a typical stormwater catch basin illustrating invert drop, crown matching, and frost depth.

are small. The *Modern Sewer Design* (AISI, 1999) publication suggests the following rules of thumb:

- For energy loss through junctions, provide a drop of:
  - 0.05 ft for straight through connections
  - 0.15 ft for 45-degree changes in direction
  - 0.25 ft for 45- to 90-degree changes in direction
- For pipe diameter increases, match crown elevations of incoming and outgoing pipes.

The designer should use these rules of thumb with caution, always checking the reasonableness of the rule applied by considering the geometry of the junction and the design velocities present in the connecting pipes.

A reasonably safe way to determine invert elevations is to work with normal-depth water surface elevations. The water surface elevation is nothing more than the pipe invert elevation plus normal depth for the design flow. In this case, the "rules of thumb" for energy loss through junctions are applied to the water surface elevation. Using this method, the likelihood of a downstream pipe causing backwater effects on an upstream pipe are minimized, further increasing the probability that the uniform flow assumption is valid.

Cover requirements are established to protect the structural integrity of the pipe from surface loading. The loading includes dead load and live load. *Dead load* includes any weight that is applied to the pipe at all times. Soil cover, pavement, and concrete curbs are typically the only dead load most pipes experience in typical land-development design. *Live load* is typically vehicular traffic such as automobiles, trucks, and other large moving vehicles. These loadings are defined by the American Association of State Highway and Transportation Officials (AASHTO, 2004) depending on the type of vehicular traffic.

Pipe manufacturers typically supply minimum cover information, or a method to compute the minimum. The minimum cover for corrugated metal pipes as recommended by the American Iron and Steel Institute (AISI, 1999) is 1 foot for pipes up to 96 inches in diameter. The American Concrete Pipe Association (ACPA, 2004) provides a method for computing cover requirements, depending on width and depth of trench and vehicle loads. In general, however, smaller diameter pipes (up to 48 inches) do not have structural loading problems as long as a reasonable cover depth is provided, typically 1 foot. A common rule of thumb among light construction contractors is the "one plus one-fourth rule," which sets the minimum cover to one foot plus one-fourth the pipe diameter. Where heavy vehicles and shallow cover is encountered, structural integrity may be a concern and a detailed analysis of the loading should be performed.

With this information, and taking into account that all pipes have a wall thickness, a basic relation for computing minimum pipe inverts is

$$\text{Invert} \le \text{grade elevation} - \text{minimum pipe cover}$$

$$- \text{pipe thickness} - \text{pipe diameter} \qquad (11.2)$$

Frost protection is necessary in cold weather regions. Frost heaving is caused when the frost line drops below the pipe bottom. When frozen, the soil expands below the pipe causing an uplift force. This action can separate the pipe from an inlet connection. Due to its curved nature, a circular pipe is susceptible to frost action after the frost line drops below the pipe centerline. For this reason, the practice of setting the pipe centerline at or below frost line is recommended. Protection from frost conditions requires research on the designer's part to establish appropriate frost depths. Local ordinances may specify an acceptable frost-line depth for a region. Sometimes frost depth is set to an accepted value as established through experience by the local construction industry. On smaller pipe systems in cold weather regions, the frost-line condition usually controls the depth of trench needed for the storm sewer.

Once the parameters are established, invert elevations at each sewer network junction are set for all incoming and outgoing pipes, while maintaining the pipe design slope. To minimize trench depths, the process begins at the upstream end of the system, being mindful of the system's receiving-stream water surface elevation or receiving-pipe invert elevation. The invert of the discharge pipe outlet should be set at least equal to, but preferably a little bit higher than, the expected water surface elevation in the receiving stream or channel. If the system connects to an existing storm sewer system, then the rules of thumb for energy loss apply to the connection.

As inverts are set, pipe slopes are occasionally adjusted to make the system fit. When this is necessary, the design must be re-examined to make sure the design is still valid. If it is not, then a redesign must be performed for the affected elements.

Example 11.5   Using the results of Example 11.4, establish pipe inverts for the preliminary sewer design. Pipe 7–8 discharges into an inlet that has a 36-inch smooth concrete discharge pipe, with pipe invert set at 381.05 feet. Expected frost depth for the region is 3.5 feet. All pipes require a minimum of 1-ft cover above the outside crown of the pipe. Pipe thicknesses are 0.11, 0.13, and 0.16 feet, respectively, for the 15-, 18-, and 24-inch diameter pipes.

Solution: Reference is made to the data provided in Tables 11.10 and 11.12. Each pipe has an invert, water surface, crown, and grade elevation at the upstream end (I_U, W_U, C_U, G_U) and the downstream end (I_D, W_D, C_D, G_D) and these abbreviations will be used in this example. Pipe segments will be identified with a two-digit subscript number. The first digit represents the inlet number at the pipe's upstream end. The second digit represents the inlet number at the pipe's downstream end.

The process starts at the upstream end of the system working downstream to the system outfall. Minimum frost depth will be used to set the first invert in the system. Upstream water surface elevations, estimated junction losses, and downstream flow depths will be used to set downstream pipe inverts. For increasing pipe diameters at junctions, crown matching will override this invert calculation if it is found that the downstream pipe crown is higher than the upstream pipe crown. Minimum cover requirements will be checked after inverts are computed. Frost depth will not be allowed to drop below the center line of the pipe, thus, frost depth plus one-half the pipe diameter will be the minimum depth to invert line. This criterion sets the minimum invert depths below grade for the 15-, 18- and 24-inch pipes to 4.13, 4.25 and 4.5 feet, respectively. Since the frost depth is 3.5 feet, and all pipe diameters are smaller than 2 feet, the 1-foot structural cover requirement will never control and therefore will not be checked.

Pipe 1–2 (15 in). The pipe is the only pipe attached to inlet 1, so the minimum invert depth will be used to set the upstream invert.

The upstream grade elevation is taken from Table 11.10.

$$G_{U12} = 393.7 \text{ ft} \Leftarrow$$

The minimum invert depth is used to establish the upstream invert.

$$I_{U12} = 393.7 - 4.13 = 389.57 \text{ ft} \Leftarrow$$

The water surface elevation is pipe invert elevation plus flow depth from Table 11.12.

$$W_{U12} = 389.57 + 0.63 = 390.20 \text{ ft} \Leftarrow$$

The inside crown elevation is pipe invert plus pipe diameter from Table 11.12.

$$C_{U12} = 389.57 + 1.25 = 390.82 \text{ ft} \Leftarrow$$

The downstream invert of pipe 1–2 entering inlet 2 will be the upstream invert minus the friction energy lost which is slope times length from Table 11.10.

$$I_{D12} = 389.57 - 0.00833(36) = 389.27 \text{ ft} \Leftarrow$$

$$W_{D12} = 389.27 + 0.63 = 389.90 \text{ ft} \Leftarrow$$

$$C_{D12} = 389.27 + 1.25 = 390.52 \text{ ft} \Leftarrow$$

Pipe 2–4 (18 in). The inlet 2 junction is a straight-through connection and pipe diameter increases from 1.25 to 1.5 feet. Head loss should be low, so 0.05 feet of head loss at the junction is reasonable. To be conservative, we will assume the head loss through the junction to be 0.1 feet. The crown matching rule will be checked.

The upstream water surface in pipe 2–4 is the downstream water surface of pipe 1–2 minus the assumed head loss through the inlet.

$$W_{U24} = 389.90 - 0.1 = 389.80 \text{ ft} \Leftarrow$$

The upstream pipe invert is water surface elevation minus flow depth.

$$I_{U24} = 389.80 - 0.87 = 388.93 \text{ ft} \Leftarrow$$

Pipe crown is invert plus diameter.

$$C_{U24} = 388.93 + 1.5 = 390.43 \text{ ft} \Leftarrow$$

The pipe crown criterion is OK at inlet 2 since C_{D12} (390.52) is higher than C_{U24} (390.43). Thus, downstream elevations are computed.

$$I_{D24} = 388.93 - 0.0108(250) = 386.23 \text{ ft} \Leftarrow$$

$$W_{D24} = 386.23 + 0.87 = 387.10 \text{ ft} \Leftarrow$$

$$C_{D24} = 386.23 + 1.5 = 387.73 \text{ ft} \Leftarrow$$

Pipe 3–4 (15 in). Like pipe 1–2, this is the first pipe in this branch, so the minimum invert depth is used to set the invert. The upstream crown calculation is not needed.

$$I_{U34} = 391.0 - 4.13 = 386.87 \text{ ft} \Leftarrow$$

$$W_{U34} = 386.87 + 0.33 = 387.20 \text{ ft} \Leftarrow$$

$$I_{D34} = 386.87 - 0.00667(45) = 386.57 \text{ ft} \Leftarrow$$

$$W_{D34} = 386.57 + 0.33 = 386.90 \text{ ft} \Leftarrow$$

$$C_{D34} = 386.57 + 1.25 = 387.82 \text{ ft} \Leftarrow$$

Pipe 4–5 (18 in). The upstream invert of pipe 4–5 must be low enough to capture flow from both pipes 2–4 and 3–4, entering inlet 4. Therefore, the lower W_D entering the inlet is used to set W_{U45}, which is $W_{D34} = 386.90$ ft. Pipe 3–4 controls the energy calculations through the inlet. Since it goes through a 90-degree direction change a head loss of 0.25 feet is used.

$$W_{U45} = 386.90 - 0.25 = 386.65 \text{ ft} \Leftarrow$$

$$I_{U45} = 386.65 - 1.20 = 385.45 \text{ ft} \Leftarrow$$

$$C_{U45} = 385.45 + 1.5 = 386.95 \text{ ft} \Leftarrow$$

A crown check at inlet 4 shows that C_{D24} (387.73) and C_{D34} (387.82) are both higher than C_{U45} (386.95), so the crown criterion is satisfied. Downstream elevations are computed.

$$I_{D45} = 385.45 - 0.01053(38) = 385.05 \text{ ft} \Leftarrow$$

$$W_{D45} = 385.05 + 1.20 = 386.25 \text{ ft} \Leftarrow$$

$$C_{D45} = 385.05 + 1.5 = 386.55 \text{ ft} \Leftarrow$$

Pipe 5–7 (24 in). Pipe 5–7 creates a straight-through connection with pipe 4-5 with a diameter change of 0.5 feet. To be conservative, a head loss of 0.1 feet is used.

$$W_{U57} = 386.25 - 0.1 = 386.15 \text{ ft}$$

$$I_{U57} = 386.15 - 1.30 = 384.85 \text{ ft}$$

$$C_{U57} = 384.85 + 2 = 386.85 \text{ ft}$$

The crown check on C_{D45} (386.55) and C_{U57} (386.85) shows that the crown matching criterion is *not* satisfied, so C_{U57} is changed to 386.55 feet to match C_{D45}. New values of I_{U57} and W_{U57} must be recomputed from the adjusted crown elevation.

$$C_{U57} = 386.55 \text{ ft} \Leftarrow$$

$$I_{U57} = 386.55 - 2 = 384.55 \text{ ft} \Leftarrow$$

$$W_{U57} = 384.55 + 1.30 = 385.85 \text{ ft} \Leftarrow$$

Downstream elevations are now computed.

$$I_{D57} = 384.55 - 0.00500(240) = 383.35 \text{ ft} \Leftarrow$$

$$W_{D57} = 383.35 + 1.30 = 384.65 \text{ ft} \Leftarrow$$

$$C_{D57} = 383.35 + 2 = 385.35 \text{ ft} \Leftarrow$$

Pipe 6–7 (15 in). Pipe 6–7 is the first pipe in a branch, so the minimum invert criteria is used to set the invert.

$$I_{U67} = 389.5 - 4.13 = 385.37 \text{ ft} \Leftarrow$$

$$W_{U67} = 385.37 + 0.31 = 385.68 \text{ ft} \Leftarrow$$

$$I_{D67} = 385.37 - 0.00889(45) = 384.97 \text{ ft} \Leftarrow$$

$$W_{D67} = 384.97 + 0.31 = 385.28 \text{ ft} \Leftarrow$$

$$C_{D67} = 384.97 + 1.25 = 386.22 \text{ ft} \Leftarrow$$

Pipe 7–8 (24 in). This pipe accepts flow from 5–7 and 6–7. The lower down-stream water surface entering pipe 7–8 is W_{D57} (384.65 ft) and this is used to establish W_{U78}. The water surface drop from 6–7 to 5–7 is 0.63 feet and provides more than enough energy to allow the flow in 6–7 to make the 90-degree turn into 7–8. Flow from 5–7 to 7–8 will control the upstream invert of 7–8. The path is straight-through, so a conservative energy loss of 0.1 feet will be used.

$$W_{U78} = 384.65 - 0.1 = 384.55 \text{ ft.} \Leftarrow$$

$$I_{U78} = 384.55 - 1.26 = 383.29 \text{ ft} \Leftarrow$$

$$C_{U78} = 383.29 + 2 = 385.29 \text{ ft} \Leftarrow$$

A crown check of pipe 5–7 (385.35 ft) and pipe 6–7 (386.22 ft) into pipe 7–8 (385.29 ft) at inlet 7 shows that the crown criterion is met.

$$I_{D78} = 383.29 - 0.0070(100) = 382.59 \text{ ft} \Leftarrow$$

$$W_{D78} = 382.59 + 1.26 = 383.85 \text{ ft} \Leftarrow$$

$$C_{D78} = 382.59 + 2 = 384.59 \text{ ft} \Leftarrow$$

Inlet 8. The downstream invert of pipe 7–8 at inlet 8 must be checked to make sure it will connect to the upstream invert of the 36 inch concrete pipe given as 381.05 ft. The elevation drop from I_{D78} to I_U of the 36 inch pipe is $382.59 - 381.05 = 1.54$ ft. This is plenty of elevation drop to accommodate the flow from pipe 7–8. The crown elevation of the 36 inch pipe is assumed to be invert plus diameter (384.05 ft). The crown match criterion is also satisfied.

The invert design is complete and summarized in Table 11.13. Pipe slopes were not changed in the system to accommodate a cover requirement or energy loss requirement. Therefore, the preliminary pipe sizing of Table 11.12 is accepted as the final design.

In the previous example, we did not encounter any unusual conditions where the preliminary design had to be changed. If ground slope is not uniform between inlets, then minimum cover conditions along the entire pipe length should be checked. If there is a problem, pipe inverts must be lowered and pipe slopes changed. When this happens, all affected pipe segments must be checked to make sure the preliminary pipe size is still adequate. Many times they are adequate, since many designed pipes have a fair amount of excess capacity. But if they are not adequate, then pipe diameters must be changed and all inlet elevations and pipe segments affected by the change must be rechecked for validity.

11.3.3 Hydraulic and Energy Grade Lines

The hydraulic grade line (HGL) in a storm sewer defines the elevation of the flowing water surface through the system, as explained in Chapter 4. It is nothing more than pipe invert elevation plus flow depth, and it shows the elevation of water expected in the system when the system is working properly. The HGL should decrease progressively and continuously along the sewer flow line. Otherwise, the assumption of uniform flow is not completely correct, and a closer examination of flow at junction points might be necessary. The energy grade line (EGL) is important in sewer design because it sets the elevation limit to which water can rise if an obstruction in the sewer

TABLE 11.13 Summary of Invert and Water Surface Elevations for the Sewer Design of Examples 11.4 and 11.5

Pipe	Invert Elevation (ft)		Water Surface Elevation (ft)	
	Upstream	Downstream	Upstream	Downstream
1–2	389.57	389.27	390.20	389.90
2–4	388.93	386.23	389.80	387.10
3–4	386.87	386.57	387.20	386.90
4–5	385.45	385.05	386.65	386.25
5–7	384.55	383.35	385.85	384.65
6–7	385.37	384.97	385.68	385.28
7–8	383.29	382.59	384.55	383.85
8–	381.05	—	—	

occurs and partially blocks the flow. The EGL is the HGL plus velocity head, which means it is a plot of total energy through the system.

Most minor storm sewer design is simple enough in geometry that the calculation of the HGL or EGL is unwarranted. However, some development regulations require the calculation of one or the other or both. The process is reasonably straightforward for flow inside the pipes. The HGL and EGL elevation at any location inside a pipe experiencing uniform flow is computed as

$$HGL = z + y \tag{11.2}$$

$$EGL = z + y + \frac{v^2}{2g} \tag{11.3}$$

where z = elevation of the pipe invert, y = normal depth of flow in the pipe under design flow, v = velocity of the design flow. The key here is that flow must be uniform because this is one of the basic assumptions used in the design. Nonuniform flow in storm sewers is often caused by backwater effects, either from the receiving stream or a junction that is constricted in a flow transition. In these cases, a more sophisticated method must be used to analyze the flow, typically the standard-step method for determining water surface profiles.

The procedure of applying estimated junction losses to water surface elevations, as used in Example 11.5, is a method that checks the HGL in the design process. A more detailed HGL analysis requires the computation of energy losses at the junctions based upon documented loss coefficients for specific geometries. An example of this process is illustrated in *Modern Sewer Design* (AISC, 1999).

11.4 CULVERTS

A culvert is a closed conduit that is used to convey surface runoff through a roadway embankment or other stream path obstruction. In urban areas, culverts can be used to convey stormwater runoff under buildings, parking lots, and streets. In stormwater detention ponds, culverts are used to convey flow through a pond embankment.

Conventional culverts include circular, rectangular (box), elliptical, pipe arch, metal box, and arch as shown in Figure 11.4. Materials are typically concrete and corrugated metal. Some of the smaller diameter circular culverts are made of plastic. The barrel of the culvert is typically constant in shape and uniform in slope.

The basic elements of a culvert are the inlet (entrance), the barrel (pipe), and the outlet (exit) as shown in Figure 11.5. The culvert passes through an embankment or obstruction and is subject to headwater and tailwater effects.

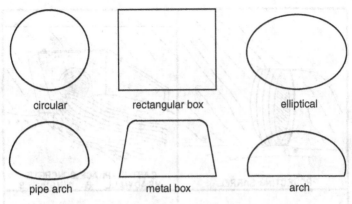

circular   rectangular box   elliptical

pipe arch   metal box   arch

Figure 11.4 Commonly used culvert shapes.

The inlet is typically designed to provide an economical or efficient entrance to the pipe. The barrel is usually designed to minimize friction resistance. The outlet should contain some type of design that dissipates the flow velocity to prevent erosion of the downstream channel.

There are all kinds of inlet configurations, but the most common are the projecting barrel, precast end sections, cast-in-place concrete headwall with wing walls, and end mitered to the embankment slope, as illustrated in Figure 11.6. The design of the inlet can significantly affect the flow capacity of the culvert. The inflow channel is often much wider than the culvert opening making the inlet edge a potential flow obstruction. A sharp edge causes a severe flow-line obstruction where a rounded edge produces a more flow-efficient inlet. In practice, sharp edges are more common because they are less expensive to build. The sharp edge often causes the inlet to become the flow control section of the culvert. There are times when the construction of a special inlet configuration is worthwhile because it increases the capacity of the culvert.

11.4.1 Culvert Flow Types

Flow through a culvert can be classified in several ways. Two common ways to classify the flow are by flow control and submergence, as referenced to the inlet and outlet.

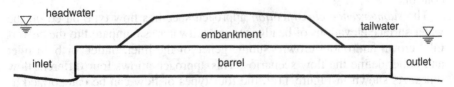

Figure 11.5 Basic elements of a culvert.

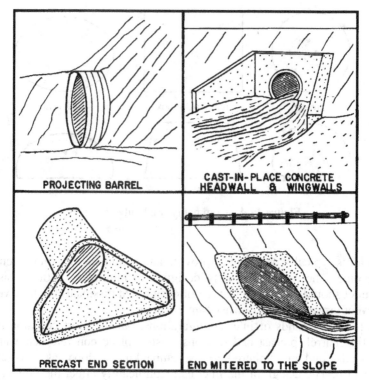

Figure 11.6 Common culvert inlet configurations (FHWA HDS-5, 2001).

The *flow control classification* defines flow type based on the basic culvert element that controls the flow. There are two flow control types—inlet control and outlet control. Inlet control means that the inlet shape and geometry controls the flow through the culvert. In essence, the inlet acts like an orifice discharging into a larger and more efficient flow channel. The length, slope, and roughness of the flow channel have no bearing on the overall culvert capacity. Instead, the geometry of the inlet and the orifice equation are used to define the flow. The other flow type is outlet control, where the entrance is efficient enough to let flow into the barrel such that barrel friction becomes the flow control. In this case, length, slope, and roughness of the barrel are important in flow modeling. Considering this explanation, inlet and outlet control might be better defined as orifice (inlet) control or friction (outlet) control.

The *submergence classification* approach specifies flow type based on the water surface elevations of headwater and tailwater as compared to the culvert inlet crown and outlet crown. Submergence of the inlet, outlet, or both inlet and outlet define the flow scenarios. This approach allows four different flow types. As shown in Figure 11.7, the four types of flow can be categorized as

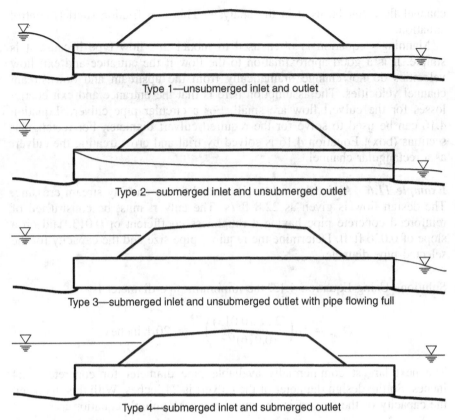

Type 1—unsubmerged inlet and outlet

Type 2—submerged inlet and unsubmerged outlet

Type 3—submerged inlet and unsubmerged outlet with pipe flowing full

Type 4—submerged inlet and submerged outlet

Figure 11.7 Four types of culvert flow based on submergence criteria.

(1) unsubmerged inlet and unsubmerged outlet, (2) submerged inlet and un-submerged outlet, (3) submerged inlet and unsubmerged outlet with pipe discharging full flow, and (4) submerged inlet and submerged outlet. Type 1 is a conduit flowing partially full, and therefore can be analyzed using the methods of open channel flow. Type 2 is also a pipe flowing partially full, but the inlet causes a constriction. Type 3 flow is very uncommon and requires very large headwater depths to cause the full flow pipe. Type 4 flow is mainly restricted by pipe friction. The majority of culvert analysis and design can be described by flow types 1, 2, and 4.

Type 1. Type 1 flow is a barrel flowing partially full with a free surface present all along the entire culvert flow path. This is a common situation in box culvert design when the top of the box is used as the base for a roadway. In this case, submergence of either the inlet or outlet would cause flooding of the roadway surface, which would defeat the purpose of the culvert. Friction along the channel length controls the flow, and the methods of open channel flow can be used in the analysis. This is a friction (outlet) control situation.

Manning's equation is often used to model this flow type because it is simple. It is a good approximation to the flow if the entrance and exit flow velocities do not change dramatically from the upstream and downstream channel velocities. The assumption here is that the entrance and exit energy losses for the culvert flow are small. For a circular pipe culvert, Equation 4.16 can be used to solve for the required culvert diameter. For rectangular sections (box), Equation 4.16 is solved by trial and error treating the culvert as a rectangular channel.

Example 11.6   A circular culvert is needed for a roadway stream crossing. The design flow is given as 22.8 ft³/s. The culvert must be constructed of reinforced concrete pipe having a roughness coefficient of 0.013, laid on a slope of 0.026 ft/ft. Determine the required pipe size and the capacity for the selected pipe diameter.

Solution: Using Equation 4.13, the minimum pipe diameter is

$$D_{min} = 16 \left(\frac{(22.8)(0.013)}{(0.026)^{1/2}} \right)^{3/8} = 20.1 \text{ inches}$$

The next largest commercially available pipe diameter for concrete is 24 inches. So the design diameter of the culvert is 24 inches. With this diameter, the capacity of the culvert is computed using Manning's equation as

$$q = \frac{1.49}{0.013} \left(\frac{\pi (2)^2}{4} \right) \left(\frac{2}{4} \right)^{2/3} 0.026^{1/2} = 36.6 \text{ ft}^3/\text{s}$$

The excess capacity assures the condition of free surface flow through the entire length of pipe, which implies that the flow must be Type 1.

Type 2. Type 2 flow is a conduit flowing partially full with a submerged inlet. The flow is being controlled by the size and shape of the inlet opening. In this case, the culvert system can be treated as an orifice using Equation 3.26, repeated here for convenience,

$$q_o = C_o A \sqrt{2gH} \tag{3.26}$$

where H is the hydrostatic head above the centerline of the culvert. Headwater, HW, is related to hydrostatic head by adding half of the vertical dimension of the culvert opening, conveniently making it the water depth above the culvert invert.

$$HW = H + \frac{D}{2} \tag{11.3}$$

Combining Equations 3.26 and 11.3 gives

$$q = C_oA\sqrt{2g(HW - D/2)} \tag{11.4}$$

For a circular culvert using $A = \pi D^2/4$, this equation can be expressed in terms of D as

$$D^5 - 2\ HW\ D^4 + \left(0.224 \frac{q}{C_o}\right)^2 = 0 \tag{11.5}$$

This equation is a fifth-order polynomial having five possible answers. Two answers will be positive. The most logical positive answer is the correct pipe diameter. Similar equations can be developed for a rectangular box or other geometric sections, but they are not as easy to solve directly.

Example 11.8   A culvert is sized to pass under a railroad track. The upstream side of the culvert experiences 7.2 feet of headwater for the design flow of 73 ft³/s. The culvert is 60 feet long on a moderate slope. Assume the culvert entrance has a flow coefficient C_o equal to 0.6. Determine the minimum reuired pipe diameter. Select a standard pipe size and compute the full capacity discharge. Assume Type 2 flow.

Solution: Equation 11.5 is solved by trial and error. The constant term is moved to the right side of the equation and the other terms with the unknown parameter D are kept on the left.

$$D^5 - 2\ HW\ D^4 = -\left(0.224 \frac{q}{C_o}\right)^2$$

$$D^5 - 2(7.2)D^4 = -\left(0.224 \frac{73}{0.6}\right)^2$$

$$D^5 - 14.4\ D^4 = -742.7$$

Trial	D (ft)	Left-Side Term	Comment
1	4	−2662	lower
2	3	−923.4	lower
3	2.8	−713.0	close
4	2.83	−742.1	close enough

The minimum pipe diameter is 2.83 feet, or 34.0 inches. The next largest commercially available pipe diameter is 36 inches. Pipe roughness is not a factor in the conveyance design.

The full capacity flow is computed using Equation 11.4.

$$q = 0.6\left(\frac{\pi 3^2}{4}\right) \sqrt{2(32.2)(7.2 - 3/2)} = 81.3 \text{ ft}^3/\text{s}$$

Type 3 and Type 4. Flow from Types 3 and 4 is a conduit flowing full with both inlet and outlet submerged. Type 3 is a special case of Type 4 where the barrel flows full, making the tailwater depth equal to the culvert vertical dimension. In both cases, there is no free surface through the culvert. Pressure flow occurs, and the methods of energy are appropriate to analyze the flow. Writing energy between the headwater and tailwater surfaces gives

$$\frac{p_1}{\gamma} + \frac{v_1^2}{2g} + z_1 - h_L = \frac{p_2}{\gamma} + \frac{v_2^2}{2g} + z_2 \tag{11.6}$$

where p_i, v_i, and z_i are the pressure, velocity and elevation at point i, and h_L is the total head loss between the upstream and downstream points. Submergence of an inlet or outlet is typically caused by the ponding of water; therefore, the flow velocities at the upstream and downstream channel ends are very slow and both v_1 and v_2 are approximately zero. At the free surface, pressure is atmospheric, so p_1 and p_2 are zero. The energy equation reduces to

$$z_1 - z_2 = h_L \tag{11.7}$$

where $z_1 - z_2$ is the difference in headwater and tailwater elevations. The minor losses h_L, include the entrance loss, friction loss, and exit loss. Therefore h_L can be expressed as

$$z_1 - z_2 = h_{\text{entrance}} + h_{\text{friction}} + h_{\text{exit}} \tag{11.8}$$

The entrance and exit losses are treated as minor losses and the combined loss is expressed as

$$h_{\text{entrance+exit}} = K_{\text{entrance}} \frac{v^2}{2g} + K_{\text{exit}} \frac{v^2}{2g} \tag{11.9}$$

For a circular culvert, v can be expressed in terms of q and A, with A expressed in terms of D.

$$v = \frac{q}{A} = \frac{4q}{\pi D^2} \qquad (11.10)$$

Setting g to 32.2 ft/s^2 and substituting Equation 11.10 into Equation 11.9, the relation becomes

$$h_{\text{entrance}+\text{exit}} = [K_{\text{entrance}} + K_{\text{exit}}] \frac{q^2}{39.7\, D^4} \qquad (11.11)$$

The friction loss can be approximated by the Manning's equation for uniform flow. To do this, Manning's equation is expressed in terms of friction slope S_f.

$$S_f = \left(\frac{qn}{1.49\, AR^{2/3}}\right)^2 \qquad (11.12)$$

Slope is the ratio of friction loss to culvert length. For a circular culvert flowing full, area and hydraulic radius can be expressed in terms of diameter.

$$S_f = \frac{h_f}{L}; \quad A = \frac{\pi D^2}{4}; \quad R = \frac{D}{4} \qquad (11.13)$$

Performing the substitutions and algebraic reduction results in the equation

$$h_f = \frac{4.64\, n^2\, q^2\, L}{D^{5.33}} \qquad (11.14)$$

Combining this result with the entrance and exit losses gives

$$h_L = \left[\frac{(K_{\text{ent}} + K_{\text{exit}})}{39.7 D^4} + \frac{4.64 n^2\, L}{D^{5.33}}\right] q^2 \qquad (11.15)$$

This equation allows the analysis of circular culverts flowing full with submerged inlet and outlet. If the equation is used for culvert sizing, several roots will result. Only one will make sense physically. Numerical methods can be used to solve this equation, but trial and error also works.

Example 11.9   A circular culvert is required for a roadway-stream crossing. At the design condition, the flow is 107 ft^3/s, upstream ponding water depth is 9.6 feet, and the downstream tailwater depth is 5.4 feet. The culvert will be reinforced concrete with a roughness coefficient of 0.013. The culvert length is 145 feet on a slope of 0.010 ft/ft. Assume that the culvert has an entrance loss coefficient of 0.5 and an exit loss coefficient of 1.0. Recommend an appropriate pipe diameter.

Solution: Equation 11.15 is solved by trial and error. The head loss h_L is the difference in water surface elevations upstream and downstream, which is upstream headwater, plus the change in invert elevation through the culvert, minus the downstream headwater.

$$9.6 + (0.010)(145) - 5.4 = \left[\frac{(0.5 + 1.0)}{39.7 \, D^4} + \frac{4.64(0.013)^2 \, 145}{D^{5.33}} \right] 107^2$$

$$5.65 = \frac{432.6}{D^4} + \frac{1301.8}{D^{5.33}}$$

Trial	D (ft)	Right-Side Term	Comment
1	3	9.07	larger
2	3.4	5.15	smaller
3	3.3	5.89	larger
4	3.33	5.66	close enough

The required pipe size is 3.33 feet, or 40 inches. A 42-inch concrete pipe is sufficient.

11.4.2 Culvert Design Aids

The above equations highlight the complexity in expressing flow through a culvert. The equations only address the circular culvert. Other section geometries are possible. Additionally, the flow type of a particular culvert is not always obvious, so choosing the correct flow equation is not readily apparent. Because of this complexity, the Federal Highway Administration (FHWA) has developed several design aids for culverts, including the publication "Hydraulic Design of Highway Culverts" (HDS-5) [FHWA, 2001] and the microcomputer program "HY8 Culvert Analysis" (HY8) [FHWA, 2004]. HDS-5 presents a series of graphical solutions, using 59 different charts for the analysis and design of a wide variety of culvert geometries and materials. Figure 11.8 is an example of one of these charts where the culvert condition is circular concrete culverts under inlet control, using U.S. standard units. In this particular graph, flow is determined based on entrance condition and headwater, where headwater is expressed in culvert diameters HW/D. The other 58 graphs present other culvert shapes under different flow conditions.

HY8 is a computer program that automates the design methods of HDS-5. The user interface, which is DOS based, is shown in Figure 11.9. Both design tools are available by download from the FHWA at *http://www.fhwa.dot.gov*. A search of this Web site for HDS-5 or HY8 should provide the download page.

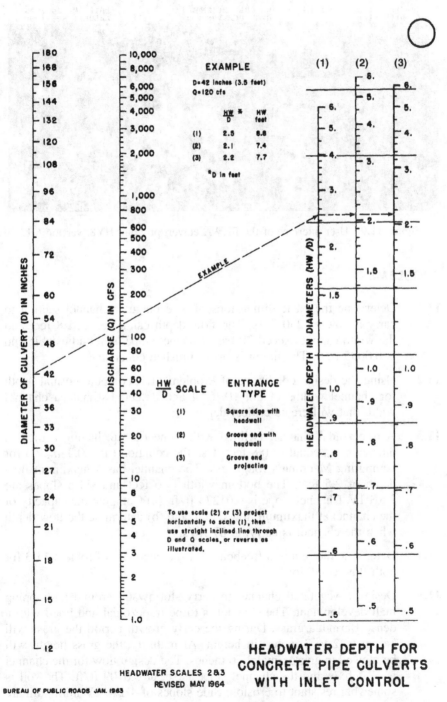

HEADWATER DEPTH FOR CONCRETE PIPE CULVERTS WITH INLET CONTROL

HEADWATER SCALES 2&3
REVISED MAY 1964

BUREAU OF PUBLIC ROADS JAN. 1963

Figure 11.8 Culvert design chart 1B from FHWA HDS-5, 2001 (p. 225).

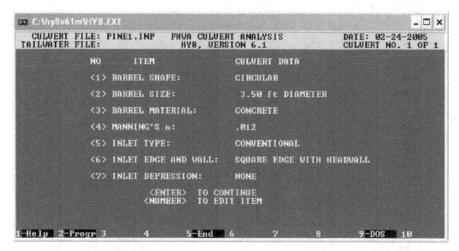

Figure 11.9 User interface of the FHWA culvert program HY8, version 6.1.

PROBLEMS

11.1 Determine the basic dimensions of a rectangular channel section to carry a flow of 230 ft^3/s. The flow depth cannot exceed 8 feet and the width cannot exceed 20 feet. Channel slope is not adjustable and is 0.0095 ft/ft. The lining is brush-finished concrete.

11.2 Using the design conditions of Problem 11.1, compute normal depth for channel widths of 20, 10, 6, 4 and 2 feet. Estimate a channel width that will create critical depth.

11.3 A trapezoidal channel is lined with stone rip-rap, having a median diameter, d_{50} equal to 0.8 feet. Use the equation ($n = 0.34d_{50}^{1/6}$) for computing Manning's roughness. The channel has a maximum flow depth of 2.5 feet. The bottom width is 6 feet and sides slopes are 2.5H:1V. Channel slope is 0.01274 ft/ft. (a) Compute the capacity of the channel at maximum flow depth, and (b) determine the flow depth when the channel is carrying 87 ft^3/s.

11.4 Determine the required freeboard for the channel of Problem 11.3 for both flow conditions.

11.5 Design a vegetated channel to carry stormwater around a shopping mall development. The channel is to be trapezoidal and lined with a dense Bermuda grass. During the early growth period the grass will be cut to 2 to 3 inches in height. At maturity, the grass height will be mowed to approximately 6 inches. The design flow for the channel is 17.2 ft^3/s and the channel slope is set at 0.0109 ft/ft. The soil is somewhat resistant to erosion. Side slopes of 4H to 1V minimum are required to accommodate machine mowing. The stormwater drainage way cannot exceed 15 feet in width, including a minimum freeboard. Make the design such that top width is minimized but the bottom of the channel can be mowed with a 36-inch-wide mowing machine.

11.6 For the channel described in Problem 11.5, design the channel to minimize flow depth.

11.7 For the purposes of this problem, the schematic diagram of Figure 8.12 represents a large parking lot drained by three inlets connected with three segments of pipe. A concrete curb surrounds the lot, which captures and directs all runoff to the inlets. Subareas 2 and 3 are paved with bituminous asphalt in good condition and subarea 1 is covered in vegetated pervious paver blocks. Rainfall IDF curves are in Figure 6.5. Specific watershed and drainage system information is provided in Table 11.14. (a) Compute design flows for each pipe segment and (b) compute a preliminary pipe size for each segment. Assume pipe slopes will parallel the average ground slopes between inlet tops. Use corrugated metal pipe having an *n* value of 0.024. The minimum allowable pipe diameter is 12 inches.

11.8 Using the results of Problem 11.7, set the inverts of the pipes at inlets 1, 2, and 3. The upstream invert elevation of the discharge channel at headwall 4 is 79.50 feet, and pipe 3–4 must match inverts or slightly above. Use the rules of thumb suggested by AISI to help set inverts.

11.9 A circular culvert is needed for a highway-stream crossing where the design flow is 38 ft^3/s. The culvert is required to be N12 plastic pipe and the design roughness is 0.012. The culvert slope is 0.037 ft/ft. Assume the culvert is flowing under Type 1 culvert flow. Determine the required pipe size and the capacity for the selected pipe diameter.

11.10 A concrete culvert is sized to pass under an office building in an old commercial district. The design flow is 147 ft^3/s and the design headwater depth is 8.1 ft. The culvert is 90 feet long. Determine the min-

TABLE 11.14 Data for Problems 11.7 and 11.8

Inlet	Area (ac)	C	t_c (min)	Pipe	Gr. Elev (ft)	Length (ft)
1	3.67	0.42	8.4		100.05	
				1-2		385
2	3.5	0.90	5.0		94.83	
				2-3		370
3	3.4	0.90	5.0		89.15	
				3-4		315
4					79.50	

imum required pipe diameter using Figure 11.8. Using trial and error, starting with $HW/D = 4$, solve for D, then check the initial assumption of HW/D. Select a standard pipe size and estimate the full capacity discharge.

11.11 Solve problem 11.10 using Equation 11.5. Assume the entrance flow coefficient is 0.6. Compare the result with the Problem 11.10 method.

11.12 A circular culvert is required to carry a flow of 370 ft³/s. The headwater depth is 11.5 feet, and the tailwater depth is 6.1 feet. The culvert is reinforced concrete with a roughness coefficient of 0.013. The culvert length is 175 feet and is laid on a slope of 0.008 ft/ft. Assume that the culvert has an entrance loss coefficient of 0.5 and an exit loss coefficient of 1.0. Select an appropriate pipe diameter. Assume flow is Type 4.

REFERENCES

AISI. 1999. *Modern Sewer Design*, 4th ed. 344 pp. http://www.steel.org.

ACPA. 2004. *Concrete Pipe Design Manual*, downloadable PDF file, *www.concrete-pipe.org*.

American Society of Civil Engineers. 1992. *Design and Construction of Urban Stormwater Management Systems.* ASCE Manuals and Reports of Engineering Practice No. 77.

AASHTO. 2004. *A Policy on Geometric Design of Highways and Streets.* 5th ed. http://www.transportation.org/.

Brater, E. F., and H. W. King. 1976. *Handbook of Hydraulics,* 6th ed. New York: McGraw-Hill.

Chin, D. A. 2000. *Water-Resources Engineering.* Upper Saddle River, NJ: Prentice-Hall.

Chow, V. T. 1959. *Open Channel Hydraulics.* New York: McGraw-Hill.

Daugherty, R. L., J. B. Franzini, and E. J. Finnemore. 1985. *Fluid Mechanics with Engineering Applications,* 8th ed. New York: McGraw-Hill.

FHWA. 2001. *Hydraulic Design of Culverts.* HDS-5, Publication No. FHWA-NHI-01-020.

FHWA. 2004. *HY 8 Cuvlert Analysis Program.* Version 6.1, downloadable EXE file, http://www.fhwa.dot.gov.

French, R. H. 1985. *Open Channel Hydraulics.* New York: McGraw-Hill.

Henderson, F. M. 1966. *Open Channel Flow.* New York: Macmillen.

McCuen, R. H. 2005. *Hydrologic Analysis and Design,* 3rd ed. Upper Saddle River, NJ: Pearson Prentice-Hall.

Ramser, C. E. 1929. *Flow of Water in Drainage Channels.* USDA Technical Bulletin 129.

Scobey, F. C. 1939. *Flow of Water in Irrigation and Similar Canals.* U.S. Department of Agriculture, Technical Bulletin 652.

Street, R. L., G. Z. Watters, and J. K. Vennard. 1996. *Elementary Fluid Mechanics,* 7th ed., New York: John Wiley & Sons.

USDA NRCS. 1986. *Engineering Field Handbook—Chapter 7, Grassed Waterways.* NTIS No. PB86-197449/AS.

USDA. 1954. *Handbook of Channel Design for Soil and Water Conservation.* SCS TP-61. Washington, DC, March 1947, Revised June 1954.

CHAPTER 12

MULTIPLE-EVENT DETENTION DESIGN

12.1 INTRODUCTION

Detention design is the conventional solution to stormwater management for typical land development activities. It is probably the least desirable method for handling stormwater runoff, yet it is hard to avoid even for the most cleverly orchestrated designs. Innovative methods should be used to reduce increased runoff generated by landscape change. Design tactics such as disconnected impervious area, reduced impervious area, decentralization of runoff, dispersion of runoff, and minimization of altered landscape are all much more desirable than the uninspired tactic of clear-build-pave followed by capture-store-release.

There are many best management practices (BMPS) that should be incorporated into a design as preliminary remediation efforts. These BMPs include but are not limited to overland flow (vs. piping), vegetated swales, bioretention basins, vegetated infiltration beds, curbless streets, narrower paved streets, shorter-set back lines (to reduce paved driveway surfaces), and reserved green space. Each BMP by itself can reduce runoff by a small amount. Several BMPs combined in an orchestrated fashion can reduce runoff by a significant amount. The goal is to eliminate as much runoff on-site as possible through creative, on-site management. Once this is done, the remaining increase runoff is then handled by a detention facility, which is most likely considerably smaller in size because of the addition of BMPs to the design. It is possible to reduce all runoff increase by innovative design, but it is very difficult and often requires the selection of a suitable site. However, conceding that stormwater management almost always means storage detention, the goal of any stormwater management plan should be to minimize the volume of storage that must be detained.

12.2   DETENTION VOLUME ESTIMATES

Before any hydrographs can be routed through a detention facility, the facility must be sized to meet the requirements for control. Preliminary estimates of storage can be performed in several ways. Some popular methods are (1) runoff difference, (2) hydrograph subtraction, and (3) NRCS TR-55, Chapter 6, 1986.

12.2.1   Runoff Difference Method

This method is based on the assumption that storage required for stormwater detention is equal to the postdevelopment runoff volume minus the predevelopment runoff volume. This difference represents the increase in total runoff due to development, so this is a logical assumption and it is simple to determine. The universal way to determine storage loss when using hydrograph analysis is to determine the predevelopment hydrograph volume (area under the curve) and the postdevelopment hydrograph volume and look at the difference. If NRCS runoff procedures are being used, then a more direct and simpler method would be to subtract the predevelopment direct runoff from the post development direct runoff. Direct runoff is computed using the curve number method of Equation 8.1 or 8.4. In this case, volume of storage required is computed as

$$V_S = A(Q_D - Q_N) \tag{12.1}$$

where V_S is the required storage volume in ac-in, A is the site drainage area in acres, Q_D is the runoff depth for the developed condition in inches, and Q_N is the runoff depth for the natural (predevelopment) condition in inches.

Example 12.1   A 62-acre natural watershed located in Virginia will be developed into the Pine Hills residential subdivision. The predevelopment *CN* for the site is 68. The postdevelopment *CN* is 76. For a design event equal to 4.2 inches of rainfall, estimate the volume of storage required for detention design.

Solution:

$$Q_N = \frac{\left(4.2 - \dfrac{200}{68} + 2\right)^2}{\left(4.2 + \dfrac{800}{68} - 8\right)} = 1.33 \text{ inches}$$

$$Q_D = \frac{\left(4.2 - \dfrac{200}{76} + 2\right)^2}{\left(4.2 + \dfrac{800}{76} - 8\right)} = 1.89 \text{ inches}$$

$$V_S = A(Q_D - Q_N) = 62(1.89 - 1.33) = 34.72 \text{ ac-in}$$

This volume is about 2.89 ac-ft, or about 126,034 ft³. A 1-acre pond with an average pond depth of 3 feet would be a good first estimate, or a 0.5-acre pond with a average pond depth of 6 feet is also a good first guess.

12.2.2 Hydrograph Subtraction

Hydrograph subtraction is similar to the loss of storage method, except it looks at runoff hydrographs a little differently. Instead of subtracting total runoff of the two hydrographs, hydrograph subtraction takes a plot of the predevelopment and postdevelopment hydrographs, and determines the volume difference between the two from time $t = 0$ to the time when the hydrographs first cross on the postdevelopment graph falling limb. Figure 12.1 shows the region that is used to compute the storage estimate. As can be seen in this figure, the volume of storage estimate in this method can be very close to the volume estimated using loss of storage. However, there are times where the falling limb of the predevelopment hydrograph is significantly higher in flows, as compared to the falling limb of the postdevelopment hydrograph. In cases such as these, hydrograph subtraction would most likely give a better estimate of storage required than the loss of storage method.

The procedure for differencing the hydrographs is reasonably simple. Both hydrographs are assumed to have tabulated ordinate data based on a common time step. Each ordinate of the predevelopment hydrograph, beginning with the first, is subtracted from the associated predevelopment hydrograph ordinate until the difference becomes negative. All of the positive differences represent required storage volume. These ordinate differences are summed

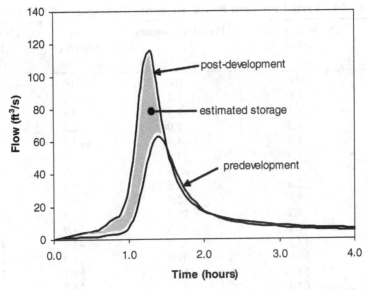

Figure 12.1 Hydrograph subtraction method for detention storage estimate.

and multiplied by the time step to give volume. Units must be consistent. Usually, flow is expressed in ft³/s, so the time step in the calculation should be expressed in seconds.

Example 12.2 Portions of the 100-year, predevelopment and postdevelopment hydrographs for the Pine Hills subdivision are shown in Table 12.1. An estimate of detention storage for the 100-year event is required.

Solution: The computations are shown in Table 12.1. The fourth column is the difference between the third and second columns. This difference is performed until a negative number is encountered. The positive values are summed and the sum is found to be 271.1 ft³/s. This sum is used to compute the total volume required:

$$V_S = 271.1 \text{ ft}^3/\text{s} \times 0.1 \text{ hrs} \times 3600 \text{ s/hr} = 97{,}596 \text{ ft}^3$$

12.2.3 NRCS TR-55

NRCS TR-55, 1986, has six chapters, each of which deals with a particular element of urban runoff analysis and management. Chapter 6 presents a method for estimating detention storage requirements based on NRCS 24-hour rainfall distribution types, runoff depths, and peak flows. It is developed through the study of average storage conditions for many structures with

TABLE 12.1 Partial Pre- and Postdevelopment Hydrographs for Example 12.2

Time (hour)	Predevelopment Flow (ft³/s)	Post-development Flow (ft³/s)	Flow Difference (ft³/s)	Cumulative Flow (ft³/s)
0.0	0.0	0.0	0.0	0.0
0.1	1.0	1.1	0.1	0.1
0.2	1.1	1.9	0.8	0.9
0.3	1.2	3.0	1.8	2.7
0.4	1.4	4.4	3.0	5.7
0.5	1.5	4.9	3.4	9.1
0.6	1.7	5.5	3.8	12.9
0.7	2.4	8.9	6.5	19.5
0.8	3.0	12.3	9.3	28.7
0.9	3.7	15.7	12.0	40.7
1.0	7.4	32.3	24.9	65.6
1.1	17.3	65.9	48.6	114.3
1.2	36.0	107.0	71.0	185.3
1.3	55.5	115.2	59.7	244.9
1.4	63.4	87.7	24.3	269.2
1.5	57.2	59.0	1.8	271.1
1.6	45.6	41.7	−3.8	
1.7	35.0	31.1		
1.8	27.2	24.1		
1.9	22.3	20.4		
2.0	17.5	16.6		

single-stage flow devices, some with orifice control and some with weir control. Estimates should be viewed as preliminary. To begin the procedure, the volume of post-development runoff is computed using Equation 12.2.

$$V_R = 3630 \, AQ \tag{12.2}$$

In this equation, V_R is volume of runoff in ft³, Q is runoff depth in inches, and A is drainage area in acres. The coefficient 3630 is simply a conversion factor for units. Figure 12.2, or Equations 12.3 or 12.4, is used to determine the ratio of storage volume to runoff volume. The equations are chosen according to NRCS rainfall distribution.

$$\left(\frac{V_S}{V_R}\right)_{I,IA} = 0.660 - 1.76\left(\frac{q_o}{q_i}\right) + 1.96\left(\frac{q_o}{q_i}\right)^2 - 0.730\left(\frac{q_o}{q_i}\right)^3 \tag{12.3}$$

$$\left(\frac{V_S}{V_R}\right)_{II,III} = 0.682 - 1.43\left(\frac{q_o}{q_i}\right) + 1.64\left(\frac{q_o}{q_i}\right)^2 - 0.804\left(\frac{q_o}{q_i}\right)^3 \tag{12.4}$$

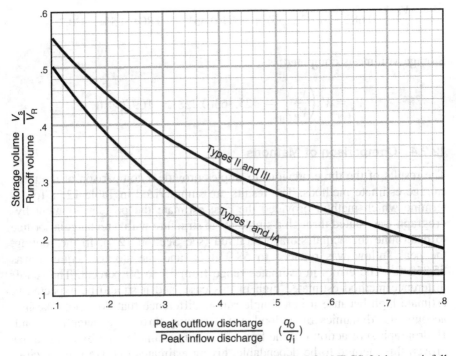

Figure 12.2 Approximate detention basin routing effects for NRCS 24-hour rainfall types I, IA, II, and III (USDA NRCS TR-55, 1986).

where V_S = volume of estimated storage, V_R = volume of runoff, q_o = target release flow, and q_i = peak basin inflow. Storage required is determine by multiplying the volume ratio by the volume of runoff computed in Equation 12.2.

Example 12.3 For the Pine Hills residential subdivision in Examples 12.1 and 12.2, compute the storage estimate using the NRCS TR-55 method. From Table 12.1, the target release rate is 61.4 ft³/s and the pond inflow is 115.4 ft³/s.

Solution:

$$V_R = 3630\ AQ = 3630 \times 62 \times 1.89 = 425{,}363\ \text{ft}^3$$

$$\frac{q_o}{q_i} = \frac{61.4}{152.7} = 0.550$$

Virginia is located in type II rainfall region, so Equation 12.4 is used.

$$\frac{V_S}{V_R} = 0.682 - 1.43(0.55) + 1.64(0.55)^2 - 0.804(0.55)^3 = 0.258$$

Storage volume is computed as

$$V_S = V_R\left(\frac{V_S}{V_R}\right)_{II} = 425,363(0.258) = 109,744 \text{ ft}^3$$

12.2.4 Comparison of Methods

The results of the three previous examples provide a comparison of the three storage estimate methods. The results are summarized in Table 12.2. To determine which method provided the best estimate the postdevelopment hydrograph was routed through a single-stage structure with a rectangular orifice to determine the actual storage required (see Section 12.4). In the routing, the peak inflow was reduced to 58.9 ft^3/s, and the storage required was 85,250 ft^3. The errors in estimates range from 15 to 50 percent. The runoff difference method estimated high in this case, and it should be expected to estimate high because it is a simple runoff difference that does not take into account the dynamics of a flood wave moving through a detention pond. Hydrograph subtraction did the best job in this example, and experience has proven this method to be dependable, giving estimates that are usually close to the correct volume. NRCS TR-55 has been accused of giving estimates that are consistently high by 25 to 40 percent. For very small sites of a few acres or less, this accusation may be true. However, the method is a good one, and in many cases provides an estimate that is within a few percent of the final result.

12.3 MULTIPLE-STAGE OUTLET FLOW ANALYSIS

Storage detention for land development activities typically requires the management of several runoff events based on frequency of occurrence. Land-development regulations typically call for three to five controlled events,

TABLE 12.2 Comparison of Results of Examples 12.1 through 12.3 for the Pine Hills Subdivision

Method	Storage Estimate	% Error
Runoff difference	126,034	+47.8
Hydrograph subtraction	97,596	+14.5
NRCS TR-55	109,744	+28.7
Modified-Puls routing	85,250	—

chosen from the standard list of the 1-, 2-, 5-, 10-, 25-, 50-, and 100-year return periods. In practical terms, the 1-10-100 criterion is probably more than adequate. If a detention structure can handle these three events, it is probably doing a pretty good job on the remaining four. Nevertheless, the designer must create a combination of outlet points in the detention pond outlet structure to meet the requirements of a particular regulation. Multiple outlets in a single structure is the common approach to this design problem. The process is presented in Section 12.4.

Before design can be performed, it is important to understand the process of analyzing a multiple outlet structure. In general, the hydraulics of culvert flow, orifice flow, and weir flow are adequate to analyze a structure. There are situations where energy methods are required to analyze flow, and the computations then become more complicated.

The fundamental equations used are the orifice and weir equations, Equations 3.26 and 4.19.

$$q_o = C_o A\sqrt{2gH_o} \tag{3.26}$$

$$q_w = CLH_w^{3/2} \tag{4.19}$$

Specific flow relations for each opening in the outlet structure are created in terms of water surface elevation, instead of water depth, above the opening. Flows are tracked in reference to water surface elevation, and all flows created by a particular water surface for individual openings are summed to get the total flow through the structure. The analysis is illustrated by example.

Example 12.4 Figure 12.3 shows a sketch of a three-stage outlet structure for a small detention pond. It consists of a 2-feet-by-4-feet concrete riser box with three inflow holes (stages 1, 2, and 3) and one outflow hole (outfall culvert). The culvert does not control flow through the structure, nor does is cause backwater to occur in the riser box. The specific geometry of each opening is summarized in Table 12.3. Create an outflow versus elevation (E-O) curve for this structure, for the elevation range of 592.00 feet to 597.00 feet, using an elevation step of 0.20 feet.

Solution: Since the outfall culvert does not control flow, the analysis begins with the first stage.

Stage 1. The rectangular orifice will initially act like a weir until the pond depth exceeds the vertical dimension. After water depth covers the entire opening, the weir flow stops and the orifice flow occurs. Therefore, this stage requires the development of two equations.

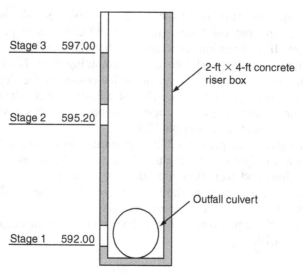

Figure 12.3   Schematic drawing of the three-stage outlet structure of Example 12.4.

1. For water surface elevations (WSEL) 592.00 ft to 592.55 ft: The orifice acts like a weir, where $L = 0.55$ ft, headwater depth of the weir is expressed in terms of $WSEL$ as $H_w = WSEL - 592.00$ ft.

$$q_{w,1} = CLH_w^{3/2} = 3.1(0.55)(WSEL - 592.00)^{1.5}$$

$$= 1.705(WSEL - 592.00)^{1.5}$$

2. For WSEL 592.55 to 597.00 ft: Orifice flow occurs where $A = 0.28$ ft^2, $C = 0.60$, and $H_o = WSEL - 592.28$ ft.

$$q_o = C_o A \sqrt{2gH_o} = 0.6(0.28)(64.4)^{0.5}(WSEL - 592.28)^{0.5}$$

$$= 1.444(WSEL - 592.28)^{0.5}$$

Flows are computed for the valid range and are shown in Table 12.4. $WSEL = 592.55$ feet is the breakpoint between the two flow types. Break-

TABLE 12.3   Geometric Characteristics of the Outlet Structure Analyzed in Example 12.4

Stage	Geometric Shape	Flow Coefficient	Dimensions	Invert Elevation (ft)
1	rectangular orifice	0.6	0.55 ft × 0.55 ft	592.00
2	rectangular orifice	0.6	0.53 ft × 0.53 ft	595.20
3	constricted rectangular weir	3.1	2.25 ft wide	597.00

TABLE 12.4   Summary of Flow Calculations of Stage 1 of Example 12.4

WSEL (ft)	$H_{w,1}$ (ft)	$q_{w,1}$ (ft^3/s)	$H_{o,1}$ (ft)	$q_{o,1}$ (ft^3/s)
592.00	0	0		
592.20	0.20	0.15		
592.40	0.40	0.43		
592.55	0.55	0.70	0.28	0.75
592.60			0.33	0.82
592.80			0.53	1.05
593.00			0.73	1.23
. . .			. . .	. . .
597.40			5.13	3.27
597.60			5.33	3.33
597.80			5.53	3.39
598.00			5.73	3.45

points usually give different answers, and the disparity is probably caused by uncertainty in the flow coefficients. The lower value of the two is accepted as the correct flow rate, simply as an arbitrary choice. An average value may be equally valid.

Stage 2. Again, this rectangular orifice acts first like a weir, and then as an orifice.

1. For WSEL 595.20 to 595.73 feet: The orifice acts like a weir, where $C = 3.1$, $L = 0.53$ feet and $H_w = WSEL - 595.20$ ft.

$$q_{w,2} = 1.643(WSEL - 592.00)^{1.5}$$

2. For WSEL 595.73 to 597.00 feet: Orifice flow occurs where $C = 0.6$, $A = 0.53$ ft^2, and $H_w = WSEL - 595.46$, substituting into the orifice equation, gives

$$q_{o,2} = 1.348(WSEL - 595.46)^{0.5}$$

Using these two equations, the appropriate values of WSEL are used to compute flow. Results are in Table 12.5.

Stage 3. This is a simple rectangular weir with $C = 3.1$, $L = 2.25$ ft, and $H_w = WSEL - 597.00$ ft.

1. For WSEL 597.00 to 598.00 ft, the weir equation gives

$$q_{w,3} = 6.975(WSEL - 597.00)^{1.5}$$

TABLE 12.5 Summary of Flow Computations for Stage 2 of Example 12.4

WSEL (ft)	$H_{w,2}$ (ft)	$q_{w,2}$ (ft³/s)	$H_{o,2}$ (ft)	$q_{o,2}$ (ft³/s)
595.20	0	0		
595.40	0.20	0.15		
595.60	0.40	0.42		
595.73	0.53	0.63	0.27	0.70
595.80			0.34	0.78
596.00			0.54	0.98
596.20			0.74	1.15
. . .			. . .	. . .
597.40			1.94	1.87
597.60			2.14	1.97
597.80			2.34	2.06
598.00			2.54	2.14

Using this equation, the appropriate values of WSEL are used to compute flow. Results are in Table 12.6.

The results of the analysis of the three stages are merged into one table, and all flows associated with a particular *WSEL* are added to get the total flow through the outlet structure. The final outflow rating table is shown in Table 12.7 and the E O curve is plotted in Figure 12.4. The figure shows the distinct break points where one flow equation ends and the next begins. Weir curves are concave upward and orifice equations are concave downward.

This is the basic analysis process for establishing a rating curve for a multiple-stage outlet structure. In practice, the simplicity of the structure, in terms of hydraulic calculation, is not always possible. As backwater effects in the riser box affect the flow, more complex analysis methods are required. To perform these complex calculations on the desktop or with even with an electronic spreadsheet is difficult. Most analyses in practice are done with the aid of commercial software, specifically designed for stormwater detention design.

TABLE 12.6 Summary of flow computations for Stage 3 of Example 12.4

WSEL (ft)	$H_{w,3}$ (ft)	$q_{w,3}$ (ft³/s)
597.00	0.00	0.00
597.20	0.20	0.62
597.40	0.40	1.76
597.60	0.60	3.24
597.80	0.80	4.99
598.00	1.00	6.98

TABLE 12.7 Outlet Rating Table Summary Calculations for Example 12.1

WSEL (ft)	Stage 1 $q_{w,1}$ (ft³/s)	Stage 1 $q_{o,1}$ (ft³/s)	Stage 2 $q_{w,2}$ (ft³/s)	Stage 2 $q_{o,2}$ (ft³/s)	Stage 3 $q_{w,3}$ (ft³/s)	Total Discharge (ft³/s)
592.00	0.00					0.00
592.20	0.15					0.15
592.40	0.43					0.43
592.55	0.70					0.70
592.60		0.82				0.82
592.80		1.05				1.05
593.00		1.23				1.23
593.20		1.39				1.39
593.40		1.53				1.53
593.60		1.66				1.66
593.80		1.78				1.78
594.00		1.89				1.89
594.20		2.00				2.00
594.40		2.10				2.10
594.60		2.20				2.20
594.80		2.29				2.29
595.00		2.38				2.38
595.20		2.47	0.00			2.47
595.40		2.55	0.15			2.70
595.60		2.63	0.42			3.05
595.73		2.68	0.63			3.31
595.80		2.71		0.78		3.49
596.00		2.78		0.98		3.76
596.20		2.86		1.15		4.01
596.40		2.93		1.30		4.23
596.60		3.00		1.43		4.43
596.80		3.07		1.56		4.63
597.00		3.14		1.67	0.00	4.81
597.20		3.20		1.77	0.62	5.59
597.40		3.27		1.87	1.76	6.90
597.60		3.33		1.97	3.24	8.54
597.80		3.39		2.06	4.99	10.44
598.00		3.45		2.14	6.98	12.57

12.4 STORAGE AND OUTLET DESIGN PROCEDURE

Regulating flow for several frequency events requires the design of a multiple-opening outlet structure for the detention facility. The typical structure is a riser box attached to the upstream end of a discharge culvert laid underneath the detention pond embankment. Outlet openings are placed at different elevations along the riser box to allow the correct amount of flow to be released to the outfall culvert for each design event. The procedure for designing a

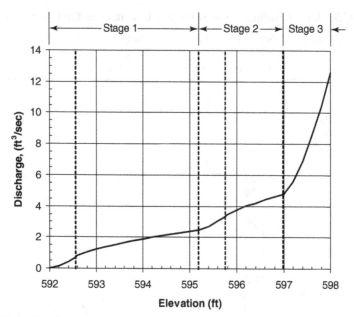

Figure 12.4 Elevation-outflow curve for the outlet structure of Example 12.4. Dashed lines show locations where a stage changes from weir to orifice flow, or where a new stage begins to add flow.

multiple-stage stormwater detention facility is a multistep process that is summarized as follows:

1. *Runoff and hydrographs*

    1.1 For the predevelopment condition of the site, perform hydrograph analyses for each controlled event. See Chapter 9.

    1.2 For the post-development condition, perform hydrograph analyses for each controlled event. See Chapter 9.

    1.3 Establish target release outflows for each event. Some local and regional regulations require target release flows to be a percentage of the pre-development peak flow.

2. *Preliminary storage estimate*

    2.1 Estimate storage required for each event. See Section 12.2.

    2.2 Make a preliminary design of detention pond shape and size according to the maximum storage required and site grading plan.

    2.3 Create an elevation-storage relationship for the detention pond.

    2.4 Determine the approximate water surface elevation in the pond for the storage requirement of each event, based upon the detention storage estimates of step 2.1.

3. *Preliminary outfall culvert*
   Size a culvert to carry the largest controlled event through the outlet structure and out of the pond, keeping the headwater elevation less than or equal to the pond bottom, if possible.
4. *Preliminary outlet structure geometry*
   4.1 Begin the design by addressing the first design event.
   4.2 For the design event, size an outlet opening in the riser box based on the expected water surface elevation in the pond (Step 2.4) and the target release outflow (Step 1.3).
   4.3 Create an elevation-outflow relationship for the outlet structure, taking into account all hydraulic elements of the design stage, riser box, outfall culvert, and any previously sized outlet openings.
   4.4 Route the post-development hydrograph through the pond.
   4.5 Verify that the target release rate has not been violated. If it has, repeat steps 4.2 through 4.5.
   4.6 Establish storage required to handle the previously routed event hydrograph, and note the maximum water surface elevation in the pond during the routing.
   4.7 Using the maximum water surface elevation. Determine the flow that the next stage must handle, considering the additional flow capacity of all previously created openings in the riser box.
   4.8 Size the opening for the next stage and place the invert at, or slightly above, the water surface elevation determined in step 4.6.
   4.9 Repeat steps 4.3 through 4.8 until all controlled events are handled correctly by the geometry of the outlet structure.
   4.10 If the storage capacity of the pond is found to be insufficient during the design of any of the outlet stages, the geometry of the pond must be adjusted and the design returns to step 2.2.
5. *Emergency Spillway*
   5.1 Determine the maximum flow that must be handled by the emergency spillway.
   5.2 Find a location for the construction of the spillway that will not put the pond embankment at risk if it begins to erode.
   5.3 Size the emergency spillway.

Detention design with multiple outlets requires this trial-and-error solution in several steps. The above process just described minimizes the number of trials required to design the structure.

12.5 DESIGN EXAMPLE

The best way to understand the step-by-step process of multiple event detention design is to go through a design example. The following example is completed with the aid of the Virginia Tech/Penn State Urban Hydrology Model (VTPSUHM) (Seybert et. al, 2005), a computer program written at Penn State University and Virginia Tech specifically for the solution of common hydraulic and hydrologic procedures used in stormwater management design. In this example, VTPSUHM is used to compute average curve numbers, time of concentrations, runoff hydrographs, and estimated detention volumes. It is then used to size the multiple outlets in the detention basin riser box, create the outlet structure rating curve, and route the postdevelopment hydrographs through the detention basin.

Example 12.5 Aron Meadows is a proposed residential subdivision located in southeastern Pennsylvania. A multiple-event detention facility must be designed to manage the increased runoff. The following data and design criteria are provided.

Watershed

- Drainage area is 13.6 acres.
- Soils are hydrologic soil group C for the entire site.
- Predevelopment conditions:
  t_c = 34 minutes, CN = 71 (meadow and some trees)
- Postdevelopment conditions:
  t_c = 19 minutes, CN = 80 (1/2 acre residential lots)

Design Criteria

- For the 1-, 10-, and 100-year events, reduce the postdevelopment peak flows to 100 percent of the predevelopment peak flows.
- Design rainfall depths for the 24-hour storm are 2.40, 4.56, and 7.44 inches for the 1-, 10-, and 100-year events, respectively.
- The NRCS tabular method must be used for the runoff modeling.
- Detention-pond side slopes must be 3H:1V maximum, with 5H:1V preferred for ease of maintenance.
- Pond depth cannot exceed 8 feet of water.
- Pond freeboard must be 1 foot minimum.
- Pond embankment must have a minimum top width of 10 feet.
- The outlet structure must be a concrete riser box with a concrete pipe used for the outflow culvert.
- The outfall culvert slope is 0.010 ft/ft.
- Tailwater on the outfall culvert will be zero because it discharges to a trapezoidal swale that eventually leads to a receiving stream.

Solution: The remainder of this chapter covers the solution to Example 12.5.

12.5.1 Runoff and Hydrographs

With the data given, the design begins with creating predevelopment and postdevelopment hydrographs. The NRCS tabular method in VTPSUHM is used to create six hydrographs. The resulting graphs are shown in Figures 12.5 and 12.6. The peak flow data and total runoff depths for the post-development condition are summarized in Table 12.8.

12.5.2 Preliminary Storage Estimates

With this hydrograph data, an estimate of detention storage is made for each event. The NRCS TR-55 method is used because it is simple, quick, and reasonably good. For the 1-year event, the ratio of flows is 0.32. Using Figure 12.2, the volume ratio is 0.37 and the estimated storage volume is

$$V_R = \left(\frac{V_S}{V_R}\right)3630 \, AQ = (0.37)3630(13.6)(0.82) = 14{,}978 \text{ ft}^3$$

Similar calculations are made for the 10- and 100-year events, and the results are shown in Table 12.9.

Required storage of the pond is approximately 61,000 ft³. The geometry of the pond depends on site topography. For the purposes of this example it is assumed that a relatively flat site with mild slopes and approximately 0.5 acres of surface area has been reserved for the detention basin.

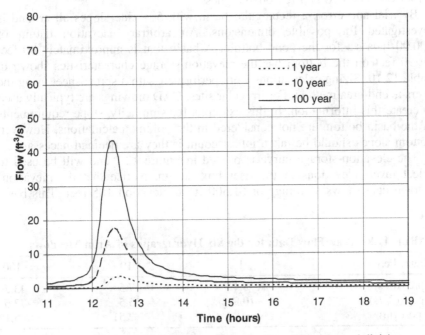

Figure 12.5 Predevelopment hydrographs for Aron Meadows subdivision.

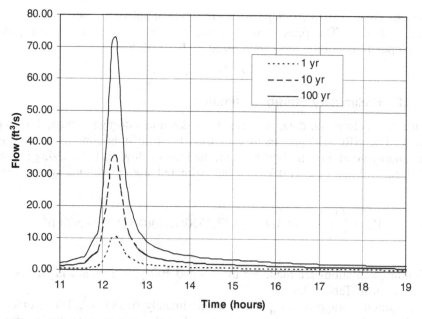

Figure 12.6 Postdevelopment hydrographs for Aron Meadows subdivision.

With 21,700 ft² of surface area and 5:1 side slopes, a pond 6 feet deep with 1 foot of freeboard is a reasonable guess.

By trial and error, a rectangular basin with 5:1 side slopes all around is investigated for possible dimensions. An arbitrary elevation datum of 100.00 ft is set for the pond bottom. A basin that is approximately 80 feet by 90 feet on the bottom has the elevation-storage characteristics shown in Table 12.10. Sizing calculations were performed with a spreadsheet using the average end-area method. For irregular sites, CAD drawings are typically used to create this information. In this example, for simplicity, slope requirements of the basin bottom are not considered in the volume calculations. However, bottom slopes should be taken into account if they are deemed necessary.

The elevation-storage curve is plotted in Figure 12.7 and will be used to select invert elevations in the riser box design. Notice that the elevation-storage data shows a storage of 61,500 ft³ at elevation 105 feet. This basin

TABLE 12.8 Peak Flow Data for the Six Hydrographs of Aron Meadows

Return Period (yr)	1	10	100
q-pre (ft³/s)	3.4	17.5	43.2
q-post (ft³/s)	10.5	35.5	72.6
Q-post (in)	0.82	2.51	5.10

TABLE 12.9   Storage Estimates for the Three Design Events of Aron Meadows

Return period (yr)	1	10	100
Flow ratio q_o/q_i	0.32	0.49	0.60
V_S/V_R	0.37	0.28	0.24
V_R	14,980	34,700	60,430

provides excess capacity for the routing design. This is always a good approach. It is much easier to reduce the original basin size than it is to increase the size once routing has shown it to be inadequate.

12.5.3 Preliminary Outlet Structure Geometry

The outlet structure design begins with a concrete riser box. The final dimensions will be determined once the outlets and outfall culvert are sized. The design is sequential, beginning with the outfall culvert, stage 1, stage 2, and finally stage 3.

Preliminary Outfall Culvert Size. The outfall culvert must carry the 100-year target release flow of 43.2 ft³/s. In addition, the backwater level in the riser box should be kept below the invert of the first stage. This condition will guarantee that all openings in the riser box will discharge freely to the atmosphere for all design events. This condition, although desirable, is not often possible. In order for this to happen, the crown of the culvert exiting

TABLE 12.10   Elevation-Storage Data for the Preliminary Detention Pond

Elev (ft)	Side Dim. (ft × ft)	Area (ft²)	Volume (ft³)	Total Vol. (ft³)
100	80 × 90	7,200		0
			8,100	
101	90 × 100	9,000		8,100
			10,000	
102	100 × 110	11,000		18,100
			12,100	
103	110 × 120	13,200		30,200
			14,400	
104	120 × 130	15,600		44,600
			16,900	
105	130 × 140	18,200		61,500
			19,600	
106	140 × 150	21,000		81,100
			22,500	
107	150 × 160	24,000		103,600

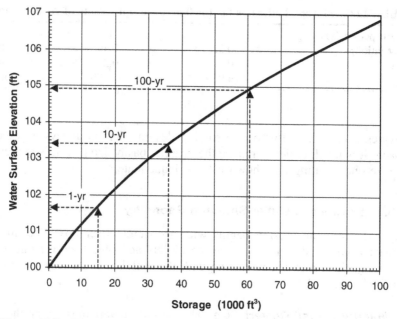

Figure 12.7   Elevation-Storage curve for the Aron Meadows detention pond.

the riser box most likely must be below the invert of the first stage. Many times there is not enough elevation to allow this, so a compromise is usually made, where backwater is allowed to cover the lower stage, but kept from affecting the flow of the upper stages. As a first guess, the invert of the outfall culvert is set to 98.00 feet.

The first stage in the outlet structure will be placed at elevation 100.00 feet, making this a dry pond design. The volume estimate for storage controlled by the first stage was determined to be 15,000 ft³. Using this information with the E S curve of Figure 12.7 reveals that the approximate water surface elevation (WSEL) in the pond necessary to control the first event will be about 101.7 feet. The second stage invert will be near this elevation. Therefore, to keep backwater effects away from the second stage, the headwater on the outfall culvert should be kept to 3.7 feet or less. It is assumed that the culvert is acting under inlet control simply because this is a common condition for riser-box outfall culverts. With this information and assumptions, a trial HW/D ratio of 1 is used to estimate the culvert size. Figure 11.8 is the FHWA HDS-5 chart for circular concrete pipe under inlet control. If inlet control is assumed, and a square edge entrance condition is used with $HW/D = 1$ and $q = 43$ ft³/s, Figure 11.8 indicates that the required pipe diameter is about 40 inches. The next closest commercially available diameter is 42 inches. If a 42-inch culvert is used, then Figure 11.8 shows that the HW/D will be close to 0.88. This means that the headwater needed to send 43 ft³/s of flow through a 42-inch (3.5-foot) outfall culvert is about

0.88 × 3.5 ft = 3.08 ft, which would make the WSEL in the pond 101.08 ft. This is acceptable since it is below the expected water surface controlled by the first stage (101.7 ft), so a 42-inch culvert with square-edge entrance condition is used to start the design. Figure 12.8 shows the configuration of the riser box at this point in the design.

The length of the culvert must be about 80 to 85 feet (5 to 6 feet deep pond with 1 foot of freeboard, 5H:1V embankment slopes, and 10 feet across the top of the embankment).

Note: At this point, it is not known if the culvert acts as inlet control or outlet (friction) control. However, we do know that inlet control is typically more constricting than outlet control. If the culvert is friction control, the design is most likely still functional. If we desire, we can return to the outfall culvert design and try to reduce this diameter after the riser is designed.

Stage 1. 1-year Event. The invert of the first stage is 100.00 feet. The target release rate is 3.4 ft³/s, and the estimated required storage is 14,980 ft³. As mentioned earlier, the estimated storage is used with the E-S curve to estimate the maximum WSEL in the pond while controlling the first event. The WSEL is estimated to be 101.7 feet. This indicates that 1.7 feet of water will be available in the pond to drive flow through the first stage orifice.

A rectangular orifice is chosen as the outlet geometry and the flow coefficient C_o is assumed to be 0.6. The size of the opening is estimated using the orifice equation, Equation 3.26, solving for area.

$$A = \frac{q_o}{C_o\sqrt{2gH_o}} = \frac{3.4}{0.60[2(32.2)(1.7)]^{0.5}} = 0.54 \text{ ft}^2$$

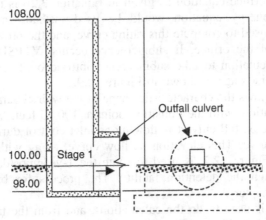

Figure 12.8 Riser box configuration for the outfall culvert and first stage in Example 12.5.

With this area, a rectangular orifice of 0.75 feet wide and 0.72 feet high provides the estimated area. However, note that H_o is defined with respect to the center of the orifice, and H_o used in this solution is to the orifice bottom. So, a better estimate of H_o might be about $1.7 - 0.72/2 = 1.34$ feet. With this value A becomes 0.61 ft². An opening of 0.80 feet wide by 0.75 feet high is a better estimate.

The opening first acts like a constricted weir ($C_w = 3.1$) during the stages 100.00 feet to 100.75 feet, and then like an orifice ($C_o = 0.6$) during stages 100.75 feet and up. H_w is measured from the weir invert and H_o is measured at the orifice centerline. These parameters are expressed in terms of WSEL as

$$H_w = WSEL - 100.00$$

$$H_o = WSEL - 100.375$$

The weir and orifice equations (Equations 4.19 and 3.26) become

$$q_w = CLH_w^{3/2} = 3.1(0.80)H_w^{3/2} = 2.48(WSEL - 100.00)^{3/2}$$

$$q_o = C_o A\sqrt{2gH_o} = 0.6(0.61)\sqrt{2gH_o} = 2.93(WSEL - 100.375)^{1/2}$$

These equations are used to create the elevation-outflow curve for the first stage. WSELs at even intervals—starting at 100.00 feet and ending at 108.00 feet—are used to compute flow through the opening. The WSEL of 108.00 feet is the maximum expected elevation in the pond exceeded by 2 feet, just to be conservative. During the calculations, it is typically assumed that backwater does not affect the flow of the first stage. However, to be accurate, flow depths in the outfall culvert should be checked at every computation interval to determine if backwater exists on the orifice opening. If it does, then the orifice equation as given in Equation 3.26 is not valid. Some form of the energy equation would be used instead. In this example, VTPSUHM is used to compute this rating curve, and the program checks for submergence of the orifice. If submergence occurs, VTPSUHM makes an appropriate calculation to take submergence into account. The rating curve result for the first stage is shown in Figure 12.9.

The figure shows the characteristic shape of the weir equation followed by the orifice equation, with the transition point at 100.75 feet. VTPSUHM also verified that the outfall culvert is flowing as inlet control during this portion of the rating curve. This elevation outflow curve, along with the elevation-storage curve Figure 12.7, is used to route the 1-year postdevelopment hydrograph through the detention facility. The process for basin routing is presented in Chapter 9.

VTPSUHM is used to do the calculations, and from the tabulated output (not shown) the routing results show that the peak flow out of the basin is 3.04 ft³/s at 12.7 hours. This outflow meets the target release criteria, but

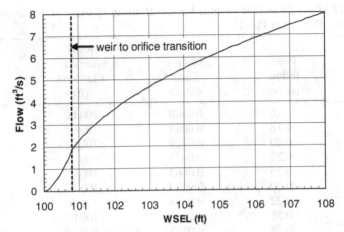

Figure 12.9 First-stage rating curve for the first estimate of required opening size in Example 12.5.

could be increased. So a second trial is performed, increasing flow area by about 15 percent. The first-stage geometry is adjusted to $A = 0.69$ ft^2, with opening size of 0.833 by 0.833 feet. A new rating curve is generated, and the 1-yr postdevelopment hydrograph is routed again. This time the peak outflow is 3.36 ft^3/s at 12.7 hours. This is very close to the target release, and this opening size is accepted as good. The inflow and outflow hydrographs for the routing are shown in Figure 12.10.

VTPSUHM provides information on storage and WSEL as part of the routing output, and the first portion is shown in Table 12.11. At the peak basin outflow of 3.36 ft^3/s (second one in the table), the maximum WSEL in

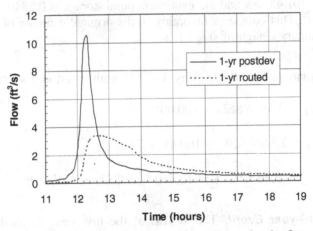

Figure 12.10 Summary hydrograph results of the routing for the first stage in Example 12.5.

TABLE 12.11 VTPSUHM Output for the Routing of the 1-yr Hydrograph through the Detention Pond

Event Time (hrs)	Pond Inflow (ft³/s)	Storage Used (ac-ft)	Water Surface Elevation (ft)	Basin Outflow (ft³/s)
11.0	0.16	0.0000	100.00	0.00
11.1	0.18	0.0014	100.01	0.01
11.2	0.20	0.0029	100.02	0.01
11.3	0.22	0.0045	100.02	0.02
11.4	0.26	0.0063	100.03	0.03
11.5	0.29	0.0083	100.04	0.04
11.6	0.32	0.0104	100.06	0.05
11.7	0.55	0.0136	100.07	0.06
11.8	0.78	0.0185	100.10	0.08
11.9	1.00	0.0250	100.13	0.13
12.0	2.33	0.0372	100.20	0.23
12.1	5.49	0.0663	100.36	0.56
12.2	9.67	0.1209	100.65	1.37
12.3	10.51	0.1880	101.01	2.57
12.4	8.14	0.2419	101.24	3.04
12.5	5.51	0.2723	101.38	3.27
12.6	3.95	0.2840	101.43	3.36
12.7	3.00	0.2849	101.43	3.36
12.8	2.37	0.2795	101.41	3.32
12.9	2.02	0.2704	101.37	3.26
13.0	1.68	0.2591	101.32	3.17

Remaining VTPSUHM output is truncated from this table.

the pond is 101.43 feet and the maximum pond storage is 0.2849 ac-ft, which is 12,410 ft³. This compares favorably to the original estimate of 14,980 ft³. The summary design of stage 1 is:

Square orifice: 0.833 ft by 0.833 ft, with invert at 100.00 ft

$$q_{w,1} = 2.58(WSEL - 100.00)^{3/2} \tag{12.5}$$

$$q_{o,1} = 3.34(WSEL - 100.417)^{1/2} \tag{12.6}$$

$$q_{peak} = 3.36 \text{ ft}^3/\text{s}, \ S = 12,410 \text{ ft}, \ WSEL = 101.43 \text{ ft}$$

Stage 2. 10-year Event. The WSEL of the first stage is used to set the invert of the second stage. Elevation 101.45 feet is chosen. The target release rate is 17.5 ft³/s, and the estimated required storage is 35,930 ft³. Estimated storage is used with the E S curve to estimate the maximum WSEL in the pond while controlling the second event. Figure 12.7 indicates that this WSEL is about 103.4 ft. This suggests that about 1.95 ft (103.4 − 101.45) of head is available to drive flow through the second stage and 2.98 ft (103.4 − 100.417) of head is available to drive flow through the first stage. The design flow for the second stage is the target release flow for the 10-year event minus the flow passing through the first stage. The first stage flow is estimated using Equation 12.6 as

$$q_{o,1} = 3.34(2.98)^{1/2} = 5.77 \text{ ft}^3/\text{s}$$

The design flow for the second stage becomes $17.5 - 5.77 = 11.7$ ft³/s. Like the first stage, rectangular orifice geometry is chosen for design. The required area is computed as in the first stage, and consideration for the half-height of the orifice is subtracted from the available head. A guess at the opening dimensions is 1 foot in height and the remainder in width. So the available head is better estimated as $1.95 - 0.5 = 1.45$ foot, and the area estimate becomes

$$A_2 = \frac{q_o}{C_o \sqrt{gH_o}} = \frac{11.7}{0.60[2(32.2)(1.45)]^{0.5}} = 2.02 \text{ ft}^2$$

Therefore, a rectangular orifice that is 1 foot high and 2 feet wide, with invert at 101.45, is the first guess at the second-stage opening size.

A new outlet structure rating curve must be generated. The final rating curve for the first stage is updated with the addition of this new opening. The outflow calculations are restarted at elevation 101.45 feet, and four equations will apply: Equations 12.5 and 12.6, which apply to the first stage, and the orifice and weir equations for the second stage. These four equations become

$$q_{w,1} = 2.58(WSEL - 100.00)^{3/2} \tag{12.5}$$

$$q_{o,1} = 3.34(WSEL - 100.417)^{1/2} \tag{12.6}$$

$$q_{w,2} = 6.20(WSEL - 101.45)^{3/2} \tag{12.7}$$

$$q_{o,2} = 9.63(WSEL - 101.95)^{1/2} \tag{12.8}$$

These equations are used as appropriate to compute total flow through the riser box for elevations ranging from 100.00 to 108.00 feet. VTPSUHM is used to perform these calculations, and the results are shown in Figure 12.11.

VTPSUHM is used once again, this time to route the 10-year event through the basin with the two-stage outlet structure. The results are graphically shown

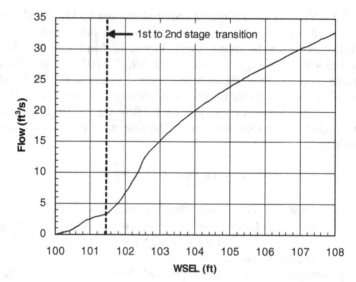

Figure 12.11 Rating curve for first trial geometry of first plus second stages, Example 12.5.

in Figure 12.12. The tabular results (not shown, but similar to Table 12.11) show that the peak pond outflow was 17.4 ft³/s at 12.5 hours. This is a very good result on the first trial, since the target release flow is 17.5 ft³/s. The sizing is accepted as good. From the tabulated computer results, the maximum WSEL in the pond during this routing is 103.40 feet with a maximum storage of 0.8261 ac-ft, which is 35,985 ft³.

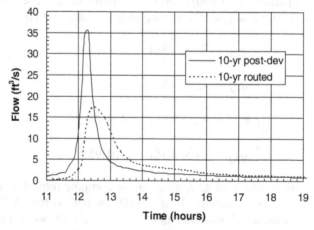

Figure 12.12 Inflow and outflow hydrographs for second-stage routing, Example 12.5.

The summary design of Stage 2 is:

Rectangular orifice: 2.00 ft wide, 1.00 ft high, invert at 101.45 ft

Rating curve equations: Equations 12.5, 12.6, 12.7, and 12.8

$q_{peak} = 17.4$ ft³/s, $S = 35,985$ ft, $WSEL = 103.40$ ft

Stage 3. 100-year Event. The maximum WSEL of the two-stage routing is used to set the invert of the third stage. Elevation 103.45 feet is chosen. The target release rate is 43.2 ft³/s and the estimated required storage is 60,430 ft³. Once more, estimated storage is used with the E S curve to estimate the maximum WSEL in the pond while controlling the third event. Figure 12.7 indicates that this WSEL is about 104.9 feet. This suggests that about 1.45 ft (104.9 − 103.45) of head is available to drive flow through the third stage, 2.95 ft (104.9 − 101.95) of head for the second stage, and 4.48 ft (104.9 − 100.417) to drive flow through the first stage. The design flow for the third stage is the target release flow for the 100-year event minus the flow passing through the first and second stages. The first stage flow is estimated using Equation 12.6.

$$q_{o,1} = 3.34(4.48)^{1/2} = 7.07 \text{ ft}^3/\text{s}$$

The second stage flow is estimate using Equation 12.8.

$$q_{o,2} = 9.63(2.95)^{1/2} = 16.54 \text{ ft}^3/\text{s}$$

The third-stage design flow becomes $43.2 - 16.54 - 7.07 = 19.59$ ft³/s.
The last stage will be a weir since it is at the top of the riser. The weir length (width) is estimated by solving the weir equation for L.

$$L = \frac{q}{C_w^{3/2}} = \frac{19.59}{3.1(1.45)^{1.5}} = 3.62 \text{ ft}$$

This weir could be one weir of 3.6 feet width or, two weirs of 1.8 feet width each, installed on opposing sides of the concrete riser box. The second design keeps the possibility of a 2-by-4-foot riser box, which is a standard concrete box dimension. In either case, the weir flow length will be 3.60 ft for the first sizing trial. This opening is modeled by one equation.

$$q_{w,3} = CLH_w^{3/2} = 3.1(3.6)H_w^{3/2} = 11.16(WSEL - 103.45)^{3/2} \quad (12.9)$$

Once again, a new outlet structure rating curve must be generated. The final rating curve of the second stage design is updated with the addition of the third opening. The outflow calculations are restarted at elevation 103.45 feet, and five equations will apply: Equations 12.5 and 12.6, which apply to the first stage, Equations 12.7 and 12.9, which apply to the second stage, and Equation 12.9 which applies to the third stage, summarized here for convenience.

$$q_{w,1} = 2.58(WSEL - 100.00)^{3/2} \tag{12.5}$$

$$q_{o,1} = 3.34(WSEL - 100.417)^{1/2} \tag{12.6}$$

$$q_{w,2} = 6.20(WSEL - 101.45)^{3/2} \tag{12.7}$$

$$q_{o,2} = 9.63(WSEL - 101.95)^{1/2} \tag{12.8}$$

$$q_{w,3} = 11.16(WSEL - 103.45)^{3/2} \tag{12.9}$$

These equations are used as appropriate to compute total flow through the riser box for elevations ranging from 100.00 to 108.00 feet. Once again, VTPSUHM is used to perform these calculations. The resulting elevation-outflow file is used to route the 100-year hydrograph through the pond. The routing shows that the peak flow out of the basin is 48.1 ft³/s at 12.4 hours. This flow exceeds the allowable release flow of 43.2 ft³/s, so the weir is resized. A few more trials on the size of the weir length results in a final weir length of 2.4 feet that produces a routed peak outflow of 42.8 ft³/s, maximum storage of 1.509 acre-ft (65,732 ft³), and maximum WSEL of 105.22 ft. This design is accepted as good. The routed 100-year hydrograph is shown in Figure 12.13. The final equation used to model flow through the third stage is changed to Equation 12.10.

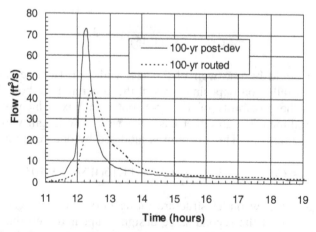

Figure 12.13 Inflow and outflow hydrographs for third-stage routing, Example 12.5.

$$q_{w,3} = 7.44(\text{WSEL} - 103.45)^{3/2} \tag{12.10}$$

The final outlet structure geometry establishes the final design rating curve for the outlet structure and it is plotted for the working elevation range of 100 ft to 107 ft. It is shown in Figure 12.14.

An abridged version of the tabulated output from VTPSUHM for the rating curve of Figure 12.14 is shown in Table 12.12. The original file used in the model had 0.1 hour time steps. Table 12.12 has 0.5 hour time steps simply to reduce the length of the table. The table shows two things of interest. First, the water surface elevation in the riser box, which is backwater caused by the 42-inch outfall culvert, does not exceed 101.45 feet through the riser-box design operating range (100.00 to 105.22 ft), and therefore does not submerge the second or third stage, as was desired early in the design. Second, the assumption of inlet control of the outfall culvert is verified by the program. Third, up to a WSEL of 105.5 ft, the normal depth in the outfall culvert never exceeds 2.82 ft. Thus, a smaller diameter culvert may work and should be evaluated. In this example however, the 42 inch culvert is used in the final design. The final outlet structure design is summarized in Table 12.13 and Figure 12.15.

Emergency Spillway. The detention pond requires an emergency spillway. Typically, it is good practice to provide enough flow area to pass the 100-year postdevelopment hydrograph through the pond, assuming the entire riser-box structure is plugged and nonoperational for the entire routing period. A broad-crested weir is typically used in the design ($C = 3.0$), with flow depths kept to a minimum. The outlet structure rating curve becomes a one stage structure, with the invert set slightly above the maximum water surface elevation determined in the routing of the 100-year event with the three-

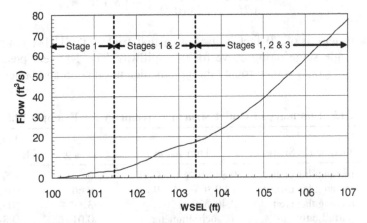

Figure 12.14 Final rating curve for the outlet structure in Example 12.5 showing regions of stage performance.

TABLE 12.12   Outlet Structure Rating Curve Calculations for Example 12.5 from VTPSUHM

Basin WSEL (ft)	Basin Outflow (ft³/s)	Riser Box WSEL (ft)	Tailwater Elevation (ft)	Outfall Culvert Control Type
100.00	0.00	98.00	N/A	INLET
100.50	0.92	98.34	N/A	INLET
101.00	2.55	98.59	N/A	INLET
101.50	3.55	98.70	N/A	INLET
102.00	6.74	98.98	N/A	INLET
102.50	11.96	99.32	N/A	INLET
103.00	15.24	99.50	N/A	INLET
103.50	18.10	99.64	N/A	INLET
104.00	23.61	99.88	N/A	INLET
104.50	30.62	100.17	N/A	INLET
105.00	38.87	100.49	N/A	INLET
105.50	48.13	100.82	N/A	INLET
106.00	58.07	101.18	N/A	INLET
106.50	67.12	102.30	N/A	INLET
107.00	77.28	102.91	N/A	INLET

opening riser box. The invert elevation is chosen to be set at 105.25 feet. The length of weir is estimated by setting the available head (flow depth) to 0.5 feet. This is an arbitrary flow depth through the weir, chosen simply on erosion concerns. In general, lower depths mean less chance for scour to occur in the emergency spillway channel. The estimated spillway length is computed using Equation 4.19 solved for L.

$$L = \frac{q}{CH_w^{3/2}} = \frac{72.6}{3.0(0.5)^{1.5}} = 68.4 \text{ ft}$$

A spillway length of 70 feet is used as a first trial. VTPSUHM is used to create a single stage rating curve for this spillway. The 100-year postdevelopment hydrograph is then routed through the detention pond and outlet struc-

TABLE 12.13   Summary of Outlet Structure Geometry for Example 12.5

Stage	Geometric Shape	Dimensions	C or n	Invert Elevation (ft)
1	rectangular orifice	0.833 ft × 0.833 ft	0.60	100.00
2	rectangular orifice	2.00 ft W × 1.00 ft H	0.60	101.45
3	rectangular weir	2.40 ft W	3.1	103.45
4	outfall culvert	42 inch diameter	0.013	98.00

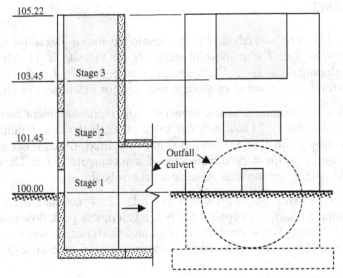

Figure 12.15 Outlet geometry for the final design of the riser box of Example 12.5.

ture to determine the actual water surface elevation obtained while passing the 100-year event. The results of the routing from VTPSUHM shows that the maximum water surface elevation in the routing is 105.71 feet, which creates a flow depth through the spillway as approximately 0.49 feet. This size is adequate if the dimensions can be made to fit the site. If either the flow depth or width is unacceptable, the dimensions must be changed. For example, if a spillway width closer to 25 feet is more desirable, it can be examined very quickly in the computer model. VTPSUHM shows that a 25 foot wide spillway results in a maximum water surface elevation of 106.10 feet, creating a spillway flow depth of about 0.85 feet.

The depth of flow in the emergency spillway channel will be something less than the estimated flow depth (water surface elevation minus spillway invert elevation), since the static energy in the pond will be converted to flow depth plus velocity head in the spillway channel. The flow velocity should be checked to make sure it is not erosive. If it is erosive, or near erosive, an erosion resistant liner must be placed in the spillway to protect the pond embankment from failure.

There are other aspects of pond design that should be considered, such as, embankment stability, outfall culvert piping, riser box trash racks, and anti-vortex devices. For very small ponds, some of these elements may not be critical. However, all of these elements should be considered, taking into account the potential for property loss or damage to downstream property if the pond or outlet structure was to fail.

PROBLEMS

12.1 A 151-acre watershed is to be developed into a 1-acre-lot residential subdivision. The predevelopment CN for the site is 71. The postdevelopment CN is 79. For a design event equal to 6.7 inches of rainfall, estimate the volume of storage required for detention design.

12.2 A 1-acre commercial site transforms the predevelopment surface from a CN value of 71 to a new CN value of 92. If the design rainfall is 5.4 inches, estimate the detention storage required. Based on your answer, suggest preliminary dimensions of a rectangular basin for detaining this runoff on the site. Assume a relatively flat site.

12.3 For the hydrograph presented in Table 12.14, estimate the volume of storage required to control the postdevelopment peak flow using runoff difference. The watershed drainage area is 165 acres, and is in a NRCS Type II rainfall region. Express the storage estimate in ac-ft.

TABLE 12.14 Hydrographs for Problems 12.3 through 12.5

Time (hrs)	Pre-q (ft^3/s)	Post-q (ft^3/s)	Time (hrs)	Pre-q (ft^3/s)	Post-q (ft^3/s)
0.0	0.0	0.0	7.8	9.7	10.4
0.3	4.6	9.2	8.1	9.4	9.9
0.6	6.2	12.6	8.4	9.1	9.5
0.9	9.0	20.6	8.7	8.7	9.1
1.2	20.1	70.1	9.0	8.4	8.8
1.5	113.4	258.0	9.3	8.1	8.5
1.8	176.8	185.9	9.6	7.9	8.3
2.1	114.4	90.7	9.9	7.7	8.1
2.4	69.7	54.0	10.2	7.4	8.0
2.7	45.6	38.0	10.5	7.2	7.8
3.0	34.1	30.8	10.8	7.0	7.6
3.3	27.4	26.3	11.1	6.7	7.4
3.6	22.9	22.8	11.4	6.2	6.9
3.9	20.1	20.7	11.7	5.7	6.3
4.2	18.1	19.2	12.0	5.2	5.7
4.5	16.9	18.0	12.3	4.7	5.2
4.8	15.8	16.9	12.6	4.2	4.6
5.1	14.7	15.8	12.9	3.7	4.1
5.4	13.8	14.7	13.2	3.2	3.5
5.7	12.9	13.8	13.5	2.7	3.0
6.0	12.1	13.0	13.8	2.2	2.4
6.3	11.6	12.5	14.1	1.7	1.9
6.6	11.1	12.2	14.4	1.2	1.3
6.9	10.7	11.8	14.7	0.7	0.7
7.2	10.4	11.4	15.0	0.2	0.2
7.5	10.0	10.9	15.3	0.0	0.0

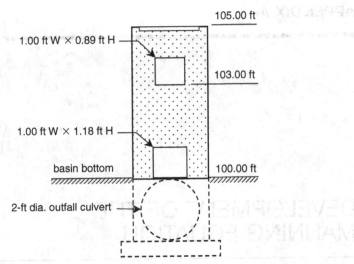

105.00 ft

1.00 ft W × 0.89 ft H

103.00 ft

1.00 ft W × 1.18 ft H

basin bottom   100.00 ft

2-ft dia. outfall culvert

Figure 12.16   Riser box of Problem 12.6. (Courtesy of T. Smith, PE, PLS, Conver and Smith Engineering, Royersford, PA.)

12.4   Repeat Problem 12.3 using hydrograph subtraction.

12.5   Repeat Problem 12.3 using NRCS TR-55.

12.6   The multiple-stage outlet structure shown in Figure 12.16 consists of two rectangular orifices mounted in a 2-feet-by-4-feet concrete riser box. The open top (no grate) acts like a weir for water surface elevations up to 105.50 feet. Determine the rating curve for this structure for elevations ranging from 100.00 feet to 105.50 feet. Assume the orifices have discharge coefficients of 0.6 and flow freely without experiencing any submergence. The weir has a discharge coefficient of 3.1 and a weir length equal to the 12-foot perimeter of the box opening.

12.7   For your location, find the government agency that regulates stormwater management and get access to the land regulation documents. Determine the number and frequency of events that must be controlled in stormwater management design based on these criteria.

REFERENCES

Seybert, T. A., and D. F. Kibler. 2005. *VTPSUHM: Computational Methods in Stormwater Management.* Continuing education short course notes, Office of Outreach, Conferences and Institutes, Penn State University, State College, PA.

USDA NRCS, 1986. *Urban Hydrology for Small Watersheds,* TR-55, Engineering Division, Washington, DC.

APPENDIX A

DEVELOPMENT OF THE MANNING EQUATION

From Section 4.5, Equation 4.4, we begin with

$$F_f = w \sin \theta \qquad (4.4)$$

Water weight, w, can be expressed as the product of volume and specific weight, γV. For a very small channel segment length, Δx, the volume, V, is expressed as Δx times the flow area, A_f. Thus

$$w = \gamma \Delta x A_f \qquad (A.1)$$

The slope of the channel is expressed using the angle θ. This angle is always small, usually less than 10 degrees (slope of 17.6 %). The $\sin\theta$ can be approximated very well by $\tan\theta$ when θ is small. From Figure 4.5, $\tan\theta$ is expressed as vertical drop, Δh, divided by length of the channel, L. This is the definition of channel bottom slope as provided in Equation 4.7. Thus

$$\sin \theta \approx \tan \theta = \frac{\Delta h}{L} = S \qquad (A.2)$$

Combining Equations A.1 and A.2 gives

$$w \sin \theta = \gamma \Delta x A_f S \qquad (A.3)$$

The friction force, F_f, is equal to the shear stress of the water, τ, acting over the surface area in contact with the water, A_s. This area, A_s, can be expressed as the wetted perimeter, P times Δx. Thus

$$F_f = \tau A_s = \tau P \Delta x \tag{A.4}$$

Shear stress is known to be proportional to the velocity squared, v^2, through a friction coefficient, C_f.

$$\tau = C_f v^2 \tag{A.5}$$

Combining Equations A.4 and A.5 gives

$$F_f = \tau \Delta x P = C_f v^2 \Delta x P \tag{A.6}$$

Equating Equations A.6 and A.3

$$C_f v^2 \Delta x P = \gamma \Delta x A_f S \tag{A.7}$$

Solving for v^2

$$v^2 = \frac{\gamma \Delta x A_f S}{C_f \Delta x P} = \frac{\gamma}{C_f} \frac{A_f}{P} S \tag{A.8}$$

Recognize that A_f divided by P is hydraulic radius, R_h. Also, the ratio of γ / C_f can be combined into one coefficient, C. Solving for v

$$v = \left(\frac{\gamma}{C_f}\right)\left(\frac{A}{P}\right)^{1/2} S^{1/2} = C R_h^{1/2} S^{1/2} \tag{A.9}$$

From experimental research, Robert Manning proposed that C in Equation A.9 is equal to $R_h^{1/6}/n$, where n is a surface roughness coefficient that represents frictional resistance.

$$v = \frac{R_h^{1/6}}{n} R_h^{1/2} S^{1/2} \tag{A.10}$$

Combining like terms gives the Manning equation in SI (metric units).

$$v = \frac{1}{n} R_h^{2/3} S^{1/2} \tag{A.11}$$

In this version of Manning's equation, R_h is in meters and S is dimensionless in m/m. For the equation to remain dimensionally homogeneous $1/n$ must be assigned the units of seconds divided by meters to the one-third power, or $s/m^{1/3}$, if the velocity is to be in the units of ft/s. In U.S. Standard units, the conversion of meters to feet is 3.2808 ft/m. Equation A.11 must be multiplied by $(3.2808 \text{ ft/m})^{1/3}$ to create an equivalent U.S. Standard version of Manning's equation. The resulting equation becomes

$$v = \frac{1.49}{n} R_h^{2/3} S^{1/2} \qquad\qquad (A.12)$$

DEVELOPMENT OF THE MUSKINGUM ROUTING EQUATIONS

To develop a storage relationship for a channel, it is assumed that channel inflow, I, channel outflow, O, and channel storage, S, varies with flow depth, y, according to similar power functions:

$$I = O = ay^c \tag{B.1}$$

$$S_I = S_O = by^d \tag{B.2}$$

If the hydraulic properties of the channel are constant then it is reasonable to assume that the coefficients a, b, c, and d remain constant along the channel reach as well. The flow Equation B.1 can be solved for y and substituted into the storage Equation B.2 to yield respective equations for inflow (upstream) and outflow (downstream) sections. For the inflow section

$$S_I = b\left[\left(\frac{I}{a}\right)^{1/c}\right]^d = b\left(\frac{I}{a}\right)^{d/c} = b\left(\frac{1}{a}\right)^{d/c} I^{d/c} \tag{B.3}$$

and thus

$$S_I = KI^{d/c} \tag{B.4}$$

where

$$K = b\left(\frac{1}{a}\right)^{d/c}$$
(B.5)

Similarly for the outflow section

$$S_O = KO^{d/c}$$
(B.6)

The Muskingum method assumes that the average storage in the channel reach is a weighted function of the storage at the upstream and downstream cross sections. Using a simple weighting parameter, X, the average storage relationship can be expressed as

$$S = XS_I + (1 - X)S_O$$
(B.7)

If Equations B.5 and B.6 are substituted into B.7, the average storage relationship takes the form of

$$S = XKI^{d/c} + (1 - X)KO^{d/c}$$
(B.8)

or

$$S = K[XI^{d/c} + (1 - X)O^{d/c}]$$
(B.9)

For simplicity, the ratio of d/c is assumed to be unity, which reduces the relationship for K in Equation B.8 to b/a. With these assumptions, the storage relationship of B.9 takes on the familiar form of the Muskingum relationship

$$S = K[XI + (1 - X)O]$$
(B.10)

The conservation of mass relationship, also known as the continuity equation, is combined with Equation B.10 to solve for the routed hydrograph. Conservation of mass is expressed as

$$I - O = \frac{\Delta S}{\Delta t}$$
(B.11)

In differenced form, with n representing the beginning of a time step and n+1 representing the end of a time step, Equation B.11 becomes

$$\left(\frac{I_n + I_{n+1}}{2}\right) - \left(\frac{O_n + O_{n+1}}{2}\right) = \left(\frac{S_{n+1} - S_n}{\Delta t}\right)$$
(B.12)

The differenced form of Equation B.10 is also necessary and is

$$S_{n+1} - S_n = K[X(I_{n+1} - I_n) + (1 - X)(O_{n+1} - O_n)] \qquad \text{(B.13)}$$

Equations B.12 and B.13 can be combined to eliminate the storage terms, S_n and S_{n+1}.

$$\left(\frac{I_n + I_{n+1}}{2}\right) - \left(\frac{O_n + O_{n+1}}{2}\right) = \left(\frac{K[X(I_{n+1} - I_n) + (1 - X)(O_{n+1} - O_n)]}{\Delta t}\right)$$

$$\text{(B.14)}$$

Equation B.14 can be algebraically manipulated to create a working form of the equation. By combining like subscripts and solving for outflow at the end of the Δt time step, the equation takes the form of

$$O_{n+1} = \left(\frac{-KX + 0.5\Delta t}{K - KX + 0.5\Delta t}\right)I_{n+1} + \left(\frac{KX + 0.5\Delta t}{K - KX + 0.5\Delta t}\right)I_n$$

$$+ \left(\frac{K - KX - 0.5\Delta t}{K - KX + 0.5\Delta t}\right)O_n \qquad \text{(B.15)}$$

The leading coefficient of every term on the right side of Equation B.15 is expressed in terms of the routing parameters K, X, and Δt. These parameters are considered known values since they can be estimated or calculated prior to the routing process.

Equation B.15 can be written in a simplified form as

$$O_{n+1} = C_0 I_{n+1} + C_1 I_n + C_2 O_n \qquad \text{(B.16)}$$

where

$$C_0 = \left(\frac{-KX + 0.5\Delta t}{K - KX + 0.5\Delta t}\right) \qquad \text{(B.17)}$$

$$C_1 = \left(\frac{KX + 0.5\Delta t}{K - KX + 0.5\Delta t}\right) \qquad \text{(B.18)}$$

$$C_2 = \left(\frac{K - KX - 0.5\Delta t}{K - KX + 0.5\Delta t}\right) \qquad \text{(B.19)}$$

These three routing coefficients, C_0, C_1, and C_2, are dimensionless. Therefore, the time units of K and Δt must be the same. Also, mathematical integrity requires the sum of the three coefficients to be equal to unity.

ADDITIONAL DETAILED CALCULATIONS FOR EXAMPLE 11.4

These calculations are a continuation of the solution to Example 11.4, detailing the preliminary sizing of pipe segments 5–7, 6–7, and 7–8.

Pipe 5–7. The drainage area is the sum of subareas 1 through 5, which is 11.99 acres. The t_c for this pipe segment is the largest of five choices: (1) overland flow time to inlet 1 plus pipe travel time through pipe segments 1–2, 2–4, and 4–5; (2) overland flow time to inlet 2 plus pipe travel time through pipe segments 2–4 and 4–5; (3) overland flow time to inlet 3 plus pipe travel time through segments 3–4 and 4–5; (4) overland flow time to inlet 4 plus pipe travel time through pipe segment 4–5; and (5) overland flow time to inlet 5. These values are

$$t_1 = 8.9 + 0.1 + 0.6 + 0.1 = 9.7 \text{ min}$$

$$t_2 = 10 + 0.6 + 0.1 = 10.7 \text{ min}$$

$$t_3 = 17.0 + 0.2 + 0.1 = 17.3 \text{ min}$$

$$t_4 = 11.9 + 0.1 = 12.0 \text{ min}$$

$$t_5 = 8.1 \text{ min}$$

Again, the path from subarea 3 to the pipe inlet controls, t_c is 17.3 minutes, and the design rainfall intensity remains as 3.4 in/hr. The weighted coefficient C_w is

$$C_w = \left[\frac{(1.98 + 2.83 + 3.85 + 1.22)(0.36) + (2.12)(0.12)}{11.99}\right] = 0.318$$

The peak flow is computed.

$$q = CiA = (0.318)(3.4)(11.99) = 12.96 \text{ ft}^3/\text{s}$$

The minimum pipe diameter is

$$D_{min} = 16\left(\frac{qn}{S^{1/2}}\right)^{3/8} = 16\left[\frac{(12.96)(0.012)}{0.0050^{1/2}}\right]^{3/8} = 21.50 \text{ inches}$$

A 24-inch diameter pipe is required for segment 5–7, and pipe full capacity is

$$q_f = \left(\frac{24}{16}\right)^{8/3}\left(\frac{0.0050^{1/2}}{0.012}\right) = 17.37 \text{ ft}^3/\text{s}$$

The full flow area is

$$A_{24} = \frac{\pi(2^2)}{4} = 3.142 \text{ ft}^2$$

Using the hydraulics elements graph with $q/q_f = 0.75$ leads to the following: $y/D = 0.65$, $y = 1.30$ ft, $A/A_f = 0.71$, $A = 2.23$ ft², $v = 5.81$ ft/s, and $t_{5-7} = 0.7$ min. The velocity is above the minimum for scour.

Pipe 6–7. This segment is a pipe spur, so the design of this pipe segment is solely based on the design flow of inlet 6, which is 0.94 ft³/s. Like segment 3–4, this pipe diameter is almost certainly the minimum allowable, but the calculations are done to verify the assumption.

$$D_{min} = 16\left(\frac{qn}{S^{1/2}}\right)^{3/8} = 16\left[\frac{(0.94)(0.012)}{0.00889^{1/2}}\right]^{3/8} = 7.22 \text{ inches}$$

The minimum diameter is verified as 15 inches. Pipe full capacity is

$$q_f = \left(\frac{15}{16}\right)^{8/3}\left(\frac{0.00889^{1/2}}{0.012}\right) = 6.61 \text{ ft}^3/\text{s}$$

The hydraulic elements graph is used once again with $q/q_f = 0.14$, $y/D = 0.25$, $y = 0.31$ ft; $A/A_f = 0.20$, $A = 0.245$ ft², $v = 0.94/0.23 = 3.84$ ft/sec, $t_{6-7} = 0.2$ min.

Pipe 7–8. The drainage area is the sum of all subareas, which is 15.22 acres. The t_c for this pipe segment is the largest of seven choices, each being inlet time plus pipe travel time to point 8 for inlets 1 through 7.

$$t_1 = 8.9 + 0.1 + 0.6 + 0.1 + 0.7 = 10.4 \text{ min}$$

$$t_2 = 10.0 + 0.6 + 0.1 + 0.7 = 11.4 \text{ min}$$

$$t_3 = 17.0 + 0.2 + 0.1 + 0.7 = 18.0 \text{ min}$$

$$t_4 = 11.9 + 0.1 + 0.7 = 12.7 \text{ min}$$

$$t_5 = 8.1 + 0.7 = 8.8 \text{ min}$$

$$t_6 = 15.4 + 0.2 = 15.6 \text{ min}$$

$$t_7 = 7.7 \text{ min}$$

As could be guessed, the path from subarea 3 controls and t_c is 18.0 minutes. The design rainfall intensity from Figure 6.5 is 3.3 in/hr. The weighted C coefficient is

$$C_w = \left[\frac{(1.98 + 2.82 + 3.85 + 1.22 + 1.05)(0.36) + (2.12 + 2.18)(0.12)}{15.22} \right]$$

$$C_w = 0.292$$

The peak flow is computed.

$$q = CiA = (0.292)(3.3)(15.22) = 14.67 \text{ ft}^3/\text{s}$$

The minimum pipe diameter is

$$D_{min} = 16 \left[\frac{(14.67)(0.012)}{0.0070^{1/2}} \right]^{3/8} = 21.15 \text{ inches}$$

A 24-inch diameter pipe is required for segment 7–8. Once again, all the supporting data is collected and computed: $q_f = 20.56 \text{ ft}^3/\text{s}$; $q/q_f = 0.71$; $y/D = 0.63$, $y = 1.26$ ft, $A/A_f = 0.66$, $A = 2.073 \text{ ft}^2$, $v = 7.08 \text{ ft/s}$, and $t_{7-8} = 0.2$ min. Once again the velocity satisfies scour requirements. The results of the pipe sizing are summarized in Table 11.12.

APPENDIX D

MOODY DIAGRAM

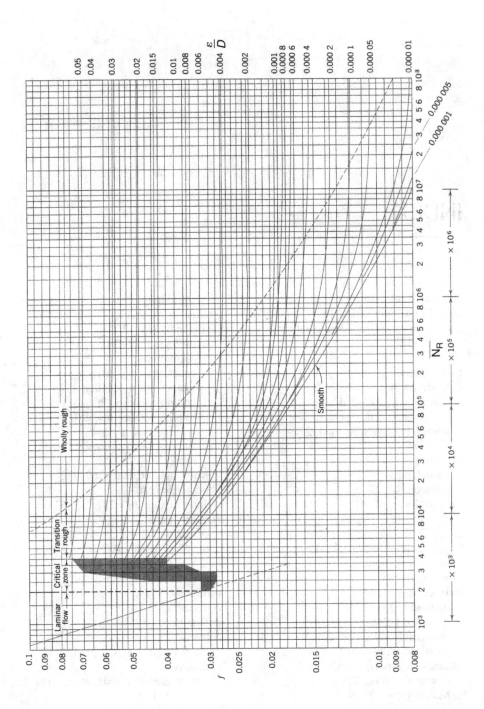

INDEX